VISUAL
AND
AUDITORY
PERCEPTION

Gerald M. Murch

The Bobbs-Merrill Company, Inc.
Indianapolis • New York

VISUAL
AND
AUDITORY
PERCEPTION

Copyright © 1973 by The Bobbs-Merrill Company, Inc.
Printed in the United States of America
Design by Anita Duncan
First Printing

Library of Congress Cataloging in Publication Data

Murch, Gerald M   1940—
 Visual and auditory perception.

 Includes bibliographical references.
  1. Optics, Physiological. 2. Visual perception.
3. Hearing. I. Title.
QP441.M87   612'.84   74-172349
ISBN 0-672-61333-6 (pbk)

Preface

Historically, the study of perceptual processes provided a catalyst that transformed scientists from physicists, philosophers, physiologists, and anatomists into experimental psychologists. Until the rise of Nazi Germany, the study of perception remained the major task of European experimentalists in psychology; their American counterparts tended to focus their attention on the learning process. Research in perception in the United States was left primarily to a minority of hard-working German scientists who had emigrated between the wars.

More recently, a new generation of psychologists has developed an interest in perception, an interest motivated in part by familiarity with advances in the physiology of sensory systems and in part by dissatisfaction with present research trends in human learning. The approaches to the problems of perception of this new generation differ markedly from the theoretical backgrounds of the preceding generation; nevertheless, a combination of the outlooks of both has produced some fascinating contributions to the study of perception.

This book provides an introduction to the area of psychology called perception. It attempts to interrelate the classical, phenomenological approaches of the earlier perceptual scientists with the empirical approach of the newer generation. The research discussed is presented in terms of a model of the perceptual process; this model is very general, yet it provides a meaningful framework through which new questions about perception can be generated.

I am greatly indebted to the researchers whose experimental observations are reported in this book. In particular I wish to express my thanks to the following individuals, societies, agencies, publishing firms, and journals from which I have drawn material for a number of graphs, drawings, tables, and photographs:

Academic Press (*Journal of Verbal Learning and Verbal Behavior*)
Allyn and Bacon
American Association for the Advancement of Science (*Science*)
American Journal of Optometry
American Journal of Physics
American Psychological Association (*Journal of Experimental Psychology, Psychological Bulletin, Psychological Review, American Psychologist*)
Appleton-Century-Crofts
Archivio di Psicologia, Neurologia e Psichiatria
Basic Books
British Journal of Psychology
Canadian Journal of Psychology
Dee Carlin
David Linton, photographer
The Dorsey Press
Duke University Press (*Journal of Personality*)
The Escher Foundation, The Hague
W. H. Freeman and Company (*Scientific American*)
Harper and Row
Harvard University Press
Hirzel Verlag (*Acustica*)
Holt, Rinehart and Winston
Houghton Mifflin Company
John Wiley and Sons
Journal of the Acoustical Society of America
Journal of the Optical Society of America
The Journal Press (*Journal of Psychology*)
Henry Kimpton Publishers

Macmillan Journals, Ltd. (*Nature*, London)
C. V. Mosby and Company
Munsell Color Company
National Aeronautics and Space Administration
National Academy of Sciences
Perceptual and Motor Skills
Pergamon Press
Psychological Record
Psychologisches Institut, Universität Göttingen
Psychology
Psychonomic Journals (*Psychonomic Science, Perception and Psycho-physics*)
Quarterly Journal of Experimental Psychology
Scandinavian Journal of Experimental Psychology
Scandinavian Journal of Psychology
Cord B. Sengstake
Speech Transmission Laboratory
Springer Verlag (*Psychologishe Forschung, Studium Generale*)
Society for Research in Child Development (*Child Development*)
University of Illinois Press (*American Journal of Psychology*)
University of Toronto Press
Van Nostrand Reinhold Publishing Company
Verlag fur Psychologie Hogrefe
William Vandivert, photographer
George Weidenfeld and Nicholson, Ltd.

I would also like to express my thanks to Irvin Rock and William H. Ittelson for their helpful comments on an earlier version of the manuscript. I am greatly indebted to my editor, Jared Carter, for his hard work and persistence in seeing this work to completion. Finally, I am grateful to Juanita Valberg for her aid in proofreading and typing the manuscript, and Barbara Breck for comments on the manuscript as well as typing assistance.

Gerald M. Murch

Portland State University
Portland, Oregon
June 1972

Contents

VISUAL
AND
AUDITORY
PERCEPTION

CHAPTER 1

The Perceptual Response

Man moves through a world of constant external and internal stimulation. Affected by the objects and events of his surroundings, he interprets them in terms of his experience and modifies his behavior accordingly. This constant interaction with the environment and the associated mental process of interpreting the impact and import of external events characterize the process known as perception.

The psychology of perception, then, involves the study of the way an observer relates to his environment—the way in which information is gathered and interpreted by an observer. This relationship is the result of a continuing process of learning, judging, interpreting, and reacting to the environment which begins at birth and continues throughout the life span of the individual.

Traditionally we speak of five channels which convey information about the external environment to the individual: vision (sight), audition (hearing), gustation (taste), olfaction (smell), and tactile-kinesthesis (touch-body position). Unquestionably the one through which the most information can be obtained is the *visual* channel. In fact, the other senses often modify their responses in accordance with the visual input. A classic experiment by Gibson (1933) demonstrates this overriding function of vision. Subjects viewed a straightedge ruler through a pair of distorting glasses that made all objects of the environment appear curved to the left. When presented with the ruler, the subjects reported it appeared to be bent or curved to the left; upon closing their eyes and running their fingers along the edge, they felt it to be straight. However, if the subjects looked at the ruler through the distorting glasses and ran their fingers along the edge, the ruler not only looked curved, it also *felt* curved.

The effect of the visual system on other senses, such as taste and smell, can be observed in a variety of everyday situations. Food invariably tastes better when served attractively and consumed in a pleasant environment. That beverages, such as beer, improve in the same manner is implied by the German expression "Das Auge trinkt mit" (The eye also drinks). The Campbell's beans at the Hilton, in other words, seem far more flavorful than those at Joe's Bar and Grill.

Hearing, the second sense of major import, through which much of our environmental information is gathered, is still subordinate to vision when seen and heard events conflict. At a drive-in movie one is aware that the speaker is hanging in the window and that the sounds do not emanate from their visual sources on the screen during the early part of the picture. After several minutes they appear localized on the screen and the discrepancy goes unnoticed. Nonetheless, we are more influenced by hearing than by the three remaining senses. For this reason we shall confine ourselves to a discussion of the processes of visual and auditory perception in this book.

Basic Problems for Perception

Before we proceed to a discussion of specific aspects of the perceptual process, several questions must be considered. These involve the meaning of the term *stimulus*, the subjective or phenomenological nature of perception, the distinction between *sensation* and *perception*, and the essentially active process of perceiving.

What is a stimulus?   In the classical sense, the term *stimulus* is half of a pair of correlative terms. The other half is the term *response* (Hocutt, 1967). This means that any object or event which elicits a response can be considered as a stimulus for that response. To function as a certain kind of stimulus then

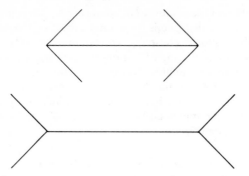

Figure 1.1
The Müller-Lyer illusion.

becomes a property of a particular object. An object, therefore, can take on the property of being a stimulus only in relation to a specific response. Neither term can be defined independently of the other. Naturally it is possible to describe an object or an event without relating either to a response. But such a discussion would be confined to the physical properties of the object or event and would not mention a response by a perceiving organism. "If a tree falls in the forest with no one to hear it, does it make a sound?" asks a famous philosophical query. The answer is clearly no, for a sound is a stimulus for hearing, and if no one hears it, the event cannot be called a stimulus.

Obviously, if psychologists were to adhere to such a strict use of the term *stimulus*, a major limitation would be imposed on the kind of observations that could be made. This concept of stimulus would force us to regard the response as dependent on the object or event (stimulus) and the stimulus as dependent on the response. Such a definition is clearly circular.

The great German physicist, physiologist, and philosopher Hermann von Helmholtz sought to avoid this circular definition by introducing the concepts of *distal stimulus*—the external object or event—and *proximal stimulus*—the sensory representation of the stimulus by the nervous system (1866). In vision, for example, the distal stimulus is a pattern of ambient light reflected from objects in the environment and the proximal stimulus a pattern of neuronal responses within the visual system initiated by that ambient light. Yet this distinction failed to resolve the issue, as demonstrated by the Müller-Lyer illusion in Fig. 1.1. Both the distal and proximal stimuli should indicate horizontal lines of equal length, but the resulting percept is one of unequal horizontal lines. The distal stimulus gives rise to the proximal stimulus which in turn contributes to the building of a percept representative of the initial distal stimulus.

J. J. Gibson (1960, 1967) has offered a clearer distinction between distal and proximal stimuli by introducing the terms *potential stimulus* and *effective stimulus*. Any object or event in the environment is a potential stimulus. When such a potential stimulus stands in a constant relationship with a given response, it is an effective stimulus. Thus we are able to describe the environment independently of the responses of an observer. This is particularly important when we consider that one is often unaware of all the responses elicited by a stimulus. The response chosen by an experimenter is often arbitrary and may be only one of a multitude of responses occurring simultaneously in the presence of an effective stimulus. Furthermore, the environment contains a continuous flow of potential stimuli, some of which are or will become effective stimuli, and others which will not. The determination of which objects or events become effective stimuli and which do not is central to the understanding of the process of perception.

The Subjective World of the Perceiver

Another problem basic to the study of perception evolves from the nature of the process itself. If we consider perception to be dependent on the interaction of effective stimuli and the sum total of all the previous experiences of the individual, then each individual's perception of an effective stimulus would be unique and different from those of another individual. No two persons have had exactly the same experiences, nor can any two individuals experience exactly the same effective stimulus. Each individual moving through the array of potential stimuli responds to a finite number of stimuli. If you are waiting at an airport the stimulus configuration of a relative would most likely evoke a perceptual response. For a person having had no previous experience with your relative, the stimulus would probably remain a potential stimulus—unless your relative were Raquel Welch. In this case she would most likely be an effective stimulus for both you and the stranger. However, the response to the effective stimulus would be different for each of you.

We are saying that perception is personal or subjective; to speak of an objective perception would be a contradiction in terms. But how can we observe a person's perceptions and accurately measure them if they are all personal and subjective? This problem arose early in the study of perception and still plagues research today. Presently four solutions are attempted.

The first solution to the subjective perception problem—and the first solution historically—is known as the *phenomenological approach*. Quite simply, it acknowledges the subjective character of perception and states that the only possible method of assessment is to ask the subject to relate his perceptions. Unfortunately, the observer is frequently unable to do this. Interviews with individuals who have witnessed an accident produce a number of versions usually equal to the total number of persons asked. In addition, an observer often does not wish to report all his perceptions. He may decide to report only some aspects, or actually to deceive the experimenter by reporting false observations, or to mention only those observations which he feels the experimenter wishes to hear. With the phenomenological approach, we have no control over the accuracy of the subject's report. Furthermore, even when observers report the same thing, we can never be sure that they have in fact had the same perceptual experience.

A second approach, which avoids the pitfalls of phenomenology, is the behaviorist's *functional approach*, which is concerned primarily with mapping the relationships between effective stimuli and overt, observable responses. This provides objective data and allows quantitative analysis. The proponents of the approach place emphasis on the fact that, although perception is subjective, certain common denominators exist between perceivers. Since all individuals are faced with the same basic problem of orienting themselves in a complex environment, the perceptual response tendencies developed by different individuals should show basic similarities. However, such an approach cannot observe the unique aspects of perception, and can only record the common aspects.

A third solution to the problem involves a combination of the phenomenological and the functional approaches. If we measure overt responses to effective stimuli and simultaneously record the individuals' reported perceptions, we can compare for inconsistencies. For example, take a male student asked to describe a recent *Playboy* centerfold. His subjective report indicated he did not find the young lady particularly attractive. However, an accompanying measure of variations in pupil size and of the galvanic skin response showed that he was quite attentive to the photograph and displayed an emotional response to it.

A final solution to the subjective problem is to use highly trained observers who have practiced accurate reporting in unambiguous terms. They are trained to attend to important aspects of a stimulus and to communicate their perceptions.

In actual perceptual research the problem often dictates the method of assessment to be utilized. The functional method can be used to seek simple effective stimulus-response relations, while the phenomenological approach is better suited for studying general relations or unique individual responses. Specific aspects of unique stimulus arrays can also be studied by means of highly trained observers. Both the functional and phenomenological methods often rely on a "safety in numbers" principle, compensating for their shortcomings by recording large numbers of independent observations.

In the research discussed in this book we shall see that although all methods have found application, in more modern work two approaches seem to predominate: purely functional observations involving large numbers of subjects, and the use of small numbers of highly trained observers.

Sensation and Perception

Another problem plaguing perceptual psychology stems from the dichotomy between sensation and perception. The term *sensation* has been used to refer to a response of a sensory receptor to a stimulus. Perception, on the other hand, is considered a more complex process, one which involves the encoding of sensory message by the higher centers of the brain. In a single sentence we might say: *To sense is to respond, to perceive is to know.* A sensation occurs when neural impulses are transmitted along the afferent (incoming) pathways of the nervous system; perception involves the processing of this input. As

W. R. Garner (1966) has pointed out: "Perceiving is a cognitive process involving knowing, understanding, organizing, even cognizing. Most of our current research on the topic would suggest that perceiving is responding, naming, discriminating, and analyzing" (p. 11).

Historically, the concept of sensation developed from the structuralists' mid-nineteenth-century notion of *specific nerve energies*. They held that for every sensation a specific receptor and neuron existed which fired to indicate the presence of a physical stimulus. But neurophysiology has shown that this is not the case. Rather than specific nerves, the important variables seem to be the portion of the cortex to which the receptor reports and the other brain centers that are activated in processing the input. The term sensation, suggests von Fieandt (1966), "can be used for denoting the *functional interaction process* between peripheral end organs and the corresponding loci in the brain" (p. 4). Sensory psychology is therefore a matter of the physiology of neural transmission in the senses, while perception can be considered the response of the organism that utilizes the message. Von Fieandt also believes that the task of perceptual psychology "is to discover and refine the regularities and lawful connections governing the central coding and experiencing of sensory messages" (p. 3). This, as we shall see, is only part of the process of perception.

Not all perceptual psychologists agree with such a description of perception and sensation. In his book on visual perception, William Dember (1960) rejects the attempt to separate sensation from perception by asserting that both are part of the same continuous process. Gibson (1966), on the other hand, prefers to widen the dichotomy, considering incoming sensory information as only a part of perception. More than the encoding of sensory messages, perception is an active process of *extracting* information from the environment. To perceive is not to interpret a sensory message, says Gibson; rather, it is a process of exploring, seeking out, and responding in continual interaction between organism and environment.

The active perceiver.   A study by Bruner and Potter (1964) illustrates this extracting nature of the perceptual process. Subjects viewed out-of-focus colored slides of common objects (e.g., a fire hydrant, a pile of bricks) which were slowly brought into near focus. Some groups of subjects began with a very blurred image which was slowly brought toward focus, while others viewed the slides starting only slightly out of focus and moving slowly into near focus. The final level of focus was set the same for both groups. Those subjects starting with a slightly blurred slide showed a 73-percent recognition of the final level; but those who started with an extremely blurred slide achieved only 25-percent recognition at the same final level. Bruner and Potter conclude: "Exposure to a substandard visual display has the effect of interfering with its subsequent recognition" (p. 425). The authors explain their results by assuming that during the active process of attempting to identify the objects pictured, the subjects formed hypotheses about the displays that were continually checked against incoming information. The hypotheses tended to modify the kind of information extracted and to influence its analysis; poorer recognition was the result of erroneous interpretation and checking of the information selected. When the information was less ambiguous at the onset and less time was allowed for developing and testing hypotheses—less time to form false assumptions about the picture—recognition was better. As Gibson pointed out, perception is more than interpreting sensory messages; it involves constant interaction between the organism and the environment.

The efference theory of perception.   At this point a final aspect of perception must be mentioned. This view of the process of perception dates back to the late nineteenth century. In 1899 Münsterberg developed the theory that perception was more than a response to incoming sensory or *afferent* messages; he suggested that the response was only part of a continuing process that also involved outgoing motor or *efferent* intervention. Montague stated in 1908 that "perceptions are presumed to arise synchronously with the redirection in the central nervous system of afferent currents into efferent channels" (p. 128). Historically the theory did not fare well and most psychologists readily accepted the view of William James (1890), which held that the motor end of perception was implausible. Recently the theory has been revitalized in an excellent monograph prepared by Festinger, Ono, Burnham, and Bamber (1967).

Let us briefly reconsider Gibson's finding (1933) that straightedged objects viewed through distorting glasses not only appeared curved but also felt curved. According to the efference theory the straight edge feels curved because the arm is being instructed via the efferent system to move in a curved path. The conscious experience of perception does not depend on the input of the tactile receptors in the fingers, but on the output of motor neurons *directing* the arm movement.

In its present form the efference theory states that the perception of effective stimuli depends on the afferent sensory input and the set of preprogrammed efferent instructions activated by the input. The constant interplay of afferent and efferent intervention leads to the resulting perception.

Consider once again the study by Bruner and Potter with the blurred slides. As the individual processes the sensory input from the blurred stimulus array, hypotheses are formed and the perceptual system is directed to test these hypotheses. The oculomotor search pattern is directed to extract information relevant to the present interpretation of the sensory input. Thus motor activity changes as a function of sensory input and sensory input varies as motor direction changes. We have a feedback system testing and modifying its direction with respect to the environment.

A Model of Perception

We can now attempt to interrelate the foregoing points in a basic model of the perceptual process. Each individual observer is an active perceiver engaged in extracting information from his environment. The kinds of information extracted and the resulting analysis and redirection of search develop as a function of the observer's interactions (experiences) with the environment. The programs of motor activity and the properties of effective stimuli required for a

Figure 1.2
Painting by Dee Carlin. (Reproduced by permission of the artist and the owner.)

direction of attention depend on these past developments. Each person is an individual perceiver who interacts with his own subjective world.

We are viewing perception as a dynamic process in which sensory messages play an integral but subordinate part. Of greatest import are the programmed experiences of the perceiver in the form of hypotheses, motor actions, interrelationships between inputs, and so on. Perception is not the passive processing of information through specific channels; obviously it is an active process. Other models of perception—particularly those based on a computer simulation of the coding and encoding of input—have often failed to acknowledge the active role of the perceiver (Gyr, Brown, Willey, and Zivian, 1966).

Although it is often dangerous to engage in introspection, let us attempt to observe the process of actual perception. For several minutes, study carefully the reproduction of a painting by Dee Carlin presented in Figure 1.2. As you examine the reproduction, new aspects appear and previously noticed ones disappear. Your attention centers on one detail while others fade away. As information is extracted, the motor activity of vision directs you to different elements of the painting. An earlier perception disappears and cannot reappear due to a different processing of the same effective stimulus. The owner of the original painting still reports the perception of new and unnoticed figures even after several years.

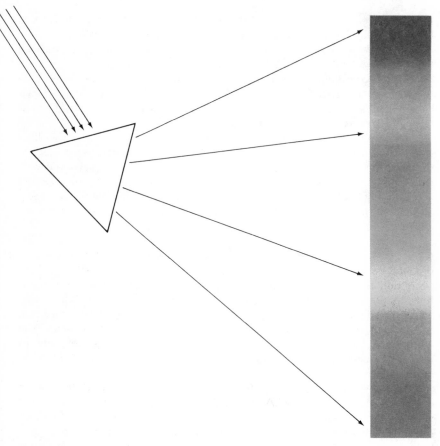

Figure 1.3
Sunlight or white light from a tungsten lamp passes through a prism and is bent into the visual spectrum.

In the following discussions of the observations of perception, we shall consider the applicability of this model to various perceptual responses and study its ability to explain and predict such phenomena. First, however, we should consider the media of sensory input in vision and audition, and the receptor systems for light and sound.

Visual Stimuli

One of the greatest advances in physics has been the understanding of the nature of light and its relationship with solid matter. The present concept of light is very similar to Isaac Newton's description of light as a stream of particles traveling in a straight line. First advanced in 1704, Newton's theory, known as the *corpuscular theory of light,* survived until the nineteenth century, when

James Maxwell introduced a new explanation of many of the characteristics of light. Maxwell's *electromagnetic theory* evolved from the observation that light did not travel in a straight line, but rather as an oscillating wave. Maxwell thought of light in terms of the mechanical forces of electricity and magnetism; rather than considering light to be composed of oscillating particles, he described it as a change in the electromagnetic field surrounding the particles. Such a field is generated by the oscillation of the charged particles and travels through space as an independent entity.

Modern physics still holds that such postulated relationships between light and electromagnetism are essentially correct. Today, however, waves of electromagnetic energy are also thought to consist of particles that display the energy and momentum characteristic of all elements of matter. Modern quantum mechanics holds that all matter, including light, can be described as a stream of particles. In the case of light, the particles are known as *photons;* in matter, *electrons.*

The two physical properties of light of primary interest in the study of perception are *wavelength* and *intensity.* Wavelength is a measure of the physical distance between the peaks of the photon waves. The wavelength of a light beam derives from and is in inverse proportion to the momentum of its photons; momentum in turn is a function of the energy of the particles. Actually, wave movement is characteristic of each of the individual particles in a beam of light—the product of the movement of all the component particles. The intensity of light, on the other hand, depends on the number of photons in a particular beam and on the highest point (peak amplitude) in the wave motion of the particles.

That portion of the wide spectrum of radiant energies to which the human eye is sensitive is quite small. Visual sensations are evoked by photon waves with lengths between approximately 420 and 700 millimicrons (mμ).[1] If a beam of white light (one that contains all visible wavelengths) passes through a right-angle prism, the beam is broken into the various wavelengths comprising the white light. Figure 1.3 shows such a beam of sunlight directed through a narrow slit and onto the prism, which bends the light waves in proportion to their lengths. The shorter waves are bent to a greater degree, the longer waves to a lesser. The resulting pattern presents the range of the visible spectrum from the shortest to the longest perceivable wavelengths. Sunlight also contains nonvisible waves that are broken down in the same manner. Immediately above the visible spectrum are the *infrared* rays (above 700mμ) and immediately below are the *ultraviolet* rays (below 400 mμ). The visual sensation evoked by the various waveforms between these two extremes is one of color. As we shall see in Chapter 2, however, the perception of color is more complex than the presentation of a specific portion of the visible spectrum.

The interaction of light and matter. We seldom respond to direct light stimulation; rather, light is reflected by objects and thus transmits information about certain characteristics of the objects. If a beam of white light strikes the

---

[1] Alternatively, wavelengths may also be measured in nanometers (nm). The two units, millimicron and nanometer, are interchangeable.

surface of an object, either it is reemitted without any change in the frequency characteristic of the wave, or part (if not all) of the waves are absorbed by the material.

The basic interaction between light and solid matter occurs when component electrons of an object respond to the bombarding photons of the light beam. Weisskopf (1968) has described the actual effect of a photon on an isolated atom in an object:

> Quantum theory tells us that light comes in packets called photons; the higher the frequency of the light (and the shorter the wavelength) the more energy per packet. Quantum theory also tells us that the energy of an atom (or a system of atoms such as a molecule) can assume only certain definite values that are characteristic for each species of atom. These values represent the energy spectrum of the atom. Ordinarily the atom finds itself in the ground state, the state of lowest energy. When the atom is exposed to light of a frequency such that the photon energy is equal to one of the energy differences between an excited state and the ground state, the atom absorbs a photon and changes into the corresponding excited state. It falls back to a lower state after a short time and emits the energy differences in the form of a photon (p. 60).

Later in the same article Weisskopf considers the response of atoms in terms of the *oscillator model*. Electron oscillators are described as systems vibrating with specific frequencies in response to the light stimulus. The oscillator responds in accordance with the kinds of energy changes in the individual atoms described above. The motion of the oscillating atoms also causes friction, which in the case of the response to light usually produces heat. With this model we can describe the response of the electron in the light-stimulated matter as an oscillatory response to the specific frequencies contained in the light beam.

Light strikes the matter and causes a sympathetic response. Some of the light is reemitted by the object in the form of photons and these are picked up by the eye. This light transmits information about the shape, texture, and color of the object. Other waves are absorbed and transformed into heat motion, depending upon the characteristics of the solid object. The photons reemitted by the object provide the initial stimulus for a specific visual sensation.

We have now traced a light beam to an object and noted that the reflected beam will convey information about the object to the eye. Our next step is to consider briefly the response of the eye to this photon stream.[2]

Light and the Eye

The reflected light ray enters the eye along the pathways depicted in the drawing in Figure 1.4. After passing through the cornea and aqueous humor, the photon beam enters the inner eye through the pupil. The amount of light

---

[2] An interesting and understandable presentation of the physical aspects of light has been provided in a special issue of *Scientific American* (September 1968) to which the interested reader should turn for further information.

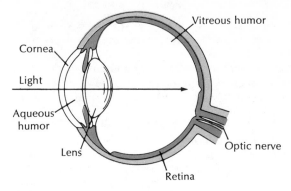

Figure 1.4
Diagram of the human eye.

allowed to enter is regulated by the pupil; the lens focuses the light on the sense cells of the retina. Between the lens and the retina is a semicolorless, viscous material called the vitreous humor; some frequencies of the wave forms contained in a light beam are absorbed by this substance.

The actual light-sensitive cells of the retina are of two types: *rods* and *cones*. Each retina contains some 100 million rods and 5 million cones (Jones, 1968). The photons of a light beam cause the rods and cones to respond. They in turn translate the input into nerve impulses which are transmitted up the optic nerve, through several substructures, to the visual cortex of the brain.

Although it is not entirely certain how the information is received by the higher centers of the visual system, it appears that the impulses are organized and analyzed at several levels of the system. At the retinal level we know that the rods are sensitive to very low light intensities and are relatively insensitive to detail. The cones are densely packed in the central portion of the retina and provide information on detail if the level of intensity of the light beam is great enough. The cones are also the first analyzers of color, brightness, and contour.

Auditory Stimuli

The stimulus for vision was found to be a stream of particles moving in an electromagnetic field. The stimulus for hearing is the physical change of a medium produced by a vibration or mechanical disturbance. A *sound wave* is a vibration or disturbance traveling through a medium that distends in a wave form in response to the disturbance. Naturally the speed with which the wave form is propagated depends on the density of the medium: the denser the medium, the faster the wave will travel.

If such vibrations are produced in a medium with a fairly low density, such as air, the disturbance will cause increases in pressure, density, particle displacement, and particle velocity around the area of the disturbance. Prior to the introduction of the disturbance, the transmitting medium is in a state of equilibrium relative to the variables just mentioned. The wave causes a disruption of the equilibrium and produces the changes in these variables. The wave produced by such a disturbance assumes a characteristic pattern. The medium is compressed in one direction and then in the opposite direction, varying around the neutral state of equilibrium. Using air pressure as an example, one would observe positive and negative changes around the base level of atmospheric pressure. Because the distension of the medium causes friction, the wave form will not be propagated indefinitely. Rather, the amount of disturbance decreases slightly on each successive swing as one moves farther from the source of the sound, much in the same way that ripples on a quiet lake attenuate as they move from the source of the disturbance. These waves of sound are referred to as *dampened* or *attenuating sinusoids*. The decreasing magnitude of the swing represents a reduction in the intensity of the sound wave. *Amplitude* is defined physically as the highest point of deflection of the wave from the base level equilibrium of the conducting medium. The number of completed positive and negative displacements of the medium over a given period of time represents the *frequency* of the sound wave. Traditionally frequency has been measured in terms of the number of completed cycles per second (cps); more recently the *hertz* (Hz), equal to one cps, has been accepted as the international unit of frequency measurement.

Figure 1.5 provides several examples of various pure waves, each of which exhibits a single frequency and intensity or amplitude. Pure tones similar to those shown in the figure can be produced under special conditions with devices such as tuning forks. Usually, however, a sound is a combination of a number of waves of varying frequencies and amplitudes. Such tones are known as *complex tones*. Complex sounds can be reduced to a collection of single frequencies by the technique of *Fourier analysis*, which represents, on a graph, the relative energy content of a sound as a function of frequency. Generally speaking, two kinds of complex tones are distinguished. First there are *discrete tones*, in which a collection of separate frequencies are found; second, there are *continuous tones*, which contain all the frequencies in some portion of the range of audible tones (20 to 20,000 Hz).

Continuous and discrete tones may be broken down further into *periodic tones* and *impulsive tones*. The former are sounds showing a repetition of wave form; the latter, no matter how complicated, are sounds that do not repeat themselves periodically. Periodic tones are usually discrete and possess individual frequencies related to one another harmonically. Such harmonic waves can be visualized with reference to a guitar string. If the string is plucked, a discrete, periodic tone is produced—a combination of tones with a *fundamental* tone and *harmonic* tones. The fundamental tone, after which the entire complex tone is named, is the lowest frequency or the frequency of the string vibrating as a whole. The harmonics are the tones produced by the string vibrating in halves, thirds, fourths, and fifths, as illustrated in Figure 1.6.

Many tones in our auditory environment are neither periodic nor continuous. Such short duration or impulsive tones—such as those produced by a knock on a door or the crash of a falling object—also contain a number

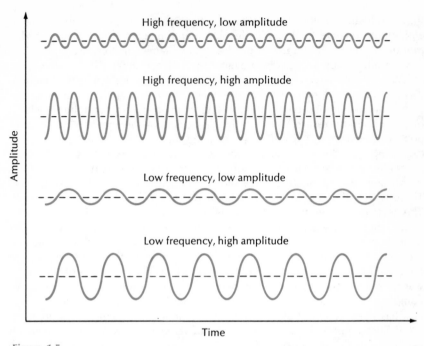

Figure 1.5
Pure waves of various frequencies and amplitudes.

of frequencies. The frequencies are not related to one another harmonically, however.

To conclude the discussion of the physical attributes of sound we need to mention *noise*, which is a continuous flow of sounds occurring simultaneously. The components of noise usually stem from varied and unrelated sources; the roar of city traffic and the breaking of waves on a beach are typical examples. In studies of audition, one usually relates a critical tone (signal) to the background noise. The signal stands out against the noise and can be described in terms of the ratio of the strength of the signal to the intensity of the noise.

We shall now turn to a brief consideration of the organs of auditory per-

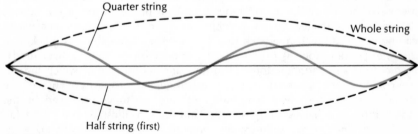

Figure 1.6
String vibrating in wholes, halves, and quarters.

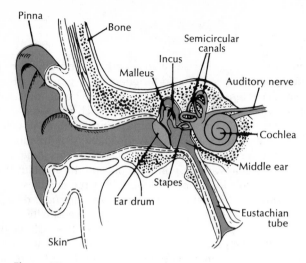

Figure 1.7
Diagram of the human ear.

ception before considering some of the aspects of the perception of sound and light.

The Ear

Figure 1.7 is a schematic drawing of a cross section of the human ear. The initial processing of sound waves is relatively simple. The wave of disturbance is transmitted through the air and into the external meatus to the eardrum; the net movement of the latter is translated as a vibration to the three bones (the ossicles) of the middle ear. These are located in an air-filled cavity that—by means of the *eustachian tube* opening in the mouth cavity—maintains an air pressure similar to the external air pressure. From the ossicles the vibrations are transmitted via the oval window to the *cochlea.*

Up to this point the disturbance in the external medium has been conducted with only minor changes, which are due to the fact that some of the ear's components transmit frequencies and intensities better than others.

The actual process of hearing begins in the cochlea. The vibrations are transmitted through its three fluid-filled canals as a wave of movement along the membranes separating the individual canals. On one of the membranes of the cochlea (the *basilar membrane*) is a cell complex known as the *organ of Corti,* which contains rows of hair cells embedded in the membrane. These respond to the physical movement of the traveling wave and translate information concerning its frequency and intensity into impulses in the auditory nerve. The information is then conducted to the cortex by way of a number of substructures of the auditory system.[3]

---

[3] For further information concerning the physiology of hearing the interested reader should consult Chapter 8 of Morgan (1965).

The Concept of Threshold

A visual or auditory sensation occurs if an *adequate* or *effective* stimulus is presented to the appropriate system. To be effective, a potential stimulus must display certain characteristics—for example, it must be of sufficient intensity and duration to evoke a response. If the values of such attributes of an effective stimulus are systematically reduced, at some point the observer will no longer be able to detect the stimulus. Traditionally the inability of the subject to report the stimulus is said to be a result of crossing a *sensory threshold*. If the values of the stimulus are too low, no response occurs and the stimulus is said to be *subthreshold* or *subliminal* (limen = threshold). If the stimulus is reported— that is, if it remains effective—it is said to be *above threshold* or *supraliminal*.

The problem of ascertaining the lower limit of sensitivity for a stimulus was first approached empirically by Gustav Fechner in 1860. Although he introduced several methods for the study of threshold, two kinds of thresholds have received extensive attention in the ensuing years: the *absolute threshold*, which is defined as the lowest value of a stimulus detectable; and the *difference threshold*, characterized by the smallest amount of detectable change in a stimulus.

Let us consider the basic problems of threshold with an example utilizing Fechner's *method of limits* and the absolute threshold for a tone. If we are interested in measuring the threshold for the intensity of a tone, all other aspects of the stimulus (e.g., duration, frequency, phase, distance from the observer, etc.) must be held constant. The variations in intensity will extend over a range beginning well below the probable threshold (near zero intensity) and continue in equal intervals or steps of intensity well above the expected threshold. In the actual experiment we will start with a low or subthreshold intensity value and increase the intensity by one unit on each successive trial. The task of the observer on each trial is to indicate whether or not he hears the tone by saying "Yes, I hear it" or "No, I don't hear it." If we start with the lowest value, the subject will answer "no" on each step until at some point he hears the tone and responds with a "yes." We then repeat the procedure; this time, however, an intensity value well above threshold is chosen and on each successive trial the intensity is reduced by one unit. The subject responds with "yes" until he no longer hears the tone. In this manner we can conduct a number of measurements (e.g., 100) using an *ascending series* for one half and a *descending series* for the other. Care must be taken not to start each series at the same level of intensity so that the subject cannot simply give the same number of "yes" and "no" responses each time.

Table 1.1 contains a sample of the kind of data obtained in such an experiment. Notice that the point at which the first "yes" occurs in the ascending series or the first "no" in the descending series is not always the same for successive measurements; a great deal of variation occurs between successive measurements. If the data are averaged—compute the sum of the intensity values at which the subject first reported "yes" or "no" and divide by the total number of measurements—we obtain a value at which the observer said "yes" 50 per-

Table 1.1

The method of limits used to establish the sensory threshold for the intensity of a tone

Intensity	Measurements							
	A	B	C	D	E	F	G	H
1	no							
2	no				no			
3	no		no		no			
4	no		no		no		no	
5	no		yes		no		no	
6	no	no			yes		no	no
7	no	yes				no	no	yes
8	yes	yes				yes	yes	yes
9		yes		no		yes		yes
10		yes		yes		yes		yes
11		yes		yes		yes		
12		yes		yes		yes		
13		yes				yes		
14		yes						

cent of the time and "no" 50 percent of the time. By counting the frequency of "yes" and "no" responses for each intensity value above and below the mean, it is possible to determine the probability of a "yes" or "no" response for all values in the series. An example of such a calculation for "yes" responses is provided in Figure 1.8. The curve is an ogive (s-shape), which is an indication of an underlying normal probability distribution. This means that if a tone with 5 units of intensity is presented it will be reported about 25 percent of the time, whereas a tone with 10 units of intensity will be reported 85 percent of the time. Threshold, then, can be considered a statistical concept rather than a point separating sensation from the lack of sensation.

Among other techniques for threshold assessment introduced by Fechner was the *method of constant stimuli*. Returning to our sample experiment in which a measure of sensitivity for the intensity of a tone was attempted with the methods of limits (Table 1.1), we can demonstrate the method of constant stimuli. Rather than presenting an ascending or descending series of intensities, under the method of constant stimuli various intensities are presented in random order and the subject is asked to respond with "yes" or "no" with regard to the detectability of the stimulus. Again, the stimulus value for which the subject says "yes" 50 percent of the time is considered to be the threshold.

Those persons interested in the area of psychology known as *psychophysics* faced an imposing task when they sought ways to describe adequately

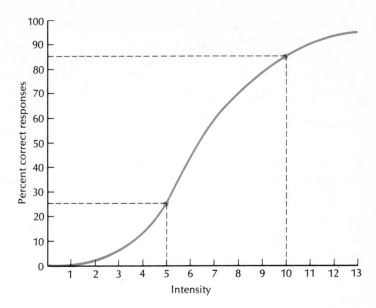

Figure 1.8
Normal curve of the threshold of intensity for a pure tone scaled by the method of limits.

the normal curve data obtained in threshold experiments. Obviously at least two factors influence whether a subject will respond with "yes" or "no" at any given level of intensity in the experiment just described. First, the response will depend on the actual sensitivity of the subject to the stimulus. Second, however, the subject's sensitivity is clouded by variations in subjective criteria for reporting "yes" or "no." In order to assess the threshold, these two factors must be separated. One solution to the problem has been offered by a technique based on *signal detection theory*.

Signal detection theory.[4]   Tanner and Swets (1954) originally approached the problem of assessing the criteria used by an observer to detect a stimulus or signal by specifying mathematically the upper limit of performance imposed by the environment. Using what they termed the *theory of ideal observers*, Tanner and Swets considered, in theoretical terms, how well a perfect observer should be able to perform under any given set of stimulus conditions. They demonstrated that a comparison of the performances of real observers with the ideal performance provides information about the response characteristics of the human observers. One difference observed was that the curve relating

---

[4] For detailed discussion of signal detection theory the interested reader should consult the following: Hake and Rodwan (1967); Swets, Tanner, and Birdsall (1961); and Swets (1961*b*).

the proportion of correct responses to intensity of the stimulus is steeper for real observers than for ideal observers. For some reason, real observers do poorer at the lower levels of intensity.

The basic experimental design in studies of signal detection requires a decision by the observer concerning the presence or absence of a specific signal during a previously defined interval. The interval is known to the observer, as is the critical signal. During the interval external noise is usually present, provided by the experimenter as a measurable background against which the signal is judged. (Noise—in the sense of that which interferes or blocks out—is also considered a property of the sensory system. Examples of noise understood in this sense are: fatigue, motivation, stimulus adaptation, changes in attention, and spontaneous, random neural activity within the sensory system.) On any given trial the observer must decide to respond with "yes" or "no." Notice that he decides only if he prefers to respond with either answer; he is not required to state definitely that "yes, a signal occurred," or "no, a signal was not present." The observer is also aware of the probability that any interval may contain a signal.

Let us consider the observer's task. During a particular interval he is aware of the probability of the occurrence of a signal plus background noise or of background noise alone; he bases his "yes" or "no" in part on the ratio of these two quantities. This ratio is known as the *likelihood ratio*. Notice that we say that the observer's response is based *in part* on the likelihood ratio. It is also based on the kind of sensory information received and on other factors such as motivation and experience.

Signal detection theory assumes that the observer establishes a response criterion that will dictate the observer's report. This criterion is based on the likelihood ratio exceeding the critical value established by the observer. Exactly what the critical value will be depends on the detection goal of the observer. For example, if the observer is only interested in never missing a signal, he will be most concerned with the probability of the occurrence of a signal at any interval. If, on the other hand, the observer is interested in his total performance, he must consider the probabilities associated with the four possible outcomes of his decisions, which are outlined in Table 1.2. Assuming that the observer's response criterion reflects the probabilities associated with each outcome, we can calculate two independent measures from his performance: his *response criterion* and his *sensory sensitivity*.

The identification of these two components is accomplished by forcing the observer to change his established criterion during various subsets of trials. If this is done, one can plot on a graph the frequency of correct "yes" responses SN_y on one axis and the frequency of incorrect "yes" responses N_y on the other axis. As the observer is forced to vary his criterion, we can plot the proportion of correct and incorrect "yes" responses as a single curve running from 0 to 1.0. The curve obtained for any observer would then depend on the attributes of the signal and of the noise as well as the observer's sensitivity. The slope of the curve at any point would give the likelihood ratio from which, as mentioned earlier, the subject's response criterion can be derived. With a knowledge of the response criterion of the observer, a measure of sensitivity

Table 1.2

**Probabilities associated with four possible outcomes
of an observer's decisions**

Observer's decisions	Stimulus condition	
	Noise (N)	Signal plus Noise (SN)
Yes (y)	$P_{N(y)}$ False alarm	$P_{SN(y)}$ Identification (hit)
No (n)	$P_{N(n)}$ Rejection (hit)	$P_{SN(n)}$ (miss)

can be obtained independently from the response criterion. Research has shown that the obtained curves for any single observer can be described by a single measure known as d'. This represents the difference between the means of the normal probability distribution associated with the signal-plus-noise condition and the noise-alone condition divided by the standard deviation of the noise distribution:

$$d' = \frac{M_{(SN)} - M_{(N)}}{\sigma_{(N)}}$$

Now let us consider the application of these techniques to an actual experiment. An observer is required to detect a tone burst (signal) against a background noise; he is aware of all of the signal's salient features. Figure 1.9 displays the proportion of correct versus incorrect "yes" responses for the five probabilities used by the experimenter. The curve is the line that best fits the data points. The insert at the lower right of the figure shows the distributions of the effect of the noise alone (left distribution) and the signal plus noise (right distribution) on the sensory system in question. This abscissa of the insert is labeled "central effect." On the trials containing noise a central effect is produced in the auditory system, the magnitude of which—that is to say, the observer's sensitivity to this central effect—is represented as a value on the abscissa E of the insert. The value of E on the occasion of each presentation of noise is expressed as a conditional probability density function (ordinate of insert). The mean of the probability function for noise is shown as the solid line marked M_N. Similarly the mean of the probability function for the signal plus noise condition is marked M_{SN}.

The observer must respond "yes" or "no" on any trial. To do so he selects a criterion on the E axis (1, 2, 3, 4, or 5). The criterion selected by the observer depends, as we have seen, on the ratio of the probability of a hit, $P_{SN(y)}$, to the probability of a false alarm, $P_{N(y)}$. These probabilities are varied by the experimenter (in the present study five probabilities were utilized) and are known to the observer. The criterion actually utilized by the observer for the

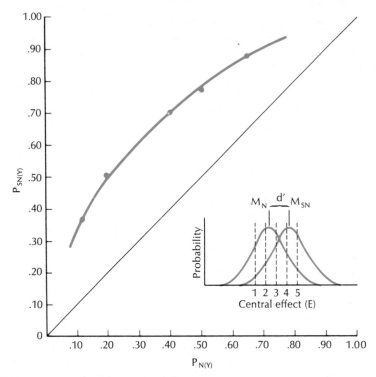

Figure 1.9
Proportion of correct versus proportion of incorrect "yes" responses in a
signal detection experiment. (After Swets, 1961. Copyright 1961 by the
American Association for the Advancement of Science.)

different proportions is given by the curved line in Figure 1.9 and is known as
the *receiver-operating characteristic*. The five criterion levels are shown as
dotted lines in the insert. If on any trial the value produced on the central effect
axis (observer's sensitivity) is great enough to fall above the criterion level
presently in use (e.g., level 2) the observer will respond "yes." If the value
falls below this level he responds "no."

The sensory performance of the observer is then given by the amount of
separation of the two distributions. This is computed as a standard score d';
in the present experiment the value of d' was 0.85.

With these procedures we have estimated the observer's sensitivity and
the criterion used to respond. We then know for this observer the probability
of a "yes" or "no" response for the auditory stimulus used, as well as the relationship between the criterion level and sensitivity.

Perhaps the most important observation is that the obtained measure of
the subject's sensitivity does not change as a function of the criterion level.
This becomes clearer when we consider another approach employed by signal detection theorists: *the forced-choice technique*. To cite another example

from Swets (1961b), subjects were asked to view a uniformly illuminated background during four temporal intervals. The signal was a small spot of light projected on the background during one of the intervals. The task of the subject was to choose which interval contained the signal. The important aspect of the experiment was, however, that the observer was given a second choice if an error was made on the first choice. According to the traditional view of a static threshold, one would expect only chance behavior on the second choice. If the original interval were above threshold it would be reported on trial one. If it were below threshold it would not be reported and the probability of correctly identifying which of the three remaining intervals contained the signal would be chance or $p = 0.33$. In actuality the probability averaged over various criterion measures was $p = 0.51$.

In light of the observations of signal detection theory, we are left with the view that a subject's response to a stimulus depends on his response criterion, the characteristics of the signal, and the amount of external and internal noise in the sensory system. In short, the concept of a fixed sensory threshold must be discarded and replaced by the concept of a variability in an organism's response to a potential stimulus. If we wish to retain the concept of threshold, we can at best speak of response thresholds but not of sensory thresholds.

We began this discussion by considering the method of limits for the measurement of threshold. Obviously this technique will provide little information about an observer's sensitivity to a stimulus. Generally speaking, the best technique would appear to be the forced-choice technique, which does not require an estimation of the observer's response criterion, because the observer is expected always to choose the interval most likely to contain a signal.

Statistical Decision Theory

On the one hand, signal detection theory has provided a new view of sensation and developed a method of measuring observer sensitivity independent of the observer's response criterion. On the other hand, it cast doubt on the validity of the enormous bulk of material collected with the traditional techniques of sensitivity assessment such as the method of limits and the method of constant stimuli. In view of the dependency of the *response threshold* on the decision criteria employed by the observer, the generality and applicability of all information gathered with these techniques is questionable. Treisman and Watts (1966) have offered a solution to part of the problem by reconsidering the interpretation of data collected under the traditional methods.

Using the example provided by Treisman and Watts, let us consider the establishment of a *differential threshold* with the method of constant stimuli. On each trial the observer listens to a standard tone of a given intensity, together with a comparison tone of greater or lesser intensity. Each of a wide range of comparison tones is paired randomly with the standard tone. The observer responds on each trial with a judgment of "greater," "lesser," or "doubt-

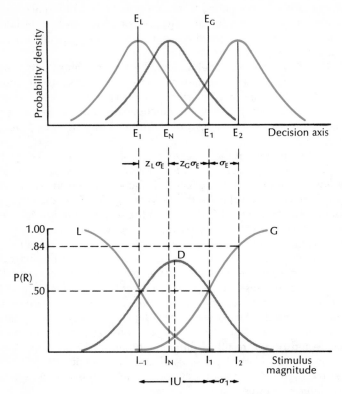

Figure 1.10
Difference thresholds for tones determined with the method of constant stimuli and three categories of response. (After Treisman and Watts, 1966.)

ful"; the last category indicates the observer's inability to make a judgment. In this manner it is possible to find the limits of sensitivity for judgments of differences between signals. The type of data obtained in such an experiment is outlined in the lower portion of Figure 1.10. The figure relates the magnitude of the difference between the standard tone I_N and the comparison tones I_{-i} to I_{+i}, to the frequency of "greater" (G), "lesser" (L), and "doubtful" (D) judgments. Notice that the curves for L and G responses are again ogives, indicating a normal probability function. The "doubtful" responses show a normal distribution around the intensity value representing the standard stimulus. The "50 percent threshold" for a "greater" response is found to be I_{+i}, the value on the P(R) scale at which the G curve intersects with the D curve. By the same token, the point at which the L curve intersects with D provides the "50 percent threshold," for a "lesser" response. The area between the two points I_{-i} to I_{+i} is called the *interval of uncertainty*. The probability of a "greater" response P(G) for a comparison tone with the value of I_{+2} is 0.84. Due to the characteristics of a normal curve, this value represents a difference between I_1 and I_2 in the probability of a "greater" response of one standard deviation. The same holds true, of course, for the L ogive, with the difference in P(L) between I_{-1} and I_{-2} equaling one standard deviation.

The statistical decision model outlined by Treisman and Watts is shown at the top of Figure 1.10. The presentation of a tone produces a central effect displaying some value along the decision axis E. Repeated presentations of the stimulus result in a normal probability function with a mean on the E-axis corresponding to the intensity values I of the tones $E_{-1} = I_{-1}$; $E_N = I_N$; $E_1 = I_1$; $E_2 = I_2$.

During the experiment the observer establishes one response criterion for "greater" and one for "lesser." Assume a comparison tone with the stimulus value of I_i which has the central effect E_i. If the value E_i on the decision axis is greater than the criterion value for the decision "greater" E_G, then the observer will respond with "greater." If E_i is less than the second criterion E_L, a response of "lesser" is expected. The failure to exceed either value on any trial places the value of E_i within the area of uncertainty. With the diagram in Figure 1.10 we can predict the probability of the response as a function of the magnitude of the difference between the standard and the test stimuli. The central effect E_{-1} would evoke the response of "lesser" 50 percent of the time, indicating that this is the observer's criterion for "lesser." We can therefore establish the subject's response criterion and observe the degree of sensitivity for any given stimulus difference. The response criteria are considered stable in this model; variations would be the result of different stimulus effects (changes in sensitivity). Although a number of measures of sensitivity are possible, Culler (1926) proposed the use of the standard deviation of the two resulting ogives (L and G) as the difference threshold.

One can also determine the response criterion for measurements of absolute threshold under the method of constant stimuli. These considerations are depicted in Figure 1.11. In this application of statistical decision theory, the stimulus value I_N is considered the constant level of background noise corresponding to the central effect E_N on the decision axis (top of figure). The lower portion of Figure 1.11 relates the probability of a "yes" response P(Y) to the various stimulus intensities I employed in the experiment. The distribution of central effects E for each stimulus intensity is shown at the top of the figure. As with the difference measurements, the observer's response criterion E_c is represented as the distribution on the E axis (decision axis) corresponding to a P(Y) of 0.50. Treisman and Watts suggest that the threshold of $I_i - I_N = \Delta I$ (incremental threshold) be used, whereas the standard deviation of the incremental threshold is given by $I_2 - I_1$.

The determination of the response criteria is described by Treisman and Watts as follows:

We see from Figure 1.11 that $I_i - I_N = \Delta I$ corresponds to $z\sigma_E$, and $I_2 - I_1 = \sigma\Delta_1$ corresponds to σ_E. Therefore, the ratio between these two measures should correspond to $z\sigma_E/\sigma_E = z$, and should be the measure of the criterion, expressed as a standardized normal deviation from the mean of the noise distribution (p. 445).

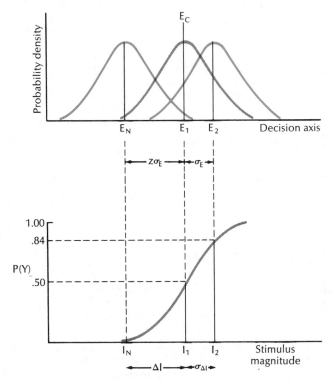

Figure 1.11
Response criteria for measures of absolute threshold determined
with the method of constant stimuli. (After Treisman and Watts,
1966.)

The statistical decision theory does not differ greatly from signal detection
theory. Although Treisman and Watts argue the application of their model for
thresholds measured with the other Fechnerian methods, such as the method of
limits, they conclude that the measures did fail to establish exact measures of
incremental thresholds and to determine the interval of uncertainty.

In conclusion, the method of constant stimuli remains useful in the assessment of observer sensitivity, and most of the older data assembled with the
method can be analyzed in terms of statistical decision theory. Nevertheless,
the independent assessment of observer sensitivity and response criterion afforded by signal detection theory makes the newer techniques most useful for
future work.

Psychophysical Scaling

The classical technique of threshold assessment and the detection approaches
are concerned with the presence of sensations and with their absence. Once

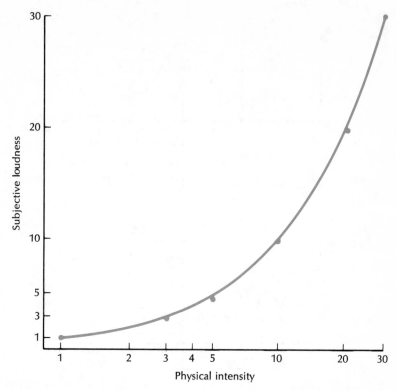

Figure 1.12
Fechnerian relationship between subjective loudness (arithmetic progression) and physical intensity (logarithmic progression).

a sensation occurs, however, further increases in the magnitude of the effective stimulus serve to modify that original sensation. For example, if we were to establish the observer's sensitivity for the presence of an auditory stimulus by varying the intensity of the stimulus, a *receiver operating characteristic* could be derived for the various probabilities of the occurrence of the signal. Further increases in intensity would result in a quantification of the stimulus; the subject would report the stimulus to be louder and louder.

The problem at this level is one of scaling the relationship between the physical intensity of the stimulus and the *perceived* or subjective intensity of the stimulus. Unfortunately this relationship is seldom a simple direct correspondence, since an increase in physical magnitude is seldom accompanied by an equal increase in subjective magnitude. Gustav Fechner suggested in 1860 that the relationship was *logarithmic:* as the magnitude of the sensation increases arithmetically, the corresponding physical value increases logarithmically. This relationship is depicted in Figure 1.12.

Faced with the task of measuring the amount of subjective change in the observer's sensation, Fechner developed the concept of *just noticeable differ-*

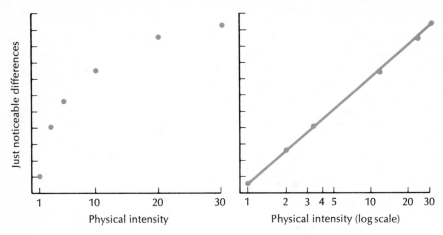

Figure 1.13
Left, just noticeable difference estimates for increasing values of stimulus intensity. *Right,* just noticeable difference estimates for the same values plotted on a logarithmic scale.

ence or *jnd.* One jnd was defined as the amount of change in value of the physical stimulus (i.e., increase in stimulus intensity) required to produce a noticeable change in the quality or quantity of the stimulus. For example, with the differential threshold, pairs of tones could be presented and the subject asked to judge which was the more intense of the pair. By varying the amount of difference between the tones and by presenting pairs of tones over a wide range of intensities, and by counting up jnds, one could derive a scale of loudness. As Fechner had expected, it was found that the relationship between perceived loudness (as assessed by jnds) and physical intensity was logarithmic. Figure 1.13 provides an example. The curve on the left demonstrates that the discriminable differences with increases in physical intensity require much less change in physical intensity per jnd at the lower intensity levels, but that the necessary increment required to produce a jnd increases as the level of physical intensity increases. If we plot the jnds in equal units and the increases in physical intensity in log units of intensity (right figure), the relationship is essentially a straight line.

Fechner's work was accepted for nearly a hundred years and has been applied successfully to a number of scaling problems. The most frequently used scale of loudness, the *decibel scale,* is based on Fechner's logarithmic formulation.

One major assumption stemming from Fechner's work is that jnds obtained anywhere along the entire scale represent subjectively equal intervals. Stevens (1936) demonstrated that this assumption was not correct for many of the physical dimensions that had been scaled by the Fechnerian techniques. In particular Stevens found that the jnd intervals in loudness judgments tended to increase in subjective magnitude as the physical intensity increased. That is, the subjective scale was not a simple arithmetic function, as had been assumed by Fechner.

For those sensations that do not produce equal interval jnds—sensations known as *prothetic continua*—Stevens (1964) has developed a descriptive function which seems to apply to a very wide range of subjective magnitudes. The function is known as *Stevens's power function.* It describes the relationship between subjective intensity and physical intensity with the formula $\Psi = K(\gamma - \gamma_0)^n$, where

$\Psi =$ subjective stimulus magnitude
$K =$ constant (depends on units of measurement to be scaled)
$n =$ exponent (depends on the sensation being scaled)
$\gamma =$ value of the physical stimulus
$\gamma_0 =$ physical value from which the scale begins
(usually determined as the absolute threshold for a sensation)

The power function will predict the relationship between the physical and psychological values of any sensory response. It provides a straight line representing the relationship of physical to psychological magnitude, whereby the slope of the line is given by the exponent of the sensory system under study. Because the power function does not assume equal intervals for the psychological scale, it is drawn with both the ordinate and abscissa in logarithmic units. In actual application, one plots the physical intensity against the observed magnitude judgments on log-log paper, a variety of paper printed with the coordinates scaled in logarithmic units.

Over the last thirty years S. S. Stevens and his co-workers at Harvard have concerned themselves with the development of scaling techniques for a large number of sensations ranging from the subjective intensity of coffee odors (Reese and Stevens, 1960) to the magnitude of electric shocks (Stevens, Carton, and Shickman, 1958).

The empirical construction of a scale and the description of the relationship between the physical and psychological variables follows two basic methods: the *method of fractionation* and the *method of direct magnitude estimation.* Let us consider the former as applied to the problem of the subjective intensity or loudness of a sound. We have already mentioned Stevens's observation (1936) that the decibel scale of loudness was inadequate at higher levels of noise due to the inequality of successive jnds. Using the method of fractionation, Stevens (1936) and Stevens and Davis (1947) developed a new scale of loudness, the *sone scale.*

The first task was to define the starting point from which the measurement was to begin (γ_0). One sone was designated as the loudness of a 1,000-Hz tone, at 40 decibels above the absolute threshold for hearing. Subjects were presented with a reference tone of a given intensity and asked to adjust a second tone to be one-half as loud as the reference tone. By presenting reference tones from the entire spectrum of intensities, a scale of loudness starting with the effective value of one sone could be constructed. The scale at the left in Figure 1.14—the sone scale in relation to the decibel values—demonstrates the inequality of successive intervals, since the decibel value asso-

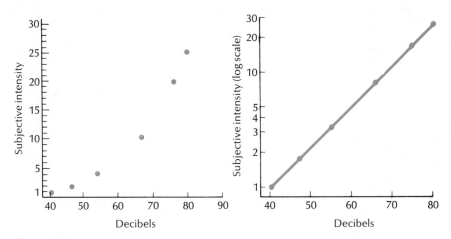

Figure 1.14
Left, the sone scale of loudness. (After Stevens, 1936.) *Right,* the inequality of successive intervals of the scale on the left plotted on log-log continua.

ciated with the interval between successive sones becomes increasingly smaller as physical intensity increases. Obviously the data cannot be described by the Fechnerian formulation, but they do follow Steven's power function. The scale at the right in Figure 1.14 shows the same data plotted on log-log continua; both the ordinate and abscissa are in logarithmic units. The power function describes the line relating the physical and subjective intensities.

With the *method of direct magnitude estimation* the experimenter selects a stimulus of a given magnitude and assigns some fixed number to represent the subjective magnitude of that stimulus. The subject is then given various physical values of the stimulus taken from the continua of values to be scaled and is required to assign a number (whole number, fraction, or decimal) to each physical stimulus value. The subject is therefore directly estimating the subjective magnitude of each stimulus.

Direct magnitude estimation was used by Stevens (1959) when subjects were asked to estimate the magnitude of the vibration produced by a device attached to the middle finger of the left hand. The subject was first stimulated by a vibration of moderate intensity and told that this vibration was to be numbered 10. Thereafter the subjects were presented with vibrations over the range from 10 to 40 decibels above threshold and asked to number them in relation to the magnitude of the first vibration (number 10). As can be seen in Figure 1.15, the subjective magnitude estimations follow the expected straight-line power function when the physical amplitude (decibels) is plotted against the direct magnitude estimation on log-log plots.

Cross-modality matching. Perhaps the true test of the power function for assessing subjective scales of intensity is to be found in the attempt to equate subjective magnitudes of one sensation with magnitude estimates of a different sensation. As an example of such comparative judgments, let us consider loudness as one sensation and vibration amplitude as the other. The task of

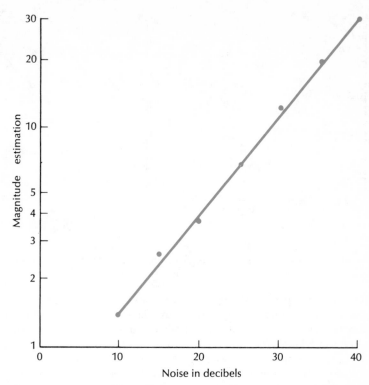

Figure 1.15
Subjective magnitude of the vibration of a finger reported by the method of direct magnitude estimation. The exponent of the power function is 0.96. (After Stevens, 1959.)

comparing them is rather like judging the size of pears by looking at a big orange. Stevens (1959) required subjects to match the level of a sound to the magnitude of a finger vibration. First a sound was presented and the subjects asked to vary the vibration until they felt the subjective magnitude of the two to be equal. A second set of measurements was taken with the magnitude of the vibration given and the loudness variable.

If the power function is a true estimator of the subjective magnitude of sensations, then a graphic plot on log-log continua of the vibration amplitude against the auditory intensity should yield a straight-line function. The exponent or slope of the line would be given by the ratio of exponents of the two scales. For vibration versus loudness, the ratio of the exponents equals 0.6. Figure 1.16 shows the empirical data produced by the experiment. The power function, as represented in this figure, describes the relationship quite well.

The technique of cross-modality matching has been utilized by Rule (1969) to test the underlying assumption of the method of direct magnitude estimation. Subjects viewed a number of circles varying in equal logarithmic steps from 0.52 to 7.74 inches. Each circle was studied for one second, after

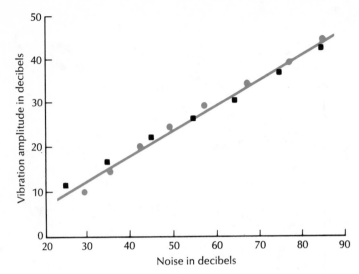

Figure 1.16
Cross-modality matching of the amplitude of finger vibration based on
adjusting the intensity of a tone. (After Stevens, 1959.)

which the experimenter stated a number. The task of the observer was to indicate whether the magnitude of the number was greater or lesser than the
magnitude of the circle. Figure 1.17 shows the results of the experiment in
which the size of the circle is compared to the numbers. The relationship between the two variables follows a straight line, which led Rule to conclude that
scale values for size judgments based on the magnitude of a number follow the
power function. The experiment not only demonstrates a cross-modality match
(magnitude of a number presented orally versus size of a visually presented
circle), it also demonstrates the validity of the method of direct magnitude estimation. Observers are in fact able to assign numbers to variations in the subjective magnitude of sensory impressions.

In summary, the power function has been able to describe a wide variety
of magnitude estimations of subjective sensations. Corso (1967) suggests that
while it is able to describe sensory processes involving the accumulation or
buildup of successive neural excitations (e.g., brightness judgments), it is not
able to describe sensory responses involving the substitution of one excitation
for another (e.g., the pitch of a tone). In many cases such relationships between the physical attributes of a stimulus and the subjective estimation of
their sensory magnitude can be described by the logarithmic relationship proposed by Fechner in 1860.

We have now considered the nature of the perceptual response and several characteristics of the effective perceptual stimulus. Armed with techniques
for assessing sensitivity and for scaling the magnitude of sensations, we can
turn to a discussion of some of the factors influencing the occurrence of sensations and perceptions as a result of simple and complex patterns of stimuli.

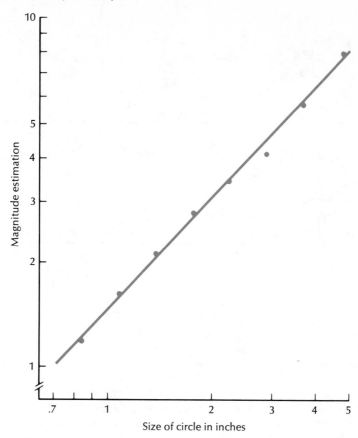

Figure 1.17
Median magnitude estimations of number plotted against the physical size of circles. (After Rule, 1969.)

CHAPTER 2

The Perception
of Color

Color, in its everyday usage, refers to a property of most of the objects in our environment. It is frequently so characteristic of an object that we define and describe the object in terms of its color. Due to our experience with objects of specific colors, it is often difficult to consider the aspects of color without reference to an object of some kind. The term *red* is an abstract concept, yet when asked to think of red, we usually have a mental image of some object that is characteristically red.

The color perception evoked by an object appears to be the result of at least seven factors:

1. A physical characteristic of the object itself—the capacity to reflect and absorb certain elements of light.
2. The properties of the light source and the reflected light from the object.
3. The medium through which the light travels as well as the distance it travels.
4. The properties of the surrounding objects or area.
5. The biochemical state of the eye and the visual system when stimulated.
6. The transmission characteristics of the receptor cells and neural centers.
7. The subject's previous experience with the object or the sensation.

Three avenues of research have been opened in the study of color perception: the physical, psychological, and physiological approaches. The following discussion is primarily concerned with the psychological aspects of color perception, but the physical and to some extent the physiological aspects must also be considered.

The Psychology of Color Perception

Our willingness to say that an object is a particular color derives from at least three aspects of the stimulus. A distal stimulus for a color sensation can be described in terms of the dominant *wavelengths*, the *intensity* of the waves, and the *purity* (proportion of white light or the number and proportion of reflected waves) of the light reflected by the object. The identification also depends on a multitude of learning variables, such as previous experiences with the object and the association of specific sensations with color names. The perception is also affected by the context in which the color occurs and by the characteristics of the surrounding area or the colors of other objects. The study of the first three variables is always compounded by the experiences of the observer with colors in general; because the perception of color is a subjective or personal experience, its aspects can be described only in terms of the subject's report of his perceptions. The color perceptions themselves vary along the corresponding psychological dimensions of hue, saturation, and brightness.

Hue.   It has long been known that the color sensations reported by an observer with normal color vision vary as a function of the wavelength of the stimulus. This holds true for the range of wavelengths falling between approximately 420 and 700 mμ. The sensations reported by observers exposed to these various wavelengths are known as *hues*. An example of research into the nature of hue is the study by Boynton and Gordon (1965). Subjects were presented with flashes of light containing single wavelengths (monochromatic light) ranging between 440 and 660 mμ and asked to identify the resulting sensations using

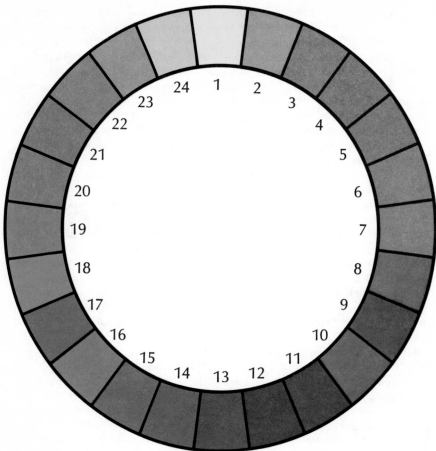

Figure 2.1
Circle of hues. (After Ostwald, 1921.)

the terms blue, green, yellow, and red. For the range of wavelengths between 440 and 490 mμ subjects reported the sensation of blue. The response green was assigned to wavelengths between 490 and 570 mμ, yellow for 570 to 600 mμ, and red for the wavelengths between 600 and 660 mμ.

Between each sensation lies an area of hue combination in which agreement between observers is less prominent. For example, stimuli ranging in wavelength from 480 to 510 mμ are described as blue-green, greenish blue, or aquamarine. Although agreement on the proper name for a given sensation is slight, the number of different hues that can be discriminated is large. Several systems have been developed in which discriminable hues are shown in relation to one another. Figure 2.1 provides an example of one of these systems developed by Ostwald (1921). Each of the hues evoke a different sensation; however, most observers with normal color sensitivity would call all the numbers 13 through 18 blue, 21 through 24 green, and so on.

The order of the hues is dictated by the wavelengths, which start with the shorter wavelengths (approximately hue 13) and increase around the circle to the area of longer wavelengths (approximately hue 11). Each different hue represents a wavelength increase of more than a single millimicron. For example, hue 13 represents a wavelength of about 440 mμ, whereas hue 14 equals a wavelength with 463 mμ. Furthermore, the intervals between hues are not equal; they are adjusted to intervals that appear to be equal, rather than on the basis of an increase in a specific wavelength. Since Ostwald developed the color circle of hues using Fechner's method of just noticeable differences, it is not surprising to find inequalities in the size of the intervals around the scale. Hue 16 represents a wavelength of approximately 481 mμ, while hue 20 equals 492 mμ; hue 5 corresponds to about 617 mμ, with hue 6 corresponding to 642 mμ.

Hue, then, is the basic component of color and is primarily responsible for the specific color sensation. While the color names or hues evoked by different portions of the visual spectrum show a close relationship to certain wavelengths, it should be remembered that hue is a psychological variable, and wavelength a physical one. Although all individuals with normal color vision would name a sector of the visual spectrum red, disagreement would occur in deciding which was the reddest red or at what point red becomes orange. These differences probably reflect varying experiences with color as well as intrinsic differences in the color mechanisms of each individual's visual system.

Saturation.   We are seldom presented with a pure monochromatic light source that evokes the sensation of a single hue. Rather, the light reflected by different objects is multichromatic. Figure 2.2 shows the range of wavelengths reflected by a ripe tomato. Notice that while the most reflected light is in the red end of the spectrum (650 to 700 mμ) many other wavelengths are also reflected to a lesser degree.

If we start with a narrow band of wavelengths, we will be able to identify a dominant hue. This dominant hue remains the same even though we increase the width of the band of wavelengths. Increasing the bandwidth causes the sensation to be modified, however; the hue becomes less distinct or clear, and we say then that the hue is less saturated. *Saturation* refers to the purity of the wavelength contributing to a color sensation. The narrower the band of wavelengths (e.g., 510 to 512 mμ), the more highly saturated is the resulting color sensation. By the same token, the wider the band of wavelengths, the less saturated will be the resulting color (e.g., 510 to 590 mμ). From the subjective point of view, saturation varies as a function of the number of hues producing the color sensation. This means that a mixture of the Ostwald hues 17, 18, and 19 would produce a less saturated color with hue 18 dominant. Mixing hues 4, 5, and 6 would produce a color with an equal degree of saturation and a dominant hue 5. In the first case the band of wavelengths only covers a range of 483 to 487 mμ; in the second, however, hues 4, 5, and 6 cover the much wider range of 593 to 642 mμ.

If the number of hues added to the sensation becomes great enough, the resulting sensation approaches gray. If we were to mix the entire range be-

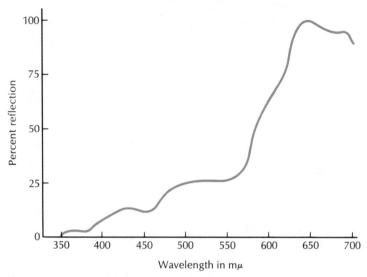

Figure 2.2
Spectral energy distribution analysis. Percentage of wavelengths reflected by a ripe tomato.

tween hues 1 and 13, the resulting sensation would no longer have a dominant
hue, but would be a neutral gray.

As was the case with hue, saturation is a psychological aspect of color,
one that depends primarily on the purity of the contributing wavelengths.
Several scales of saturation have been developed to describe the subjective
change in a sensation resulting from an increase in the number of hues. Much
in the same manner as the sone scale of loudness was developed with modern
scaling techniques (see Chapter 1), Indow and Stevens (1966) have developed
a saturation scale based on a unit called a *crome*.

Brightness.   The third aspect of a color sensation comes from the amount of
white or black mixed with the hue. This gives variations along the continuum
of *brightness*. The visual sensations of black through varying degrees of gray
on to white make up the scale of brightness. Such sensations are referred to as
achromatic colors or stimuli, while those containing a dominant hue are known
as *chromatic colors* or stimuli. Naturally the addition of white or black to a
given hue reduces its purity and brings about a reduction in saturation.

The brightness of a color corresponds most closely to the physical intensity
or radiometric units of energy of the light wave. However, the phenomenal
brightness of color also depends on hue, as can be seen in Figure 2.3. If
subjects are asked to judge the brightness of hues or to arrange them in
order of increasing brightness, some hues are perceived as brighter than others.
This is true even when the various hues exhibit the same physical intensity.
Characteristically, yellow appears the brightest (hue 1 of Figure 2.1) and blue
the least bright (hue 13 of Figure 2.1). The other hues fall in between: hues 2

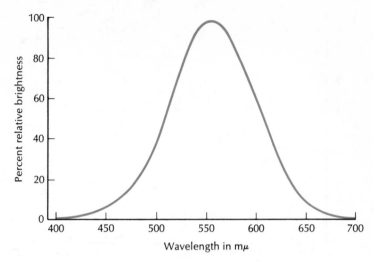

Figure 2.3
Phenomenal brightness of hues. The apparent brightness of each portion of the spectrum is expressed in terms of a percentage reduction in brightness away from the portion of maximum phenomenal brightness (555 mμ).

through 12 show decreasing phenomenal brightness, and hues 14 through 24, increasing brightness.

The fact that we are more sensitive to light waves in the central portion of the spectrum (510 to 600 mμ) presents a problem for the study of the relationship of phenomenal brightness and the physical intensity of the light wave. If we measure the amount of physical energy necessary to match light waves of varying wavelength to a standard achromatic stimulus, we obtain a curve similar to the one shown in Figure 2.4, which shows that we are most sensitive to light waves with a length of about 555 mμ. As this is the most sensitive portion of the spectrum, we can assign it the relative value of 1 unit of energy required to produce a match of the standard stimulus. This provides an anchor point with which the physical energy required to match the brightnesses of the other portions of the spectrum can be judged. The curve, known as a *luminosity curve,* indicates the relative sensitivity of the entire spectrum and informs us how much more intense one wavelength must be than another (e.g., 500 mμ compared to 550 mμ) in order to produce apparently equal brightness (0.70 unit of intensity).

If you compare Figures 2.3 and 2.4 you will note that the curves are really the same. In Figure 2.3 we have related the psychological variables of judged brightness and hue; in Figure 2.4 we have related the physical variables of wavelength and intensity.

For the purposes of research we can derive a unit of measurement referred to as *luminous energy,* which is the product of multiplying the physical amplitude of the light wave by the relative sensitivity of the typical human visual system for the wavelength to be utilized. This gives us a unit of sensitivity applicable to the entire visual spectrum.

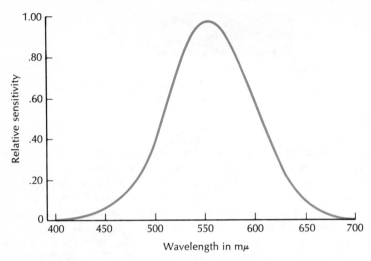

Figure 2.4
Spectral sensitivity of the average observer. Peak sensitivity at 555 mμ has been set at a value of 1. Sensitivity values at all other points along the spectrum reflect proportional reductions in sensitivity.

A study by Ball and Bartley (1966) employed these luminance levels to observe the effect of an increase in luminance on the apparent brightness of different hues. They presented narrow bands of light with dominant wavelengths of 500, 580, and 660 mμ at a number of different luminance levels. The experiment demonstrated that a given increase in luminance levels showed the greatest brightness increase for the 500 mμ stimulus and the least for the 660 mμ stimulus; the 580 mμ stimulus showed a brightness midway between the extremes. The intricacy of the relationship between brightness and hue is underscored by an apparent shift in hue that occurs with increasing brightness. This observation, known as the *Bezold-Brücke effect,* holds for all but three areas of the spectrum (478 mμ—blue, 503 mμ—green, and 572 mμ—yellow). In the study by Ball and Bartley the hue of 660 mμ was reported to shift in the direction of the shorter wavelengths at high luminance levels. Several subjects also experienced a hue shift with the 500 mμ stimulus.

Although the interrelation of hue, saturation, and brightness appears to be complex, several models have been developed to indicate their interaction.

The Munsell color tree.   Any given chromatic color sensation exhibits some value along the three dimensions of hue, saturation, and brightness. The relationships among the three are such that a variation along one dimension necessarily causes a change in the value of the other dimensions. A. H. Munsell (1941) developed a model for representing the relationships of these three dimensions. A modification of the basic model by Newhall, Nickerson, and Judd (1943) brought the system into closer agreement with empirical observation of perceptual tendencies. Let us start with the brightness dimension. Brightnesses or achromatic colors range from black to white in steps of gray, as shown in Figure 2.5.

Figure 2.5
Scale of achromatic colors ranging from white through various shades of gray to black.

The relationships among hues were shown in Figure 2.1. Hue and brightness can be related to each other in the manner shown in Figure 2.6. This figure indicates that the phenomenal brightness of a sensation depends on the amount of white or black (brightness dimension) and on the particular hue (circle of hues). The yellow and orange hues are found to exhibit a higher degree of phenomenal brightness and the reds and blues a lesser degree.

Finally, the dimension of saturation can be added as the distance between the circle of pure hues and scale of brightnesses. This is shown in Figure 2.7. A color sensation containing many hues will be less saturated and on our model will be situated close to the center of the disc. If enough hues are in the sensation, the color becomes very unsaturated and approaches gray.

Figure 2.8 shows a three-dimensional model of a color tree prepared by the Munsell Color Company. With this model we can make some definite statements about the hue, saturation, and brightness of any color sensation:

1. An increase or decrease in brightness will cause a reduction in saturation.
2. A change of hue will cause a change in brightness (e.g., a change from blue to green will cause an increase in brightness, from yellow to red a decrease).
3. An increase in the number of hues contributing to the color sensation will cause a reduction in saturation. Conversely, a reduction in saturation will involve an increase in the number of hues contributing to the sensation.

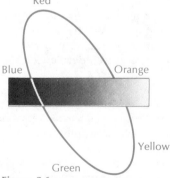

Figure 2.6
Relationship between achromatic colors (brightness) and hue.

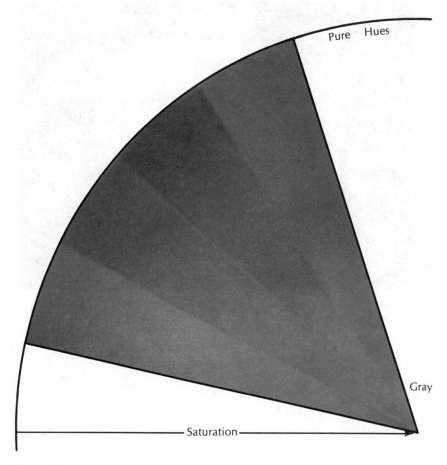

Pure · Hues

Gray

Saturation

Figure 2.7
Relationships between hue and saturation. As the saturation values of the pure hues on the outside of the circle are reduced, the colors approach a neutral gray.

It should be noted that the Munsell system was designed to describe the relationships among different color samples distributed along the psychological dimensions described above; it provides a standard by which specific color sensations can be related to each other. Unfortunately, the model cannot take into account all of the empirical observations related to the mixture of color or of the phenomenal appearance of colors under differing viewing conditions. What Katz (1935)—and also Hurvich, Jameson, and Krantz (1965)—pointed out about Ostwald's system also applies to the Munsell color arrangement: that the appearance of colors under differing conditions of illumination or context may vary greatly despite their equality along the dimensions of the model. Therefore we must turn to another system for a description of the laws and relationships of color mixture.

Figure 2.8
Relationships among hue, saturation, and brightness as represented by the Munsell color tree. Each cross-section of the color tree displays a gray scale in the center and hues of varying degrees of saturation toward the outside. (Courtesy of the Munsell Color Company, Inc., Baltimore, Maryland.)

Color Matching

With the Munsell system we have observed the relationships among hue, saturation, and brightness. Now we are interested in the effect of the addition of colors to one another on the chromatic sensation of an observer. Because we are centering our attention on the physical aspects of light, we will be dealing with the variables of wavelength and luminance.

If light sources of different dominant wavelengths are cast on a common surface, an additive process within the observer's visual system produces a chromatic sensation containing the elements of the contributing wavelengths. This is known as *additive color mixture.* Our primary concern will be with this kind of mixture; however, we should also note that a second kind occurs, known as *subtractive color mixture,* in which the contributing light sources absorb or eliminate wavelengths in each other. The mixture of paint pigments follows the relationships found in subtractive color mixture.

Trichromatic relations of color.   In his classic studies of color vision, Helmholtz (1896) reported that, given an appropriate set of three monochromatic (single wavelength) light sources, which we will call W_1, W_2, and W_3, one could mix a fourth light source W_x with any one of the first three and produce a match to the mixture of the remaining two light sources: $W_x + W_1 = W_2 + W_3$.

The only necessary stipulation to this relationship is that none of the three, W_1, W_2, or W_3, is a match for the mixture of the other two.

Any three wavelengths capable of producing such color matches are known as a set of *primaries*. The choice of three primaries is arbitrary, so long as one observes the stipulation that the mixture of any two will not match the third. Helmholtz chose three areas of the spectrum to serve as primaries: *red, green,* and *blue.*

Having chosen our three fixed primaries, R, G, and B, we can go on to consider changes in luminance. This means that through the variation of the amounts and relative proportions of each of the three primary colors it is possible to produce all the color sensations found on the Munsell color tree. The following basic formula is used for this matching of colors:

$$W_x + W_{RGB} \equiv R + G + B$$

W_x represents a color that we wish to match or produce and W_{RGB} the proportion of our three primaries to be combined with this color. The wavelengths of R, G, and B are fixed and their intensity or energy variable. The symbol $\equiv$ is used in color vision research to express visual color matches.

It should be noted that the addition of W_{RGB} to one side of our color matching equation is required to produce a reduction in saturation of the matched color equal to the reduction that occurs through the mixture of R, G, and B. Saturation, it will be recalled, refers to the purity of the hue, and is reduced by the mixture of hues.

Turning to the empirical application of these relationships, in which observers actually match color sensations, Wright (1928–29) recorded the necessary contributions of each of the primary colors to produce matches of the various spectral sensations. His results provided the distribution coefficients for a red of 650 mμ, a green of 530 mμ, and a blue of 460 mμ. In the actual experiments the subjects matched the color of one viewing area to the color presented in a second viewing area. The second presented any combination of amounts of the three primaries; in the first, any one of the three primaries could be presented alone with a fourth monochromatic light source. Using each of the primaries in turn, Wright determined the necessary contributions of each to match mixtures of spectral components with a primary color. The average data for the matches of ten subjects are presented in Figure 2.9.

The graph shows the relative amounts of each of the three primaries needed to match any given wavelength. A negative value indicates that some of that particular primary had to be added to the to-be-matched sample in order to reduce its saturation to the point where it could be matched with a mixture of the two remaining primaries.

These data make possible the development of a chart of the matching relationships among the various wavelengths—a chart of chromaticity space. The one derived by Wright, shown in Figure 2.10, gives the proportional amounts of each of the three primary colors (P_1 = red, P_2 = green, P_3 = blue) relative to the total of all three. Axis c_1 gives the proportional amount of red and axis c_2 the proportional amount of green. The third proportion c_3 is not shown since the drawing can depict only two dimensions; c_3 can easily be

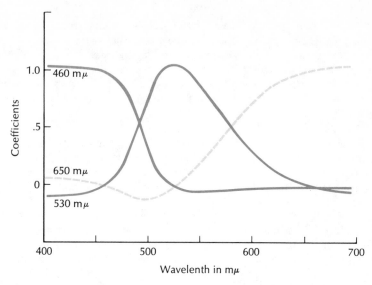

Figure 2.9
Trichromatic coordinates for ten observers. The three primaries were mono-chromatic light sources of 460, 530, and 650 mμ. (After Wright, 1928–29.)

deduced from any given c_1 and c_2. Matches for colors are usually given in terms of x,y, and z, which correspond to the c_1, c_2, and c_3 axes of the figure when the proportions have been corrected for the spectral properties of the three primary colors established by the Commission Internationale de l'Eclairage. This was done in order to avoid the negative values required by Wright in his matches (see Figure 2.9). The central triangle indicates matches that produced white for the subjects in Wright's experiment. The curved outer boundary indicates matches to single wavelength light (parts of the visual spectrum). In all, the chart is designed to display the following characteristics of hues:

1. All mixtures and matches of color can be produced with the chromaticity space.
2. All colors located within the triangle formed by connecting the three primaries, P_1, P_2, and P_3, can be produced by the appropriate mixture of the three primaries.
3. All colors along any straight line in the space can be produced by the binary mixture of the two connected wavelengths.
4. All points in the space can be made to appear identical by varying the amounts of the contributing wavelengths.

Finally, we should consider the kind of information the chart of chromaticity space does *not* provide:

1. The distance between points in the space does not provide any information about the magnitude of the difference in appearance of the two colors.
2. The chart provides no information on the effects of luminance.

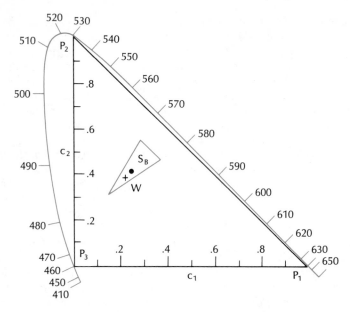

Figure 2.10
Chart of chromaticity space. (After Wright, 1947.)

Wright's classic contributions to the psychology of color perception were presented in the years before 1928. In 1931 a special commission on illumination (Commission Internationale de l'Eclairage, abbreviated as CIE) adopted a set of standard primary wavelengths: 700, 546.1, and 435.8 mμ. These three primaries were selected because they are easier to produce than those utilized by Wright and others. They also display several advantages for experiments with color mixture.[1] Accordingly, they are often invoked to describe color stimuli in a concise way that does not require specifying the amounts of all wavelengths present.

The Mixture of Colors

Taken together, the Munsell system of sample colors and the color matches obtained through the CIE chromaticity space provide a basic system for identifying perceptual units of color vision. Consider once again the relationship of hue, saturation, and brightness in the Munsell color tree: through the application of the trichromatic relationships of hues as provided by the chromaticity space, we can use the Munsell system to predict the sensation resulting from the mixture of any of the sample colors on the tree.

If we connect two hues on the outside edge of the color circle and note the color sample at the point inside the circle halfway between the two

[1] For a detailed discussion of color mixture, the reader should consult Graham (1965).

hues, a mixture of these hues in equal proportions will produce that color sensation. These relations are shown in Figure 2.11. If the amount of one hue is increased, the resulting mixture changes in dominant hue proportionately in the direction of the greater hue. If the two hues are diametrically opposed on the color circle, the halfway point between the hues will be located in the center of the circle. The color sample found in the center is an achromatic gray. Such opposing colors whose mixture produces an achromatic gray are known as *complementary colors*. Hues that do not produce an achromatic gray when mixed are *noncomplementary colors*.

If more than two hues or hues with more than single wavelengths are mixed, the resulting color sensation on the color tree is given by the center of a triangle produced by connecting the three, or by the boundaries of the band of wavelengths on the color circle. If the amount of each hue or the width of the contributing wavelengths is disproportionate, the center point of the triangle shifts toward the dominant hue.

Up to this point we have considered only the mixture of hues and the accompanying changes in saturation. What is the effect of mixing hues of varying brightness? The brightness of the resulting sensation will fall between the brightnesses of the contributing hues. If one of the contributing hues is present in a greater amount, the brightness of that hue will influence the brightness of the mixture of the hues to a greater degree.

In summary, color mixtures can be predicted with the color tree by finding the color sensation located between the contributing hues. The exact sample will depend on the brightness, saturation, and proportion of each contributing hue. After determining the values of each of the contributing elements of the sample, one can consult a chart of chromaticity space to find the mixtures of hues which will provide a color match.

Having examined these basic relationships of the attributes of colors and the interrelation of colors, we can now move on to a study of the perception of color in context. Until now we have discussed color in an abstract sense, without considering the fact that color occurs as an attribute of objects and that colors occur together under varying conditions.

Colors in Context

The phenomenal appearance of colors.   Lawns are green and fire engines are red. The color of the object is also a property; it belongs to the object and is not imposed on it. Colors as attributes of objects have been described by Katz (1935) as *surface colors*. A particular color seems to coat or to be within the object itself. As we shall see, part of our perception of such surface colors remains invariant, although the physical properties of the colors may vary greatly.

Katz also identified several other modes of the phenomenal appearance of colors. The visual perception resulting from the stimulation of the eye by homogeneous, unpatterned light evokes a sensation of color described as *film color*. The color is not perceived as part of an object; rather, it is seen as

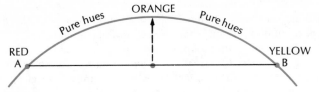

Figure 2.11
Mixture of pure hues. Combining any two hues will produce
the hue halfway between them. The saturation of the resulting mixture will be lower than that of the original hues. The
farther apart the two hues on the color circle, the greater
the reduction in saturation of their mixture. Diametrically opposed hues when mixed produce a neutral gray.

independent of the object, as though it were located in space somewhere
between observer and object. Von Fieandt (1966) cites the perception of a
cloudless sky as an example of film color: the blue is located at some distance
from the observer. The color of a specific object often takes on the quality of a
film color if we are unable to view the entire object. Roll a piece of paper into
a tube and look with one eye at a flat, uncontoured, colored wall. The color
of the wall appears closer to you and independent of the wall.

A third phenomenal mode of color can be described as *space color:* a
room illuminated by a red light seems filled with a reddish glow. Tinted glasses
provide another example of the experience of space color in which the entire
scene appears surrounded by or filled with a specific color.

Finally, a fourth variety of color can be described as *illumination color.*
A light source such as a slide projected on a screen provides a color sensation
located entirely on the surface. The color is superimposed: not part of the
surface, but located immediately in front of it.

Unquestionably the most common color perceptions are of surface colors.
Most colors are related to a specific object; unfortunately, many laboratory
studies of color have disregarded this relationship and have utilized film colors
and illumination colors for observations of color perception. This is probably
due to the tendency to regard color as a sensation rather than as an element of
perception.

Color constancy.   Hering (1920) noted that many surface colors remain unchanged despite a wide range of conditions of illumination and context. Although the physical aspects of the distal stimulus varied, the phenomenal perception of the stimulus remained constant. Hering described this perceptual
tendency as a result of the influence of *memory colors.* Because of our experience with the object we tend to retain a constant perception of its hue, independent of surrounding conditions. This tendency is known as *hue constancy.* For example, a green lawn retains its hue throughout the day and well
into the evening. Often we still perceive the lawn as green even though the
level of illumination is so low that a stimulation of the color receptors of the eye
is not possible. By the same token, other situations can be cited in which a
perceived hue changes with variations of illumination or surrounding condi-

tions. A dress purchased under the artificial illumination of the interior of a shop appears quite different when viewed in the sunlight.

A simple demonstration of hue constancy can be developed with a pair of normal sunglasses. Hold them at arm's length and note the hue of an object seen through the lens: The object takes on the tint of the glass and appears greenish in hue. If the glasses are worn, the object and surrounding objects appear to display their natural hues.

Similar situations involving brightness and saturation can be described in which the phenomenal sensation of a stimulus remains invariant despite changes in the physical aspects of the stimulus. Taken together, the maintenance of perceived color under various conditions in which hue, saturation and brightness remain constant is known as *color constancy;* a change in such perceived color is known as *color variance.*

It would appear a simple task to discover the conditions producing color constancy and color variance. To date the empirical attempts, however, have been less than successful. Usually one finds color variance rather than invariance. The constancy effect contributes to the reduction of variance but seldom minimizes it. For example, if one views two spinning discs, each of which is half white and half black, a medium gray is observed. Illuminating one disc with sunlight and leaving the second in shadow produces a variance in brightness so that the illuminated disc appears brighter. By varying the proportion of white and black on the shadowed disc, a condition of physical equality in intensity can be produced, yet the discs do not appear phenomenally equal in brightness. Subjective equality in brightness is produced by a setting somewhere between the illumination/shadow condition and the illumination/equal-intensity condition. The shadowed disc reflects less light than the illuminated disc. Yet the increase in the amount of white added to the shadowed disc to produce phenomenal equality in brightness is less than the amount required to match the physical intensity of the two discs. The constancy effect allows the two stimuli to appear equal, although physical measurements of intensity would indicate marked differences between the two distal objects.

Constancy effects are the result of numerous factors. Although some researchers might disagree, past experience with specific objects probably plays an important role in constancy. Such experiences would seem to influence the perceptual interpretation of incoming sensory information so that objects *known* to be similar are *perceived* to be similar despite variations in surrounding stimuli.

The discussion of brightness constancy and constancies of shape and size will be reserved for a later section. At this point we are still concerned with the influence on color perception of colors that appear in a chromatic context.

Color contrast.   If the perception of one hue is modified by the presence of a second, we have an example of *simultaneous color contrast.* A recent study by Oyama and Hsia (1966) serves to illustrate this phenomenon. Subjects viewed a circular test field which subtended a visual angle of 4°. A monochromator—a device producing narrow portions of the spectrum—set at a bandwidth of 7 mμ and displaying a range of settings from 450 to 700 mμ illuminated the test field. The subject adjusted the monochromator until he felt the field showed the "best possible" blue, green, yellow, or red. Color contrast was demonstrated when the tendency of the subjects to select a best color (e.g., blue) shifted in the direction of the surrounding field (e.g., yellow). That is, the wavelength selected as the best possible blue would be shifted toward yellow if the surround were yellow. Furthermore, Oyama and Hsia noted that the magnitude of the compensatory shift depended on the proximity of the surround to the test field. The largest shift occurred when the borders of the surround and the test field touched (zero degree of separation) and decreased steadily as the degree of separation increased.

In two other studies (Akita, Graham, and Hsia, 1964; Akita and Graham, 1966) subjects varied the settings of the test field to maintain an absolute hue (e.g., green) against varying background colors. By measuring the amount of compensatory shift necessary for the maintenance of the absolute hue, it was possible to obtain quantifiable data on the degree of contrast evoked by each surround.

Induced colors.   Simultaneous color contrast studies deal with the influence of a colored surround on the perception of a colored test field. If the test field is neutral (i.e., gray) or dark, and is perceived to be colored due to the presence of a colored surround, one speaks of *induced colors*. The general effect of the inducing surround on the neutral test field is a coloration of the test field in the direction of the hue complementary to the inducing field (Graham and Brown, 1965). Sometimes, however, the neutral region will assume the hue of the inducing field, particularly if the luminance of the inducing field is high and that of the gray test area low (Edridge-Green, 1914).

Figure 2.12 provides examples of induced color. The gray circles should take on the complements of their surrounding hues, although it may be necessary to cover the page with a sheet of thin tissue paper in order to observe this kind of coloration.

A series of experiments on the factors influencing induced colors has been reported by Jo Ann S. Kinney (1962, 1965, and 1967). Subjects viewed a vertical dark strip imposed on a circular induction field; this surround could be blue, green, yellow, or red. They were required to match the color induced on the dark strip with those shown on a comparison strip which could be varied in hue, saturation, and brightness. Kinney reported that the best induction occurs with a blue inducing field. The actual colors reported depended on the size of the test field, the purity of the inducing color, and the luminance ratios of the inducing field to the test area. Brightness differences of the inducing field alone produced a wide variety of hues. For example, with a blue surround varying along the brightness dimension, subjects reported colors including canary yellow, antique gold, toast, and Indian red (Kinney, 1962).

Observations such as those by Kinney have thrown light on the controversy regarding the demonstrations by Edwin Land (1959a, b). Land prepared two black and white transparencies of a scene, one photographed through a green filter and the other through a red filter. Both transparencies were then superimposed on a screen. The red-filter slide was projected with a red lamp and the

Figure 2.12
Induction of color in a neutral gray area by means of a surrounding hue. Each gray circle should appear lightly tinted with the
complement of the hue of its enclosing rectangle.

other with the white light of a tungsten lamp. The resulting composite picture
of the scene (Figure 2.13) displayed a wide range of colors.

In his discussion of the results, Land (1959c) postulated a new mechanism
of color vision. He emphasized the interplay of brightness differences associated with the wavelengths produced by the two filters. Land's theory has
failed to gain widespread acceptance, perhaps as a result of comments by Judd
(1960) and Walls (1960), who explained his results in terms of trichromatic
color matching. Belsey (1964) has provided examples of the Land colors and
demonstrated that the perceived hues correspond to the hues characteristic
of specific objects. The effect of memory colors coupled with the diversified
hues produced by brightness differences, as in Kinney's study, would indicate
that the Land demonstrations are the result of simultaneous color contrasts,
induced colors, and memory colors. Land's emphasis on studying color perception in natural images, rather than requiring observers to respond to patches
of colored light, does point to an important area for future research.

Chromatic Afterimages

If the intense light of a flashbulb stimulates the retina of the eye for a brief
period, a visual sensation persists long after the primary stimulus (flash) has
faded. The spot of light seen floating in space is called an afterimage. Such
a brief flash of high-intensity light produces a number of after-sensations. Ac-

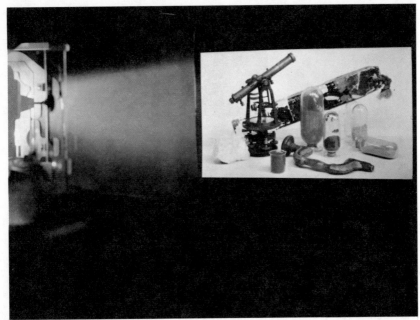

Figure 2.13
Phenomenal appearance of Land colors. The photograph has been retouched in order
to simulate the colors reported by observers of the demonstration. (Land, 1959c. Photograph by William Vandivert.)

cording to Dittler and Eisenmeier (1909), seven phases of the afterimage can
be identified; these alternate between positive sensations in which the original
stimulus is perceived after its physical cessation, and negative phases in which
the brightness relations are the opposite of the original stimulating conditions.
Assuming a stimulus with a bright center, a positive sensation would be white
center area with a dark surrounding area; a negative sensation would be a dark
center with a light surround.

Afterimages produced by flashes of a colored light of medium intensity
and short duration characteristically display three phases (Brown, 1965): a positive phase, in which the color of the primary stimulus continues for several
seconds; an intermediate phase, in which no color is reported; and finally a
negative phase, in which the color of the afterimage is close to the complement
of the primary stimulus. If the duration of the primary stimulus is around 400
msec, the first positive phase may last up to 10 seconds and the negative phase
as long as 30 seconds. As the duration of the primary stimulus increases, the
length of the positive phase decreases. With a primary stimulus lasting over 6
seconds, one is usually unable to observe a positive afterimage (Miller, 1966).

A number of primary and secondary stimuli for producing afterimages are
to be found in Figure 2.14. Fixate the black dot in the center of the red square
for approximately 15 seconds; next, fixate the black dot in the center of the

Figure 2.14

Chromatic stimuli for the demonstration of negative afterimages. (After Evans, 1948. Reproduced by permission of John Wiley and Sons, Inc.)

gray square. The gray square should appear a greenish color. Follow the same procedure with the yellow and blue squares. The afterimage should be close to the complement of the primary stimulus (see Figure 2.1).

The effect of viewing a chromatic primary stimulus and a chromatic secondary stimulus can also be demonstrated with Figure 2.14. Fixate the red square for 15 seconds followed by the yellow or the blue field. The after-sensation is the result of the combination of the complementary color of the primary stimulus and the color of the secondary stimulus. Through the various combinations of the remaining stimuli, the effect of the interrelation of primary and secondary colors on the afterimage may be observed.

A great many investigators have isolated a number of interesting variables affecting the afterimages. For example, once the afterimage has faded, a shift in fixation or an eye blink may cause it to return. Helmholtz (1866) reported that movements of other bodily parts often sufficed to reactivate the afterimage. Other experiments have studied the size of the afterimage. Place Figure 2.14 at a distance of about three feet and fixate the black dot in the center of the red field for 15 seconds. Now close your eyes and move forward about one-half the distance to the figures. Open your eyes and fixate the black dot in the center of the gray square. You will note that the greenish field now covers only a small portion of the gray secondary stimulus. That the size of the afterimage depends on the distance of the secondary stimulus was first observed by Emil Emmert in 1881. The formal version of his studies, known as *Emmert's law,* holds that the apparent size of the negative afterimage is directly proportional to the distance of the secondary stimulus.

Induced color and afterimages.   In the experiments with induced color the neutral gray square usually assumes the complementary hue of the surrounding field. Chromatic afterimages also display the complementary color of the stimulating hue. King and Wertheimer (1963) have attempted to relate these similar occurrences in a study that produced afterimages of induced colors. Subjects first viewed an 8-inch gray disc surrounded by a 28-inch green ring; the phenomenal impression was that of a green ring surrounding a light magenta disc (induced color). Next a green light was added to the achromatic disc, neutralizing the induced magenta coloration and causing the disc to appear gray again. (Note that the combination of primary afterimages with a secondary color occurs in the same manner.) After viewing one of these targets for 30 seconds the subjects stared at a blank wall and reported the after-sensations they experienced. For the ring and induced color they reported an afterimage of a magenta ring and a green disc; that is, they perceived an afterimage of both the ring and the induced coloration of the achromatic disc. Under the neutralized condition the subjects also reported a green central disc, which was, however, less saturated than the afterimage produced by the first condition.

King and Wertheimer conclude that the underlying mechanism of induced color must function in much the same manner as when the eye is stimulated by an actual color. Although some disagreement (Swink, 1963) exists as to their conclusion, the fact that an induced color produces an afterimage would indicate a similar mechanism underlies both phenomena.

McCollough effect.   An interesting new kind of color effect has been described by McCollough (1965). She presented a pattern of black vertical lines on an orange background followed by a pattern of black horizontal lines on a blue background. The two patterns were shown alternately for 5 seconds each followed by a 1-second dark interval. The alternations continued for several minutes, ending with a test pattern of a white background with vertical lines on the left and horizontal lines on the right. McCollough's subjects reported a bluish coloration on the vertical lined portion of the test pattern and an orange coloration of the horizontal portion. In other words, complementary colors were seen on the two orientations of the test patterns. Initially it was proposed (Harris and Gibson, 1968) that the McCollough effect might be a special case of complementary afterimages. However, a number of studies have noted important differences between McCollough's effect and the more common complementary afterimages. Hajos (1967) reports that the McCollough effect persists for periods up to forty-eight hours, while negative afterimages decay after several minutes. Murch (1968, 1969) tested the application of Emmert's law for the McCollough effect. The results showed that the colored area on the test patterns always extended over the entire test pattern irrespective of the distance of the test pattern.

The physiological basis of the McCollough effect is still unclear; that something more than complementary afterimages is involved would appear to have been demonstrated. In fact, Murch and Hirsch (1972) showed that the McCollough effect could be evoked using complementary afterimages as the inducing stimuli. Subjects viewed an unlined red square followed by a pattern of vertical lines on a white background. Due to the complementary afterimage of red (green), the white background appeared greenish. Following the vertical pattern was an unlined green square which induced a red complementary afterimage on still another following pattern of horizontal lines. The sequence of unlined red, vertical lines on white, unlined green, and horizontal lines on white was repeated for several minutes. At the end of this inspection period, subjects viewing test patterns of vertical and horizontal lines on white backgrounds described the vertical pattern as pink and the horizontal pattern as green. That is, on the test patterns they reported hues complementary to those induced during inspection. Therefore the McCollough effect must be due to an adaptive process other than the one underlying complementary afterimages.

Subjective Colors

The sensation of color depends on stimulation of certain visual receptors, on central mediators found along the visual pathways of the optic system, and probably on the influence of cortical memory elements based on the previous experiences of the individual. The initial stimulus for the sensation is usually light composed of a combination of wavelengths of various intensities. We have noted, however, that color sensations can be evoked in the absence of appropriate light stimulation, as in the case of induced colors, for example, or afterimages. Furthermore, the same sensation can often be evoked by a wide variety of stimuli.

Due to the various possibilities of the interaction of chromatic sensations it becomes necessary to distinguish between objective, physical stimulation and subjective, phenomenal sensation. A subjective color perception results when the appropriate visual receptors are activated. Any stimulus capable of activating the receptor brings about the perception of color. A physical blow to the eye, for example, causes a color sensation in the absence of light stimulation.

One of the most intriguing methods of evoking color sensations without varying wavelength involves achromatic (black and white) stimuli, which are referred to as subjective, or Fechner, colors (Cohen and Gordon, 1949).

In 1838 Fechner reported some interesting perceptions evoked by a spinning disc containing a black-and-white section (see Figure 2.15). If spun at a high speed the disc's surface appeared to be a uniform gray. However, if the disc was rotated at a speed below the fusion frequency, lines of color were seen extending from the center of the disc toward the periphery.

Subsequently several other black-and-white discs (see Figure 2.15) were discovered that were capable of producing the sensation of color. The most distinct colors were produced by the Benham disc, which originally appeared in the shape of a child's top (Benham, 1894, 1895). Half of the top was black and the other half was white with short, curved, black lines. As the top spun, various colors could be seen, depending on the speed of rotation, direction of rotation, and illuminating light. Unfortunately the success of the popular toy was marred by the discovery that prolonged viewing frequently caused nausea. In 1902 Bagley produced 96 variations of the Benham disc for use in his studies of subjective colors.

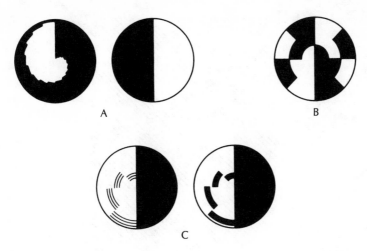

Figure 2.15
Discs for the demonstration of subjective colors as developed by: *A,* Fechner; *B,* Helmholtz; *C,* Benham.

Another variation of subjective colors was reported by Rood (1860). He noted that the colors of objects viewed through a spinning disc with a half-inch slit cut over one quarter of the circumference varied as a function of the speed of rotation. At 600 rpm white clouds viewed through the disc took on a reddish coloration.

An explanation of subjective colors based upon physical theories of light proved difficult. Colenbrander (1933) noted the following discrepancies between subjective colors and the physical qualities of light:

1. Subjective colors distort under a convex lens and chromatic colors do not.
2. Subjective colors appear even when the disc is illuminated by light of a single wavelength (monochromatic light).
3. Subjective colors change as a function of the intensity of the illumination.

Perhaps the most telling demonstration of the fact that wavelength plays no role in subjective colors is obtained by observing them through the medium of television. In an unpublished study by the author three of the discs in Figure 2.15 were taped with a television camera and the tape shown on a normal black-and-white closed-circuit television set to a group of 35 students. Presented with four different speeds of rotation for each disc, the subjects were asked to describe the discs at each speed. Colors were reported by all subjects for the Benham disc, by 29 for the Helmholtz disc and by only 6 for the Fechner disc. The colors reported varied as a function of the speed of rotation; at slower speeds blues and greens were frequently seen, at higher speeds reds and pinks, although much individual variation occurred among observers with regard to the colors reported.

Figure 2.16
Stationary pattern for the demonstration of subjective colors.

Subjective colors can also be produced by a pattern of thin black lines on a white background (Luckiesh and Moss, 1933). View the lined pattern in Figure 2.16 from a distance of approximately 12 inches and do not attempt to fixate a particular point. Look for veins of light, unsaturated colors in the white spaces between the lines; similar effects can be seen in the moiré patterns of contemporary op art.

The theoretical explanation of subjective colors can be drawn from a more general theory of color vision. A consideration of this theory remains the task of the last section of this chapter.

A Theory of Color Vision

Over the last one hundred years a number of theories of color vision have been advanced. Of the six listed by von Fieandt (1966), two have received the most attention: the *Young-Helmholtz theory* and the *Hering opponent-processes theory*. The bulk of recent anatomical and neurophysiological studies appear to support the Young-Helmholtz theory as that which best explains color vision at the level of the retina. Beyond that level little information on color vision has been gathered. However, some phases of the central processes seem to fit Hering's system (Hurvich and Jameson, 1957, 1966).

In the present discussion we will limit ourselves to the Young-Helmholtz theory, which seems to be able to account for most of the facts of color vision discussed in the present chapter. Obviously color vision involves much more than the stimulation of a color-coded receptor in the retina. However, at present the knowledge of the central mediators of color perception is deficient.

The Young-Helmholtz or *trichromatic theory* was originally suggested by the Englishman Thomas Young in 1801, and later formalized by Helmholtz in 1866. It assumes that three different kinds of color receptors are to be found in the vertebrate eye, each maximally sensitive to a specific portion of the visual spectrum. The first receptor is considered maximally sensitive to red; the degree of sensitivity declines the more the color varies from pure red. The second receptor is maximally sensitive to green and the third to blue and violet. Again, the degree of sensitivity depends on the closeness on the spectrum of a given stimulus to a particular color receptor's maximum responsiveness.

If the stimulating color is red, the response of the proper receptor will be maximal and the accompanying sensation will be red. If the color is an orange yellow (between red and green), the red and green receptors will be equally active. If more yellow than orange is present in the sensation, the proportion of green receptors responding will be greater than that of the red. In this way, through the appropriate contributions of each receptor, stimuli of all colors can be processed for transmission to the central visual system.

The theory can explain the relationships of color mixing and color matching, in which only three primary colors are necessary to produce all other colors. In fact, Helmholtz developed the theory with the principles of color mixture in mind. However, the theory has trouble with several phenomenal aspects of color perception. As MacNichol (1964) has pointed out, "psychological investigation tells only what the visual system can do and not how it does it" (p. 48). He goes on to say that in order to study the generation of impulses in the retinal receptors one must first measure the effect on the receptor cells of light of a given wavelength. In experiments, MacNichol and others have found three receptors, each maximally sensitive to different portions of the visual spectrum. The sensitivity distributions of three such receptors in the primate eye are shown in Figure 2.17, which shows the peak sensitivities of 477 mμ (blue-violet), 540 mμ (green), and 577 mμ (yellow-red). Note that each receptor is maximally sensitive to a specific portion of the spectrum and displays decreasing curves of sensitivity for the surrounding portions of the spectrum.

Until now we have explained the transmission of information in terms of chromatic stimuli. But how does the Young-Helmholtz theory explain the sensations of achromatic colors (white, gray, black)? The theory holds that the sensation of white is a result of the simultaneous stimulation of all three receptors. White light contains all wavelengths of the visual spectrum and therefore evokes a response in all receptors. The sensation of black indicates the failure of the receptors to respond, and gray is an intermediate condition in which a response of lesser magnitude occurs. The Hering theory, in contrast, assumes the existence of separate receptors for white and black.

The trichromatic theory and the phenomena of color perception.   We have already noted that the Young-Helmholtz trichromatic theory handles the color

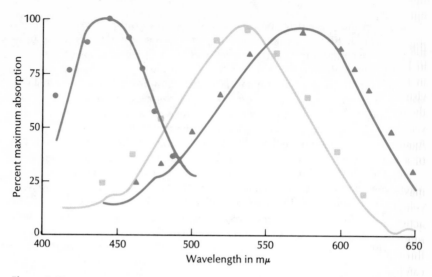

Figure 2.17
Sensitivity distributions for three types of cones in the eye of the primate. (After MacNichol, 1964. Copyright 1964 by Scientific American, Inc. All rights reserved.)

matching and color mixing data quite well. The theory can also explain after-images, color contrast, induced colors, and subjective colors.

Afterimages.   The observation of positive afterimages has been explained by a process referred to as the *residual stimulation effect*. The response evoked by the initial stimulus continues after the cessation of actual stimulation. After a short period the receptors involved in the positive sensation become fatigued —the receptor's ability to respond is reduced. If at this point a white or achromatic stimulus (medium gray) is presented, all three receptors should respond with equal fervor. Because the receptor fatigued by the original stimulus is unable to respond, the white light evokes a response in the two remaining receptors. If the original chromatic stimulus were red, the receptor for red would become fatigued, and upon presentation of the white light only the green and blue receptors would respond. The negative phase would be a blue-green sensation. We should note, however, that in many cases the actual color of the negative image is somewhat displaced and does not conform exactly to the expected combination of remaining receptors. This may be due in part to the coloration of the humor and sclera of the eye (Hartridge, 1945). Also the actual points of maximum sensitivity differ from individual eye to eye. Hence the reports of the after-sensation vary.

One problem still unanswered is the observation of afterimages in the absence of a second stimulus. After exposure to a chromatic stimulus an after-image of negative coloration may be perceived in total darkness. Barlow (1956) explained the negative afterimage with no second stimulus by assuming a base level of retinal activity occurring in the absence of stimulation. The depressed level of sensitivity for the receptor stimulated by the primary stimulus falls below the base level. Cessation of stimulation after the fatigue of the primary receptor (e.g., red) causes the base level response of the remaining receptors to initiate an afterimage (blue and green).

McCollough effects prove difficult to explain in terms of retinal receptors. The observation that the effects do not conform to Emmert's law would indicate that something beyond the level of the retina is involved. McCollough (1965) believes the effects are the result of the selective adaptation of color-coded edge-detectors. Edge-detectors that respond to lines of specific spatial orientation have been found in the cortex of the cat (Hubel and Wiesel, 1962). If the effect is the result of the chromatic adaptation of receptors to contour, one would expect a lessened effect in the absence of sharp contour. However, Gibson and Harris (1968) found McCollough afterimages even when the contours of the vertical and horizontal lines were blurred. They propose a mediating mechanism called a *dipole*, which receives information from different portions of the retina and displays selective spectral adaptation. Neither the edge-detector nor the dipole theory would appear entirely adequate to explain the McCollough effect, and further research is needed to identify its underlying mechanism.

Subjective colors.   Fechner used the trichromatic theory (1838) to explain his observations of subjective color. The rotating disc causes the retina's receptors to be stimulated by white and immediately thereafter by black. The white light causes all receptors to discharge and the black none. If we assume that the rise-and-fall response times of the three receptors is different, then after several rotations the cadence of responding will be disrupted. For example, if the red receptor responds quickly and the blue receptor slowly, the response of the red receptor may have ceased during the presentation of the black section of the disc. The blue, however, might not have ceased responding through the brief period of the black section and would therefore not be restimulated by the subsequent white sector of the disc. The white would stimulate only the red, causing the disc to appear reddish. In the case of the line pattern (Figure 2.16) the intrinsic movements of the eye would cause receptors to be alternately stimulated by white and black in much the same manner as with the rotating disc. Again, assuming different decay times for each receptor, colored responses would occur due to recurrent stimulation by the white spaces between lines.

Color contrast and induced colors.   At the level of the retina the explanation of color contrast and induced colors proves difficult for all theories of color vision. Consider a red disc surrounded by a yellow ring: the disc takes on a slightly bluish-red hue. According to the trichromatic theory the constant stimulation would cause receptors of red and yellow to fatigue. The eye is in constant motion, even if the individual attempts a strict fixation on the red disc; this motion would cause some cells to be stimulated alternately by red and yellow. Such a constant interaction of the two hues would influence the sensitivity of the red receptors and cause a shift in perceived hue. With induced

Figure 2.18
Koffka's gray ring.

colors the complementary hue of the gray central portion can be explained on the basis of the adaptation or fatigue of the receptor for the surrounding color. If the surround is red and the disc gray, then the gray can only stimulate the green and blue receptors, since eye movement allows red-adapted receptors to be stimulated by the gray. The disc would appear somewhat blue-green. The process is similar to the inducement of negative afterimages.

The phenomena associated with color contrast and induced colors involve much more than the selective adaptation of retinal receptors. The wide number of colors perceived in the Land demonstrations are probably induced in more central regions of the visual system. Our memory of the colors of objects probably influences color perception. An example of nonretinal influences in contrast phenomena can be seen in Figure 2.18—Koffka's gray ring (1935). Despite the different backgrounds, the ring displays the same brightness (shade of gray) on both backgrounds. However, if you cover the intersection of the two colors with your finger, the gray on the blue background appears lighter than the gray on the yellow background. Such effects are very difficult to explain in terms of retinal receptors.

In this chapter we have considered the phenomenal aspects of a color sensation in terms of the perceptual dimensions of hue, saturation, and brightness; we have also considered how a distal stimulus for color in the physical world may be described in terms of wavelength, purity, and intensity. The hue, saturation, and brightness of individual color sensations were interrelated on the Munsell color tree, while color-matching techniques for wavelength and luminance led us to an examination of the trichromatic nature of color stimuli.

An understanding of the complexity of color perception depends on several aspects of the phenomenal appearance of colors in context. Under some conditions, color sensations remain invariant despite marked changes in their context. Under others, the sensations vary directly with changes in context.

Many aspects of color perception, such as color matching, color mixing, induced color, color contrast, and chromatic afterimages can be explained by the trichromatic theory of color vision. Other aspects (e.g., McCollough effect and the phenomenal appearance of colors) conform more to the expectations of the opponent-process theory. Finally, certain elements of color are not clearly understood in terms of any contemporary theoretical formulation.

The work of the neurophysiologists has provided support for the Young-Helmholtz theory of color vision at the level of the retina. More recent evidence indicates that an opponent-process color system exists in the lateral geniculate nucleus (DeValois et al., 1966, 1967). The observations by Hubel and Wiesel (1968) that the orientation-sensitive cells of the monkey's cortex are not color sensitive has rendered untenable McCollough's explanation of the McCollough effect. However, these advances have aided in the search for explanations of color perception. Further research on color vision will depend to a great extent on knowledge of the visual system provided by neurophysiology.

CHAPTER 3
A Sensory Basis for Perception

In the first chapter we outlined a general, active-perceiver model of perception. The present discussion will attempt to clarify some of the details of this model. We are concerned here with the first stages of the processing of effective stimuli and will describe some of the variables influencing the selection of effective stimuli from the array of potential stimuli.

Shiffrin and Atkinson (1969) have developed a model of the memory process that can also serve to describe perception. Figure 3.1 presents a slightly modified diagram of their model. This diagram can be followed as a flow chart of the processing pathways of perceptual information. The actual char-

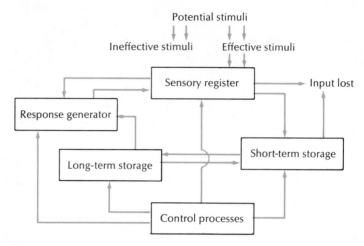

Figure 3.1
A model of the perceptual process. (Developed from a similar model by
Shiffrin and Atkinson, 1969.)

acteristics of the system vary, depending on the sensory modality (vision or
audition); however, the directions of processing are considered the same for
all modalities.

A potential stimulus may follow three possible pathways. First, it may fail
to gain entrance to the system and be relegated to the *ineffective stimuli*
category. Second, the stimulus may actually enter the sensory register but flow
out to the *input lost* category. As one moves through a complex environment
many sights and sounds evoke momentary sensations that quickly pass out
of the system. A third possible direction for a potential stimulus is to become
an effective stimulus passing into the sensory register and on to *short-term
storage*.

In the present chapter we will be concerned primarily with the sensory
register and the short-term storage aspects of the model. The other portions of
the diagram will be discussed in detail at a later time. For the moment, however, we can note that an effective stimulus in short-term storage either continues to long-term storage or passes out of the system altogether as input
lost. The model shows a two-way interaction between short- and long-term
storage, which means that information can flow in both directions. Information
from the permanent storage banks of long-term memory can influence the
processing of information in short-term storage; it can also be influenced by the
current contents of short-term storage. The perceiver is able to generate responses directly from both short- and long-term storage. Note also the interaction between the sensory register and the response generator. Conceivably a
response may be generated directly from the sensory register; such a response
would have an effect on the kinds of stimuli to which the sensory register
would be directed. It is also interesting that the system postulates no information loss from long-term storage.

Superimposed on each of the components of the system are the *control
processes*. This complex of variables, which directs the search procedures of

Figure 3.2
An example of figure-ground
segregation.

the perceiver, is based primarily in the physiological makeup of the individual. Influences such as general state of health, basic drives and needs, and physiological capacities and limitations constitute the control processes. On the one hand long-term storage provides influences on perception derived from the past experiences or learning of the perceiver; on the other, the control processes represent influences innately characteristic of the individual or based on aspects of the individual's physiology.

Let us now consider the empirical characteristics of the elements of the model, and the behavior of potential stimuli proceeding along one of the three processing routes.

Figure-Ground Segregation

That some potential stimuli become effective while others remain ineffective is easily observed. The task of identifying the attributes of the former proves more difficult. Nevertheless, one rather obvious attribute is that effective stimuli appear to stand out against the background of potential stimuli. Such stimuli become figures, whereas the other stimuli provide a background. While listening to a complex musical piece one often hears a specific instrument against the background provided by the rest of the orchestra. In viewing a complex scene some objects are held in the focal point of perception and others are relegated to the periphery of vision.

For many investigators the segregation of figure and ground provides the basis for perception. In order to convey information about the environment a stimulus must be differentiated from that environment. Metzger (1966) describes the characteristics of figures as elements of the perceptual field having some form and appearing to be separate from the background of stimuli. The outline in Figure 3.2 provides an example. The black blob stands out from the white background and has a specific form or shape.

Freeman (1929) observed the effect of the brief exposure of figures simi-lar to that of Figure 3.2. An inkblot was flashed for several milliseconds and the subjects asked to report their perceptions. Thereafter the duration of exposure was successively lengthened, and additional reports required of the subjects for each increase. Generally they first reported that certain portions of the field appeared darker than others. As the duration increased they began to notice ill-defined shapes and forms. Finally, clearly contoured figures were reported.

For most students of perception the tendency to perceive figures segre-gated from grounds is considered an innate property of the organism. Hebb (1949) has referred to this tendency as *primitive unity*. He believes that the per-ceptual process begins with a simple figure-ground separation that can occur independently of the actual identification of the figure. In terms of our model the identification of the specific attributes of a figure, such as exact form or color, requires the influence of control processes; often it may require specific experience stored in the perceiver's long-term memory banks.

Hebb cites the data reported in 1932 by von Senden in which anecdotal information on the first moment of restored sight for blind patients was col-lected from medical records dating back over a period of several hundred years. Newly sighted persons tended to report the perception of figures differ-entiated from background, but they showed an inability to remember specific shapes. More recently, London (1960) described the observations of the Rus-sian surgeon A. I. Pokrovskii, who studied the postoperative perceptual re-sponses of newly sighted patients. The patients usually reported seeing a "some-thing" which could not be identified on the basis of visual cues. A nine-year-old girl was shown a kitten which she described as a "gray" blob such as she had never before experienced. Upon touching the object the girl immediately iden-tified it as a kitten. Pokrovskii also found that newly sighted patients experi-enced difficulty in judging the distance of objects. For example, they frequently collided with the furniture around them.

We can consider stimuli displaying certain figural characteristics as candi-dates for entrance into the sensory register. If individuals respond spontaneously to figures, what would be the effect of providing a subject with a completely homogeneous stimulus field entirely lacking in figures?

The Ganzfeld or homogeneous field.   The perceptual experience of a figure-less ground should provide information on the importance of the structured elements of normal vision. However, the initial construction of such an envi-ronment proved rather difficult. Metzger (1929) seated subjects within a white-washed box 4 meters square and illuminated its smooth inner surfaces with neutral light. Observers looking within reported the experience of a "sea of light" characterized by a lack of depth and spatial orientation. Metzger called such an environment the *Ganzfeld* (homogeneous field); it has retained that name in most of the scientific literature.[1]

---

[1] For a more detailed review of this literature the interested reader should consult the paper by Avant (1965).

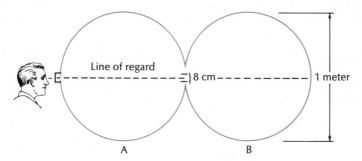

Figure 3.3
Diagram of the Cohen-Brown Ganzfeld.

Although Metzger's design produced a fairly homogeneous background, some structure was provided by the corners of the box. A series of studies by Cohen (1957, 1958) attempted to avoid this shortcoming. His method of creating a Ganzfeld is shown schematically in Figure 3.3. Cohen constructed two adjoining spheres, each 1 meter in diameter, connected by an 8-cm opening. Subjects viewed the field through a monocular eyepiece mounted in the wall of sphere A and aligned so that the 8-cm opening to sphere B was directly in front of the eye. The spheres were constructed of a translucent material and their surfaces homogeneously illuminated from without. Each sphere could be illuminated independently.

Cohen (1957) supported Metzger's observations of a lack of depth perception within the Ganzfeld. He asked subjects to estimate the distance to the homogeneous field; the average report was 2 inches, and only one observer estimated the distance to be greater than 6 inches. The actual distance was, of course, 2 meters.

By varying the brightness relations between the two spheres, Cohen could produce a figure at the 8-cm aperture joining them. At low levels of illumination, when sphere B was slightly darker than sphere A, subjects reported a dark spot located somewhere *behind* the fog or sea of light. The observance of an homogeneous field or ground in front of the darker figure constitutes a reversal of the usual figure-ground relationship. Increasing the intensity difference between spheres A and B produced an apparent decrease in the distance of the spot; it then appeared to be located several inches in front of the sea of light.

Unfortunately, it is difficult to describe the Ganzfeld experience verbally. Skiers often experience the effect in the so-called whiteout which involves a loss of visual orientation. Hochberg, Triebel, and Seaman (1951) suggest that one can approximate the Ganzfeld effect by placing half of a Ping-Pong ball over one eye and covering the other eye.

Obviously observers experience great difficulty in orienting themselves under homogeneous stimulation. Miller and Hall (1962) found some subjects actually hallucinating after periods of prolonged Ganzfeld experience. Uncertain about where they are looking, subjects seek some point on which to fix their gaze. Frequently a *blanking-out* experience is reported characterized by a complete lack of visual experience. Cohen (1960) flashed geometric designs into the Ganzfeld during these blanked-out periods and found the subjects unable to identify the designs.

The disorientation and lack of depth experience in the Ganzfeld indicates the importance of structure and texture as prerequisites for effective perceptual stimuli. The sensory mechanism appears unable to cope with completely uniform stimulation and requires structured differences for adequate orientation. If ground alone is inadequate for perceptual orientation, what would be the effect of a simple figure introduced in the Ganzfeld? Katz (1967) approached this question with the design shown in Figure 3.4. The task of the subject was to position a small circular spot of light, subtending 8' of visual angle, at the geometric center of the field. The spot of light was to travel along a horizontal plane starting 23° to either the left or the right of center. The subject was to indicate when the spot arrived at the geometric center of the field. Several conditions of testing were set up so that different degrees of information on the accuracy of centering could be provided to the subject. If performance in centering was to improve, then some degree of orientation in the homogeneous field would appear possible. Although the variation between and within subjects was rather large, improvement did occur after several trials. This indicates that individuals are able to locate figures in a homogeneous field.

In an earlier experiment by Katz, Petlay, and Cirincione (1965) it was reported that subjects found it difficult to center the target due to the apparent movement of the spot of light. The light appeared to jump about in a random manner. This effect, which was not mentioned in the experiment just described, might mean that the observers were not experiencing a true Ganzfeld. Apparent movement seems to be the result of presenting figures without adequate backgrounds. This phenomenon provides the next topic of discussion.

The autokinetic effect. If a small point of light is presented against an otherwise homogeneous background, observers frequently report that the light appears to be in motion. The effect was first noted by the astronomer von Humboldt in 1799. He reported an apparent movement of stars after prolonged periods of attempted visual fixation. Later, extensive laboratory studies were carried out by Aubert (1887), who is also responsible for naming the phenomenon the *autokinetic effect.*

Early work on the phenomenon described the effect of projecting a small point of light in a completely black room or in front of an untextured background. Gibson (1954) concluded that the slightest texture on the background or the slightest room illumination eliminated the effect.

The light seems to move in all directions and at varying speeds. Fleischl (1892) attempted to measure the amount of movement perceived by requiring subjects to trace the movement of the light on a piece of paper. Such tracings have often shown a paradoxical relationship between the distance covered by the spot of light and the reported speed of movement. The amount of movement traced is frequently less than the speed would indicate. Moustgaard (1963) concluded that displacement and speed in autokinetic movement are at least in part independent of each other.

While the autokinetic effect readily appears when a single point of light is used, some question remains concerning the effect of placing additional points

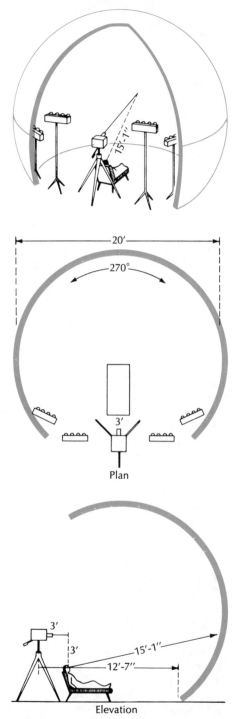

Figure 3.4
Ganzfeld developed by Katz (1967).

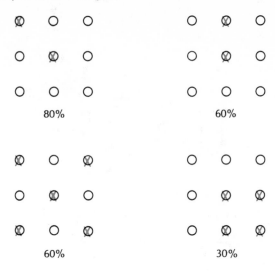

$\textcircled{Q}$ = Light on

$\bigcirc$ = Light off

Figure 3.5
Complex light arrays for the evocation of autokinetic
movement. Figures accompanying each array indicate the percentage of observers (N = 10) reporting
autokinetic movement. (After Royce, Stayton, and
Kinkade, 1962.)

of light in the array. Royce, Stayton, and Kinkade (1962) tested the latter with
a 3-by-3 matrix of nine lights located 9 inches apart. Individuals viewed varying
combinations of the lights. Some of the combinations, with their corresponding
percentages of subjects reporting autokinetic movement, are shown in Figure
3.5. Presenting a single center light produced phenomenal movement for 90
percent of the subjects, while the presentation of all nine lights at once produced such movement for only 20 percent. Generally speaking, the results
demonstrated that the greater the number of lights, the less frequently autokinesis was reported. The spatial arrangement of the lights seemed to make
a difference; lights forming points of simple geometric figures (e.g., the pattern
at the lower right in Figure 3.5) remained fairly stable.

One of the most popular explanations of the autokinetic effect was originally proposed by Hoppe (1879), who emphasized the relationship between the rapid intrinsic movements of the eyes and the apparent movement
of the dot of light. Lehman (1965) photographed eye movements and found
them correlated with the onset of reported autokinetic movement as well as
related to changes in the direction of movement cessation. Using the technique of image stabilization, Matin and MacKinnon (1964) tested for the visual

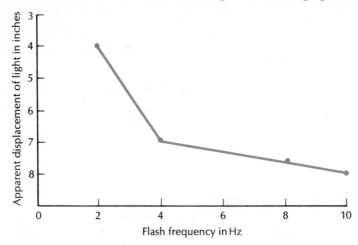

Figure 3.6
Autokinetic effect produced by a flashing light. (After Page, Elfner, and
Jamison, 1966.)

autokinetic effect under conditions minimizing eye movement. The effect was
shown to be greatly reduced, and in some cases eliminated altogether.

While the exact role of eye movements is still unclear, Worchel and
Burnham (1967) have advanced the hypothesis that a misinterpretation of the
relationship between retinal position and efferent signals to the extraocular
muscles underlies the effect. They suggest that the retinal position of the light
is processed through the sensory pathways. However, attempts by the efferent
system to localize the light in space fail, due to the lack of a fixed relationship
between the light and other objects.

Rock (1966) has theorized that the effect may lie in the inability of the
visual system to discriminate adequately between the movement or drifting of
the eye and the drifting of an object in space. Given no other information from
the visual field, the sensory system is unable to determine whether the source
of movement is in the eye or in the visual field; the autokinetic effect arises
from this ambiguous situation.

We must also consider the possible effects of continuous stimulation by
the same figure. Perhaps such instability (i.e., movement or drifting) occurs
due to the sensory mechanism's failure to continue processing the same external stimulus. This line of reasoning led Page, Elfner, and Jamison (1966) to
expect a reduction in autokinetic movement if the light was flashing and not
continuous. Their results relating the amount of displacement of the light to
the number of flashes of the light per second are presented in Figure 3.6.
They found that higher flash frequencies produced greater amounts of displacement. While such results are somewhat confusing, the authors (Page
et al.) conclude that the effect is reduced at low levels of flash frequency due
to the increased amount of time allowed for the development of a clear figure.
Following this reasoning, increases in displacement would be expected up to
a critical flash frequency, after which a decrease would be expected.

Table 3.1

Number of subjects reporting movement of sound (N = 10)
(Cautela and McLaughlin, 1960)

Group	Instructions	35 db tone	70 db tone
1	Trace	10	10
2	Describe	10	10
3	Characterize	1	5
4	Notice	0	2

Again, as noted in conjunction with the Ganzfeld, more than the presence of a simple figure is required for stable perception and effective stimulation. Figures must be perceived in relation to textured or well-defined backgrounds.

The discussion of Ganzfeld effects and of autokinesis has been limited to the visual channel; however, analogous phenomena have also been reported for the auditory system. The effects on auditory perception of background noise without figures will be discussed in detail under the topic of *sensory deprivation*. With regard to the autokinetic phenomenon, Bernadin and Gruber (1957) seated blindfolded subjects in a dark room and sounded pure tones of moderate intensity. Prior to this, subjects were provided with one of three sets of instructions. The first requested the subjects to report anything they noticed about the sound. The second required reports on perceived changes in pitch and loudness, and the third asked for indications of changes in the source of the sound. Although the amount of reported displacement of the sound was greatest under the third instruction, which focused the attention of the subject on possible sound movement, all subjects under all conditions reported some sound displacement.

Cautela and McLaughlin (1960) attempted a more controlled demonstration of the *audioautokinetic effect*. They fastened blindfolded subjects to a head restraint and presented two sound sources: a 500-Hz, 35-db tone followed after a brief interval by a 550-Hz, 70-db sound. The source of the sound was located along the midline of the subject's head in a manner ensuring that the tone would reach both ears simultaneously. As in the earlier experiment Cautela and McLaughlin varied the instructions to the subjects. Group 1 was told that a moving tone would be presented and that they were to trace its movement on a piece of paper located in front of them. Group 2 was asked to describe the movement of the sound but not required to trace its displacement. Groups 3 and 4 were instructed, respectively, to characterize the sound or to report anything they noticed about the sound. The numbers of subjects reporting movement of the sound in each group are recorded in Table 3.1. Obviously an audioautokinetic effect was obtained, but it does not appear to occur as spontaneously as the visual effect (Sherif, 1936). Furthermore, since head position was restrained in this experiment, possible movement of the ears cannot be considered a source of the phenomena analogous to visual autokinetic displacement caused by eye movement. The results shown in Table 3.1

may simply reflect a degree of suggestiveness in the instructions, one that led the observers to expect a movement of the sound.

The influence of suggestion is also readily demonstrated by experiments involving visual light stimuli. Several researchers (e.g., Rethlingshafer and Sherrer, 1961), having informed subjects that the light source would spell out words, collected numerous reports of such words from the subjects—usually simple three-letter words such as *and, the,* and *one.* However, some subjects reported four-letter words of lower frequency and social acceptance. Some work has been done utilizing the direction connoted by the light source. Comalli, Werner, and Wapner (1957) asked subjects to report the direction of movement of illuminated transparencies of a running horse, a running boy, and an arrow. Each picture was shown facing left and facing right. As would be expected, the direction of perceived motion corresponded to the orientation of the picture.

The influence of such extrinsic and intrinsic instructions on autokinetic and audioautokinetic effects suggests that the control processes and long-term storage are integrally involved. Faced with an ambiguous stimulus situation the subject produces a perceptual response from his own repertoire of responses. If the information contained in the external stimulus is insufficient for processing, then the percept will develop from information stored at some advanced level and involve memory and expectation. If this explanation is correct, the importance of eye movement in the case of the visual auto-kinetic response is unclear. Quite possibly an autokinetic response resulting from suggestion does not depend on eye movement, just as the suggested audioautokinetic response does not require movement of the ears. Unfortunately, research on this question is presently unavailable.

Eye movements. If an observer is asked to fix and hold his gaze on a specific point, he is able to do so with minimum difficulty. Subjectively, during such periods of strict fixation, the eyes seem to be motionless. Nonetheless, continual involuntary eye movements are occurring. In 1738 Juring and in 1866 Helmholtz reported such eye movements. Their magnitude has been estimated by more recent techniques such as that employed by Riggs, Armington, and Ratliff (1954). Their method involves fitting the subject with a plastic contact lens to which a plane mirror is attached. A beam of light is reflected by the mirror onto a screen where a continuous photographic record of the beam movements and hence eye movements is obtained. The kinds of eye movements recorded by these techniques have been summarized by Young (1963):

1. *Saccadic eye movements:* rapid, voluntary eye movements between fixation points. They occur at irregular intervals averaging about 2 to 4 times a second. The angle of movement may vary between 2° and 50° with reaction times between 100 and 250 msec. For a saccade of 10°, a reaction time of approximately 100 msec is required.
2. *Slow drift movements:* slow, involuntary, random movements around a fixation point. Such continuous movements range between 1' and 5' of arc per second.

3. *Rapid tremor eye movements:*   rapid, involuntary movements around
    the fixation point. These occur as rapidly as 30 to 150 times per sec-
    ond and at intervals as short as 30 msec. The rapid tremor is usually
    superimposed on the slow drift movement and keeps the line of
    regard within several degrees of the fixation point. An interesting ob-
    servation by Riggs and Ratliff (1951) regarding such tremor move-
    ments shows them to be independent for each eye. That is to say, the
    tremor movements of one eye do not affect such movements in the
    other.

In order to assess the importance of such eye movements a method was
required for eliminating their influence on retinal displacement. If such a technique could be developed, then the effects of a motionless eye on the perception of figures could be observed. A number of techniques have been developed and are discussed by Heckenmuller (1965). The most popular technique,
developed by Riggs, Ratliff, Cornsweet, and Cornsweet (1953), is diagramed in
Figure 3.7. A beam of light from a projector containing a figure (e.g., a thin vertical line) is reflected by a mirror mounted on a contact lens onto a screen. The
image on the screen is reflected back to the eye through a series of mirrors
placed at appropriate distances to compensate for the angle and distance of
the projection beam. Any movement of the eye now produces a corresponding movement of the projected image. The result is a stabilization of the
image on one portion of the retina.

With this apparatus, Riggs and his co-workers projected fine lines of
varying thickness to the eye. They found no impairment in the initial perception of the line, but a fading and disappearance of the line after several seconds of stabilized viewing; the line tended to reappear and disappear.
This appearance-disappearance occurred frequently for fine lines and much
less frequently for wider lines.

That the function of eye movements is to maintain the stimulus and not
to aid in the initial perception of the lines was demonstrated in a second
of the Riggs experiments. Lines were flashed for one of four brief durations (30,
100, 200, or 450 msec). A comparison of the results obtained with those of a
control series, in which the eye was allowed normal movement, revealed that
for short fixed-eye durations, identification was actually enhanced by the
stable image.

Subsequently a large number of reports on various aspects of stabilized
eye movement have appeared. Pritchard (1961) has explored the effects of
stabilizing more complex patterns on the retina. Frequently he has found that
such figures tend to fade in parts rather than as wholes. In addition, the parts
dissolving from a typical figure do not seem to disappear in a random fashion,
but follow meaningful sequences. Some examples from Pritchard are shown in
Figure 3.8.

Pritchard, Heron, and Hebb (1960) have also shown that meaningful targets tend to disappear more slowly than meaningless targets, and that directing a subject's attention to aspects of a complex pattern makes that pattern
less susceptible to fading. With a technique introduced by Evans (1967), these

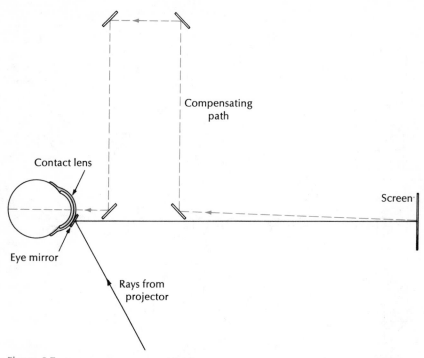

Figure 3.7
Diagram of an apparatus for stabilizing images on the retina. (After Riggs, Ratliff, Cornsweet, and Cornsweet, 1953.)

effects may be demonstrated with a minimum of difficulty. Find a room which
can be made very dark and open the book to Figure 3.9. Illuminate the patterns
with a high-intensity lamp. Now turn off the lamp and all other room lights
and allow yourself time (about 5 to 10 minutes) to become dark-adapted. Illuminate the book and fix your gaze on the point centered in one of the
patterns. After 15 seconds turn off the light and look at a blank wall in the
dark room. You should have a white negative afterimage of the pattern stabilized on your retina. Note whether all or parts of the image fade at once. Once
the image disappears, several rapid eye blinks should restore it.

Krauskopf and Riggs (1959) observed the effect of a line stabilized on one
eye on the perception of a line stabilized on the same portion of the other eye.
In perceptual terminology, the stimulus was presented to the *ipsilateral* eye
and the test figure to the *contralateral* eye. That vision was found impaired in
the contralateral eye indicates some binocular interaction beyond the level of
the primary receptors of the retina.

The exact function of eye movements in the perceptual process is still unclear. That they do not aid in the initial perception of a stimulus appears to
have been demonstrated. Cornsweet (1956) noted the effects of target disappearance or target displacement on different kinds of eye movements. The

Figure   Reported disappearance

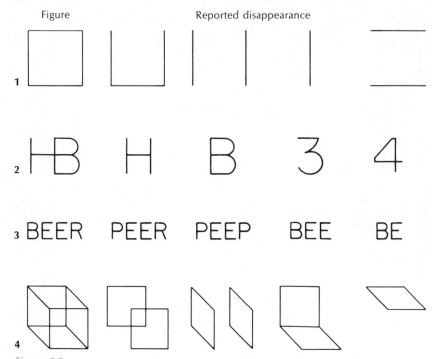

slow drift movements were not influenced by target disappearance or by target displacement. Such movements may simply represent an inherent instability of the oculomotor system—an observation fitting nicely with the attempted explanation of the autokinetic movement effect. The saccadic movements, on the other hand, were affected by target displacement. Both the direction and amplitude indicate that changes in the visual field exhibit an adjustive function; that is, they return the target to the portion of the retina allowing clearest vision.

The nature of voluntary eye movements has been explored further by Crovitz and Daves (1963). They flashed arrays of letters of the alphabet across the horizontal visual field; the center of each array contained a fixation point. They noted a relationship between eye movements occurring *after* the presentation of the array and the tendency to identify the letters correctly in that portion of the field. Note that the eye movement occurred after the exposure and therefore could not aid in the perception of the physical stimulus; rather, such movement made a contribution during the postexposure period.

While at this time it is not possible to specify the exact function of eye movements in perception, it would seem that the experimental results are compatible with a view emphasizing an active perceptual system, one in which information is gathered and processed at numerous levels. Both the effects of suggestion on the autokinetic and audioautokinetic effects and the role of

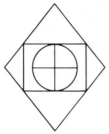 

Figure 3.9
Patterns for the demonstration of stabilized afterimages.

attention and figure meaningfulness in the disappearance of stabilized images demonstrate the ways in which elements of the perceptual system influence one another. Certainly complex control processes are in effect at each level of the system.

Visual Acuity

The term *visual acuity* refers to the ability or capacity of an observer to perceive fine detail. While the degree of visual acuity varies greatly among observers, a number of variables influencing their capacity to respond to detail have been identified. We will be using the term visual acuity to refer to the capacity of an observer to recognize or identify specific visual figures. With regard to our perceptual model, this means that a perception of a figure is required rather than a mere sensation. Such stimulus configurations entering the sensory register must be evaluated and interpreted on the basis of information maintained in the long-term storage and imposed by the control processes.

Assessing visual acuity. Before considering the factors influencing visual acuity, we must view some of the methods for assessing it in the typical observer. Basically four types of tasks are most commonly employed by researchers: tasks of *recognition, resolution, detection,* and *localization.*

For most persons the *recognition* variety of acuity task is most familiar. One technique, introduced by Snellen (1862), requires an observer to identify letters of the alphabet that vary in size. Each letter is constructed so that the thickness of the line segments is one-fifth the height of the letter. In assigning a measure of visual acuity, the minimum visual angle that can be discriminated at a distance of 20 feet is multiplied by 20. Hence the standard for normal visual acuity of 20/20 means the ability to recognize a letter whose line segments subtend 1' of arc at a distance of 20 feet. By the same token, visual acuity of 20/10 would indicate the recognition of line segments subtending 0.5' of arc, whereas 20/400 would mean recognition of line segments subtending 20' of arc.

Unfortunately, the discriminability of all the letters of the alphabet is not the same. Some letters, such as *b* and *d*, are easily confused, whereas others,

Table 3.2

Mean recovery time as a function of flash duration
(Miller, 1965)

Duration (seconds)	0.04	0.10	0.24	0.34	1.40
Mean recovery time (seconds)	14.22	27.89	51.97	74.19	109.71

such as *w* and *k*, are easily recognized. This observation led Landolt (1889) to introduce another recognition task in which the figure **C** is presented with the gap either up, down, left, or right. The subject must indicate the position of the gap. As with the Snellen chart, the gap is one-fifth the size of the figure, allowing the same kind of measurement of acuity provided by the Snellen chart.

In measurements of *resolution* acuity the observer is required to respond to the separation between elements of a pattern. A typical test involves the presentation of a vertical or horizontal grating of black bars ⦀ ☰ in which the width of the bars equals the white space between the bars. By systematically reducing the visual angle subtended by the bars a point is reached at which the observer can no longer divide the figure into bars and spaces. This point is known as the *minimum angle of separation* or MAS (Riggs, 1965).

In the *detection* task, the observer is confronted with the problem of identifying the presence or absence of a stimulus in a visual field. Usually a bright object of a given size must be detected against a dark background. Often the brightness relationships between the test object and background are varied so that the subject must detect a dark object on a darker background.

Finally, the *localization* task involves the capacity of the observer to discriminate the displacement of one element in a visual array. Usually a test of *vernier acuity* is given in which one segment of a vertical line is displaced slightly to the left or right. The amount of displacement can be varied and the level can be established at which the subject can no longer indicate the position of the offset element.

In attempting to relate visual acuity to attributes of effective stimuli, tasks are frequently utilized which fail to fall clearly within the domain of these four basic types of acuity measurement. Often subjects are required to identify an object or a word as a function of some stimulus attribute (e.g., duration of presentation or size of object). Such a task would involve recognition, resolution, and detection. Since our main concern is to identify the properties of effective stimuli and to observe some of the response characteristics of the sensory system, several of the conditions that contribute to visual acuity are discussed below.[2]

The adaptive state of the eye. When the eye responds to beams of light, there are continual changes in the general level of the sensitivity of the visual receptors. If the eye is exposed to light of a fairly high intensity, a corresponding

---

[2] For a more complete review of the literature on this subject, the reader should consult the paper by Lit (1968).

Table 3.3

Mean recovery time as a function of flash size
(Miller, 1965)

Flash size (degrees of visual angle)	10°	7.5°	5°	2.5°
Mean recovery time (seconds)	52.99	54.00	56.35	59.08

adaptive state is produced whereby it becomes relatively insensitive to weak stimuli. This continual process is known as *light adaptation*. The return of sensitivity after a period of time in darkness is called *dark adaptation*. That the light or dark adaptive state of the eye relates directly to visual acuity can be attested by anyone having attended a movie in the afternoon. On entering the theater visual acuity is impaired. After several minutes, however, the eye becomes adapted to the low level of light intensities and acuity improves. The reverse process of light adaptation can be experienced on leaving the darkened theater and reentering the sunlight. Again, acuity is markedly reduced until an appropriate level of light adaptation is reached.

It is important to note that the level of adaptation is constantly changing as a function of the intensity of each successive light stimulus. Even a brief flash of light has a marked influence on the acuity level of the eye. Miller (1965) presented a flash of light subtending 10° of visual angle and observed the capacity of her subjects to identify Snellen letters as a function of the duration of the flash. The mean recovery time, or time required to return to the pre-exposure level of acuity, is presented for each flash duration in Table 3.2.

Note that with a flash duration just under a quarter of a second almost a full minute was required for readaptation. Miller also observed the effect of the size of the flash on the ability of her observers to identify Snellen letters subtending 16.3′ of visual angle. In Table 3.3 the mean recovery times as a function of flash size are given for the four longest durations (0.10, 0.24, 0.34 and 1.40 seconds) combined. For all sizes, recovery times just under one minute are generated. It is interesting that the smallest field produced the longest recovery time. Perhaps this is a result of a concentration of energy on a smaller portion of the fovea.

Retinal position.   An important element of the visual system, unrelated to the attributes of the external stimuli, is the portion of the retina stimulated by the optical array. Presenting the stimulus to the central portion of the fovea fosters the highest degree of acuity; such acuity decreases rapidly, however, as the stimulus is presented to more peripheral sections of the eye. Figure 3.10 relates the level of visual acuity to the position of the test stimulus in degrees of visual angle from the center of the fovea.

That the range of high-acuity vision is very narrow can be demonstrated with Figure 3.11. Cover your left eye with your left hand and look directly at the point marked 0° on the right end of the figure. Your eye should be approximately 5 inches from this point. If you attempt to read the letters at the positions to the left of the fixation point without moving your right eye, you will

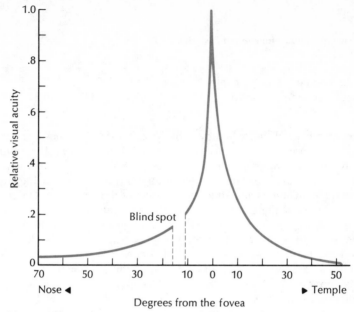

Figure 3.10

Visual acuity as a function of retinal position. Acuity decreases in proportion to the distance from the center (0 degrees) of the fovea.

note that clear vision extends only less than 10°. The letters at 20°, 30°, 40°, and 50° are very unclear.

Hershenson (1969) has recently attempted to measure the ability of subjects to identify English letters presented to different portions of the retina. He was concerned with locations close to the fovea within which acuity should be fairly high. Seven-letter arrays subtending a visual angle of 3.5° were flashed for approximately 20 msec and subjects attempted to identify as many of the seven letters as possible. In order to insure that the influence of retinal position was the prime variable, rather than postperceptual factors of memory, a fixation point at the position of either the second, fourth, or sixth letter was presented prior to the display of the seven letters. The probability of correctly identifying a stimulus letter at a given position was then traced for each of the three fixation points. Hershenson's results are reproduced in Figure 3.12. Absolute retinal locus obviously affects acuity, as the figure demonstrates. The farther the position of the letter from the fixation point, the poorer the performance.

Figure 3.11

A simple test of visual acuity in the periphery of the eye.

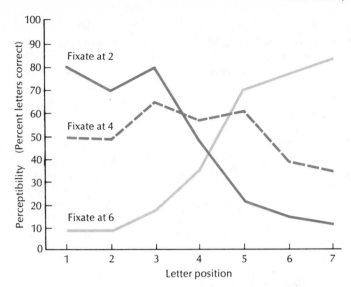

Figure 3.12
Perceptibility as a function of letter position for fixation points at positions 2, 4, and 6. (After Hershenson, 1969.)

An interesting controversy has developed around the question of the superiority of the right or left visual fields in identifying peripherally presented figures. Ayres and Harcum (1962) found the left portion of the horizontal visual field to be superior to the right portion. In terms of recognition accuracy, they also found the top or north portion of the vertical visual field to be superior to the south portion. Ayres (1966) has argued that these results may represent artifacts of method rather than higher levels of acuity for the left field and north field. He reasoned that we are used to reading and looking from left to right and from up to down and would tend, therefore, to report our perceptions in similar fashion. As a result subjects would make errors for the right and south portions due to forgetfulness rather than faulty perception.

Winnick and Bruder (1968) supported the artifactual nature of the earlier work by applying a signal detection task to the problem—a method designed to reduce or eliminate the influence of the subject's order of report. A vertical or horizontal array of eight letters was flashed, followed by a card containing eight dashes representing the positions of the previously flashed letters. A single letter was shown on the test card at one of the eight positions and the subject was asked to indicate whether the single letter was the same as (signal) or different from (noise) the letter occupying that position in the preceding array of eight letters. The horizontal array was flashed for 100 msec, the vertical array for 200 msec. A fixation point was located between the fourth and fifth letter position for both arrays. The results indicated no difference between left and right portions of the visual field or between north and south.

Finally, Freeburne and Goldman (1969) tested the order of report hypothesis directly by requiring subjects to respond to six-letter arrays and indicate the letters perceived from left to right, right to left, or in any order chosen. The results of the unspecified and left-to-right orders of report clearly showed the left retinal field to be superior to the right; under such instructions, in fact, twice as many correct letter identifications were made from the left portion as the right. Exactly the reverse was true when the instructions required a report of the letters perceived from right to left. The right field of vision proved to be superior by a factor of two to one.

In summary, the most recent research on left or right retinal dominance indicates that the differences uncovered in earlier studies were due to the tendencies of subjects to report letters in the favored left-to-right or up-to-down order. Such a tendency would appear to be the result of experience in reading printed material that is usually processed from left to right and up to down. Similar experiments with individuals raised in cultures that present written materials from right to left have supported this explanation. Thus Harcum and Friedman (1963) found improved performance in the right retinal field for Israelis.

Stimulus variables and visual acuity.   Visual acuity has been shown to depend on a number of stimulus variables. In the following sections we will consider briefly the relationships between acuity and *stimulus intensity, stimulus duration, stimulus frequency,* and *interstimulus interval.* Unfortunately, the relationships between acuity and these four aspects frequently vary as functions of the particular acuity task applied. For our purposes we shall limit the discussion to acuity as defined by means of the recognition task. While this limitation is somewhat arbitrary, it does fall in line with our consideration of perception as an active, information-seeking process. Only in the recognition task is the delineation between sensation and perception clear. By having to recognize the stimulus and to identify certain of its attributes, the observer must rely on previous experience and on perceptual response tendencies previously accrued.

Stimulus intensity.   With increases in the intensity of the stimulus, corresponding increases in the level of acuity are observed. Figure 3.13 reports the data for single subjects highly trained in the detection of the Landolt C as a function of luminance level (Shlaer, 1937).

While the relationship between intensity and acuity for a recognition task seems clear, we should note that this is not true for some of the other estimates of visual acuity. Wilcox (1932), for example, developed a resolution task in which the intensity of the bar stimulus to be resolved was varied, while the background level of intensity was held constant. He reported a U-shaped function in which the resolution threshold steadily decreased and then increased, with further increases in the intensity of the stimulus. This meant that the ability of subjects to resolve the target improved as the intensity of the target increased; however, at the higher levels of intensity a reduction in resolution acuity occurred.

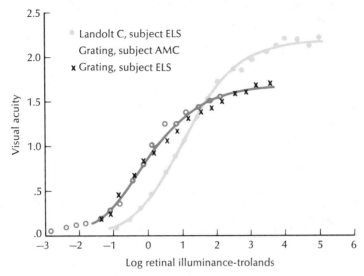

Figure 3.13
Visual acuity for a grating and a Landolt C as a function of retinal illuminance. (After Shlaer, 1937.)

Stimulus duration.   The importance of the duration of a stimulus in visual acuity has been of considerable interest for both early and modern investigators of the process of perception. Most of this consideration deals with the perception of complex forms and will be discussed at the onset of the next chapter. As was the case with intensity, recognition acuity is found to increase as the duration of the stimulus increases. If acuity increases steadily with increases in duration and with increases in intensity, one might expect a reciprocal relationship between these two variables. That is to say, one should be able to hold the level of acuity constant by increasing the stimulus duration and correspondingly decreasing the stimulus intensity. With regard to duration, this expected reciprocity is known as *Bloch's law,* which states that within the confines of a critical duration, a short, intense stimulus should have the same effect as a longer stimulus of lower intensity. Kahneman, Norman, and Kubovy (1967) sought to determine the critical duration within which Bloch's law would hold. Using the Landolt C, they established an acuity level at which the position of the C would be identified correctly 60 percent of the time. By successively decreasing the intensity and increasing the duration, this level of acuity could be maintained up to a total duration of about 160 msec. After this point increases in duration with corresponding decreases in intensity produced sharp reductions in recognition acuity.

Stimulus frequency.   With a reciprocity established for intensity and duration, Haber and Hershenson (1965) undertook the measurement of the relation-

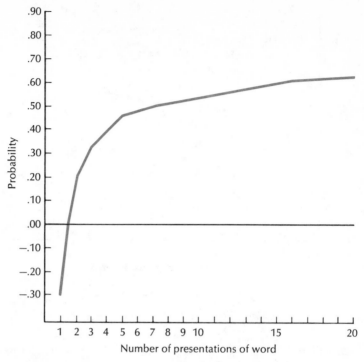

Figure 3.14
Probability of identifying a seven-letter word as a function of presentation frequency. (After Haber and Hershenson, 1965.)

ship between stimulus frequency and duration. They flashed seven-letter English words subtending 2.5° of visual angle 1, 2, 3, 4, 5, 10, 15, or 25 times at one of seven durations ranging from 5 msec to 35 msec in steps of 5 msec. That frequency of presentation contributed to recognition accuracy can be clearly seen in Figure 3.14. The probability of correctly recognizing the word flashed is shown as a function of presentation frequency. Improvement occurs up to about 10 presentations, after which further presentations appear to contribute little to acuity.

Having demonstrated that acuity depends on frequency, Haber and Hershenson investigated the relationship between frequency and duration by comparing the percentage of correct word recognitions for total flash durations composed of varying frequencies of word exposure. These data are shown in Table 3.4. Note that the left-hand column shows total duration and that each successive column to the right indicates the duration of each component flash. For example, with a total duration of 60 msec, six flashes of 10 msec provided 7 percent correct word identification, three flashes of 20 msec 68.3 percent, and two 30-msec flashes 93.7 percent.

Table 3.4 clearly indicates that a simple reciprocity for duration and frequency does not exist. Recognition acuity evidently depends on a minimum

Table 3.4

Percentage of words perceived when the total number of milliseconds of duration is divided into one or more exposures
(Haber and Hershenson, 1965)

Total duration	Flash exposure duration				
	10	*15*	*20*	*25*	*30*
20	3.1		42.0		
40	9.2		67.5		
60	7.0	37.7	68.3		93.7
90	8.5	37.0			97.3
100	9.1		81.7	91.2	
120	9.5	42.0	83.0		89.7
150	10.1	47.4		95.5	96.3

duration (Bryden, 1966) for each stimulus presentation which cannot be counterbalanced by a number of shorter presentations. Simply stated, the effect of one long flash is not the same as a number of shorter flashes equaling the same total duration. Possibly a critical minimum duration could be identified above which a duration × frequency reciprocity exists. According to the longer flash durations listed in Table 3.4, the effect of 5 flashes of 30 msec each appears equal to the effect of 6 flashes of 25 msec each.

Interstimulus interval. Recent work has also demonstrated the contribution of interstimulus interval to recognition acuity. Perhaps the effect of 5 flashes of 10 msec per flash also depends on the interval between the successive flashes. In Figure 3.15 the probability of identifying a seven-letter English word presented either 3, 5, or 10 times is shown as a function of the interval between presentations. Since the interstimulus interval is the variable of interest here, each data point represents an average probability in which the effects of brief flashes of a specific duration were combined (Murch, 1969c). The effect on recognition acuity of 3, 5, or 10 flashes separated by 25 msec is obviously greater than the effect of the same frequencies separated by longer interstimulus intervals (e.g., 500 msec). With this observation in mind, one might be able to establish a reciprocity for duration × frequency × interstimulus interval, although such a possibility has not yet been explored.

The relationships between recognition acuity and stimulus frequency, stimulus duration, stimulus intensity, and interstimulus interval hint at some of the characteristics of the sensory register proposed in our model of perception. These observations, coupled with research designed specifically to uncover the attributes of the sensory register and the short-term storage mechanism, can provide information about the initial steps in the perceptual process.

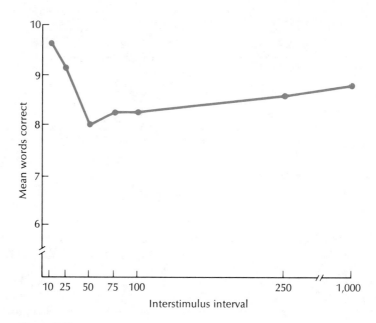

Figure 3.15
Probability of identifying a seven-letter word as a function
of interstimulus interval. (Murch, 1969c.)

The Visual Sensory Register

The model of the perceptual process we considered at the beginning of the
present chapter appears to be generally compatible with the experimental
observations reported in the pages that followed. At this point we must consider more carefully the various stations of perception postulated in Figure
3.1 and attempt to assess the attributes of each mechanism of the model. We
assumed, it will be recalled, that a potential stimulus could follow one of three
possible pathways. One, a potential stimulus might remain unnoticed and
therefore be classified as an ineffective stimulus. Two, it might pass into the
sensory register but no farther. And three, it might become an effective stimulus and pass through to short-term storage.

Before we examine the attributes of the sensory register, we shall consider
the evidence in support of the separation of the first stages of perception
into a sensory register and a short-term storage bank. Some support can be ob-

tained from a study by Smith and Carey (1966) in which subjects were required to read rows of six letters presented tachistoscopically. The number of trials required to read all rows of letters was counted. Of particular interest among the several conditions studied were the continuous presentation of the stimulus array for 100, 200, or 400 msec and the 20 msec presentation followed by a second 20 msec presentation after a delay interval of 60, 160, or 360 msec. Comparing the effects of the two conditions, Smith and Carey found no differences in the number of letters correctly reported.

To account for the lack of differences, at least two stages of perceptual processing must be assumed. Registration in the first stage would appear to occur very rapidly, followed by a slower transfer to the second stage. Information is processed at stage two even when the original stimulus array is no longer present; this indicates that some trace of the original stimulus must be maintained in the first stage during the delay interval.

Sperling (1960) was one of the first to attempt a systematic exploration of the sensory register. In the introduction to his monograph, Sperling discusses the response to brief presentations of complex visual displays. Typical observers are unable to report all they see. Initially, visual information is recorded very rapidly, but it cannot be maintained long enough for the subject to process it all. This subjective experience of seeing more than one can identify is readily demonstrable if one looks at a complex scene such as a city skyline or a bed of flowers. The visual experience cannot be adequately described—nor all the details reported—when physical stimulation ceases. Immediately after closing one's eyes, a rather vivid image of the scene seems to remain briefly. After several seconds, however, only a few specific points can be recalled. Much of the information entering the sensory register appears to be lost very quickly.

Averbach and Coriell (1961) tried to measure the duration of the storage of visual information in the sensory register. They first presented subjects with two rows of eight letters. After a short delay, a line appeared over the position of one of the letters in the previous display. The subject's task was to identify this letter. The capability of an observer to reproduce the letter decayed steadily as the interval between stimulus array and test line increased. With this method, Averbach and Coriell established the limit of the sensory register at 200–300 msec. They interpreted their results to indicate the presence of a sensory holding mechanism, from which visual image rapidly decays and information is lost unless it passes into the short-term memory store.

The work of Sperling and Averbach and Coriell served as the catalyst for a number of subsequent studies. C. W. Eriksen and his co-workers undertook a series of experiments designed to assess the notion of a sensory register. In an early paper, Eriksen and Steffy (1964) advanced a criticism of Averbach's and Coriell's study. They pointed out the possible disrupting effect of presenting line markers after the exposure of the rows of letters. This second stimulus might erase or blot out (mask) the information currently stored in the register. (Masking refers to a reduction in the recognition capability of an observer when a critical stimulus is closely followed by a second stimulus.) The line marker used by Averbach and Coriell may have functioned as such a masking stimulus.

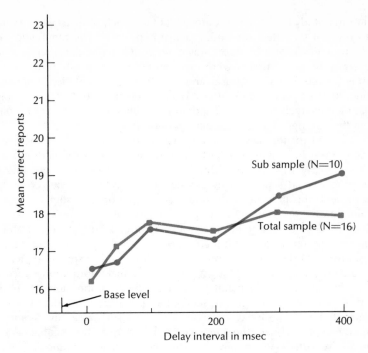

Figure 3.16
Accuracy of report as a function of the delay of the indicator. (After Eriksen and Steffy, 1964.)

Eriksen and Steffy then tested this possibility with their own design. The first stimulus they presented to subjects was a pattern of Xs and Os arranged at the even hours of an imaginary clock. This display was followed by a dark interval of either 10, 50, 100, 200, 300, or 420 msec. Next an arrow briefly pointed to one of the clock positions of the previous display. The subject was asked to indicate whether the arrow pointed to a position occupied by an X or an O in the original display. The results of the experiment are shown in Figure 3.16.

Clearly the presentation of the arrow reduces recognition accuracy. The effect is strongest at the shorter intervals and appears to level off after about 100 msec. Performance at delays greater than 100 msec stays at about the same level up to 420 msec. While this experiment demonstrates the possible masking effect of the second stimulus, it offers no evidence of the presence of a sensory register mechanism similar to that indicated by the work of Averbach and Coriell. Their results would lead one to expect a further reduction in accuracy at 200–300 msec as the time limit for storage in the sensory register is reached.

Perhaps Eriksen and Steffy were unable to find evidence of a sensory register due to the limited amount of information contained in their stimulus display. If, as Sperling has suggested, the sensory register is capable of holding

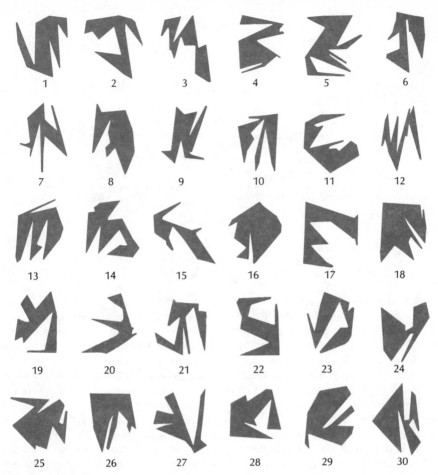

Figure 3.17
Examples of the nonsense figures of Vanderplas and Garvin (1959).

complex materials for a brief interval, the simple task of positioning an arrow relative to a preceding field of Xs and Os would not test the limitations of the sensory register. Steffy and Eriksen (1965) explored this possibility with an experiment in which a triangular arrangement of nonsense forms was briefly presented. Next, after a delay of from 10 to 700 msec, they showed a form identical with one of the preceding three nonsense forms. Subjects were required to identify which of the three stimulus forms was the same as the test form.

Examples of the type of nonsense forms used in this experiment are shown in Figure 3.17. Such material offers several advantages over that used in the earlier studies. First, rather complex visual displays can be presented. Second, the use of nonsense forms seems to insure that the subject remembers a visual image rather than a verbal indicator of the display. (That is to say, if we present

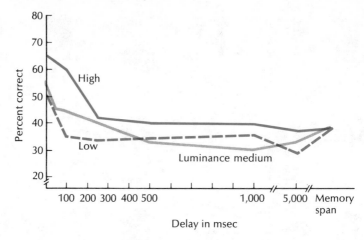

Figure 3.18
Stimulus luminance and the percentage of correct identifications for
complex displays. (After Keele and Chase, 1967.)

a simple square, a delay interval, and a triangle and ask the observer if the
second figure matched the first, we receive correct responses even after very
long delays. This method does not test *visual* memory, however, since we do
not know whether the subject has maintained a visual image of the square
during the delay or if he has encoded the stimulus and remembered the term
square following the delay. Since there are no ready-made terms or cues for
forms such as those shown in Figure 3.17, it can be assumed that the subject
is required to rely on visual memory of the stimulus.)

For half of the subjects the three forms were followed by the test form
after delays ranging from 10 to 700 msec. The other half of the subjects received the test form first and then, after a delay, the three nonsense forms.
Actually, Sperling's visual memory theory would predict no difference between
the two conditions; visual memory should be able to hold the information in
both orders equally well. Steffy and Eriksen found no reduction in performance
over the entire 700-msec range for the condition in which the test form preceded the alternatives, but a marked performance decrement up to 100 msec
for the condition in which the three nonsense forms came before the test.

These results indicate the absence of a visual memory or sensory register,
yet they may still be considered evidence of an observer's ability to hold some
critical aspect of a nonsense form in immediate or short-term storage. Steffy
and Eriksen point out the similarity of their results with research on the short-
term memory mechanism for verbal materials. Murdock (1961), for example,
found perfect retention for single words over long delay periods, but marked
decay within the first few seconds for three words. Although the time bases
(milliseconds for visual displays and seconds for words) are quite different, the
effects seem to follow similar basic principles.

Keele and Chase (1967) have followed up the problem of complexity of
visual materials with a modification of the Eriksen and Steffy (1964) experiment.

Figure 3.19
Example of the dot patterns used
by Eriksen and Collins (1967,
1968).

Instead of using Xs and Os, they arranged ten letters and digits like the face of
a clock. Using all letters of the alphabet and digits 1 through 9, they constructed forty-two different visual arrays. Delays from 0 to 5,000 msec inter-
vened between presentation of the clock design and an arrow pointing to one
of the elements in the display. Three levels of stimulus intensity (3.7, 16, and
70 footlamberts) were used. Figure 3.18 presents the results of their study.

The work of Keele and Chase lends support to the theory of visual sensory
registration and points out the importance of stimulus intensity in maintaining
the visual image. At high levels of luminance the image was maintained up to
250 msec, and at lower levels, up to 100 msec. Haber and Standing (1968) developed an intensity measure of the persistence of a visual image by repeatedly
flashing a simple black circle and varying the interval between flashes. When
the inter-flash interval was less than 250 msec, subjects reported that the
circle never faded completely during the interval. The luminance level in this
experiment corresponded closely with the level described by Keele and Chase,
and a similar period of visual persistence was observed.

Recently Eriksen and Collins (1967, 1968) introduced a novel approach
to the study of the sensory register. They showed a subject a pattern of apparently random dots followed after a delay by a second dot pattern. Presented alone, the patterns, as can be seen in Figure 3.19, produce no meaningful
form. However, if presented simultaneously the patterns produce a legible
nonsense syllable. At very short delays between presentations of the two patterns (up to 25 msec), performance in syllable identification shows little de-

cline. As the delay is increased, performance decreases and levels off somewhere around 300 msec.

Eriksen and Collins also varied the intensity of the stimulus patterns. Under one condition both stimulus halves were presented with an intensity of 5 millilamberts (mL). Other conditions displayed the first dot pattern at an intensity of 5 mL and the second at 2 mL; the reverse (2 mL followed by 5 mL); and a 1-mL stimulus followed or preceded by a 5-mL pattern. In the experiment each pattern half was displayed for 6 msec separated by delays of 25, 50, 75, and 100 msec. The 6-msec display period for each pattern half was established prior to the actual experiment as the value allowing 85-percent correct syllable identification when both halves were presented simultaneously. Figure 3.20 shows the effect of the luminance of the stimulus halves on performance as a function of the interpolated interval.

Eriksen and Collins (1968) suggest that another factor besides the decaying visual image appears to play a role in the reduction in accuracy when the delay interval between stimulus halves is increased. In a control situation it was found that observers correctly identified 92 percent of the syllables with simultaneous exposure of the two patterns when the intensity level of each pattern was held at 5 mL. With 2-mL intensity and simultaneous exposure, an 88-percent accuracy level was obtained; and with a 1-mL intensity, 80 percent. By increasing the intensity of the two dot patterns, a higher percentage of correct syllable identifications could be observed. This could be interpreted to mean that the speed of decay of the visual image (trace) increases as stimulus intensity decreases. If the decaying image alone were responsible for the performance decrement, then with increasing intervals between stimulus halves, presenting a 5-mL pattern followed by a 2-mL pattern should yield a level of identification accuracy higher than the simultaneous presentation of the pattern at 2 mL. The same should be expected of a 5-mL pattern followed by a 1-mL pattern. Figure 3.20 clearly shows this is not the case. Performance at all intervals is below the control accuracies listed above. One would have expected, for example, that a 5-mL pattern could be followed after a given delay by the 1-mL pattern and still yield a level of accuracy equal to the simultaneous presentation of both patterns at 2 mL. Presenting the bright stimulus half first does seem to retard the rate of decay—a result analogous to the intensity effect observed by Keele and Chase (1967).

To explain the data of Figure 3.20, Eriksen and Collins reason that a second process beyond the decay of the visual image may be involved: the basic temporal resolving unit of perception. This suggestion, often referred to as the concept of the *psychological moment*, has been discussed in perceptual literature for a number of years (see White, 1963). It assumes that incoming sensory stimuli are not processed in strict temporal order; instead, they are stored for brief periods and processed together. The length of the storage period makes up the psychological moment. With regard to the Eriksen and Collins study, the incoming patterns are stored briefly and then processed together. The sooner they arrive—that is, the shorter the delay interval between halves—the greater the probability that both halves will be processed in the same psychological moment. Due to the decay of the visual image, the first stimulus to arrive would

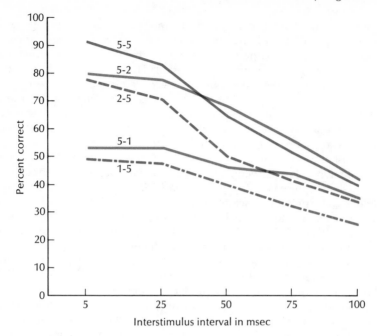

Figure 3.20
Percentage of correct nonsense syllable identifications as a function of the luminance of the corresponding stimulus halves and the interstimulus interval. (After Eriksen, 1968.)

have decayed to some degree before the second stimulus arrives in the sensory register. Although processed together, the two stimulus halves would mismatch in brightness because of the decay of the first image. Such mismatches would lead to the kinds of data displayed in Figure 3.20.

In summary, two processes seem to influence the processing of input in the sensory register. On the one hand, the visual image starts to decay as soon as or very shortly after the distal stimulus is removed. The proximal representation of the distal stimulus (visual image) must be processed before the decay process is complete or else the input is lost. On the other hand, inputs separated by very short time intervals seem to be processed simultaneously. The greater the interval between two successive elements entering the sensory register, the greater the probability that they will not be processed simultaneously.

The psychological moment.   Improvements in the technology of measurement have made it possible to divide the continuous flow of time into very minute elements. The degree to which time can be sectioned depends on the calibration of the particular measuring device. The typical wristwatch divides time into minutes and seconds, but more sophisticated devices break seconds into milliseconds and milliseconds into microseconds. Hylan (1903) was one of the first to investigate the human perception of simultaneity (or the passage of zero time) in the perception of ongoing events. If one event precedes a second by a given duration, how large does the interval between events have to be in order for an observer to perceive succession? Hylan flashed six letters in succession, varying both the interval between each letter and the order of presentation. The observers reported perceiving all letters simultaneously as long as the total duration for all six letters was less than 80 msec. Later Stein (1928) flashed the letters of a German word to German-speaking subjects, starting alternately with the first or last letter of the word. When the total duration of successive flashes was no greater than 100 msec, subjects reported seeing the word in its entirety; all letters seemed to occur simultaneously, independent of the order of letter presentation. More recently Fraisse (1966) modified Hylan's older design by presenting six-letter words in which the letters 1-3-5 formed a meaningful three-letter word; letters 2-4-6 formed another word. In one experiment, letters 1-3-5 were flashed for 15 msec. After delays varying from 0 to 320 msec, letters 2-4-6 were flashed and the number of responses of simultaneous perception of all six letters of the word was recorded as a function of the delay interval. For total durations (duration of letters 1-3-5 + duration of letters 2-4-6 + interpolated delay) under 80 msec, almost 100-percent simultaneity of perception was reported. Conversely, if the total duration exceeded 200 msec, almost all subjects reported perceiving the letters in succession.

Such observations have led to the assumption that at some point in the process of perception incoming sensory information is lumped together and processed simultaneously. The temporal size of these *chunks* of input would appear to fall somewhere between 50 and 100 msec. It is as if the sensory register were storing input over successive 50- to 100-msec intervals and then sending the combined units on to be processed at some higher perceptual station. A problem arises concerning the initial temporal order in which successive stimuli enter the sensory register. Assume that stimulus A is followed after 10 msec by stimulus B. One variation of the psychological moment hypothesis holds that both stimulus A and stimulus B will be processed together as a single unit (White, 1963). In this case no temporal order can be assigned; any incoming stimuli separated by an interval of time less than a psychological moment are phenomenally simultaneous. This conception of the psychological or perceptual moment has been termed the *discrete moment hypothesis* by Allport (1968). He also proposes an alternative interpretation of the psychological moment which he calls the *traveling moment hypothesis*. Rather than assume that input processing occurs in discrete moments defined by a particular duration, events are considered to be processed in succession. Thus all events processed at one time reside within the same psychological moment. Allport distinguishes between the two hypotheses with an analogy involving a train passing through a railway station. On the one hand, a man in the station is able to view the contents of each compartment as a unit; his glimpses of the contents are clearly discontinuous. Such a situation is analogous to the discrete moment hypothesis, with each train compartment representing one psychological moment. On the other hand, for a man riding within the train and looking out the window, the content of one moment contains all elements

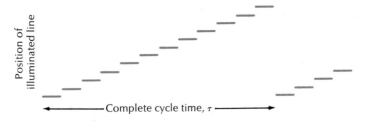

Figure 3.21
Oscilloscope line patterns used by Allport (1968).

presently in the field of view. New elements enter and others pass from the moment continuously as the train moves forward. This situation is analogous to the traveling moment hypothesis.

Allport reports several clever tests of the two possible variants of the psychological moment. In one experiment twelve short lines were presented in rapid succession on the face of an oscilloscope. The arrangement of lines is shown in Figure 3.21. The lower left-hand line was flashed briefly, followed by the next line above and to the right, and the next, until all twelve lines had appeared. Line one followed the twelfth line immediately so that a continuous cycle was set up. If the speed of presentation was slow, subjects reported successive perception of each line. With reductions in presentation duration, a point was reached at which all lines appeared to be on the screen simultaneously. All lines were contained in the same psychological moment. At this point the screen appeared to show a stationary array of horizontal lines. Subjects reported seeing a shadow move successively across the lines, briefly obscuring each line. All subjects reported the shadow to be moving in the direction of the actual order of line presentation. Allport (1968) points out that this observation is consistent only with the traveling moment hypothesis:

> Let the steps be numbered 1, 2, 3, . . . , 12 in the order in which they (the lines) occur within the cycle. According to the discrete moment hypothesis, all the steps within the cycle will be phenomenally simultaneous when they are included within the same discrete moment. When the moment length just includes, say, 11 of the 12 steps, the shadow presumably represents the excluded ith line. Then in successive discrete moments the ith line will be replaced by line $i - 1$, $i - 2$, $i - 3$, etc.; and the shadow will appear to travel in the direction *opposite* to that of the sequence of line positions.
>
> If, on the other hand, the span of simultaneity is determined by a continuous traveling moment, again including $n - 1$ of the n steps at any instant, the excluded ith line will be, successively, $i + 1$, $i + 2$, $i + 3$, etc. The reader should verify this statement for himself, if necessary, by visualizing the sequence of integers given above moving past a window which exposes $n - 1$ at a time. Consequently the shadow will appear to travel in the same direction as the sequence of line positions (pp. 403–4).

Thus the line shadow's observed direction of travel is consistent with the traveling moment hypothesis. A theory suggesting that sensory information is continuously processed in *moving* blocks is more consistent with a model of perception emphasizing the active role of the perceiver. To the initial phase of the perceptual process, the discrete moment hypothesis seems to add a mechanical element which does not fit our model of an information-extracting organism interacting meaningfully with the environment.

Visual masking.   The concept of a psychological moment has several important implications for the processing of visual information. Such implications have received a great deal of attention in recent years. One area of particular interest has been the investigation of the effect of a potential stimulus on an immediately preceding potential stimulus. *Visual masking* refers to the impaired perception of a potential stimulus when a second stimulus occurs simultaneously with or follows the first closely in time.

We shall consider several variations of the basic visual masking paradigm. One kind involves the presentation of a test stimulus followed closely by a flash of light. Deficiencies in the perception of the stimulus are referred to as the result of *luminance masking*. Two other kinds of visual masking involving two patterns have been extensively studied. In the first the perception of a test form is impaired by a second stimulus (*backward masking* or *metacontrast*). In the second, a masking form precedes and hinders the perception of a following test stimulus (*forward masking* or *paracontrast*).

An experiment by Eriksen (1966) serves to clarify the phenomenon of luminance masking. A fixation point was presented in field one of a three-field tachistoscope. After fixing the point, the subject pressed a trigger which caused either the letter A, T, or U to be flashed at a duration that would allow 80 to 85 percent recognition accuracy of the letter. Each letter appeared randomly at the corners of an imaginary square of 1.25° of visual angle centered about the fixation point. Simultaneously with the presentation of the letter, a flash of 0.00, 0.09, 0.20, or 0.40 mL was presented for the same duration as the letter. The light, Eriksen reasoned, would effectively reduce the contrast ratio or figure-ground brightness of the letter. Under the control condition with no luminance mask (0.00 mL), the contrast ratio for the letter to the background is 22:1 (luminance of the letter 0.09 mL, luminance of the ground 0.20 mL $= 0.20/0.09 = 22$). Adding the flash of light (e.g., 0.40 mL) would produce a reduction in contrast ($0.20/0.40 + 0.09 = 0.4$). In Figure 3.22 the percentage of correct letter identifications is related to the effective log ratio of the luminance of the ground to the luminance of the figure. As the effective luminance ratio increased, so did identification accuracy. Notice that for a log contrast ratio of 0.2 (0.40-mL flash), performance approached chance recognition of the letter (0.33). Eriksen's experiment indicates that luminance masking is the result of a *summation* of light energy entering the system and reducing figure-ground contrast.

If the luminance summation hypothesis is correct, a limit to summation should be provided by varying the interval between the test stimulus (letter) and the flash of light (mask). This prediction follows from the psychological moment hypothesis—that all stimuli falling within the confines of the moment will interact. The smaller the interval between successive stimuli, the more

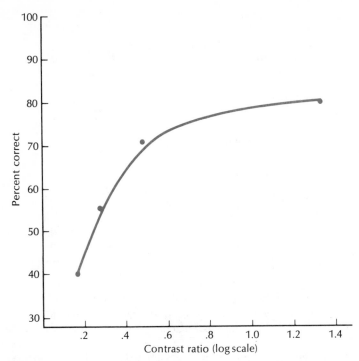

Figure 3.22
Percentage of correct form identifications as a function of the log ratio
of the luminance of the ground to the luminance of the figure. (After
Eriksen, 1966.)

highly probable will be the summation. If the interval increases, then the reduction in contrast will decrease, as the degree of summation between letter
and mask will lessen. Thompson (1966) provided support for the theory in
a study in which the letter A, T, or U was followed by a light flash of one of
four luminance levels (0.200, 0.102, 0.067 or 0.040 ft L). The flashes were presented at one of six delays interpolated between the letter and the flash (0, 5,
10, 25, 50 or 75 msec). Table 3.5 shows the percentage of correct letter identifications as a function of luminance level and delay interval. The base level of
identification was set at 90-percent accuracy for a control condition without
a masking light flash. Notice the interaction between delay interval and luminance: performance impairment is greatest for short intervals and bright
flashes. Increasing the interval and holding the flash luminance constant improves performance, as does reducing flash luminance and leaving the interval
unchanged.

If luminance masking derives from an energy summation between test
figure and masking flash, then presenting the mask before or after the figure
should make no difference. Eriksen and Hoffman (1963) tested this prediction
and found it to be accurate: performance in recognition accuracy was impaired
equally under both conditions.

Table 3.5

Percentage of correct letter identifications in luminance masking
(Thompson, 1966)

Delay interval	Luminance of mask			
	.200	*.102*	*.067*	*.040*
0	30	47	63	79
5	41	58	66	83
10	50	60	72	82
25	66	76	80	86
50	80	81	82	90
75	84	85	86	91

Unfortunately, these results become less clear in the light of an observation by Kahneman (1966). Using the Landolt C as a test stimulus followed or preceded by a flash of light, he related acuity to the duration of the light flash. If the flash was longer than 400 msec, acuity performance actually *improved* in comparison with a condition lacking such a flash. This result is most puzzling in the light of the studies by Eriksen and his co-workers. Perhaps the difference is to be found in the kind of acuity task utilized. Kahneman used the Landolt C, whereas Eriksen measured the capability of observers to identify letters of the alphabet.

Let us now turn to the effect of a second form or pattern on a preceding or following test stimulus. Werner (1935) provided early information on this phenomenon of metacontrast. He briefly flashed a solid black circle followed after a short delay by a black ring. The figures were constructed so that the outer edge of the circle coincided with the inner edge of the ring. If the interval between the two figures was very short (e.g., less than 20 msec), most subjects failed to report the circle at all. Reversing the procedure and presenting the ring before the circle did not produce a masking of the ring. Werner's interpretation of these results did not emphasize a psychological moment. Rather, he was of the opinion that form perception, with the contours or outlines of the shapes viewed sharply defined, required time. Since the outer edge of the circle coincided with the inner edge of the ring, the presentation of the ring inhibited the development of the contours of the circle, and the subject was therefore unable to perceive the circle. Reversing the order did not mask the ring, since its outer edge had been allowed enough time to be clearly perceived.

A complete superpositioning of contours, as in Werner's studies, is not a prerequisite for masking. Eriksen and Collins (1965) presented the letter A, T, or U for durations allowing 70-percent recognition accuracy in a forced-choice situation. On half the trials a ring surrounding the letters was flashed first at delays ranging fom 0 to 250 msec. For delays below 50 msec, recognition accuracy for the letter was reduced from 70 to about 46 percent. Allowing the ring to precede the letter by a given interval resulted in the same performance detriment for intervals up to 50 msec. For delays greater than 50 msec, rapid improvement in accuracy developed, with performance returning to the 70-percent base level for periods greater than 90 msec.

These results are, of course, compatible with the concept of a psychological moment. Two successive stimuli separated by less than 50 msec will be processed in the same moment. The recognition of a letter surrounded by a ring Ⓐ is much more difficult than the recognition of the isolated letter A. As the time interval between the appearance of ring and letter increases, the probability decreases that the ring will fall in the traveling moment at the same time the letter is present. The explanation is enhanced by Eriksen's and Collins's (1965) observation that the performance impairment was the same for delays of 0 to 50 msec as for trials when letter and ring were flashed simultaneously.

While the visual masking of a form can be instigated by light flashes that reduce the contrast of figure to background, and by patterns that reduce the legibility of the preceding form, most evidence indicates that these two effects are mediated by different sensory mechanisms. Recently Spencer (1969) compared the effects of a pattern mask (metacontrast) with a luminance mask (luminance masking). Figure 3.23 shows performance in the identification of single letters in relation to the interval between mask and letter for both kinds of masking. Clearly, for the pattern mask, performance is equally poor when the pattern is simultaneous and when it follows after a 50-msec delay. Recognition improves, however, reaching the no-mask control level for delays in excess of 150 msec. In contrast, for delays of both 25 and 50 msec a luminance mask diminishes performance to a lesser degree than under the simultaneous condition, but performance returns to the control level after a delay of only 75 msec. This is not surprising if we assume that the psychological moment hypothesis applies only to the pattern mask, and that the luminance summation hypothesis is most applicable to the luminance masking condition. When a pattern closely follows the test stimulus, recognition accuracy is impaired, as the two elements are combined and perceived as a single unit. When a flash of light closely follows the test stimulus, contrast between the test stimulus and background is reduced, and recognition accuracy decreases.

Further evidence for the existence of separate mechanisms of luminance and metacontrast masking is supplied by an experiment conducted by Schiller and Smith (1968). They showed that presenting a test figure to one eye and a luminance mask to the other brought about no reduction in recognition performance. But the presentation of a patterned mask to one eye produced recognition impairment for a figure presented to the other eye. Such results imply that metacontrast occurs at a stage in the visual system sensitive to input from either eye. Luminance masking, in contrast, does not occur when the test figure is shown to one eye and the mask to the other, indicating that the effect must occur at the level of the retina, prior to the mixing of input from each eye. The exact manner by which acuity is reduced in the metacon-

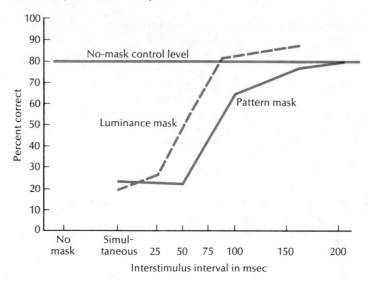

Figure 3.23
Percentage of letters identified under conditions of pattern masking and luminance masking. (After Spencer, 1969.)

trast situation is not clear. Weisstein (1968) has recently offered a theory based on the neurophysiological mechanism of lateral inhibition which accounts for a number of metacontrast observations.

Visual summation.   If letters followed in rapid succession by masking patterns reduce identification capability, it follows that repeated presentation of the same form should produce an improvement in recognition accuracy. If we assume that two stimuli fall within the same psychological moment, then the combined information should produce a clearer percept of the stimulus. Standing, Haber, Cataldo, and Sales (1969) demonstrated the summation effect by presenting an English word ten times. The interval between successive brief word flashes was initially very long and the word was shown at a speed that did not permit word recognition. When the interval between successive flashes was reduced, the accuracy of word recognition increased.

Using the letters A, T, and U, which have gained such popularity in Eriksen's laboratory, Eriksen and Greenspoon (1968) studied the summation effect under conditions of binocular presentation. The test letter was presented to one eye and simultaneously, or after brief delays, to the other eye. Increases in recognition accuracy for the letters were observed if the interstimulus interval was 10 msec or less. At intervals greater than 50 msec no evidence of summation was demonstrated.

The observation of a binocular transfer of summation by Eriksen and Greenspoon indicates that the concept of summation should not be taken too literally. Summation is evidently not the result of the stimulation and re-stimulation of the exact same receptors in the retina of the eye. This can be

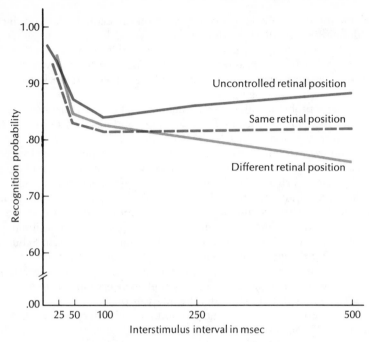

Figure 3.24
Percentage of words identified as a function of the duration of the interval between repeated presentations of the same word. (Murch, 1969c.)

demonstrated by a recent experiment (Murch, 1969c) in which seven-letter words subtending fairly large visual angles (13°) were flashed either 3, 5, or 10 times, at intervals of 25, 50, 100, and 500 msec. In one study (experiment 3) subjects were required to maintain a strict fixation point during the presentation of the word; this increased the likelihood that each word would be flashed to the same portion of the retina on successive trials. In another study (experiment 4) the word was moved between flashes to a new position relative to the fixation point. This insured that the word would *not* fall on the same retinal area. The results of the studies are graphically depicted in Figure 3.24. Also included in the figure are the combined results of two other studies (experiments 1 and 2) in which subjects were not required to maintain a fixation point and the word did not move.

The results of these trials indicate that visual summation facilitates recognition accuracy at interstimulus intervals below 100 msec. Furthermore, summation occurs even if the word is moved between flashes to a different part of the fovea. It is also interesting that when the subjects were allowed to change their fixation point between flashes (experiments 1 and 2), they identified more words with the longer interstimulus intervals than when the strict fixation point was required (experiment 3). The worst performance for long intervals occurred when the word was moved between flashes (experiment 4). Probably these observations are due to the fact that the subjects in experiments 1 and 2 could look at the first few letters of the word on the early flashes and the last letters during the final flashes. Thus the word could be pieced together. For experiment 3, however, subjects could not use this technique, since they were required to hold a fixation point. For experiment 4 the word always moved to a new position between flashes and the subject did not know where to look.

One major problem with experimental observations of visual masking and visual summation still persists. In the paracontrast and metacontrast studies the masking effects are approximately the same for conditions in which the test stimulus and the masking stimulus are presented simultaneously or follow interstimulus intervals up to 50 msec. Yet in the visual summation studies, performance decreases steadily as the interstimulus interval lengthens (see Figure 3.24). The subject of considerable discussion, this discrepancy may derive from the fact that the masking situation involves the presentation of a single test stimulus followed by a single masking stimulus. In studies of visual summation, the potential stimulus is flashed several times in rapid succession. Schurman, Eriksen, and Rohrbaugh (1968) point out that the effect of a train of ten 2-msec pulses on the accuracy of recognition of the letter A, T, or U is a monotonic decrease in accuracy as the interval between each pulse is increased. Thus, for ten pulses of light separated by intervals of 2 or 4 msec, recognition accuracy is slightly above the single long-duration flash control level. As the interflash interval increases, performance gradually deteriorates, reaching about 50-percent accuracy for intervals of 28 msec and 38 percent for intervals of 48 msec.

Short-Term Storage

Incoming stimuli are channeled for very brief periods through the sensory register. Of the great quantity of such stimuli entering the sensory register, only a finite number are processed and pass to short-term storage. A kind of scanning or encoding facility reads the information in the sensory register into short-term storage. There it is held briefly and either discarded or filed in long-term memory as an image or verbal translation of the sensory image. Such information from long-term storage can be brought up into the short-term area during the processing of sensory input. Short-term storage represents the "now" of perception, since it involves the continuous processing of sensory images and the comparison of incoming images with information stored in long-term memory.

A number of models of short-term storage have been developed (Posner, 1967). For the study of perception, the most parsimonious model would be one assuming the brief storage of information read from the sensory register as well as the encoded visual input which has been translated into verbal categories. If no such verbal category exists or if none can be developed during the period the image is stored in the sensory register, short-term storage for a visual configuration is limited to the duration of the sensory image. Hence nonsense forms such as those depicted in Figure 3.17 can be "remembered"

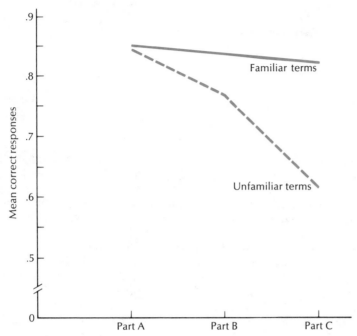

Figure 3.25
Mean proportion of correct responses in matching familiar and unfamiliar terms with comparison terms. (After Earhard, 1968.)

for only a brief period, whereas a form with a verbal label (e.g., a square) can
be maintained for a long period of time. If the availability of a name for a
visual stimulus influences the encoding and storing of the image in short-
term storage, then presenting familiar and unfamiliar images should introduce
a bias favoring the familiar material.

Earhard (1968) briefly presented familiar nine-letter English words or
strings of nine non-related letters. These were followed by a comparison
stimulus that was either identical with the preceding nine-letter array or completely different (part A). By "completely different," Earhard meant that no
letter in the stimulus term was repeated in the comparison term. Thus the subject needed to identify no more than a single letter in each term to determine
whether the comparison term was the *same as* or *different from* the stimulus
term. In part B of the study, half of the comparison terms contained from three
to five letters in common with the familiar or unfamiliar stimulus terms; in
part C, the former had from six to eight letters in common with the latter.

The ability of subjects to judge correctly whether a familiar or unfamiliar
nine-letter sequence was the same as or different from a comparison term under the three conditions outlined above (A, B, and C) is shown in Figure 3.25.
Under condition A, subjects were able to discriminate between unfamiliar

Table 3.6

Number of items retained from a 10-item display
(Mackworth, 1963. Copyright 1963 by Academic Press.)

	Digits	Letters	Colors	Shapes
Block presentation	7.2	6.2	5.5	4.9
Single presentation	5.9	4.7	4.7	4.4

and familiar terms with equal accuracy. However, when the number of letters in common between stimulus and comparison terms was increased, a marked reduction in discrimination ability developed for the unfamiliar terms but not for the familiar words. Apparently because the amount of information to be retained was much greater for unfamiliar materials, it exceeded the encoding and storage capacities of short-term memory. Obviously this limitation is not related to the total number of items to be retained, because both the familiar and unfamiliar units contained nine letters. Rather, the limitation would seem to depend on the codability of the material. A familiar word can be encoded and maintained as a unit or *chunk* of information (Miller, 1956). For an unfamiliar item all nine letters would have to be encoded separately, since each letter would represent one chunk of information. Miller proposed that the maximum number of chunks to be held in short-term memory was about seven. This proposition has become known as Miller's *magical number seven*. Therefore, items with verbal names pass from the sensory register to short-term storage. If the number of chunks of information does not exceed the capacity of short-term storage, the information can be maintained for periods of several minutes in short-term storage.

Mackworth (1963) has studied the amount of material retained in short-term storage in relation to the type of stimulus material and the mode of presentation. She flashed 10-item strings of *numbers, letters, colors,* and simple *shapes* (e.g., square, cross, etc.). The items were displayed either one at a time or simultaneously. The total time allowed for single and simultaneous presentation was the same. Table 3.6 indicates the number of items correctly recalled for a 10-second block presentation and for a single exposure rate of one item per second. The differences between the four kinds of items are much greater for the block presentation than for the single presentation. With a block presentation the observer is able to determine his own rate and technique of encoding the input into short-term storage. With a single presentation of each item, the order of the sensory input is dictated by the experimenter and each item must be encoded in the order provided. The superiority of recall for digits probably depends on our increased familiarity with numbers compared with the other kinds of items. Frequently we consult a telephone book, commit the seven digits to short-term storage, and maintain them there long enough to dial the number.

Mackworth (1963) has also shown the effect of the number of items to be recalled. She presented blocks of digits, letters, colors, and shapes for durations

Table 3.7

Number of items recalled from 10- and 15-item blocks
(Mackworth, 1963. Copyright 1963 by Academic Press.)

	Digits	Letters	Colors	Shapes
10-item block	8.3	7.2	6.3	5.3
15-item block	7.0	5.4	3.9	3.1

long enough to allow the subject to call out each item. Recall was tested immediately after the presentation of the array. Two block sizes were compared; Table 3.7 gives the average number of items recalled after exposure to 10- and 15-item blocks. Clearly the greater number of items taxed the capacity of short-term storage and impaired performance for all types of material. It would seem that overloading the short-term storage markedly reduces the number of items encoded and stored.

Before passing on to a discussion of auditory processes, one topic of current interest in studies of short-term storage should be mentioned. That some kinds of potential stimuli are encoded and maintained in short-term storage has been demonstrated. However, some question remains as to whether stimuli are encoded only in a *serial order*. It is possible that the sensory register may also process them in *parallel order*. An experiment by Eriksen and Spencer (1969) provided support for parallel processing. Their subjects were as successful at identifying a critical letter in a nine-letter sequence at intervals as brief as 5 msec as they were at much longer intervals. A serial encoding mechanism would certainly improve the processing at slower input rates and impair it at higher rates. A possible control mechanism, which will be analyzed in more detail later, has been proposed by Broadbent (1958). He assumes that instructing the subject to respond to a specific target stimulus sets up *filters* at the lower stages of the perceptual process. These allow only relevant items to pass into short-term storage. If such filters are indeed operative, high-speed processing rates such as those observed by Eriksen and Spencer would be possible.[3]

The Auditory Sensory Register

The perceptual model described in this chapter should apply to all sensory systems. While the basic interrelationships between the model's subsystems remain the same, their individual functioning depends on the sensory modality in question. There is a major difference between the ways in which sensory data is processed by vision and by audition. In vision, separate inputs are defined primarily by their spatial relationships and only secondarily by temporal factors. The temporal variable is usually imposed by the information-seeking

---

[3] For a more detailed discussion of short-term storage, the interested reader should consult the excellent book by Neisser (1967).

tendencies of the organism; a section of the visual field is fixated briefly and *followed by* the fixation of another sector. The perception of sound, however, is clearly governed by temporal factors; the relationships among sounds are provided by the temporal order of their occurrence.

Postulating the existence of a sensory register for hearing has advantages and disadvantages. If hearing is a temporal event, then the information contained in a single microsecond or even a millisecond would not provide the necessary multiplicity for complex sound perception. Each simple stimulus would be processed individually without the development of complex interrelationships. Individual stimuli would have to be pieced together in a way capable of mastering these complexities. In contrast, a psychological moment would allow temporally separated events to be combined and would facilitate the perception of complex sound patterns. However, the temporal integration of incoming information implies a loss of order, since a maintenance of temporal order is imperative for hearing. In speech perception, for example, one must maintain the proper temporal relationships in order to distinguish one word from another and to derive the proper meaning of sentences requiring that the words be perceived in a certain order. For these reasons, the hypothesis of a *traveling psychological moment*, proposed by Allport (1968), best applies to hearing. The auditory sensory register gathers and stores incoming information in the form of a composite stimulus trace which is then read out into short-term memory. The auditory and visual systems are probably organized along similar lines. In each case effective stimuli are initially processed in the sensory register and proceed to short-term storage. There the input is analyzed by calling on the long-term storage of the perceiver. However, as indicated earlier, the auditory system is organized to respond to temporally separated input, whereas vision is primarily responsive to spatially separated stimuli.

Due to the temporal nature of hearing, the *time base* of storage in the sensory register and in short-term storage are different. As R. P. Erickson (1968) has pointed out, receptor function is different in vision and in audition. In Erickson's terms, the afferent receptors of sensory information in audition are *topographic*. That is, each receptor is *tuned* to respond to a narrow band of stimulus characteristics. Slight changes in the nature of a stimulus are signaled to the brain when one set of receptors ceases to respond and another set is activated. At the level of the cochlea, for example, the receptors for various frequencies are laid out along the surface of the basilar membrane. As the frequency pattern of a sound changes, entirely different receptors are called into play. In contrast, the receptors of the retinal surface are broadly tuned and respond to almost all dimensions of a stimulus. Color perception involves receptors maximally sensitive to certain portions of the spectrum but also responsive to almost the entire visual spectrum. Such receptors can be termed *nontopographic*, for all are able to respond to a broad band of stimulus characteristics. Other visual receptors signal shapes, borders, and straight and curved lines to higher centers of the nervous system. The visual system apparently contains both topographic and nontopographic receptors. Perhaps the multifold response capabilities of the visual system stem from the existence of both kinds of sensory receptors, whereas other sensory systems are comprised almost entirely of topographic receptors.

In audition, the nature of an effective stimulus is initially represented mechanically and then translated by topographic receptors into an electrical impulse. This information is then transmitted to the higher centers of auditory perception in the cortex. In vision, however, information from a number of different types of receptors is relayed and integrated at higher visual centers.

Following comparable experiments on visual ability, several scientists have attempted to assess the capability of observers to discriminate tones separated by brief temporal intervals. Hirsh (1959) required subjects to indicate whether two tones occurred simultaneously or successively. A high degree of accuracy was reached for intervals as low as 2 msec. Gescheider (1966) obtained similar results, reporting that an interval of 1.8 msec was the smallest subjects could discriminate. However, for the listeners to determine which tone preceded which, much longer intervals were required. Hirsh found correct judgments of temporal order to approach 75-percent accuracy when the interval between successive tones was at least 17 msec. For 100-percent accuracy, an interval in excess of 40 msec was needed.

Evidently the auditory mechanism is quite unlike the visual mechanism in its ability to resolve temporal separation. The differences between simultaneous and successive inputs are perceived much more rapidly by the auditory system than by the visual. Within a psychological moment of approximately 40 msec, the auditory system outperforms the visual system in defining temporal relationships. Due to the dependency of the auditory system on time, such fine temporal discriminations are not surprising.

Auditory masking. If a test tone is accompanied simultaneously or followed closely by a second tone, the latter tends to mask the first tone. The effect of the masking tone is measured as an increase in the absolute threshold for the pure tone. Wright (1964) measured the threshold for a 1,000-Hz pure tone and assigned a value of 0 decibels as the intensity at which the tone was reported on 50 percent of the trials. The effect of a 600 msec white-noise mask of 40, 60, or 80 db on the tone's threshold was measured as a function of the interval between the onset of the pure tone and the onset of the mask. The tone preceded the noise by intervals of from 10 to 500 msec and terminated 100 msec before the end of the mask. The influence of 40- and 80-db masking noises on the 1,000-Hz test-tone threshold are presented in Figure 3.26. For very short intervals in which the pure tone preceded the mask by 25 msec or less, masking was almost complete. Before the pure tone could be perceived, its intensity had to be raised to a level close to the intensity of the mask. As the time difference between the start of the pure tone and the onset of the white noise increased, the effect lessened; the mask exerted no influence for onset differences greater than 300 msec. When the test tone preceded the mask by 25 msec and was not perceived, the integration of tone and mask was assumed to be complete. Masking in the auditory system is similar to masking in the visual system. The auditory mechanism evidently combines two signals separated by short intervals. As Wright points out, the masking effect

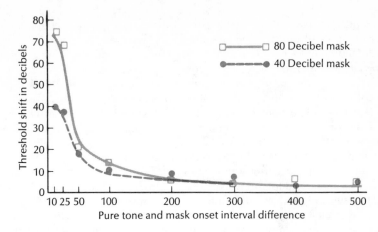

Figure 3.26
Threshold changes induced by white noise masks as a function of interval
between pure tone and mask onset. (After Wright, 1964.)

for intervals greater than 50 and less than 200 msec is independent of mask
intensity. He suggests this indicates a dual process in auditory masking. Complete temporal integration occurs below 25 msec (analogous to the period of
time-intensity reciprocity in visual backward masking) and is followed by a
second phase which lacks the intensity effect. The second phase could be considered the sensory trace phase, since some "image" of the tone is preserved
in the auditory sensory register.

In a study conducted a number of years ago, Garner and Miller (1947) presented pure tones of one of four frequencies (400, 670, 1,000, or 1,900 Hz)
in the presence of wideband masking noise. The threshold at which the
pure tones could be perceived was measured in decibels as a function of
the duration of the test tone. The decibel values for the various durations of
the lowest tone (400 Hz) and the highest tone (1,900 Hz) are given in Table 3.8.
In this case the threshold intensity decreased linearly as tonal duration increased. For durations greater than 200 msec the mask's effect seemed independent of tonal duration.

Ehmer, Ehmer, Seamon, and Cohen (1968) have reported that the frequency range of pure tones masked by a pure tone, rather than by white noise,
is very wide if the mask follows the test tone closely (below 25 msec). The
range of tones masked by the pure tone narrows rapidly for longer intervals.
This would indicate the importance of brief periods of time for the separation
of temporally close inputs—an implication previously noted in the studies of
temporal resolution.

The lower limit of the auditory sensory register seems to require intervals
greater than 20 to 40 msec for adequate perception; in comparison, the visual
system requires intervals from 50 to 100 msec. The upper limit for the storage
of the stimulus trace in the auditory sensory register must be in excess of 200
msec. Guttman and Julesz (1963) required subjects to distinguish repetitive

Table 3.8

Threshold increases of masked pure tones
(Garner and Miller, 1947)

Decibels	Pure tone duration in msec								
	12.5	*25*	*50*	*100*	*200*	*500*	*1,000*	*2,000*	*Infinite*
Low tone	34	31	27	20	18	16	16	16	16
High tone	33	31	29	23	21	21	21	20	20

segments contained in blocks of white noise. They reasoned that if such segments could be perceived, the observers must be able to retain the entire block
in the sensory register. To perceive a repetition in the pattern, subjects would
have to be able to compare all the elements of the entire block and maintain
an image of each element so that comparisons could be made. The study
showed that subjects experienced great difficulty in hearing repetitive patterns when the repeated elements were greater than one second in length.

Auditory Short-Term Storage

Information contained in the sensory register must be transferred to short-
term storage in order for the input to be maintained for periods greater than
a second. Doris Aaronson (1968) designed several clever experiments in order
to study the way auditory input is encoded and held in short-term storage.
Large groups of subjects listened to seven numbers randomly presented at
varying rates (1.5, 3, or 6 digits per second). In one phase of the study they
were required to recall as many of the digits as possible in the order presented.
In a second, under the same presentation conditions, subjects monitored digit
strings for the presence of a critical number. They pressed one key if it occurred
in the series and another if it did not. Aaronson reasoned that if the perceptual
process involves proximal representation of the distal stimulus as a trace in the
sensory register and an encoding of the input for transfer to short-term storage, then different effects of presentation speed should be observed for the
recall task and for the monitoring task. This follows from the assumption that
a subject monitors by responding directly to each successive stimulus in the
sensory register, without recourse to short-term storage. In other words, the
subject responds directly to the stimulus trace. On the other hand, recall neces-
sitates encoding and holding each unit in the proper order in short-term
storage. Aaronson found the predicted influence of presentation rate in the
recall task in which errors increased as did speed of presentation. For monitoring, errors were unaffected by presentation rate.

A further analysis of Aaronson's data suggests that auditory input is
processed *serially*. Since input in the recall task is encoded and stored, one
would expect more errors in the recall of items presented late in the sequence.

As the early items are processed, not enough time is left for succeeding items. For example, assume that the subject has successively encoded items 1 and 2 at the time items 1, 2, and 3 enter the sensory register. The sensory trace of item 3 might last long enough to allow proper encoding of this digit, but by the time encoding is complete, items 4 and 5 will have entered the sensory register. The sensory trace for item 4 and surely for item 5 will have decayed before processing can be initiated. Aaronson's experimental data support this expectation. With the exception of the last digit, which was almost always correctly reported, the number of errors tend to increase steadily as a function of position in the list.

Yntema (1964) reported results of an experiment in which a computer presented seven digits at very high speeds. At a presentation rate of ten digits a second, subjects could identify any single digit but recall only three or four. At a presentation rate of two digits a second, approximately six items could be recalled.

Regarding the number of units maintained simultaneously in short-term storage, Miller's *magical number seven* (Miller, 1956), which indicates the limits of the number of units capable of being maintained simultaneously, has been assumed to apply to both auditory and visual storage. Probably the actual amount depends more on the presentation rate and the type of material than on the total number of units presented. Miller, of course, pointed out that the magical number refers to chunks of information rather than to number of items. While listening to a meaningful sentence, we are able to retain more than seven words, since we tend to group the words into units. On the average, subjects can encode about seven unrelated items in short-term storage, provided the presentation rate is neither too slow nor too fast. This can be tested by asking a friend to read a vertical row of digits from Table 3.9 at a rate of about one digit per second. The listener should then attempt to recall the digits in order. As Ross (1969) has demonstrated, digits may be poor indicators of memory span, due to our familiarity with the material. Attempt to repeat back the vertical lists of Xs and Os also found in Table 3.9. Generally, this task proves more difficult than the task involving digits, since the subject must hold highly similar items in a specific order.

Auditory and Visual Interaction

At the level of the sensory register the auditory system seems to be able to retain information better and longer than the visual system. This is evident in a study by Posner (1967) in which pairs of digits were simultaneously presented both visually and aurally at three interstimulus intervals (750, 1,000, and 2,000 msec). Recall for the two digits was tested in two ways. First, by requesting the subject to report both digits in any order. Second, by requiring the visually presented digit to be recalled before the aurally presented digit, or vice versa. For the reports with unspecified order, the number of errors was twice as large for the visual member of the pair of digits. Delaying the report of either the auditory or the visual digit caused more errors than when the digit was

Table 3.9

Tests of immediate memory span

Digits					Symbols				
				Stimulus length					
5	6	7	8	9	5	6	7	8	9
2	7	9	3	5	O	X	X	X	O
5	2	1	5	8	X	X	O	X	X
1	9	3	8	2	X	O	O	O	O
3	5	7	2	7	O	X	X	X	X
8	8	4	1	4	X	O	O	O	O
	3	2	6	1		O	X	O	O
		6	9	3			X	O	X
			7	9				X	X
				6					O

reported first. The delayed report had a much greater negative effect on the visual digits. Generally the advantage of the auditory storage over visual storage increased as the speed of presentation increased.

A great deal of recent literature suggests a close interrelationship between the short-term storage mechanisms of vision and audition. Consider the task of recalling a list of visually presented numbers. The encoding of the numbers into visual short-term storage involves auditory as well as visual mechanisms. We store not only a visual representation of each digit but also a verbal representation. In fact, the testing of recall is frequently based on auditory storage, since subjects are required to *say* the letter recalled. Conrad (1959) has shown that subjects frequently make substitution errors when recalling lists of visually presented letters in which the letter substituted (e.g., ANQT) sounds similar to the correct letter (e.g., ANQE). Although these letters are highly dissimilar in appearance, they sound similar when spoken aloud. This visual material, Conrad suggests, must have been translated and encoded in auditory storage.

Murray (1968) reports extensive studies of short-term storage for visual and auditory items. He presented lists of letters varying in length (six to nine letters) to either the eye or the ear. These lists exhibited varieties of *acoustic confusability:* in some lists all the letters sounded similar (PBCTVG); in others, there were two kinds of similar sounds (PXNTVS); and in still others, six different sounds (PYQFOJ) were employed. Murray attempted to reduce or enhance the auditory element in storage under five different conditions:

1. *Visual suppression:*   lists presented visually with the subject required to say the word "the" as each letter appeared. (This vocal response was designed to reduce subvocal rehearsal of the letter in auditory storage.)

2. *Auditory suppression:*   lists presented aurally with subjects repeating "the" at each presentation.
3. *Visual rehearse:*   lists presented visually with subject rehearsing items silently.
4. *Auditory rehearse:*   lists presented aurally with subjects rehearsing silently.
5. *Vocalize:*   visual presentation with subject speaking each letter.

The results were computed by a technique called the *probe method.* After the presentation of each list the subject was given one letter from the list and asked to write down the following letter. For each position in the list it was possible to compute the probability that the next letter could be identified by counting the number of times that the letter following each probe letter was correctly named.

Murray's results show how the similarity of sounds affected recall of the list (acoustic similarity). Subjects made fewer errors when the sounds of the letters were dissimilar. This was the case for the *auditory suppression condition* and the *auditory rehearse condition* but it was far less observable in the *visual suppression condition.* This means that the short-term storage mechanism for vision can be separated from audition if the auditory component is suppressed. This separation was not complete, however, since acoustic similarity did show some influence under the visual suppression condition. Allowing the subject to vocalize produced acoustic similarity effects somewhere between the effects observed in the visual suppression and auditory rehearse conditions. Speaking the letters aloud added a component of motor behavior, which may have aided the subject's ability to discriminate between acoustically similar terms. As far as overall performance was concerned, the greatest number of errors occurred in the visual suppression condition and the least in the auditory rehearse condition.

In Murray's experiment, conditions enabling the auditory system to assist in the coding and storing of incoming information tend to produce superior performances; this may indicate that the auditory mechanism is generally superior to the visual mechanism in this respect. Such a superiority has been demonstrated by Murdock (1968) as well as by a number of other experimenters. Murdock presented ten-word lists visually or aurally. Testing with the probe method described above, and also with a recognition method in which subjects responded to a two-word combination with "yes" if the combination had appeared in the list, Murdock reported performance differences that clearly demonstrated the aural condition's retentive superiority.

Wickelgren (1965) has demonstrated that the presence of acoustic elements in visually presented material can influence the accuracy of recall. His subjects listened to four random letters. Next, eight letters were visually presented and copied by the subject. Finally a test of the first four aural letters was administered. Even though the interpolated material had to be copied rather than spoken, if the eight letters were similar in sound to the aural letters, performance on auditory recall was poorer than when the visual letters were quite dissimilar in sound.

Finally, Ross (1969) developed a logical test of the audio-visual interaction in short-term storage by measuring the retention of simple symbols (+ and −) either organized in patterns (e.g., − + + + − + − + −) or unpatterned (e.g., + − + + − + − − +). His subjects were congenitally deaf children and normal children, 7 to 15 years old. Each item was projected on a screen for several seconds with a one-second interval between items. Recall was measured by requiring the subjects to draw the patterns. Requiring deaf children to complete the task would ensure at least as great an auditory suppression as afforded by the conditions of Murray's experiment.

Using the symbol test, Ross found scores for the unpatterned orders ranging from 4.50 to 5.18 for normal children and 4.88 to 5.65 for the deaf subjects. In no age group were differences between groups statistically significant. Also, no differences were found in the patterned series, even though one might have expected the normal children to be superior at the patterned task due to their increased opportunity for building chunks of information based on auditory encoding. To aid in the recall of a symbol string such as − + + + − + − + − + the normal child might code the input verbally into "minus, three pluses, alternate minus and plus three times." Thus only three chunks of information would have to be stored as opposed to ten. Both groups did better with the patterned series, but their performances were well below the number of units that can be maintained by using an efficient coding strategy. Perhaps the failure to find differences between the groups does not reflect the ineffectiveness of auditory encoding of visual materials, but rather the failure of the children to adopt an efficient strategy of encoding.

Blanton and Odom (1968) did find a superiority of seeing and hearing children over deaf children in terms of the span of digits that could be recalled. However, this result may reflect greater experience with numbers on the part of the normal children.

In conclusion, the evidence for separate mechanisms of visual and auditory information processing is strong. Furthermore, under many conditions the encoding of strictly visual material or strictly auditory material involves the use of the short-term storage of both systems.

CHAPTER 4

Perceptual Organization

The preceding chapter described the initial processing of visual and aural stimuli in conjunction with a model of perception. The discussion considered certain attributes of effective stimuli, prerequisites for stable perception and aspects of the subsystems of processing. In the present chapter we will examine the perception of specific forms and shapes both in terms of the nature of the stimulus and in terms of the development of the perceiving organism. Additional topics to be considered are the perception of multidimensional figures and complex stimulus arrays, specific differences among perceivers, and the influence of experience on subsequent perceptual response tendencies.

Microgenesis of Perception

During the discussions of visual acuity and visual masking we noted several important differences between form and brightness perception. Temporal relationships characteristic of luminance masking varied considerably in comparison with those found in pattern masking. That each of these conditions involved separate processes was supported by the observation that a pattern mask to one eye successfully masked a test stimulus in the other eye, while a luminance mask to one eye failed to mask a test stimulus in the other eye. Differences are also noted when the *time-intensity reciprocity* (Bloch's law) mentioned earlier is taken into account. It will be recalled that, for the identification of the brightness of a stimulus for periods under 100 msec, decreases in the duration of the stimulus could be compensated by corresponding increases in the stimulus intensity (Kahneman and Norman, 1964). For the perception of form, however, the relationship between time (duration) and stimulus intensity appears to be more complex. First, with regard to a visual acuity task (Landolt C), Kahneman (1964) demonstrated that the relationship between time and energy depends on the level of acuity performance and on the energy levels of the stimuli employed. Even with a perceptual task as simple as the localization of the gap in the Landolt C, the duration of the stimulus seems to play a somewhat different role than intensity.

If a more complex task is required, the influence of duration on perception can no longer be offset by increases in energy. Leibowitz, Toffey, and Searle (1966) flashed a circular white disc under a number of conditions in which increases in duration were counterbalanced by decreases in stimulus intensity. The test disc was flashed for a given time-intensity value and a series of comparison discs varying in size and shape was provided. Each test disc was actually slanted away from the subject by 30°, which presented an elliptical stimulus. To match this form, subjects were asked to select a comparison disc of the same size and shape. The application of this task to the time-intensity problem in form perception is particularly interesting in light of the phenomenon of *shape constancy*. Although a detailed discussion of this tendency will be reserved for the next chapter, suffice it to say here that an observer presented with a slanted circular test figure tends to take the slant into account and select a true circle as the correct comparison figure. It is as if the subject realizes that the test figure is slanted and therefore selects a corresponding circle of the proper shape for his match. Shape constancy depends on the assumption, therefore, that the subject still sees the slanted test circle as a circle despite the elliptical pattern produced by the slant. If the subject were to select an elliptical shape as a matching stimulus, he would fail to demonstrate a tendency toward shape constancy.

The phenomenon of shape constancy is observed when a subject is given a great deal of time to make the match. In the experiment by Leibowitz,

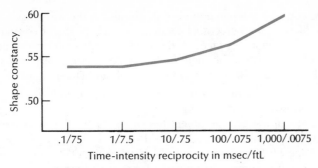

Figure 4.1
Tendency toward shape constancy as a function of time-intensity reciprocity. (Leibowitz, Toffey, and Searle, 1966.)

Toffey, and Searle, the slanted circle and the comparison discs were also presented at different time-intensity ratios. They questioned whether a reciprocity
for time and intensity exists for the estimate of the shape of a simple form. Their
results are presented in Figure 4.1. The horizontal axis of the figure shows
varying time-intensity ratios; the vertical axis measures the tendency toward
shape constancy. Along the latter, a value of 1 indicates complete shape constancy and a value of 0.50 a complete lack. Values toward 1, in other words,
indicate that subjects tended to select comparison figures closer to circles,
whereas responses toward 0.50 indicate the selection of elliptical shapes.
Figure 4.1 also shows a reciprocity between time and intensity for exposure
durations of 0.1 and 1 msec. At these values the shape judgments are the same.
As duration increased and intensity decreased, subjects displayed greater degrees of shape constancy. This means that perception of the slanted circle
was influenced more by duration than by stimulus intensity; subjects tended
to see one shape as an ellipse at shorter durations and as a slanted circle at
longer durations. One can conclude that the perception of form varies as a
function of duration.

The importance of duration in form perception has been studied by earlier
experimenters. Davies (1905) showed that form perception changes or develops as the duration of exposure increases. He illuminated simple geometric
figures with very short flashes of light and noted that subjects reported the
light flash before any notice of the forms. Freeman (1929) flashed inkblots
which were either meaningless or the outlines of simple forms. As the duration of presentation increased, three distinct stages of perception could be
inferred from the phenomenal reports of the observers. The first stage
involved the report of the existence of some kind of object in the field. In
other words, the exposed visual field displayed some inhomogeneity. Freeman
called this the *stage of the generic object*. The second stage involved the perception of contours and the location of the object in a specific portion of the
visual field. The final *stage of the specific object* involved identification of the
form in all its fine details. Further increases in duration had no influence on
perception.

If we consider the perception of brightness as the first stage and the appearance of complex perceptual tendencies such as shape constancy as the final stage, five separate stages in the development of form perception as a function of duration can be identified. This developmental process has been termed the *microgenesis of perception* (Flavell and Dragnus, 1957):

1. *Stage of light detection:* the report of a change in the brightness relations of the visual field.
2. *Stage of the generic object* (Freeman, 1929): the presence of an unspecific figure in the visual field.
3. *Stage of the differentiated object* (Vernon, 1952): a contoured figure located in some specific part of the visual field.
4. *Stage of the specific object* (Freeman, 1929): a specific form or shape with detailed outline.
5. *Stage of manipulation* (Forgus, 1966): the influence of perceptual tendencies and previous experience on the meaning or interpretation of the figure.

The final stage of microgenesis probably depends on experiences encoded in the observer's long-term storage and on the influences of numerous control processes. Stages one and two probably represent the entrance of a weak stimulus to the sensory register, whereas stages three and four involve the transfer of the input from the sensory register to short-term storage.

Kaswan and Young (1963) have reported an interesting study of duration and complex perceptual response. For brief durations they exposed rows of dots and varied the distance between alternate dots to determine if observers would organize the visual field spatially into pairs of dots. If the differentiation of perception develops as the duration of stimulation increases, it was assumed that the tendency to group the dots would increase with length of presentation. Altogether observers viewed six separate lines of sixteen dots. For three lines all dots were evenly spaced, with the distance between dots equal to either 1.1, 1.2, or 1.4 cm. In the remaining three lines, pairs were formed by making the distance between every second dot 1.2, 1.4, or 1.8 cm. The length of the entire row of dots remained constant and subtended a horizontal visual angle of 10°. Kaswan and Young used exposure durations ranging from 4 to 512 msec and eight intensity values ranging from 0.09 to 11.84 mL. They found that for the unequally spaced rows, the tendency for observers to report pairs of dots varied as a function of duration; intensity played no part in the perception of the spatial array.

Kahneman (1966) has criticized the Kaswan and Young study on the ground that it contains the basic elements of a luminance masking experiment. Since they exposed an adapting field prior to and immediately after the presentation of the dots, Kahneman reasoned that at the shorter durations, the preceding and following adapting field might mask the dot array so that performance would be poorer at shorter durations. This impaired performance would be due to luminance masking rather than to a duration insufficient for the perception of complex form. While Kahneman's own study did demonstrate a masking effect of the preceding field, he was surprised to find that the effect did not account for the magnitude of departure from the time-intensity reciprocity. As Kahneman indicated, the experiment by Kaswan and Young suffered from a methodological artifact. However, it still demonstrates that a minimal duration is in fact required for form perception.

The perception of form, shape, and spatial relations appears to be dependent on the duration of the stimulus. The microgenetic approach traces the successive development of form perception as the duration of the input increases. If, as in the case of shape constancy and spatial perception, we assume that experience plays a major role in the perception of form, we would expect differences between observers as a function of their ages. This consideration of the perception of form would be an *ontogenetic* approach.

Ontogenesis of Perception

The visual patterns striking our senses evoke complex responses based on years of experience with the perceptual environment. Familiar sights and sounds are immediately recognized and responded to or disregarded. An adult viewing a room full of furniture perceives the collection of forms and shapes in light of his experience with the objects. But what of the sensory world of a new-born infant? Does a day-old child perceive form and shape in the same manner as an adult? That the perceptual experience of the room full of furniture would be the same to an infant and to an adult is rather unlikely, due to the specific experiences of the adult with the forms observed. Early research has shown that children respond to movement and brightness at an early age. Such differentiated responses do not indicate that the newborn child perceives specific objects, for the responses may be to changing patterns of light and color. To study the initial stage of the ontogenetic development of form perception, we must assess the functional capabilities of the child's sensory system and the dimensions of the stimuli evoking spontaneous preferences in the child.

Sensory receptors at birth. Measurements of the electrochemical activity of the retina of newborn infants have demonstrated the functioning of both photopic (cone) and scotopic (rod) receptor systems (Horsten and Winkelman, 1964). Thus the primary receptors are intact at birth. Furthermore, Dayton, Jones, Steele, and Rose (1964) have shown that coordinated eye movements occur within the first few days of life. The corrective saccadic movements are greater than those of the mature adult, but they clearly function to hold a target on the fovea. Other studies indicate that convergence (aiming the two eyes together or apart in response to a stimulus moving toward or away from the observer) is underdeveloped in the newborn infant (Hershenson, 1965). Convergence does occur, but for short periods and without the control displayed by the mature adult. Hershenson (1967) points out that the lack of convergence cannot be taken as evidence that the child sees a blurred or doubled world at birth as does the adult during a failure of convergence. Perhaps the input to each eye can be processed sequentially or the input to one eye suppressed during early visual experience.

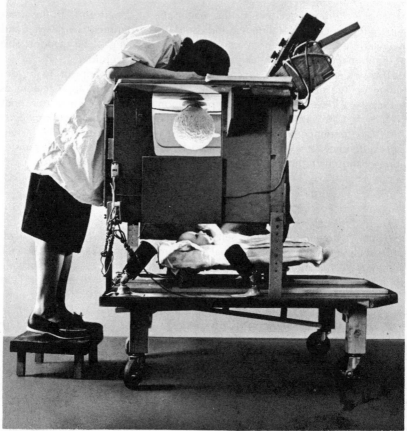

Figure 4.2
Apparatus for the study of detailed vision in the newborn child. (Fantz, 1961. Photograph by David Linton.)

With regard to visual acuity during early life, Fantz (1961) attempted to measure detailed vision in the newborn child with the apparatus depicted in Figure 4.2. Pairs of stimuli consisting of a plain gray square or gray stripes were presented on the front of a two-way mirror. The experimenter looking through the mirror could measure the amount of time that a given pattern was reflected by the eyes of the infant lying below; an unbroken reflection indicated that the infant was looking directly at a particular pattern. The first series of studies demonstrated that infants spent more time viewing a pattern of gray stripes than a plain gray square. As the width of the stripes was successively decreased, the threshold for acuity could be obtained and defined as the point at which no preference for the striped pattern was found. Presumably both stimuli appeared as plain gray squares at this point. Infants less than one month old responded preferentially to ⅛-inch stripes at a distance of 10 inches, indicating a visual acuity level of 20/200. For six-month-old children, 1/64-inch stripes were preferred, indicating an acuity-level equivalent of 20/100.

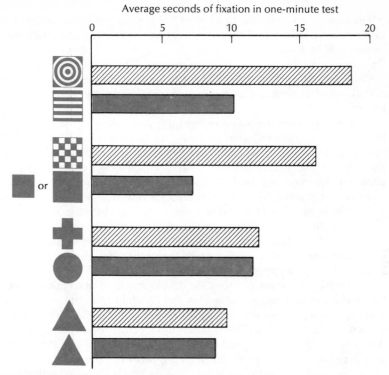

Figure 4.3
Average number of seconds fixated on various patterns during one-minute tests. Data based on twenty-two infants observed during ten-week period. (After Fantz, 1961. Copyright 1961 by Scientific American, Inc. All rights reserved.)

Such tests demonstrate that the sensory capabilities for brightness, color, and movement—as well as some degree of detailed vision—are present at birth. The resolving power of the eyes at birth is far below that of the normal adult; however, the capability for some kind of form perception appears to be present.

Perceptual capabilities at birth.   Fantz's test of visual acuity shows that the newborn child can distinguish straight lines. But the question of the infant's perception of complex forms and shapes remains unanswered. Fantz (1961) also presented pairs of forms differing in shape or pattern, some of which are reproduced in Figure 4.3. The twenty-two infants in this experiment were tested one week after birth and each week thereafter for fifteen weeks. Clearly the more complex patterns received the greater amount of attention. Even so, Fantz's study does not really demonstrate form perception. Since each pair is presented separately, we can only observe a response bias for one form or the other. Furthermore, we do not know if the infant is actually responding to the whole form or to a specific element of the pattern, such as a straight line. This problem is demonstrated by an experiment of Hershenson, Munsinger, and Kessen (1965). Solid black nonsense forms differing in the number of angles (five, ten, or twenty) were presented in pairs. The only comparison yielding a preference—defined by the length of fixation of one figure in the pair—occurred when the ten-angle figure was viewed longer than the five-angle figure.

After reviewing the literature on form perception in the newborn infant, Hershenson (1967) concluded that most research has failed to isolate the dimensions of forms to which a child may be responding. Hershenson also pointed out that little information has been collected concerning the actual degree of attention the child affords to the shapes viewed. Although an infant will frequently leave his gaze fixed on a specific object before falling asleep, this could hardly be interpreted as a preference for that object.

In conclusion, the studies of innate or spontaneous capabilities in the infant do not clearly demonstrate the presence of form perception at birth. At the same time, one could argue with equal fervor that they also fail to demonstrate a lack of form perception at birth.

A discussion of the ontogenetic development of perception must follow the changes in perceptual tendencies and capabilities as the responding organism grows older. This specific aspect of perception is usually studied under the topic of learning. E. J. Gibson (1969) has recently reviewed much of the evidence of changes in perceptual response as a function of age. Rather than present a general discussion of the learning process, specific topics related to perception will be mentioned at appropriate points throughout the remainder of the text.

Pattern Preference

The perception of specific form depends on the duration of presentation and the developmental state of the perceiving organism. In addition, individual experience seems to influence the ability of observers to respond to form. The perceptual environment seldom presents isolated sights and sounds; rather, it provides figures or patterns of stimuli to which the organism must respond. In the next few sections we shall discuss three aspects of pattern perception: *pattern preference, pattern recognition,* and *pattern organization.* The term pattern is used here to refer to sensory input containing numerous elements. As we shall see, the tendency to perceive our perceptual world organized into patterns makes distinctions between form, figure, and pattern perception very difficult.

Frequently we deem a complex visual experience or auditory pattern pleasant or unpleasant. Clearly we tend to show definite preferences for certain kinds of stimuli. Although psychologists have been aware of such preferences for a number of years, little work has been done to isolate the variables underlying an aesthetic interpretation of sensory input.

In an early study of simple forms, Fechner (1860) became specifically interested in preferences for certain shapes. He asked several acquaintances to

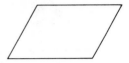

Figure 4.4
Patterns for testing preference among simple figures. (Murch, 1965.)

select the most pleasing shape from a series of rectangles with a constant length and variable width. Most individuals presented with the task selected a rectangle in which the width was six-tenths of the length (ratio of 1 to 0.62). This particular rectangle has gained renown from the early architecture of Greece and Egypt. The rectangular dimensions of the Parthenon and the stones of the great pyramids display the same ratio of width to length as the rectangular shapes preferred by Fechner's subjects. In architecture, this form has been called the *golden section*. More recently Collins and Stone (1965) collected assorted business cards, driver's licenses, picture frames, and other familiar items and found an average ratio of length to width of 1 to 0.65. They also noted that the ratio of length to width in 35 mm slides and projectors is 1 to 0.66.

Why does such a preference exist? Collins and Stone offer a rather pleasing explanation based on the observation that the vertical visual field of the eye is about six-tenths the size of the horizontal visual field. Therefore the golden section is a rectangle which fits nicely within the confines of the visual field. Schiffman (1966) tested the visual field or perimeter theory of Collins and Stone by asking subjects to draw the most pleasing rectangle possible. After finishing the drawing each subject indicated whether the longest portion of the rectangle should be vertically or horizontally oriented. Ninety-seven percent of the subjects located the long section horizontally, which conformed well to the hypothesis of Collins and Stone. Oddly enough, the obtained length-to-width ratio did not conform to the golden section (mean 0.525, standard deviation 0.104).

Distinct preferences for other forms and shapes have also been observed. The present author (1965) asked thirty-six graduate students in psychology to select one of the forms shown in Figure 4.4. The reader is invited to choose one form and compare his or her choice with the preferences of the graduate students. Of the thirty-six subjects, three selected the parallelogram, six preferred the square, and ten chose the circle. The greatest preference was for the triangle, which was chosen by over half the observers (seventeen).

Requiring subjects to visualize a combination of two simple forms demonstrates a definite bias or figural preference. Figure 4.5 contains three such problems from an experiment by the present author (1966). For several seconds subjects were shown the two figures to be combined (left portion of Figure 4.5). Immediately thereafter three possible combinations of the figures were provided and the subjects asked to select a best combination. The most frequently selected combinations were A for problems 1 and 2 and C for problem 3. As a matter of fact, 96 percent of the observers selected combination A for problem 2.

Problems   Combinations

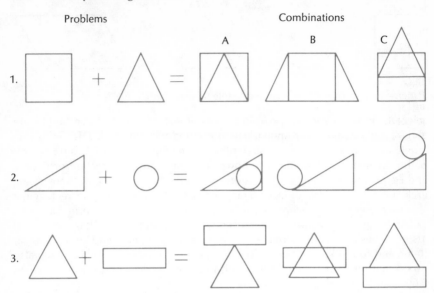

Figure 4.5
Patterns for testing preference among figure combinations. (Murch, 1966.)

The preference for some forms rather than others was explored by Koffka (1935), who postulated a natural law underlying the preference for certain shapes which he called the *law of Prägnanz* or the *law of the best figure*. The law described the tendency of observers to prefer the simplest and most stable figure available. Since the choices offered subjects in Figure 4.5 contained both stable and unstable figure combinations, as Koffka would have predicted, the simplest and most geometrical figure was usually selected. In problem 2, the ball appears about to roll from the wedge in combinations B and C; such unstable figures were seldom chosen. Although Koffka's explanation of figure preference has met with a great deal of criticism—primarily due to the lack of a clear definition of *simple* and *stable*—it does point out a noticeable attribute of preferred stimuli.

Dorfman and McKenna (1966) attempted to assess preferences for true patterns containing numerous elements. They required subjects to select the most pleasant of pairs of patterns of black and white blocks. The patterns were constructed by randomly filling in a matrix that could have either 2, 4, 6, 8, 10, or 12 blocks on a side. Whether a given block was to be black or white was determined by chance, with the probability for any block in the matrix equal to 50 percent. Figure 4.6 provides examples of the four kinds of patterns prepared for each of the six matrix grains. All twenty-four patterns were presented in pairs and every pattern was paired with every other pattern for each observer. Two groups of female subjects rated their preferences. The first group was composed of randomly selected psychology students and the second group was selected from students majoring in art. Table 4.1 presents the mean preference ratings for the six levels of complexity for both groups.

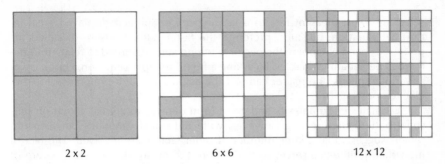

2 x 2   6 x 6   12 x 12

Figure 4.6
Patterns for testing preference among complex figures. (After Dorfman and McKenna, 1966.)

The highest preference was given a value of 1, the lowest a value of 6. Both groups of subjects agreed that the 6-by-6 matrix was the most pleasant, followed by the 8-by-8. Dorfman and McKenna also compared individual responses and found very specific individual preferences for certain complexities of pattern. The preference ratings between the two groups varied much more than the preference ratings of individuals.

Such preferences seem to relate to pattern complexity. Attneave (1957) observed that ratings of complexity of multisided figures were primarily determined by the total number of angles in the individual figures. In addition, asymmetrical shapes were judged to be more complex than symmetrical shapes exhibiting the same total number of angles. Again such preferences seem to fit Koffka's concept of the law of a best figure and to illustrate his point that the best figure is not necessarily the least complex figure.

Little work has been performed on preferences for auditory patterns. An exception is that of Vitz (1964), who asked subjects to rate the pleasantness of tone sequences varying in speed of presentation (zero to eight tones a second). Sixteen pure tones, corresponding closely to the C-major scale, were randomly presented. Vitz found that preference ratings increased monotonically with the speed of presentation. Unfortunately, he did not break the data down into individual preferences, but the monotonic relationship observed may be explained in the light of a study by Gottschaldt (1966) in which subjects were asked to

Table 4.1

Mean preference ratings for six levels of pattern complexity
(Dorfman and McKenna, 1966)

	Matrix grain					
	2 × 2	4 × 4	6 × 6	8 × 8	10 × 10	12 × 12
Art students	4.7	3.6	2.4	2.8	3.8	3.5
Psychology students	3.6	3.6	2.7	3.1	3.5	3.8

select the most pleasant rate of a tapping noise. Subjects displayed great individual variation, but most preferred the faster rates. Gottschaldt called the preferred speed of tapping the *personal tempo* and attempted to relate it to numerous personality variables. By asking a friend to tap a pencil on a book cover at various speeds, the reader can test the assumption of a preference for specific tempos.

Estimates of complexity and good form depend to a great extent on personal pattern preferences. However, wide individual variations between observers suggests that a large number of other factors are involved. The fact of individual preference serves to underscore the personal, subjective nature of the perceptual process.

Pattern Recognition

An experienced fisherman has no difficulty recognizing a particular species of fish even though individuals of that species vary greatly in size, markings, shape, and coloration. Most persons are able to read handwritten material despite considerable variation among writers. In returning to a once familiar area, we recognize not only the area but also the specific changes that have occurred in our absence. At a simpler level we recognize acquaintances despite wide ranges in apparel, hair style, or external lighting. Yet there are obvious limits to our capacity to recognize familiar objects. If a particular fish is much larger than usual, the fisherman may doubt that it belongs to a certain species; if a friend suddenly appears with a new color of hair, our recognition may be impaired.

Obviously some stored memory of previous sensory experience must be revived when the same or similar situations occur. That we are able to retain the information required for recognition over very long periods of time is something each of us has experienced. The mechanism by which such information is maintained has been the subject of much experimentation. Let us consider some of the experimental evidence concerning variables that allow or impair pattern recognition. Dearborn (1899) identified one limit to pattern recognition in an early study. Simple but unfamiliar forms were presented for examination and then later repeated among new forms either in the same orientation or tilted 180°; also, on some trials, mirror images of the forms were presented. Figures occurring a second time in the same position were recognized 70 percent of the time, whereas the inverted forms were identified 50 percent of the time. Mirror images were recognized 46 percent of the time and inverted mirror images only 32 percent of the time.

Inverting the forms certainly impaired recognition but it did not stop recognition completely. Perhaps some objects are recognized in a single orientation because they are almost always encountered in that orientation. The recognition of other objects normally viewed in a variety of orientations is not impaired by such rotation. Gibson and Robinson (1935) measured recognition accuracy for *poly-oriented forms* (objects encountered in a variety of positions, such as geometric figures, books, clothing, etc.) and *mono-oriented*

Table 4.2

Mean recognition error for mono-oriented objects
(Yin, 1969)

	Condition			
	Upright	Inverted	Up-down	Down-up
Faces	0.89	4.35	3.81	5.14
Houses	2.23	3.42	2.86	3.43
Airplanes	3.65	3.85	3.19	4.14

forms (cars, railroad trains, animals, etc.). Recognition accuracy for mono-oriented objects was markedly impaired by inversion. Gibson and Robinson also presented geographical outlines of states, countries, and continents in a variety of orientations. As one can readily discover by attempting to read an inverted map, rotating the figures greatly impairs recognition.

An interesting mono-oriented pattern is the human face. Brooks and Goldstein (1963) measured the ability of children to recognize photographs of their classmates that were presented normally or in an inverted orientation. The children found it extremely difficult to recognize the inverted faces. In a related study Hochberg and Galper (1967) noted that recognition memory for inverted faces was much poorer than for properly oriented pictures. Yin (1969) has recently studied recognition accuracy for faces and other mono-oriented objects (houses and airplanes). Subjects were shown forty pictures at the rate of 3 seconds per picture. Thereafter a series of pairs of pictures were shown, one of which was always from the preceding forty pictures and one of which was new. The observers were asked to indicate which picture in each pair had been shown among the preceding forty pictures. Yin's results are shown in Table 4.2. For the means of column one both stimulus and test figure were upright and in column two both were inverted. For the up-down condition, pictures were properly oriented during the stimulus phase and inverted during the testing; for the down-up condition the reverse procedure was followed.

Recognition accuracy for faces was better than for the other two kinds of objects when both test and stimulus figures were upright, but disproportionately worse when both were inverted. Going from a normal to an inverted orientation produced the most errors for faces, while the worst performances involved the condition in which the faces were initially upright but inverted in the test. Yin's results suggest that the subjects had great difficulty in maintaining the salient attributes of the faces. On being questioned, the subjects reported using two techniques to attempt to remember the stimulus pictures. Some searched for critical cues while others sought to gain a general impression of the whole picture. This second strategy was the favorite for identifying faces, although use of the critical cue strategy would have been more efficient. However, Köhler (1940) has pointed out that critical cues are difficult to apply to inverted faces; one frequently takes facial expression into account, but such expression is lost once the face is inverted.

Line inversion: ｛ ·ʞɔɐq s,ƃop ʎzɐʃ ǝɥʇ ɹǝʌo
pǝdɯnɾ xoɟ uʍoɹq 'ʞɔınb ǝɥʇ

Line reversal: ｛ nem doog lla rof emit eht si woN
.ytrap eht fo dia eht ot emoc ot

Line and letter reversal: ｛ .baer ot tluciffid yrev eb ot dnuof
saw noitamrofsnart ralucitrap sihT

Figure 4.7
Inversion and reversal in printed words.

The subjective reports of Yin's observers are rather interesting in the light of a study by Sekuler and Abrams (1968). Their subjects attempted to judge whether a pair of black-and-white 4-by-4 matrices were the same or different. Either 1, 2, or 4 cells were blackened and either 0, 1, 2, 3, or 4 of the same cells were blackened in each pair. One group of subjects was asked to call a pair the *same* if both matrices contained one or more of the blocks blackened in the same location; a second group was instructed to judge a pair the *same* only if all blackened blocks were in identical locations in both matrices. The results showed a superiority in speed for the second group, even though this group was required to determine if *all* blackened cells were identical in both matrices. The disadvantage of using a critical cue, as the first group did, is that each cell must be processed serially until a discrepancy is found. For the second group, the entire figure could be viewed. Pattern recognition, then, depends not only on the kind of pattern to be recognized and the orientation of the pattern but also on the strategy utilized in the process. The influences of both orientation and strategy can vary from one kind of pattern to the next.

It is important to note that only extreme changes in the orientation of mono-oriented objects produces marked recognition impairment. Radner and Gibson (1935) displayed six forms slightly tilted away from true vertical. After all figures had been shown, subjects were asked to draw the forms. None of the subjects had noticed the deviation from vertical, and all drawings showed the shapes in an upright position.

To read a book tilted at a slight angle presents no problem; however, inverting the book or tilting it 90° makes reading very difficult. As Kolers, Eden, and Boyer (1964) have demonstrated, a printed text inverted 180° can be read much quicker than a text in which each letter is reversed or in which the line is printed backwards. Although printed material is usually mono-oriented, one does occasionally attempt to recognize inverted print. The other two conditions are encountered much less frequently. Some examples of inverted and reversed printing are provided in Figure 4.7.

It is difficult to explain pattern recognition. One of the earliest and simplest theories, frequently referred to as the *template matching theory* (Gibson, 1963), dates from the late nineteenth century. It rests on the assumption that sensory experience is stored in the form of a template to which all new sensory input is compared. If the templates match, proper recognition occurs. As early as 1891 Höffding noted that a matching of templates would not handle the simple observations of pattern recognition. Any variation between the attributes of the template already filed in experience and the new sensory event would cause a mismatch. Writing on the subject of frequently encountered shapes, Deutsch (1955) has pointed out that recognition is not impaired by variations in location in the visual field, by size of stimulus, by angle of observation, or by reversals of the object, such as a mirror image. The literal version of the template theory was never taken too seriously; it has served as a scapegoat for later theorizing on the subject of pattern recognition (Hake, 1966).

One must be careful to avoid regarding the eye as a camera in which successive *pictures* are compared. Rather, the information contained in a visual image (such as color, brightness, line orientation, position in the visual field) is assembled after several stages of processing. Hence, recognition can occur with much variation as long as the total characteristics of the input are most like the characteristics of the previous sensory experience. Köhler (1940) mentions several unpublished studies in which inkblots were presented in various orientations. In one particular orientation an inkblot looked like a familiar object (e.g., a cat), but when tilted it did not seem familiar. The *attributes* of the sensory data were sufficiently similar to coded information for the pattern to be recognized as a specific object (cat), but not similar enough when the attribute of orientation was lost.

Many modern writers (e.g., Neisser, 1967) refer to the *similar attribute theory* as though it were opposed to template matching theory. In fact, the newer view can be considered to have evolved from a literal interpretation of the older. The likelihood that attributes rather than strict templates of previous experience are what is being compared is supported by the Sekuler and Abrams study discussed earlier, which involved impaired speed of recognition. Neisser (1964) demonstrates the difference nicely in an experiment in which observers were required to search for a critical letter Z in two lists of six-letter combinations. The six letters, which appeared in random order, were QDUGOC on one list and IVMXEW on the other. A Z is imbedded in both lists, which are shown in Figure 4.8. Search as rapidly as possible and measure the amount of time required to find the Z in each. A strict version of the template theory emphasizing photograph-like sensory coding would predict no difference in search time for the two lists. One would be expected to compare each letter against the Z template until the critical letter was found. However, if pattern recognition requires only a selection of attributes, then finding the Z in list A should be easier since none of the letters is made entirely of straight lines, whereas in list B all of the letters are made of straight lines. Selecting the critical attribute in list A does not require a detailed checking of each letter, but can be accomplished by rapid scanning.

Pattern recognition, then, involves extracting the attributes of new data and comparing them to previous collections of attributes in order to search out similarities. The same kind of process occurs when we view figures or complex patterns, and tap our memories for similarities with attributes of previous sensory experience.

A   B

A	B
QDUGOC	IVMXEW
OCDUGQ	EWVMIX
CQOGUD	EXWMVI
QUGCDO	IXEMWV
UCDGQO	VXEMWI
DUZGQO	MXVEWI
UCGQOD	XVWMEI
DQOCGU	MWXVIE
QDOCGU	VIMEXW
CGUDOQ	EXVWIM
OCDUGQ	VWMIEX
UOCGQD	VMWEIX
GGQCOU	XVWMEI
GCUDQO	WXVEMI
QCUGDO	EXMEWI
DUCOQG	MXIVEW
CGODQU	VEWMIX
UDGCOQ	EMVXWI
GQCODU	IVWMEX
GOQUCD	IEVMWX
GDQUOC	WMXZIE
UQDCGO	XEMIWV
GODQOC	WEIMXV
DQOCGU	IVEMXW

Figure 4.8
Visual search tasks for the critical letter Z. List A,
attributes of critical letter and noise letters are dissimilar. List B, attributes of critical letter and noise
letters are similar. (After Neisser, 1964. Copyright
1964 by Scientific American, Inc. All rights reserved.)

In passing, we can note that the attribute approach to pattern recognition
can help to explain the frequent experience of déjà vu—the feeling of having
been somewhere before, even though one is fully aware of never having been
there. The attributes of the sensory data processed at the new location must
be enough like the attributes of some other, familiar location to evoke a partial
recognition. Since the attributes of the new situation are only similar or partially identical with the old, one experiences a feeling of familiarity without
quite recognizing the exact previous situation that provided the similar attributes stored in one's memory.

Pattern Organization

Perception involves the processing of very complex stimulus patterns; due to
the volume of incoming stimuli, some kind of organization of input is necessary. Consider how chaotic the visual world would be if each stimulus and the

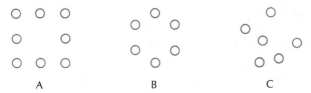

Figure 4.9
Patterns demonstrating principles of gestalt organization.

dimensions of each stimulus (brightness, color, form, etc.) required serial processing. Also, in light of the limited capacities of the sensory register and in particular the short-term storage, the establishment of relationships between input and organization of pattern would be required in order to sample more than a minute detail of the environment. The subjective experience—the fact that we do not interact with a complex environment by processing individual sensations—led a group of German psychologists to attempt to outline the principles by which the organization of input occurs. This approach to perception was led by Max Wertheimer, Kurt Koffka, and Wolfgang Köhler. Their major tenet was that perception involves the organization of sensory input into wholes or units rather than the processing of separate sensations. The logic underlying this *gestalt* concept of pattern organization has been outlined by Wertheimer:

> I stand at the window and see a house, trees, sky. Now on theoretical grounds I could try to count and say, "here there are . . . 327 brightnesses and hues." Do I have 327? No, I see sky, house, trees, and no one can really have these 327 as such. Furthermore, if in this strange calculation the house should have, say, 120 and the trees 90 and the sky 117, I have in any event *this* combination, this particular segregation; and the sort of combination or segregation in which I see it is not simply up to my choice; it is almost impossible for me to see it in any desired combination that I may happen to choose (p. 115).

Wertheimer points out that some kind of *spontaneous organization* seems to take place which is very stable and impervious to reorganization. As we shall see, the stability of perceptual organization depends on the nature of the stimulus material; certain stimuli can be organized in numerous ways. In the following section we will examine aspects of stimulus configurations that give rise to specific organizations of the perceptual field.

But first let us return to a consideration of the spontaneous organization of perceptual input. Figure 4.9 shows three separate collections of six circles; what do you see as you view each collection? In parts A and B one tends to see them organized as a square and circle (or hexagon), respectively. Even in part C a random collection of six circles provides a kind of natural organization in which subunits or groups seem to belong together. Observations such as these led Koffka to conclude that the organized whole is different from the simple sum of the separate parts. Obviously each part of Figure 4.9 contains only six circles; however, the perception of the three parts varies considerably, depending on the spatial arrangements of the circles.

Why does such an organization occur? Or, put more simply, why do things look as they do? Koffka answered his own question by observing that "things look as they do because of the field of organization to which the proximal stimulus distribution gives rise" (1935, p. 98). In other words, the relationships among stimulus elements are important only as proximal stimuli on which an organizational process is superimposed. In many cases, as Rock (1966) has argued, noting the relationships among proximal stimulus elements is sufficient to predict perceptual organization. Koffka, however, envisioned an intrinsic organizational process or natural law which we have already discussed, the law of Prägnanz. With regard to the field of organization, Koffka reasoned that "the psychological organization will always be as good as the prevailing conditions allow" (1935, p. 110). While Koffka fails to provide a clear meaning of the all-important word *good* in his definition of the law of Prägnanz, he does go on to say that the organization will be the simplest, most stable possible organization of the proximal stimuli. It should be made clear that Koffka actually considered the foregoing to be a sort of natural law or intrinsic force *causing* the organization of the field to occur. The law of Prägnanz has failed to gain support and is not considered a natural law of psychology in the way that Boyle's law concerning the behavior of gases is accepted in chemistry or Newton's laws of motion are accepted in physics.

For the moment let us put aside this topic concerning the source of sensory organization and consider the stimulus variables that give rise to certain perceptual organizations. Each of the stimulus relationships may be considered a *factor* capable of contributing to specific organizations. In many previous discussions they have been incorrectly referred to as the *gestalt laws of organization*. However, the gestalt psychologists believed the law of Prägnanz to be the only law of perceptual organization. In their opinion, the factors described in the next section give rise to the best perceptual organization.

Gestalt factors of perceptual organization.   Several reevaluations and reconsiderations of the factors of organization have occurred since the work of the first gestalt psychologists. The following explanations rely heavily on the work of Wolfgang Metzger (1966), who might be considered one of the prime students of gestalt psychology of the second generation.

Factor of similarity.   (Faktor der Gleichartigkeit, Metzger, 1937.) If a number of elements are present in the perceptual field, those with similar characteristics will be seen as though they are grouped together. The influence of this factor can be seen in part A of Figure 4.10.

Factor of proximity.   (Faktor der Nähe, Wertheimer, 1923.) Elements of the perceptual field located near one another will tend to be seen as a group or unit. This factor is demonstrated in part B of Figure 4.10.

Factor of common fate.   (Faktor des gemeinsamen Schicksals, Wertheimer, 1923.) Elements engaged in the same pattern motion or common occupation will be seen as though they are grouped together. Metzger (1966) provides an example of six house flies on a ceiling; three flies are moving about and three

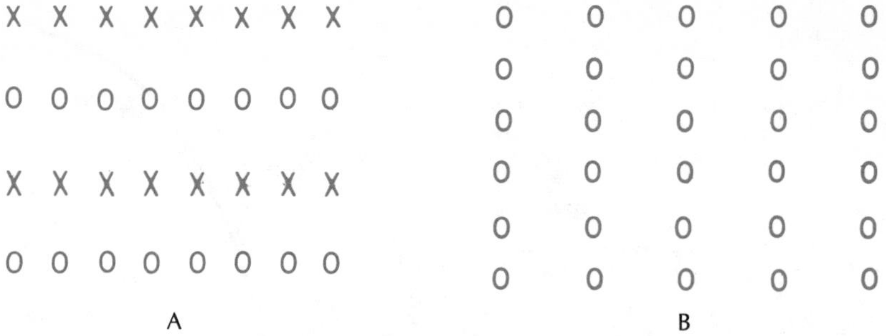

```
X  X  X  X  X  X  X  X          O      O      O      O      O

                               O      O      O      O      O
O  O  O  O  O  O  O  O
                               O      O      O      O      O

X  X  X  X  X  X  X  X          O      O      O      O      O

                               O      O      O      O      O
O  O  O  O  O  O  O  O
                               O      O      O      O      O
            A                                  B
```

Figure 4.10
Patterns demonstrating A, factor of similarity; B, factor of proximity.

are stationary. The three in motion will be seen as one group, the three not moving as another. An example from Dember (1960) can also serve to illustrate common fate. Most observers would fail to notice a deer standing immobile against the foliage of a forest; the animal is part of the background and hence enjoys common fate. If the deer moves, it becomes a single figure, and common fate is lost. One might say that to make waves is to lose common fate.

Factor of objective set. (Faktor der objektiven Einstellung, Wertheimer, 1923.) This important organizational factor describes a kind of primacy of perception in the observer. In contrast to other gestalt factors mentioned, this factor designates a condition of the observer rather than a condition of the stimulus field. Objective set is best demonstrated by an experiment conducted by Bell and Bevan (1968). Three groups of observers were asked to describe the organization of matrices of thirty-six dots arranged in vertical columns and horizontal rows. During the trials the ratio of vertical to horizontal distance between dots was varied. For one pattern the distance between horizontal dots was only half the distance between vertical dots (vertical/horizontal distance = 0.50). This was changed to a pattern in which the horizontal dots were twice as far apart as the vertical dots (vertical/horizontal distance = 2). The task of all subjects was to judge whether the dot matrices appeared to be organized as rows (horizontal lines) or columns (vertical lines). For one group E_c each of the test patterns was preceded by an anchor pattern in which the vertical columns of dots were moved very close together, while a second group E_r saw anchor patterns in which the horizontal rows were very close. A final control group judged only the test patterns unpreceded by anchor patterns. The results of the study are presented in Figure 4.11. Curve C represents the average judgments of the control group that received no anchor. As the curve shows, the percentage of row judgments increased steadily as the vertical to horizontal distance ratio decreased. At the neutral value of 1.0, in which the dots were equally spaced, about 50 percent of these subjects judged the pattern to be organized in rows. For group E_r, which viewed the anchor patterns before each judgment of rows that were very close, a much lower ratio of vertical to horizontal distance was required (0.85) before

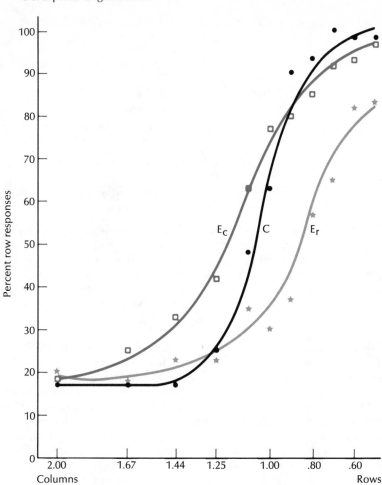

Figure 4.11
Relative frequency with which a matrix of dots was perceived to consist of a set of rows when the ratio of vertical to horizontal distance was varied from 0.60 to 2. (After Bell and Bevan, 1968.)

50 percent of the judgments indicated the test pattern to be organized in rows. On the other hand, the group receiving the column anchor E_c judged the test patterns to be organized into rows at a much higher ratio of vertical to horizontal distance. In other words, providing the subjects with a set for the judgment of rows altered their organization of the perceptual field. Bell and Bevan (1968) demonstrate similar effects for the factors of similarity, good continuation, and closure. In simple terms, then, the factor of objective set means that the perceiver will perceive what he expects or is set to perceive.

Figure 4.12
Pattern demonstrating factor of inclusiveness.

Factor of inclusiveness. (Faktor des Aufgehen ohne Rest, Wertheimer, 1923.) Of the six vertical lines shown in Figure 4.12, the central four are paired. While one frequently sees this as two narrow columns and two extra lines at the ends, the figure is also often perceived as three wide columns. This tendency of organization obviously goes against the factor of proximity but allows all elements of the field to be included in simple groups.

Factor of good continuation. (Faktor des glatten Verlaufs, Wertheimer, 1923.) If possible, the field will be organized along lines of continuous contour or flow. Figure 4.13 shows Wertheimer's example of good continuation (1945). The curve in part A is seen as continuous rather than subdivided. Part B in Figure 4.13 is an example from Metzger (1953) in which good continuation is not maintained. Whereas at point X one sees two continuous lines crossing one another, at point Y one is likely to see two lines meeting at a point— the upper one composed of straight lines, the lower one of curves—even though here, too, good continuation would favor seeing two intersecting lines. Apparently, in this case, good continuation gives way to the factor of similarity.

Factor of closure. (Faktor der Geschlossenheit, Wertheimer, 1923.) A field containing broken figure parts is usually organized to be seen as a number of closed figures. In the simplest example, one perceives the dots of parts A and B of Figure 4.9 as completed squares or circles. Although the outsides of the broken squares shown in Figure 4.14 are in fact closer together than the broken

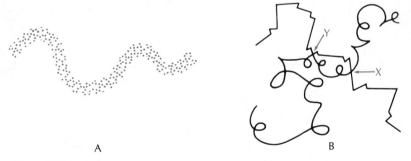

A

B

Figure 4.13
Patterns demonstrating *A*, factor of good continuation; *B*, factor of good continuation at fixation point *X* but not at *Y*.

Figure 4.14
Pattern demonstrating factor of closure.

parts, one tends to see them as completed squares. The factor of closure over-rides that of proximity in serving as the dominant organizational factor in this example; the closure factor also overrides the possible influence of the factor of inclusiveness, a variable that might come into play due to the two half squares at each end of the line, which invite the viewer to see the figure as a series of five very wide-flanged I-beams.

Other gestalt factors.   Several other stimulus variables have been shown to influence the manner in which patterns are perceived. These factors were not identified by the early gestalt psychologists, but they have been studied and formulated in the traditional gestalt psychology manner by later researchers.

Factor of fixation.   The organization of certain kinds of patterns clearly depends on where the observer fixes his attention. Figure 4.13 by Metzger illustrates the influence of this factor. Several other organizations demonstrating the importance of point of fixation are shown in Figure 4.15. Part A is a figure developed by Morinaga (1942) and part B is a steel bar illusion (Gregory 1966) made popular by *Mad* magazine.

Factor of contour.   Woodworth (1938) suggested that contour and bright-ness may influence perceptual grouping. In other words, one tends to group objects in the visual field that are much brighter or much darker than other elements of the field. In complex scenes in which organization does not occur on the basis of the preceding factors, those objects sharply distinguishing themselves from the background will probably be grouped together.

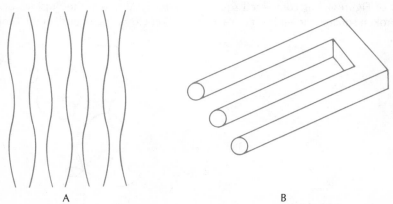

A   B

Figure 4.15
Influence of fixation on pattern organization. A, Morinaga (1942). B, Gregory (1966).

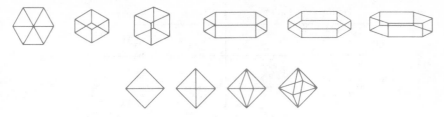

Figure 4.16
Patterns for judging bi- and tridimensionality as a function of figural complexity. (After Hochberg and Brooks, 1960.)

Factor of object interdependence.   Also prevalent in the organization of complex patterns encountered in visual experience is a tendency to group objects that are functionally rather than physically similar. We frequently see objects in this way if they display some kind of interdependent relationship. For example, we tend to see a cigarette and a lighter as though they belong together, despite their lack of physical resemblance.

Empirical evidence of the gestalt factors.   The descriptive nature of the gestalt factors makes empirical testing of their validity somewhat difficult. Wertheimer's demonstrations indicate that for certain specific patterns, grouping does occur on the basis of the factors listed. However, that the factors generally apply to a variety of patterns is a proposition that remains untested.

Researchers have long been interested in the underlying forces of organization envisioned by Koffka in the law of Prägnanz. Of particular interest are the several attempts to evaluate an observer's tendency to group elements of a visual field into the simplest, most stable organization. Perkins (1932) exposed irregular outlines for short durations and asked subjects to reproduce the figures. Their drawings exhibited greater symmetry than did the original figures. However, the tendency toward symmetry may not be due to the influence of Prägnanz; rather, it may indicate the working of a limited memory for complex forms. Wulf (1922) required subjects to reproduce simple, asymmetrical forms after intervals of thirty minutes, one day, seven days, and three months. Each successive test showed a greater simplicity and symmetry in the drawings. That memory limitation alone is not responsible for this organizational tendency has been shown by Hebb and Foord (1945), who essentially replicated Wulf's experiment but allowed subjects to reproduce the original form only once. Some subjects were tested immediately, others after several weeks. Changes toward symmetry occurred, but the changes for subjects tested immediately and for those tested after several weeks were about the same. The earlier work evidently compounded memory changes, since the subject was forced to remember each successive attempt to reproduce the original figure. Rock and Engelstein (1959) allowed subjects to study nonsense forms for twenty seconds. The subjects were then dismissed and given the impression that the experiment was over. However, they were retested on the forms after fifteen seconds, one day, seven days, or twenty-one days. Half of the subjects were required to draw the original figures while the other half were asked to

Figure	Rating	Figure	Rating
 (dot pattern)	1.09	(dot pattern)	2.94
 (dot pattern)	1.14	 (dot pattern)	4.51
 (dot pattern)	1.80	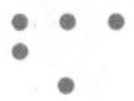 (dot pattern)	4.90
 (dot pattern)	2.06	 (dot pattern)	5.63

Figure 4.17
Ratings of figural goodness for various dot patterns. Low rating indicates a high degree of goodness. (After Handel and Garner, 1966.)

select the figures from a number of figures varying in degree of similarity to the originals. Recognition was almost unaffected by the delays, and the drawings displayed the usual tendency toward symmetry and simplification. Obviously memory factors are important here, but one can also argue that memory coding—which simplifies complex patterns—may be due to the organizational limit of the perceptual system.

Hochberg and Brooks (1960) considered the simplicity factor in more detail from a different perspective. They presented subjects with geometrical figures such as those in Figure 4.16. Measures of complexity were obtained by counting the number of interior angles of the two-dimensional drawing of each figure. As each figure was briefly exposed, subjects were asked whether it appeared to be bi- or tridimensional. The frequency of judgments of tridimensionality increased with the number of angles. For figures with a small number of angles, then, the simplest and easiest organization was bidimensional, even though with effort such figures can be seen as tridimensional. For a more complex figure, tridimensional organization was simpler, since there are fewer tri- than bidimensional angles.

Handel and Garner (1966) presented all possible arrangements of five dots in a 3-by-3 matrix and asked subjects to judge the *goodness* of the figure. Judgments were made on a scale from 1 to 7 with 1 indicating a high degree of goodness and 7 a very low degree. Symmetry was very important in the judgments, as can be seen in Figure 4.17.

Several theorists have attempted to describe simplicity and figural goodness. Attneave (1954, 1955, and 1959) has pointed out that a symmetrical figure contains much less information than an asymmetrical figure. The smaller the amount of information, the easier the encoding and storage of the organized pattern. Hence, one would expect observers to seek out the simplest organization of the field available. In attempting to remember forms, a tendency to simplify might be the result of loss of information from memory rather than a force for spontaneous organization of good figures.

Jacob Beck has reported several experiments on pattern perception and similarity. In one study (Beck, 1966a) subjects were presented with a number of patterns similar to the example in Figure 4.18. Their task was to divide each

Figure 4.18
Pattern groupings based on element similarity and orientation. (After Beck, 1966a. Copyright 1966 by the American Association for the Advancement of Science.)

figure at the most natural break. The resulting divisions were based almost entirely on *orientation* rather than similarity. That is, in the example given, almost all subjects divided the figure between the upright Ts and the tilted Ts. Ratings of the similarity of elements in the pattern were also obtained. For a comparison of the elements T and ⊼, a mean similarity rating of 8.04 was obtained (1 = the lowest similarity and 9 the highest). A comparison of the elements T and ⌐ yielded a mean of 3.83. Obviously, in the context of a pattern, similarity must include orientation, which in the present case appears to be the most important factor. Despite the ratings of similarity in which each element of the pattern was presented individually, one would be forced to conclude that in a complex pattern T is not highly similar to ⊼ .

Beck (1966b) also observed the effect of varying the brightness of combined patterns of upright and tilted Ts. Figure 4.19 provides examples. As can be seen in part A, equal brightness of the two elements fails to elicit segregation into two patterns. However, changes in brightness (part B) do produce separate figures. Beck found that as brightness differences increased, so did the subjective ratings of the degree of separation of the two groups of elements.

One might expect a similar relationship for proximity—that grouping tendencies would increase steadily as similar elements are brought closer to-

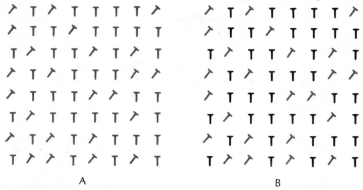

A   B

Figure 4.19
Influence of brightness on pattern groupings. (After Beck, 1966b. Copyright 1966 by the American Association for the Advancement of Science.)

Figure 4.20
Pattern groupings in random dots.
(After Drösler, 1967.)

gether. In several studies by Drösler (1967), children were asked to select five natural groups of dots, or dots appearing to belong together, from a pattern of random dots. An example of the test material is shown in Figure 4.20. Drösler analyzed the results by computing the tendency of subjects to group dots as a function of the distance of groups of dots from the center of the visual field. Proximity played an important part only for the center of the field; its influence declined rapidly away from the center. In contrast to Beck's findings —that as brightness differences between elements increased so did the tendency to see elements grouped together—Drösler found proximity important only for very closely located elements. As the distance increased, the tendency to see a group or figure dropped disproportionately.

In another experiment, Beck (1967) studied the influence of varying brightnesses on pattern grouping; he was able to develop a comparison between the effects of brightness on the grouping of similar and dissimilar units. Figure 4.21 presents the results of four such comparisons. Subjects rated the degree of division of the total figure (see Figure 4.19) from 0 to 6, with 0 indicating no clear division of the total figure into separate patterns. Beck concluded that the influence of brightness in pattern grouping is essentially the same for all kinds of figural units. The overall degree of separation increases as does the dissimilarity of the compounding elements; however, the brightness contribution is the same for all levels of dissimilarity of elements.

The factor of closure has also received experimental attention. Bobbitt (1942) flashed triangles with various sections incomplete. At very short durations, subjects would report lines and angles. However, as the duration was increased, subjects tended to report completed triangles. Several experiments (Carlson and Duncan, 1955; Holmes, 1967) have assumed that a tendency toward closure would show itself in the recall of incomplete figures. (This expectation was derived from Wertheimer's explanation of gestalt influences in memory.) Subjects viewed a circle with a gap and were tested for recognition by being asked to select the original from a series of test circles

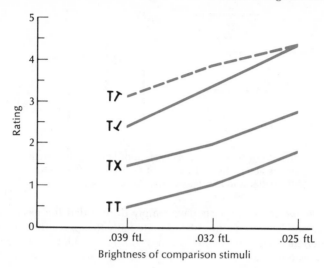

Figure 4.21
Rating of the degree of figural separation under three conditions of brightness difference between standard and comparison stimuli. Standard = 0.07 ftL. (After Beck, 1967.)

with gaps of various sizes. They tended to select circles with gaps actually *larger* than that in the original circle. The absence of a closure tendency in a memory test for forms would seem to refute the gestalt expectations; two factors must be considered, however. First, the lack of a closure effect in recalling a form does not support or refute the influence of closure in pattern perception. Second, the failure of a closure effect in *simple* figures tells us nothing about the memory for complex designs. According to the information content analysis by Attneave (1954), one must encode very little information in order to recall correctly that a circle was incomplete. In fact, one might expect an overestimation of the gap if the subject were encoding only the two pieces of information, circle and gap.

McKendry, Snyder, and Gates (1963) report one of the few studies of the influence of gestalt factors on complex stimulus material. Subjects viewed magazine illustrations for one second and then indicated groups of objects within the illustrations. Since the viewing time was very short, one can assume that groups were seen spontaneously. The study isolated four important factors. In order of importance, groupings were based on proximity, object interdependency, similarity, and contour.

That the gestalt factors do describe the organization of some figures appears to be certain. However, very little research has been devoted to assessing the general applicability of the factors in everyday situations involving perceptual response to complex environmental stimuli.

Observer experience and perceptual grouping.   For most psychologists trained in the empiricist tradition of American psychology, the gestalt assumption of spontaneous, innate organizational tendencies has been unacceptable. In fact,

Figure 4.22
Influence of set on the organization of lines. Look at both
patterns above, look at part A of Figure 4.31, then return
to the patterns in this figure. (After Boring, 1946.)

to a large degree the empiricists have simply disregarded the gestalt position
on this issue and have frequently stated quite flatly that perception is the result
of past experience. During the discussion of form perception we have encountered the question of whether the ability to perceive form is innate or learned.
Although, as we have seen, the evidence is not conclusive, some kind of form
perception seems to occur independently of prior experience.

Zuckerman and Rock (1957) have examined the controversy concerning
the learned versus the innate nature of perceptual organization. On logical
grounds they argue in favor of an innate organizing principle. In order to account for the gestalt grouping factors in terms of past experience, one might
assume that the organism *learns* to group similar and proximal objects together.
Yet this would imply, as Zuckerman and Rock point out, that prior to learning
the organism would be able to distinguish, compare, and recognize the attributes of the objects in order to perceive their similarities. It is also fallacious
to argue that such abilities are derived from experience with objects that are
interconnected or move together, since the organism would have to have the
innate ability to organize the field in order to perceive the initial "moving
together." While the problem of the innate versus the learned origins of many
perceptual processes is discussed throughout the book, at this point we are
concerned solely with the gestalt factors that affect the grouping of patterns.

The difficulty of explaining the role of experience in perception is compounded by the distinction proposed by Wertheimer (1923) between set
(factor of objective set) and experience. An example by Leibowitz (1965) under-
scores the influence of set. Look at the lines in Figure 4.22, then turn to Figure 4.31 and study part A. Return to Figure 4.22, and the organization of the
four lines will appear in three dimensions rather than two. The reason for the
change is based, in gestalt terms, on the factor of objective set.

That objective set does not always influence perception has been demonstrated by Dinnerstein (1965). Look at part A of Figure 4.23, then part B. Set
seems to havè no effect in this instance; after one studies part A one does not
see part B as a part beside a complete square. Rather, part B appears as two
complete squares, one in front of the others. This seems to challenge both
the gestalt concept of set, and the notion that perceptual organization requires
prior experience; in this example organization is independent of experience or
set, and must be due to some innate factor.

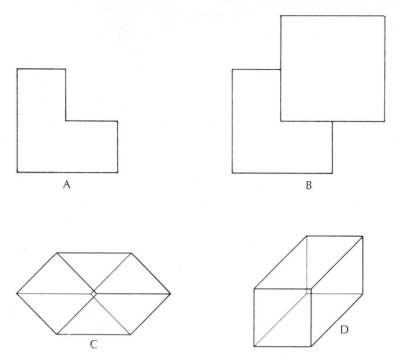

Figure 4.23
Patterns for the induction of set. (After Dinnerstein, 1965.)

Gottschaldt (1926) attempted to study the role of experience in the organization of complex geometrical designs. He showed several simple figures
(e.g., part A of Figure 4.24) either 3 or 520 times, followed by a complex figure
(part B). One of the simple figures was embedded in the complex design.
Whether subjects viewed the simple figures 3 or 520 times, there was no difference in the number of spontaneous reports of the fact that one of the simple
figures was contained in the complex design. In either test condition only a
small number of the subjects noted the simple figure's presence (approximately
6.6 percent of the observations for the subjects viewing 3 exposures of the
simple figures and 5 percent for those viewing 520 exposures). However, Gottschaldt did find that specific instructions enabled subjects to perceive the
hidden figure more readily. After 3 presentations of the simple figures, one
group of instructed subjects identified the hidden figure in 31.2 percent of the
observations; a second group, having viewed 520 presentations of the simple
figures, located the hidden figure on 28.3 percent of the trials. The instructions
for finding the figures provided a set that was independent of the amount of
prior experience with the simple figures. The percentage of correct identifications increased for both groups; however, even with such instructions, the 520-
exposure group had no particular advantage over the 3-exposure group in
spotting the hidden figure.

The experience with the simple figure did not influence the perception of
the complex designs. There is some question as to whether repeated exposure

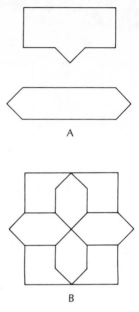

Figure 4.24
One of the simple figures of A is embedded in the complex design
of B. (After Gottschaldt, 1926.)

of the simple figures can be considered past experience and whether such an
experience could override the observer's total previous experience with the
designs. In any case, Gottschaldt does demonstrate the tendency to see figures
as *wholes* rather than as a collection of separate parts. That a proper set can play
some role in organization is demonstrated by the fact that subjects could find
the embedded figure if given the proper instructions.

Djang (1937) also sought to demonstrate the importance of past experience
in the perceptual organization of complex designs. She required subjects to
commit to memory a series of simple figures composed of dots rather than
lines, as in the Gottschaldt experiments. The subjects learned to retrieve these
figures from memory and to associate each figure with a nonsense syllable. To
test past experience, complex designs containing the previously memorized
simple figures were shown. She found that subjects could identify the simple
forms in the complex designs and concluded that Gottschaldt's assumption of
the ineffectualness of prior experience was unfounded. This conclusion seems
unwarranted, however, when one considers the instructions given the subjects
in Djang's study. She emphasized breaking the figures into parts and reproducing the previously learned figures. Such instructions would produce a set
similar to that provided by Gottschaldt's specific instructions to look for the
simple figures in the complex patterns. Djang also noted that some of the simple figures were located more frequently than others, even though the level
of learning during memorization of the sample figures was the same for all
designs. This observation would seem to imply that any variations in the diffi-

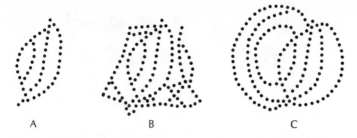

A   B   C

Djang's simple figure A embedded in the more complex design of B.
C, a complex figure by Zuckerman and Rock (1957) in which figure A
is not seen as easily as in B.

culty of finding the simple figures in the complex patterns must be due to the
strength of the organizational factors influencing the complex patterns. Figure
4.25 contains one of Djang's simple figures (part A) and one of her complex
figures (part B). Also shown is a complex design (part C) by Zuckerman and
Rock (1957) containing the same simple figure. The simple figure is much
more easily identified in part B than in part C, which must be due to the strength
of the organizational factors influencing the perception of the complex
figure.

Past experience does play a role in perception, but the role must be separated from immediate set. The following four observations attempt to assess
the role of experience in figural organization.

Past experience can ease the recognition of familiar items. Campbell
(1941) showed that subjects located simple, symmetrical parts of a complex
design more rapidly than irregular parts. Superimposed on experience, then,
are the organizational factors described by gestalt psychology: the stronger
their influence, the lesser the effect of experience. The familiar word of Figure 4.26 can be read only with difficulty, since one has a tendency to perceive
the top and bottom elements together. Covering the top half of the figure
simplifies recognition of the word.

*Memory traces in the form of perceptual sets can influence the organiza-
tion of ambiguous figures.* We will consider reversible figures in detail in
the next section; in the present discussion we are referring to figures that can
be seen in two or more ways. Dinnerstein (1965) has demonstrated the influence of perceptual set on the organization of ambiguous figures. When 43 sub-

UNIVERSITY

Figure 4.26
Influence of gestalt factors on recognition of a
familiar word.

Figure 4.27
Influence of learned figure-ground relations on word
recognition.

jects had viewed part C of Figure 4.23, 79 percent described the figure as a flat, two-dimensional design. Part D of 4.23, seen by 47 observers, was described as a cubical or three-dimensional figure by 72 percent. Another group of subjects viewed part C followed by part D. In this case, 58 percent saw part D as a flat figure. In the reverse condition, with part D preceding part C, 53 percent of the subjects reported part C as cubical. The organization of the ambiguous figure, then, depended on the set established by the preceding figure.

Past experience in the form of expectations of figure-ground relations can influence perceptual organization. We learn to expect certain kinds of figures to be figures and others to be background. This is demonstrated by Figure 4.27, where this tendency makes organization most difficult. The influence of previous experience can be overridden by placing the index finger of your left hand along the top of the black lines and the little finger of your right hand along their lower edge in order to frame the central portion of the figure. Experimentally, Nelson and Vasold (1965) have shown that figure-ground orientation affects recognition accuracy. Subjects were asked to identify common objects shown as positive or negative transparencies. The duration of presentation required for the subject to identify the object (i.e., give the same object name on three consecutive trials) was significantly shorter for the positives.

Past experience can exert a number of indirect effects. The observer's familiarity with organizational tendencies may influence the tendency brought to bear on a particular situation. For example, the organization of a painting is probably different for the art critic than for the casual art observer. The manner in which you view subsequent figures in this text will be influenced by the experience gained in studying the preceding figures.

Specific experiences are probably encoded in long-term storage and thereafter used to evaluate or to develop percepts from new incoming sensory stimulation. The preceding comments concerning the role of past experience attempt to isolate some of the ways in which specific types of past experience may contribute to the processing of sensory input.

Reversible figures. The gestalt factors are used to describe the general organizational tendencies of the perceiving organism; theoretically, under such conditions, many different possible organizations may occur. If the proper factors are brought to bear, a stable and unchanging organization occurs. For example, if dots and circles are placed in the proper relative positions, one tends to organize them on the basis of the factors of proximity or similarity. There are certain kinds of figures in which an observer may see more than one pos-

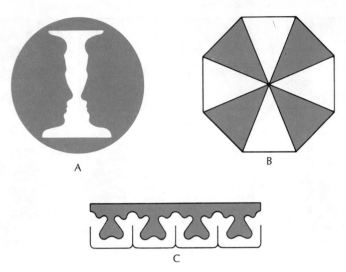

C

Figure 4.28
Reversible figures demonstrating fluctuations in figure-ground relationships.

sible organization. Such designs can be divided into two classes: those in which the figure and ground can exchange positions, and those in which the figure orientation varies.

Figure-ground reversal.   Figure 4.28 shows three figures that may be perceived in two different ways. The classic example is part A, where the figure can be seen as a white vase on a blue background or as two blue profiles on a white background (Rubin, 1921). As one can observe with all of these figures, the figure and the ground exchange positions quite frequently. The exchange is marked by a modification of the apparent *depth* of the figure; the figural portion always appears to be *in front of* the background.

Rubin (1921) studied figure-ground reversal in some detail. He projected a series of nine irregular figures, each enclosed by a black area, similar to A, B, and C in the upper portion of Figure 4.29. These were presented several times to a limited number of observers who were instructed to *see the enclosed area as the figure.* A second series of nine figures followed in which the observers were asked to *see the black enclosing area as the figure.* After a delay of about thirty minutes Rubin then presented all eighteen patterns in random order and asked the subjects to indicate whether the enclosed or enclosing portion of the pattern constituted the figure. He found that with 64 percent of the patterns, subjects saw the same portion as the figure as they had in the earlier presentation; only 33 percent reported figure-ground reversal. This tendency to see the same figure as that of the instructed period has been termed *figure persistence* (Epstein, 1967).

For gestalt psychologists, Rubin's results indicated a tendency to organize the figure in the same manner as originally perceived. The instructions of the

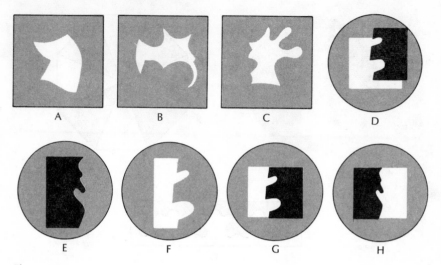

Figure 4.29

A, B, C, ambiguous figures used by Rubin (1921). D, offset figure used by Cornwell (1963). E, F, G, H, ambiguous figures used by Rock and Kremen (1957).

first part of the experiment had provided a set for the perception of the ambiguous test figure. Rock and Kremen (1957) have demonstrated that set is the important aspect here, not the mere repetition of the figures. They presented figures such as those in the lower portion of Figure 4.29. During training they showed only half of a subsequent test figure (parts E or F of Figure 4.29) and instructed observers to see that part as the figure. Rock and Kremen found no tendency to report the previously experienced half as the figure when composite figures (parts G or H of Figure 4.29) were shown. These results are similar to those of Gottschaldt with the hidden figures: previous experience with the figure parts did not influence or override the subsequent organization of the entire test figure, but specific instructions did.

Cornwell (1963) tested the necessity of providing a specific set. He reduced the ambiguity of the test figures used by Rock and Kremen by shifting either the black or white portion (part D of Figure 4.29) to the side, so that the offset portion was much more likely to be perceived as the figure. When the ambiguous patterns were presented, Cornwell's subjects tended to display the figural persistence noted by Rubin: the portion of the pattern previously experienced as the figure was reported as the figure in the ambiguous patterns. Although Cornwell (1964) failed to replicate his own result, Botha (1963) required subjects to associate the unambiguous halves with nonsense syllables and found that the previously associated half of the ambiguous pattern tended to stand out as the figure.

The conclusion here is similar to the conclusion for organizational tendencies: providing a specific set or context will influence the perception of a subsequent figure. Passive experience alone does not appear to be sufficient to influence the manner in which a complex pattern is organized.

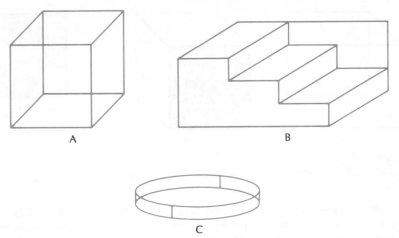

Figure 4.30
Patterns demonstrating orientation reversal. *A*, Necker cube; *B*, Schröder stairs;
C, Ebbecke ring.

Changes in orientation.   Figure 4.30 provides some classic examples of
reversible patterns which orientation changes. In all of these patterns, organization encourages a three-dimensional perception: the portion seemingly
located the farthest away can exchange position with the portion appearing
to be the closest. Study each of the patterns in Figure 4.30 and note the frequency of orientation change. In the example of the Schröder stairs, the second orientation is difficult to obtain, and in the other two it is readily seen.
Almost all such designs have a *preferred orientation* that is seen most of the
time and by most observers.

By far the most research has been conducted with the Necker cube (part
A of Figure 4.30). Cohen (1959) measured the frequency of changes in orientation reported by observers. His data indicate that the number of reversals increases steadily and, after about 60 to 75 seconds of continued viewing, levels
off at a frequency of 12 to 20 reversals a minute. The frequency varies for different observers but tends to remain rather constant for each. On the subject of
the preferred orientation of the Necker cube, most observers see it oriented
as in part B of Figure 4.31. Part C of the same figure shows the alternative
orientation.

Several factors have been identified which influence reversal rate in the
Necker cube. Lynn (1961) varied the *intensity* of a projected Necker cube and
found that the rate of change increased proportionately with increases in intensity. In an experiment analogous to research on the autokinetic phenomenon, Pelton and Solley (1968) requested subjects either to attempt to hold an
orientation of the Necker cube or to allow the figure to reverse at will. They
found a reduction in reversal rate under the hold instructions. It should be
noted that such instructions retarded but did not halt the rate of change.
Even when a subject attempts to hold an orientation, reversals occur fairly
frequently.

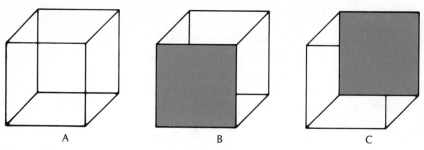

Figure 4.31
Necker cube with both orientations rendered unambiguous.

Perhaps the most widely studied theory of reversals derives from gestalt psychology. Köhler (1940) proposed that the figure-ground reversals described earlier in the chapter arise from a process of *cortical satiation*. He suggested that when an observer views an ambiguous stimulus (e.g., Rubin's face and vase), some central process controls the perception. Continued viewing causes this central process to fatigue or become satiated, and allows a reorganization of the field through a nonsatiated mechanism. While Köhler was not primarily interested in explaining the reversals found in figures such as the Necker cube, others have extended his ideas and developed arguments stressing the importance of the *satiation of orientation*. Orbach, Ehrlich, and Heath (1963) believe the reversals are a result not of the satiation of figure parts but of the satiation of a particular third-dimensional orientation. They required viewers to study a single square (the forward up or down sections of parts B and C in Figure 4.31) and then the cube itself. They interpreted Köhler's theory of the satiation of figural parts to predict an increase in the probability that a reversal would occur when the cube was presented. In other words, they thought that if a subject viewed a square representing the forward down portion of the cube followed by the entire cube superimposed on the square, he should report a reversal of that forward down portion to upward back. The experiment did not produce this result. Cohen (1959) had shown that a general condition of satiation is not responsible for changes in orientation. He required subjects to view a Necker cube for 45 seconds followed by either Rubin's vase or a continuation of the Necker cube. The number of reversals continued to rise for the cube, but fell back to a lower level for the vase. Evidently satiation is limited to a specific figure of a specific orientation.

Orbach, Ehrlich, and Heath (1963) also report the effects of a discontinuous presentation of the cube on reversal rate. In a number of conditions they systematically varied the on-time (presentation duration) and off-time of the cube. Exposure frequency ranged from 42 to 1,200 times a minute. Figure 4.32 shows the reversal of orientation related to the presentation rate. As the frequency increased from 42 times a minute, so did the reversal rate; the latter reached a peak at 105 presentations per minute—almost double the rate for continuous viewing. Further increases in frequency reduced the reversal rate toward the normal condition of continuous viewing. The two

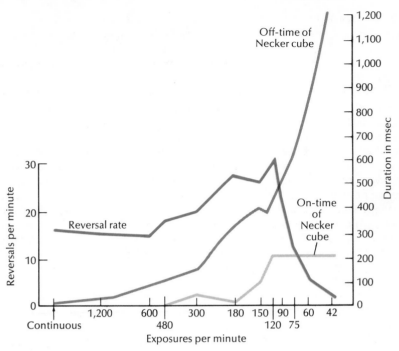

Figure 4.32
Reversal rate as a function of frequency of exposure. (After Orbach, Ehrlich, and Heath, 1963, figure 4. Reproduced by permission of authors and publisher.)

other lines in the figure represent the on-time and the off-time for each frequency; unfortunately, the relationship between these two was not held constant during the experiment. For the lower frequencies the on-time remained constant at 200 msec while the off-time increased steadily. The failure of reversals to occur at the 42-per-minute rate can be interpreted as the failure of the satiation effect to summate over the long interval. In a later paper, in fact, Olson and Orbach (1966) concluded that the satiation effect decays if the interval between successive exposures of the cube exceeds 250 msec.

The data of Figure 4.32 are compatible with an explanation of satiation of orientation in which satiation builds during the presence of the figure and decays during the interstimulus intervals. If the interval is long, the satiation dissipates, but if it is short, some summation occurs during the interval. Such summation is limited to a period of about 250 msec. This temporal boundary was identified earlier as the upper limit of sensory register storage, and it may indicate the working of a common mechanism in both conditions.

Kolers (1964) has reported an experiment that seems to support the satiation of orientation theory. In one portion of the study the rate of reversal for a cube flashing 160 times a minute was compared to the rate under continuous viewing; Kolers found an increased reversal rate similar to that of Orbach et al. He also asked observers to indicate the reversal frequency of a cube in physical motion. He reasoned that a moving cube should reduce the possibility of a satiation of the figural parts (Köhler's theory) but still have no influence on the satiation of orientation. In fact, the experimental results showed an increased reversal rate for the moving cube, thus contradicting Köhler's theory.

Several versions of a second theory of reversals of orientation have been developed, all of which emphasize *attention* as the major variable. In general, they hold that, given a stimulus with several possible organizations, variations in perception will occur as the observer's attention wavers. To account for this wavering, some theorists point to the conscious search for new dimensions of perceptual experience; others believe such variations of attention are mediated at unconscious levels. Attention would seem to have some influence on the perception of reversible figures, as indicated by the results of some of the studies mentioned above. The tendency for instructions to affect the rate of reversal would probably depend on attention mechanisms rather than a central satiation process. In addition, Kolers's finding—that a moving cube has a greater effect on reversal rate than a stationary cube—can be interpreted as the result of attention. The moving cube would hold the observer's attention and cause him to study the figure in more detail.

Confronted by various psychological phenomena, scientific investigators have developed many theories in the attempt to isolate single variables responsible for particular observations. In the case of reversible figures, neither satiation nor attention can handle all observations. However, a theory combining the two—acknowledging a satiation mechanism plus variation in the observer's attention—would seem to do well with the data.

In a rather clever study, Olson and Orbach (1966) applied the earlier observation of the effect of presentation rate on reversal frequency to an analysis of the aspects of the cube causing reversal. In a test applying the data shown in Figure 4.32, subjects viewed the Necker cube for presentation rates of 300 msec on and 250 msec off (109 exposures per minute) and for 300 msec on and 1,000 msec off (46 exposures per minute). For the 109 exposures per minute, Figure 4.32 predicts a reversal rate much greater than under continuous viewing; the 46 exposures per minute, in contrast, should yield a reversal rate close to zero. During the off intervals, Olson and Orbach presented to each group a number of figures representing different aspects of the cube. For the condition of 109 exposures, they reasoned that if the reversal rate stayed at a high level, the interpolated figure would be demonstrating no effect on that rate—the effect would be the same as no figure at all. On the other hand, if the rate decreased to a value similar to continued viewing, the interpolated figure would be equal to the cube itself—the effect would be the same as that of continued viewing of the cube. For the condition of 46 exposures, an increase in reversal rate from 0 to 12 to 18 reversals per minute would indicate that the interpolated figure produced the same effect as continuous viewing of the cube. Figure 4.33 gives the results of this testing. The numbers beside each figure indicate reversal rates for the conditions of 109 and 46 exposures when that figure was interpolated during the off interval. On the basis of this data, a number of factors influencing reversal

	Group I			Group II			Group III		
	Exposure rate			Exposure rate			Exposure rate		
Figure	109	46		109	46		109	46	
1	39.5	0.0	Blank	41.0	0.0	Blank	42.0	2.0	Blank
2	14.5	12.5		17.0	12.0		15.0	9.0	
3	13.5	10.5		13.0	13.0		16.0	8.0	
4	34.5	6.0		15.0	4.0		16.0	5.0	
5	29.0	2.5		27.0	11.0		29.0	5.0	
6	38.5	2.0		22.0	10.0		38.0	1.0	
7	29.5	6.0							

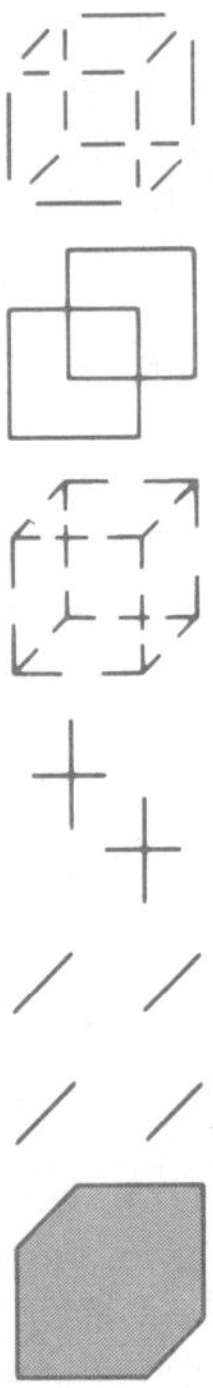

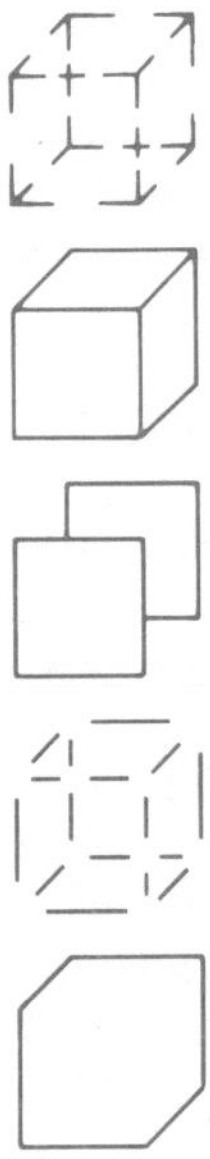

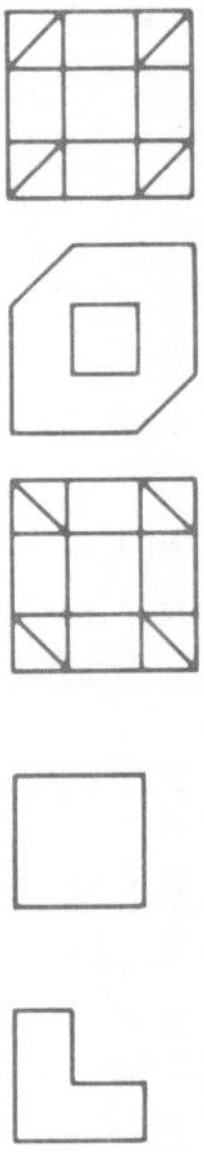

Reversals per minute

Figure 4.33
Influence of interpolated figures on reversal rate. (After Olsen and Orbach, 1966, figure 1 and table 2. Reproduced by permission of authors and publisher.)

rate can be identified. For groups 1 and 3 one can say generally that if the inter-polated figure can be seen in three dimensions with two orientations, the stimulus is an effective substitute for the cube. Limits to this generalization are imposed, obviously, by the figure's degree of completion. Although Figure 4 in group 1 was ineffective, the same figure with an extension of its lines (Figure 2 for group 2) proved to be an effective substitute for the cube. The embedded figures of group 3 also proved effective, even though these figures are not readily perceived in three dimensions. Perhaps their complexity produced an alteration in attention and hence a change in reversal rate. Note that for some figures the influence was not the same for both conditions of frequency. Perhaps this result is due to variations in the amount of attention devoted to the interpolated figures.

Auditory reversible figures.   Gregory and Warren (1958) have considered the possibility that certain auditory patterns may also be reversible. They found a number of words that, when presented singly, tended to exhibit a reversal effect. The best example was the word "say": when spoken aloud it seems to change to "ace" and back to "say." Drawing out such a word produces a number of reversals (e.g., *saaaaaay*), as does rapid repetition of the word. Any single word spoken repetitively changes so that it sounds different, often to the point that it loses all connection with the original word. This can be called satiation of meaning. Repeat any two-syllable word thirty to forty times and listen carefully. Sometimes the effect can be rather disturbing.

The Organization of Auditory Perception

In this section we will consider some of the specific characteristics of auditory perception. In turn the discussion will center on the perception of *pitch, loudness, tonal quality,* and *auditory patterns.*

Pitch perception.   In Chapter 1 it was noted that the stimulus for hearing—the sound wave—is defined by two salient variables, frequency and amplitude. While these two variables may be utilized to define a distal stimulus, they cannot be applied directly to the definition of a proximal stimulus. When the frequency of a sound wave is varied, the listener experiences changes in *pitch*, whereas changes in the amplitude of a sound wave produce perceived variations in *loudness.*

The relationship between the frequency of a sound wave and the perceived pitch of the sound is not linear. For this reason it was necessary to develop a subjective scale of pitch. Early work on this problem was conducted by Stevens, Volkmann, and Newman (1937). Using the method of fractionation they established a scale of pitch as a function of frequency known as the *mel scale.* Their method was essentially the same as that used to develop the *sone scale* of loudness, which was discussed in Chapter 1. For tones below 1,000 Hz, as the frequency of the tone increases, there is a disproportionate increase in the perceived pitch. From 1,000 to 4,000 Hz, the range of maximum sensitivity for human observers, the mel scale is linear. That is, each increase in the frequency of the tone is accompanied by an equal increase in the perceived pitch. For frequencies above 4,000 Hz a disproportionate change in pitch is again found. In 1965, after a careful consideration of the sound-absorbing characteristics of Stevens's laboratory, Siegal remeasured the mel scale. The material on the walls of Stevens's test room was rockwool, which has been found to have a greater absorbency for higher tones. Furthermore, Siegal noted that the observers in the study (Volkmann and Newman) were over 25 years of age. The hearing of individuals above 25 shows a reduction in pitch sensitivity at higher frequencies (Licklider, 1951). Figure 4.34 shows the mel scale obtained by

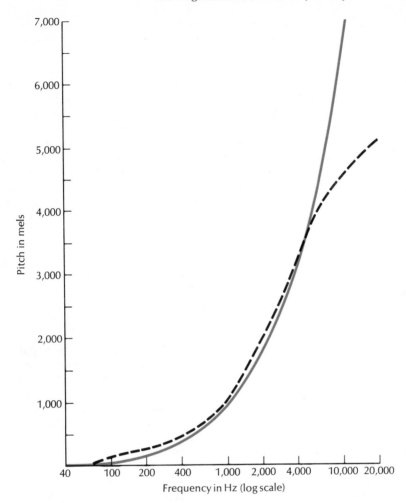

Figure 4.34
Mel scales of pitch. *Dotted line,* as measured by Stevens, Volkmann, and Newman (1937). *Solid line,* as measured by Siegal (1965).

Siegal when the factors of observer age and test room conditions were controlled. Also included in the figure is the data from Stevens, Volkmann, and Newman (1937). A comparison of Siegal's curve with the sone scale shown in Figure 1.14 indicates that their forms are basically the same.

The human ear is sensitive to sounds over the range of 16 to 22,500 Hz, although different individuals show a great deal of variation in sensitivity (Révész, 1946). By far the majority of sounds we encounter in everyday life display frequencies from the lower portion of the sound spectrum. In music, for example, the tones range from 65 to about 4,000 Hz. Figure 4.35 shows the internationally accepted definition of tones that a piano should produce as a function of frequency. This definition of tones is designed to take into account the abilities of observers to distinguish pitch as observed by Siegal (1965).

Pitch and intensity.   Pitch varies not only with frequency but also with intensity. If a tuning fork is sounded and moved closer to the ear, a change in pitch occurs. Depending on the original pitch of the tone, changes in tonal intensity will produce increases or decreases in perceived pitch. If the tone is above 3,000 mels, pitch increases as does the sound intensity. A tone below 1,000 mels decreases in pitch as intensity increases. In the range of 1,000 to 3,000 mels, pitch and intensity display little divergence. Unfortunately, many musical tones are lower in pitch than 1,000 mels and therefore increase in pitch as intensity decreases. Heard from the stands, the band on the football field frequently sounds rather out of tune. As the intensity of the component tones decreases over distance, so does their pitch. The result can often be a discordant sound.

Pitch and duration.   The relationship between duration and pitch is quite similar to that between pitch and intensity. The pitch of a very short tone is usually undistinguishable, and is perceived only as a click. However, if a tone is above a minimum duration, the listener will be able to distinguish its pitch. Bürck, Kotowski, and Lichte (1935) attempted to establish the limits of duration below which pitch could no longer be identified. Generally, they found that longer durations were required for the identification of lower frequency tones. Over the range of 1,000 to 4,000 Hz a tone needed a duration of only 10 msec in order to be assigned a pitch. Pollack (1968) required musically trained observers to adjust a matching tone to the apparent pitch of a short tone burst. As the duration of the low-frequency tones was shortened, pitch apparently increased; reducing the duration of high-frequency tones brought reports of a decrease in pitch. Once again the influence of duration was minimal for the range of 1,000 to 4,000 Hz (1,000–3,000 mels).

Pitch and complex tones.   Until now we have considered only pure tones; more frequently, however, the ear is presented with a number of tones simultaneously. Such complex sounds, as explained in Chapter 1, contain a fundamental tone (after which the tone is named) and a number of partial tones or overtones. Everyday experience shows that a number of different tones can be processed simultaneously. That is, we are able to hear out the separate components of a complex tone. Helmholtz (1863) discussed this ability and developed what he designated as *Ohm's acoustical law* (in honor of the German physicist G. S. Ohm). The law predicts the minimum frequencies that must separate component tones before they can be individually distinguished.

Stumpf (1890) studied the ability to hear out partial tones and came to the conclusion that the lower overtones (second and third) were harder to perceive than the harmonics of higher order. For some tones Stumpf reported he could hear out overtones as high as the twenty-seventh partial. More recently Plomp (1964) has systematically studied this ability in observers with normal hearing. He has established critical frequency separations for most of the sound spec-

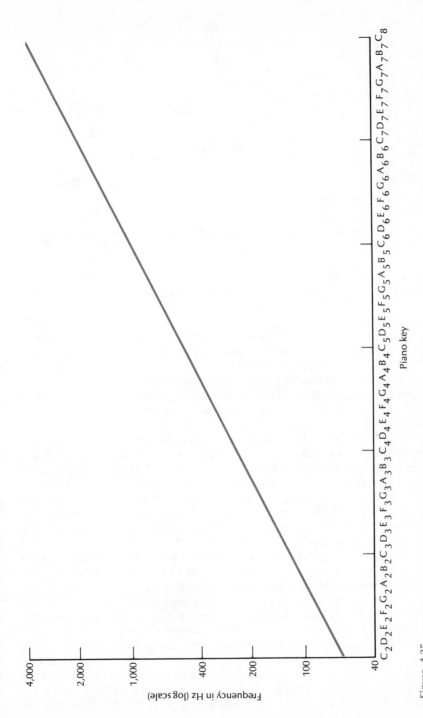

Figure 4.35
Frequencies of piano tones. (After Mörner, 1963.)

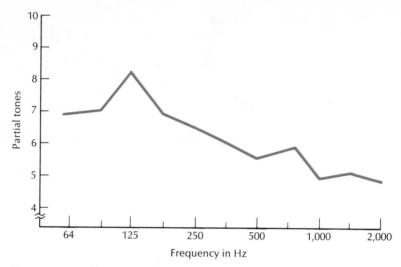

Figure 4.36
Number of partial tones reported with 75-percent accuracy as a function of tone frequency. (After Plomp, 1964.)

trum. Studying the capacity of a listener to hear partial tones, Plomp found marked differences in the number of partials heard as a function of the frequency of the lowest partial tone. Plomp's results as shown in Figure 4.36 are in marked contrast to Stumpf's early observations. Figure 4.37 provides a representative example in which observers selected the partials from a fundamental tone of 250 Hz. Performance remains perfect up to the fourth overtone, but drops to chance by the tenth.

The role of the fundamental tone in defining a complex sound was demonstrated by several experiments conducted by Fletcher (1934). Given a complex sound composed of tones of 500, 700, and 900 Hz, observers reported the fundamental tone equal to a pitch of 200 Hz. The fundamental was defined not by the average of the combined tones (700 Hz in this instance), but by the average difference (200 Hz) between the combined tones. If tones of 600, 800, and 1,000 Hz were added to the combination listed above, the resulting fundamental would drop from 200 to 100 Hz.

Finally, mention must be made of *absolute pitch*, the ability of a trained observer to name or sing a tone accurately without the aid of a reference tone. Bachem (1950) found that this ability depended on the frequency of the tone and on *tone chroma*. The latter was assumed to arise from the distinct combinations of overtone characteristics of a given sound. Korpell (1965) attempted to assess chroma and to observe whether it in fact arose from combinations of overtones. He re-recorded musical notes and played them back to subjects with extensive musical training at speeds slightly above or below that of the original recording. Korpell reasoned that if chroma stems from overtone combinations, matches to the re-recorded tones should produce the same fundamental, since the relationship among overtones would remain un-

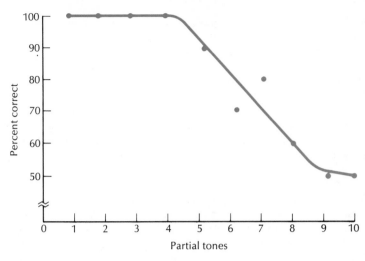

Figure 4.37
Percentage of partial tones reported correctly for a 250-Hz tone. (After Plomp, 1964.)

changed. However, if chroma depends on some transposition within the auditory system, subjects would match the tones to the new frequency produced by speeding up or slowing down the original note. The majority of musically trained observers adjusted the matching note to the new frequency. Tone chroma, then, must involve more than the characteristics of overtones. For example, when we note that a phonograph record is playing too slowly, we do so because of our knowledge of the proper key and tempo of the song and not because of our identification of a change in absolute pitch.

Loudness.   In Chapter 1 we discussed a scale for loudness, the sone scale, as an example of the application of Stevens's power function. Subsequent replications by Stevens himself (1955, 1956) as well as by many others (see Ekman and Sjoberg, 1965, for a review) have firmly established the validity of the function. In fact, Schumacher and Klingensmith (1968) have recently suggested that the power law for loudness is one of the most accepted laws in psychology.

Loudness and frequency.   The perceived loudness of a tone depends on its frequency and its amplitude. In terms of the threshold intensity at which a tone of a given frequency is reported 50 percent of the time, Fletcher (1940) found that a tone of 46 decibels was required for a frequency of 100 Hz, while a tone of 1 decibel was reported on half the trials at 1,000 Hz. Since the decibel scale was derived originally with a reference frequency of 1,000 Hz, the threshold value at 1,000 Hz by definition should be close to 0 decibels. Later research, however, found the point of maximum sensitivity for intensity to lie above 1,000 Hz and within the range of 1,000 to 4,000 Hz. While the resulting negative decibel values for the perception of tones in the maximum range is mathematically sound, it is rather confusing to define the perceived loudness of a tone as less than zero.

The changes in perceived loudness as a function of frequency in matching experiments show a U-shaped function similar to those obtained in visual threshold studies. The curves in Figure 4.38 show some examples of perceived loudness in relation to intensity (in decibels) for a number of representative frequencies. They indicate that perceived loudness depends not only on intensity but also on frequency. If increases in perceived loudness were independent of frequency, then one would expect a single line rather than the observed curves.

Loudness and duration.   A tone must sound for a minimum duration in order for its loudness to be estimated. Above this minimum, as the duration decreases the estimated loudness decreases (Békésy, 1933). Phenomenal loudness also changes if observers are required to listen to tones over long durations. Mirabella, Taub, and Teichner (1967) asked subjects to constantly adjust the loudness of a tone presented over a period of several minutes. For high-intensity tones, subjects steadily increased the intensity as the time increased, in order to maintain the same subjective loudness. For low-intensity tones, the reverse relationship was found: as time continued, the perceived loudness of the tone increased.

Loudness summation.   When presented together, two tones of different frequencies seem to be louder than either tone alone. Because of the relationship discussed previously between fundamental and complex tones in pitch perception, it is perhaps not particularly surprising to find that the perceived loudness of complex tones equals neither the sum of the combined tones nor their average. Stevens (1956a) noted that the degree of summation depends on the intensities of the combined tones as well as the frequency separation between individual tones. Again, the notion of a minimum frequency separation is relevant in this context. It can be defined as the frequency spread between combined tones necessary to produce loudness summation. Once it is reached, the degree of summation increases very rapidly. The loudest complex sounds occur when the component tones are equally loud (Scharf, 1962) and when all individual tones are separated by an equal number of critical bandwidths (Zwicker, Flottorp, and Stevens, 1957).

Tonal quality.   Several other attributes of sounds have been identified in addition to loudness, pitch, and complexity. Those attributes that refer to the qualitative aspects of sounds are grouped under the heading of *tonal qualities*. Their actual number is open to question, but at least three of them are important enough to be discussed separately.

Timbre.   Two sound sources may be perceived as dissimilar even though they are equal in loudness and pitch; each is said to have a different *timbre*. If a piano and a clarinet both play a middle C with the same loudness, the resulting tone sounds different for each instrument. The physical basis of timbre seems to lie in the presence and strength of partial tones (harmonics) produced

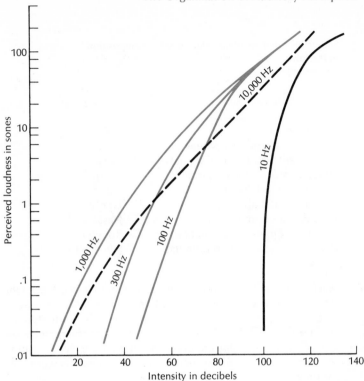

Figure 4.38
Perceived loudness of tones of various frequencies as a function of physical intensity. (After von Fieandt, 1966.)

along with the specific pitch. For middle C on the piano the first partial is most prominent. On the clarinet, however, the third partial is the most promi-nent. Helmholtz (1863) suggested that the physical characteristics of tones produced by different instruments are identifiable as timbre. He went on to attribute the subjective qualities of tones to the specific relationships among harmonics present in a tone. His observations are presented in Table 4.3.

Helmholtz's theory of harmonics has been modified to include the influ-ence of the relative location of the partials along the frequency continuum. His theory, called the *harmonic-structure theory,* has been challenged by a second conception of timbre, described by Bartholomew (1945), called the *formant theory.* It ascribes timbre to the relative strengthening of whichever partial lies within the fixed formant (region) of the musical scale. Those partials nearest the formant of a tone are strengthened. This strengthening is due to the resonant characteristics of some part of the instrument and hence is related to specific instruments.

Clear support has not been developed for either theory. In fact, the capa-bility of individuals to distingush among instruments that are not physically present is questionable. Saldanha and Corso (1964) prepared tape recordings of ten different instruments each briefly playing the notes C_4, F_4, and A_4. (See

Table 4.3

Subjective tonal quality in relation to the composition
of the tone
(Helmholtz, 1863)

Composition of tone	Tonal quality
Fundamental alone	Soft
Fundamental and first partial	Mellow
Fundamental and several partials	Broad
Fundamental plus high partials	Sharp
Dominant fundamental	Full
Dominant partials	Empty
Odd partials dominating	Nasal
Discordant partials dominating	Rough or hard
High discordant partials dominating	Screeching

Figure 4.35.) Each note was also recorded with and without a *frequency vibrato.*
The tape of these notes was played for twenty musicians who were asked to
identify the instruments producing the tones. Some were easily identified (e.g.,
clarinet, oboe, and flute) while others were frequently confused (e.g., violin,
cello, and bassoon). The musicians did better when the note was F_4 than when
it was C_4 or A_4. Over all trials only 40 percent of the judgments were correct;
however, performance did improve with practice.

Saldanha and Corso also analyzed the tonal patterns produced by each
instrument but failed to find a specific factor influencing the ease or difficulty with which an instrument producing a tone could be identified. Obviously the psychological characteristics of timbre are not yet fully understood.

Volume.   Subjectively, some tones or sounds seem bigger or larger than
others. The same note played on an organ and on a flute differs not only in
timbre but also in the dynamics of the sound. The organ note seems able to
fill the room or to occupy more space than the same note on a flute. This
aspect of a tone is referred to as *volume.* While volume has received little empirical study—perhaps because of the difficulty in describing this aspect of
sound—Stevens (1934) attempted to measure this characteristic. Subjects were
required to match the volume of tones of different pitch. With practice, subjects could produce equal matches of volume that were independent of pitch,
timbre, and loudness. As the loudness and pitch of the test tones increased,
subjects were able to hold volume constant.

Density.   Stevens (1934) studied a third attribute—the impression that
some tones are more compressed, concentrated, or *dense* than others. In
his experiment Stevens asked observers to make pairs of tones of different
frequency sound equal in apparent density by adjusting the sound-pressure

level of one tone of the pair. They were able to match such tonal densities. That the dominant physical variable related to density is the sound-pressure level has been supported by the recent work of Guirao and Stevens (1964). They found that direct magnitude estimations of density increase as a power function of sound pressure. Although the physical attribute underlying volume is somewhat uncertain, it can be distinguished from density on the basis of the fact that the relation to loudness and pitch is reversed. An increase in pitch must be accompanied by a decrease in loudness in order for density to be held constant.

Auditory Patterns.   Individual sounds can be assigned a frequency, a loudness, a duration. However, we are seldom confronted with simple sounds such as those produced in the laboratory. Typically one hears numerous sounds of changing pitch and loudness. Some sounds of similar structure mask and swallow others, while sounds of differing structure seem to exist simultaneously. In ways analogous to visual patterns, sounds are organized into meaningful patterns and are subject to figure-ground segregation. On entering a room full of people conversing in groups, you are aware of a general level of noise, but you do not pick up more than individual words if you are yourself engaged in a conversation. Let someone in a neighboring group mention your name, however, and this stimulus becomes a figure that stands out against the background of conversation.

Organization on the basis of similarity is obvious in music, where specific tonal relationships in the different musical scales provide groups. A tone not belonging to a particular scale stands out immediately. Also, sounds displaying temporal proximity are perceived to belong together. Such organization is usually referred to as *rhythm*. Fraisse (1966) has studied how varying the duration between successive beats affects auditory organization. His subjects reported an impression of rhythm or togetherness for successive patterns of notes when the temporal interval between beats did not exceed two seconds.

Recent work analyzing the complex patterns of sound produced by objects in the environment has utilized the *spectograph* to measure the components of these sounds. Each sound produces a characteristic spectogram and each can be imitated by reproducing the same combination of frequencies and intensities. This is also true of human speech, in which each noise displays a characteristic structure, despite variations among individual speakers.

Speech Perception

The complex sounds produced by and responded to by other humans provide one of man's richest sources of perceptual interaction. Most voices display a *middle tone,* which is defined as the middle of the speaking range of tones, somewhere between 65 and 1,044 Hz. Naturally the human voice varies among individuals in average loudness as well as in timbre, density, and volume.

The complexity of human speech is underscored by the difficulty in finding a basic unit of speech (Chananie and Tikofsky, 1968). In some approaches the variety of sounds produced has been calibrated in terms of the flexibility of the vocal apparatus itself. Speech sounds are classified on the basis of the part of the vocal apparatus primarily responsible for the sound. In the psychology of speech perception and linguistics, however, the types of sounds produced are usually defined on the basis of *phones*. The *phoneme*, in this classification, represents the smallest unit by which one utterance can be distinguished from another. In English, phonemes and letters are not the same: we pronounce certain letters differently in different words, such as the *o* in *boy* and *cow*. Also, English words frequently include letters that serve to differentiate in the written but not in the spoken language; examples are *here* and *hear*. While phonemes distinguish one utterance from another, *allophones* are the nondistinguishing applications of sounds in speech. For example, the *k* of *keep* and *cool* does not distinguish between the words and is therefore an allophone.

Using the spectrograph it is now possible to classify the sounds of a spoken language into distinctive units. Phonemes are broken down into vowels and consonants on the basis of the manner in which the sound is produced. Gleason (1961) identified twenty-one consonant phonemes and twelve vowel phonemes. A further subdivision on the basis of distinctive features of each phoneme has been carried out by Jakobson and Halle (1956). They divided phonemes into twelve categories on the basis of the characteristics of the distinctive features. For example, a phoneme may be voiced or voiceless (indicating the presence of a recurring low-frequency excitation), strident or mellow (the presence of more high-intensity noise or low-intensity noise, etc.). Work with the spectrograph has also pointed out the importance of temporal relationships in distinguishing sounds and demonstrated how variations in the intensity of sounds impart emotional connotations of words.

The problems of understanding speech perception are further complicated by the fact that the intelligibility of a word varies as a function of context. Pollack and Pickett (1964) played individual words from fluent streams of speech and observed the degree of intelligibility of the words for adult subjects. The larger the number of meaningfully connected words, the greater the intelligibility of each successive word. As in the case of patterns in vision, total perception depends on the context of presentation.

The identification of distinctive features in speech has received a great deal of empirical attention. Miller and Nicely (1955) developed a classification of distinctive characteristics with which to identify syllables embedded in noise. Most studies have indicated that the number of identification errors is a function of the distinctive features of the phonemes combined into syllables. Chananie and Tikofsky (1969) have also demonstrated that reaction time provides an accurate measure of the distinctive characteristics of phonemes. They measured the length of time required for listeners to judge whether a test phoneme differed from a preceding stimulus phoneme. They next compared the degree of difference to the response accuracy measures obtained by Miller and Nicely (1955). They found that subjects required longer to respond to same constants than to different constants. This finding is important in that it indicates the possibility of systematically varying the distinctive features of phonemes and measuring the speed of reaction. If observers showed longer reaction times it would indicate that the features tested did not distinguish between sounds. More rapid reactions would isolate the feature of the phoneme tested as an important characteristic in speech discrimination.

The complexities of speech have also been approached through the ontogenetic method. As is frequently the case with developmental studies of perception, the results are neither clear nor decisive. In a series of experiments Irwin and Chen (Irwin and Chen, 1946; Chen and Irwin, 1946; Irwin, 1947) studied the speech development of ninety-four infants from birth to the age of 30 months. They found that in early life vowels are uttered about five times more frequently than consonants. By 30 months the child utilizes almost all of the vowels found in adult speech and about 66 percent of the consonants. Soon after 30 months the child's speech sounds approach the pattern of adults. Using older children, Templin (1952) found that the number of correct articulations for vowels remained at about 90 percent over the span of years from 3 to 7. Consonant articulation improved from 67 percent to about 90 percent at age 7. Sex differences in speech development were also observed in the above study; girls reached a 95-percent level of correct articulation by age 7, while boys required an additional year before arriving at the same percent level. The ability to discriminate consonants has been shown to reach adult capabilities by age 7. Tikofsky and McInish (1968) asked children to make same or different judgments of test consonants following same or different stimulus consonants. The degree of difference was measured on the basis of a distinctive feature analysis. Only 2 percent of the responses were in error, and the few errors made were mostly for consonants differentiated by a single distinctive feature.

Although a number of theories of speech perception have been advanced, each fails to cover all aspects of the complex process. This is hardly surprising in light of the task imposed by the empirical observations of speech development. Since all persons do not articulate each phoneme in the same manner, for any given phoneme the listener must decide which of the known phonemes the specific stimulus is most like. Furthermore, this must be done at a fantastic speed. The studies of development mentioned above indicate that these abilities are learned over a large number of years. However, one never ceases to be amazed at the first articulate speech productions of the young child and the rapidity with which sentence and word combinations develop. The speed with which grammatical relationships and vocabulary develop indicate that the human capacity for learning is remarkable.

CHAPTER 5
The Perception of Spatial Relations

The correct perception of spatial relations provides man with information about his own position in the physical world. Due to long years of experience our responses to the three dimensions of the real world seem very natural. With little difficulty we are able to judge the distances of objects and to indicate which way is up. Nevertheless, a great deal of research has been directed at assessing the manner in which such seemingly simple orientations are possible.

The Perception of Vertical and Horizontal

Since the external world is fairly stable, we are usually able to judge the position of an object in space relative to the horizon. This frame of reference provides a definition of horizontal; lines perpendicular to the horizon are defined as vertical. A second indicator is provided by the position of the body in space. Man can judge the position of objects relative to his own upright position. Since he is able to maintain that position even in the absence of visual cues, it can be assumed that the earth's gravity is a major influence on the perception of the vertical.

The importance of each of these indicators can be measured in two ways: either tilt the visual world, or tilt the observer, and study the resulting perceptions of verticality. In normal orientation both of these indicators could be expected to influence the perception of the upright. For a number of years, however, experiments were conducted in the hope of demonstrating that either the frame of reference provided by the visual field or the position of the body provided by gravity was the primary source of spatial orientation. In the following sections we will consider these two groups of experiments involving body tilt and tilted environment.

Body tilt. As early as 1886 Aubert had become interested in the effect of body tilt on the perceived upright. In an environment providing few vertical and horizontal cues, he tilted the heads of observers and recorded their observations of an upright visual target. Generally, Aubert found the subjects tended to perceive the upright target displaced a few degrees away from the true vertical. More recent work has shown this tendency to be rather complex. Bauermeister (1964) tilted 100 subjects from 90° to the left through upright to 90° to the right, while asking them to adjust a luminescent rod in an otherwise darkened room to either true vertical or to their own apparent body position in space. Bauermeister found that with a body tilt of 10° or less, subjects tended to align the rod about 2° away from the true vertical; the error was usually in the direction of body tilt. Furthermore, increasing the body tilt to between 40° and 50° reversed the effect: subjects aligned the rod several degrees away from true vertical. Another reversal occurred when body tilt was increased toward 90°. As the amount of tilt increased, subjects adjusted the rod in the direction of body tilt. With a tilt of 90°, the apparent vertical was displaced more than 15° away from true vertical. When subjects attempted to adjust the rod to the position of their bodies, similar results were obtained. For body tilts under 20° they displaced the rod about 5° farther than the bodies were tilted. Up to 50° the effect reversed, with a tendency to adjust the rod away from the body tilt. Finally, Bauermeister found a tendency to overestimate with body tilts approaching 90°.

Another approach to body tilt has been utilized by C. W. Mann and his associates. They seated subjects in a motor-driven chair, tilted the chair, and required them to return it to true vertical. In one such experiment Mann and Dauterive (1949) found that if the degree of tilt was rather small, subjects experienced great difficulty in finding true vertical. Forcing the subjects to remain tilted for several seconds (Mann and Berry, 1949) produced a marked increase in the degree of error away from true vertical.

Wapner and Werner (1957) have applied an ontogenetic approach to the study of perception of verticality. Their early research showed that young subjects (those below 15 years of age) tend to perceive the apparent vertical—as estimated by adjusting a luminescent rod in an otherwise darkened environment—located toward the side to which the body is tilted. For subjects between 16 and 50 years of age the opposite effect is found: apparent vertical is located several degrees away from body tilt. Finally, for the oldest age group (65 to 80) the apparent vertical was again located in the direction of body tilt. Wapner (1968) has found that the point of the first reversal occurs earlier for boys (13 to 15) than for girls (15 to 17).

Tilted environment.   Of primary importance in studying the influence of a tilted environment on the perception of the vertical is an observer's ability actually to perceive a tilt. A simple way to test this ability is to ask an observer to judge the verticality of a luminescent rod in an otherwise darkened room. Gibson (1933) performed such a study and found a tendency for subjects to report the degree of tilt to diminish after periods of prolonged viewing. Once this adaptation occurred, subjects judged a line oriented to true vertical to be tipped away from true vertical in the direction opposite the original line. Such results would indicate that the subjects were assimilating the tilted line as the indicator of vertical, and misjudging a subsequent physically vertical line due to its deviation from the new frame of reference.

Evidently subjects are not equipped to make completely objective observations of true vertical. In the study by Bauermeister (1964) previously mentioned, subjects sitting in an upright position judged the degree of tilt of a luminescent rod, and almost all adjusted the rod slightly to the left of true vertical. Earlier work by Werner and Wapner (1952) had uncovered such systematic deviations in the perception of verticality. Subjects tended to *undershoot* in adjusting the luminescent rod. That is, if the rod was initially located 30° to the left, subjects would adjust the rod several degrees short of vertical and still toward the left. Starting with the rod tilted to the right, subjects undershot and located the apparent vertical position several degrees to the right of true vertical. When a study by Weintraub, O'Connell, and McHale (1964) failed to confirm the existence of such systematic deviations, a later experiment by O'Connell, Lathrop, Weintraub, and McHale (1967) attempted to isolate the reason for the discrepancy. They researched the influences of handedness, starting position of the rod (amount of turn required to reach vertical as well as direction turned), and the sex of the subject. Although gender proved to be unimportant, the choice of hand used to adjust the rod significantly influenced its positioning. Settings with the left hand tended to be located a few degrees to the right. Similarly, while the amount of turn required to reach apparent vertical had no effect, the direction of turn did. Turning the rod from right to left produced more errors than from left to right. The overall average of the various conditions showed the point of subjective verticality to be located about 1° to the right. Generally, results such as those obtained by O'Connell and his co-workers seem to indicate that the observed asymmetry in adjusting a luminescent rod depends on the method employed in testing. In the study under discussion another important variable was whether the observers were allowed to make small corrections after bringing the rod toward verticality. Such corrections provided rather exact estimates of the true vertical, with an average deviation of only 0.02° to the left.

An experiment by Wertheimer (1912) yielded an important observation concerning the influence of the position of the environment on perceived vertical. Naïve observers looked through a tube toward a tilted mirror that reflected a room in Wertheimer's laboratory, but they were not informed of the mirror's presence. Almost all the observers reported perceiving a tilted room that contained disfigured or disoriented objects. However, after a period of prolonged viewing, a righting occurred, and the room no longer appeared tilted. Asch and Witkin (1948a) carried the experiment further by requiring subjects to indicate when a rod located on a table in the reflected room was vertical. Despite a variety of conditions in which subjects were sometimes informed of the presence of the mirror and sometimes not, most subjects aligned the rod with the walls of the room reflected in the mirror, rather than in line with the true vertical defined by gravity. Asch and Witkin noted great differences among observers performing this particular task. Although most aligned the rod to the vertical defined by the tilted mirror, some aligned it relative to gravity. To a few observers the room did not appear tilted; a larger number reported the degree of tilt to disappear after the scene was viewed for some time. This result, of course, is in accord with Wertheimer's report.

The fact that a subject initially sets the rod to the vertical defined by the tilted room presents a difficult problem, since it indicates that he assumes the tilted room to represent the real world. His response to the task is to align the rod in the context of the room, rather than on the basis of some other factor, such as his own body position. Much debate has occurred concerning this point, primarily on the question of whether or not the subject must see the rod as vertical because of the tilted room. On the one hand, it is as if the room were no longer perceived as tilted; on the other hand, observers frequently report the room to appear tilted and still adjust the rod in line with the room. Further consideration indicates no need to assume that the room exerts a righting effect. Rather, the observer's response—defining the vertical in the context of the tilted room—is the most reasonable solution to the experimental problem. As Rock (1966) points out, if the subject aligns the rod to the gravitational vertical of his body, then the rod looks wrong in the mirror. If he aligns it with the vertical of the room, it looks correct, but the subject still knows that the room is tilted. The latter response would seem the best. If this is true, then one should be able to demonstrate that the subject does indeed perceive the room as tilted. Rock reports preliminary data in which subjects adjusted a rod to match the orientation of the room after the tilted room was no longer present. Subjects tended to adjust the rod in agreement with the tilt the walls of the room had as seen previously.

Another method for producing a tilted frame of reference was introduced

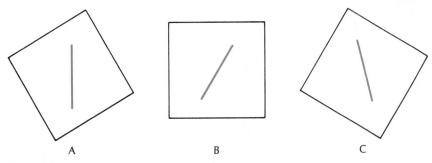

Figure 5.1
Starting positions for the rod-and-frame test.

by Witkin and Asch (1948), who used a device known as the *rod-and-frame test.* Each of their subjects sat in an upright position with the head held immobile and viewed a large luminous square containing a straight line in the center. The experimenters would turn the square, the line, or both to any desired degree of tilt. Figure 5.1 shows the three possibilities under their control: A, to leave the rod vertical and tilt the square or frame; B, to leave the frame vertical and tilt the rod; or C, to tilt both frame and rod. Once the rod and frame were positioned by the experimenter, the subject was asked to set the rod to vertical. When presented with the starting position shown in part C of Figure 5.1, many subjects adjusted the rod close to true vertical; their adjustments were only slightly influenced by the surrounding frame. Some subjects, however, consistently adjusted the rod to align with the frame. Witkin (1959) describes subjects who tend to rely on the visual cues afforded by the frame as *field-dependent observers;* those who tend to utilize gravity and to adjust the rod to the true gravitational vertical he calls *field-independent observers.*

The tendency to display either field dependence or field independence seems to relate to the sex and age of the observer. Witkin (1959) reports data obtained by administering the rod-and-frame test to male and female subjects between the ages of 8 and 21. In the experiment the frame was always tilted a constant 28° and the observers were asked to adjust ·the movable rod to true vertical. Figure 5.2 presents Witkin's data for male and female subjects at each age level. Witkin found that younger subjects were field dependent, since they tended to adjust the rod close to the 28° tilt of the frame; older subjects came closer to the true vertical (0° tilt). Although he noticed a general trend toward field independence with increasing age, he also reported that female subjects at the higher age levels displayed a tendency toward field dependence. In summary, the degree of field dependence decreases with increasing age; for adult women, however, a tendency toward increased field dependence is noticeable.

Rock (1964) introduced a technique designed to reduce the assumed influence of gravity on the positioning of the rod within the frame. Subjects lay on their backs and viewed a rod-and-frame apparatus suspended horizontally above them. The frame was tilted either 15° to the right of the body midline or 30° to the left. Subjects were instructed to adjust the rod to the *egocentric*

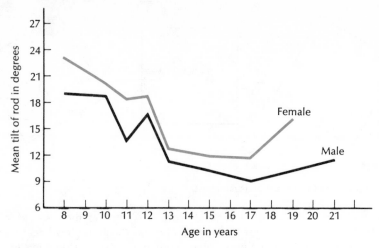

Figure 5.2

Degrees of field dependence as a function of age for male and female subjects. (After Witkin, 1959. Copyright 1959 by Scientific American, Inc. All rights reserved.)

vertical—that is, to align the rod with their body midline. Rock found that the egocentric vertical was clearly influenced by the frame. When the frame was located 15° to the right, subjects adjusted the rod an average 7.5° to the right; with a 30° tilt to the left, they adjusted the rod an average 10.3° to the left. According to these observations, the role of gravity in the orientation of two-dimensional space is open to question. It would appear that gravity itself is not important, but rather that the position of the rod on the retina relative to the vertical defined by the midline of the body is the defining factor. Gravity plays a role only when it is utilized to define true vertical by an observer who is in an upright position. Rock himself (1966) has pointed out a major difficulty with this explanation: if the subject is sitting upright and adjusts a rod to the vertical, his performance is better than when he is lying down. Brosgole and Cristal (1967) showed this by measuring the average amount of error subjects experienced in adjusting a rod to a frame while in a sitting or a supine position. The error range was 13.9° for the sitting position, 19.4° for the supine. While this effect was not statistically significant, it does show a decay in performance for the supine condition. Brosgole and Cristal point out that gravity may be only incidentally related to the superiority of judgments made in an upright position. One is much more experienced in making judgments when upright than when supine. If this is the case, then Rock's hypothesis concerning the presence of an egocentric, apparent vertical would remain a likely possibility.

In normal visual experience the orientation of objects is clearly dependent on the field. Thus when one views a vertical object (e.g., a flagpole) and tilts the head several degrees, the object still appears vertical despite a change in retinal orientation. During the Apollo space research series, the astronauts

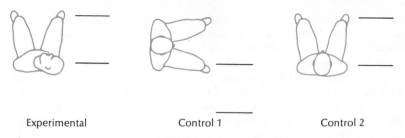

Experimental   Control 1   Control 2

Figure 5.3
Positions of body and head for subjects of three groups tested for the perception
of the vertical. Two test lines are shown, although in the actual experiments they
were not presented simultaneously. (After Begelman, 1968.)

experienced little difficulty in orienting themselves to an environment that
provided no gravitational cues. Up and down were defined by the position
of the body relative to the environment provided by the space capsule. In
the environment of reduced gravity provided by the moon, Edwin E. "Buzz"
Aldrin Jr.'s exuberant demonstration of an ability to run, jump, and even
make football cuts clearly shows that man can adapt to marked changes in
the pull of gravity and still maintain an upright position with ease.

Begelman (1968) raises an interesting question concerning the importance of the body and head in determining verticality. Is the vertical defined
by the position of an object on the retina or by the position of the object in
line with the midline of the body? In the presence of visual cues, the flagpole example previously cited would favor the body more than the retina.
In his experiment Begelman seated one group of subjects with their heads
tilted 90° toward their right shoulder—in other words, their heads were as
nearly parallel as possible to the floor. Two groups of control subjects also
participated in the study. Subjects of one group sat upright but were turned
90° to the right; those in the second group sat upright and faced the same
direction as the experimental group. Several kinds of stimuli were used in
the study. Most important for the present discussion was a straight line placed
on the floor either below the subject's right shoulder or beside his right foot.
To ascertain how observers perceived the line, Begelman asked each subject
to draw the line "just as it is seen" on a piece of paper located on a table
in front of him. For the experimental group the line was vertical relative to
the head, but horizontal relative to the body midline. For the first control
group the line was vertical for both head and body midline, while for the
second control group it was horizontal for both. The positions for head,
body midline, and the two stimulus lines for the three groups are shown in
Figure 5.3.

The drawings of the lines indicated that the first control group saw both
test stimuli as vertical lines and that the second control group saw both as
horizontal lines. These groups defined the line's position by the body midline,
since their heads and bodies were not in conflict. For the experimental group,
in which the subjects experienced a head/body conflict, the line located below
the shoulder was judged to be vertical. To define its position in space they

used the orientation of the line relative to the head rather than body mid-line. However, when the test line was placed beside the observer's foot, the experimental group then judged the line to be horizontal. In other words, they judged the line relative to the body midline. Note that the orientation on the retina was the same for the line whether it was placed below the shoulder or beside the foot. Begelman concludes that retinal orientation per se is not the determinant of orientation. Apparent orientation seems to depend on an alignment of the body and head. When the positions of the head and midline of body are in conflict, the results are ambiguous and rather unclear.

Before continuing, let us consider the observations reported thus far. The vertical and horizontal dimensions of space can be defined by the cues afforded by the visual environment, or by the position of objects relative to the midline of the head and body. The influence of gravity is reduced to providing the usual frame of reference for the alignment of the body position. Orientation to the midline does not seem to depend on gravity alone. Under laboratory conditions in which the visual frame of reference is absent or is provided by a tilted square, the midline orientation seems to prevail. Tilting the body, placing it in a supine position, or producing a conflict between head and body midline all increase the difficulty a subject experiences in attempting to adequately assess the vertical dimensions of space.

Interaction of midline and visual cues.   In the experiments reviewed in the previous section the visual point of reference provided by the frame does not appear to influence orientation to the degree expected. The studies that involve showing a room apparently tilted by a mirror produce more striking effects. One can demonstrate such effects by viewing a room reflected by a tilted mirror through a piece of rolled paper.

Asch and Witkin (1948b) also introduced a fascinating technique for the study of the interrelation of body position and visual cues. A box seven feet square was constructed to look like a small room. Within it were pictures on the walls, and lamps and chairs. The entire box was mounted and positioned by a motor so that any degree of tilt could be obtained. Subjects sat securely fastened in a chair which could also be tilted to any desired angle. In the basic test the room was tilted to one angle and the chair to another (either in the same or the opposite direction). The subject indicated the degree of tilt perceived by adjusting the position of the chair to the true vertical. Most subjects succumbed to the visual cues afforded by the room and adjusted the chair to align with the walls of the room. A smaller number were able to align the body midline with the true vertical. Bartley (1969) mentions an interesting observation obtained with the tilted room. If a plumb line is suspended from the top of the box while the room is tilted, the line hangs at an odd angle. Subjects still tend to align themselves to the vertical as defined by the walls of the room; however, they see the plumb line as a rigid rod attached at a peculiar angle from the ceiling.

While Witkin's studies (1959) have found both field-dependent and field-independent observers, a larger group of individuals demonstrate the tendency to combine the various conflicting cues. They adjust the chair closer to the vertical defined by the room, but do not align it completely with the walls of the room. In other words, the disorientation of their own body midlines enters into their calculations of the vertical.

Other investigators with tilted environments have concluded that the response initiated by the subject depends on what is requested by the experimenter. Mann (1950) found subjects capable of responding to the visual framework or to the body midline, as requested.

Fred Attneave has provided some data concerning the influence of instructions on the perception of true vertical that are also relevant to the previous discussion of the role of retinal position in the perception of apparent vertical. In one experiment Attneave and Olson (1967) presented vertical and horizontal lines in a tachistoscope. Observers were required to identify the orientation of the lines as rapidly as possible. When the heads of the observers were tilted 45°, reaction times required to identify the same horizontal and vertical lines were about the same as when the head was upright. However, if diagonal lines were flashed under the condition of a 45° head tilt—which produces a vertical or horizontal line on the retina—reaction times were markedly slowed. A few of Attneave's and Olson's subjects did respond to the diagonal lines under the condition of head tilt without an increase in reaction time. However, they represented only a small percentage of the subjects observed. Attneave and Reid (1968) followed up this latter observation with an experiment that required subjects to adopt a frame of reference in which either the walls of the test room were defined as up and down, or the top of the head was to be considered up. Reaction time required to identify diagonal lines was facilitated by these instructions.

Such results indicate that subjects are capable of utilizing all available information for the assessment of the visual vertical and horizontal dimensions. Perhaps the ambiguity of much of the earlier research could be resolved if the experimenter were aware of the particular frame of reference adopted by the subject. One could argue, of course, that studies without specific instructions assess the *natural* response tendencies of the observers. However, the natural response is probably determined by the observer's perception of what is required of him in the experimental situation. This possibility is supported by the observed changes in the adopted frame of reference as the observers increase in age. (See Figure 5.2.)

One further approach to the natural response for vertical involves the use of animals other than man. Lyons and Thomas (1968) trained pigeons to peck at an illuminated vertical line on a black background in order to obtain food. Five separate groups were trained in this manner. For groups 1 through 4 the white line provided the sole source of illumination, while group 5 learned the response in a lighted cage. After the response to the line was well established, the animals were tested with the original line and four other lines set at angles of −60°, −30°, +30°, and +60°. Testing for each group occurred under a different degree of cage tilt. Figure 5.4 shows the degrees of tilt for each of the four groups as well as the positions of the five lines under each condition of tilt. Group 5 was tested with a tilt of 24°, with the cage lights on. Again, for groups 1 through 4, only the light of the line was present.

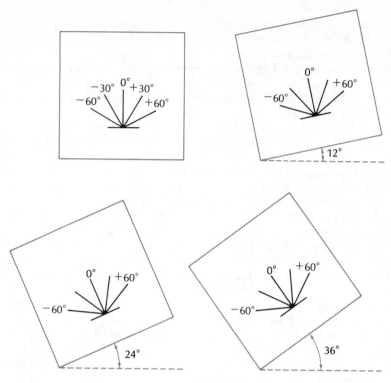

Figure 5.4
Cage-tilt and test-line positions for study of the perception of the vertical in pigeons. (After Lyons and Thomas, 1968.)

Figure 5.5 shows the results of the Lyons and Thomas experiment. The total number of responses for each line is related to the angle of the line on the test key. Note that the group experiencing no cage tilt during testing had a 30-percent response to the original 0° line (vertical) but only a 20-percent response to the lines tilted to the left or right of vertical. For cage tilts of 24° and 36°, the pigeons preferred the −30° line. True vertical was more accurately defined by the +30° lines; however, the birds tended to overcompensate the floor tilt and respond most frequently to a line tilted even farther away from vertical. In the absence of visual cues, body position seems an important determinant of vertical for pigeons and for people. Group 5 in the Lyons and Thomas study, for whom visual information was provided by the "house lights," displayed no preference for lines other than the original 0° line.

Perception and Prisms

Another approach to the perception of the vertical and horizontal, which is presently enjoying renewed emphasis, involves the use of prisms or lenses that transform the retinal images. Research with optical transformations is un-

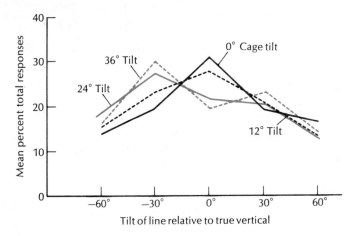

Figure 5.5
Mean percentage of total responses to the test lines for four dark-tested groups of pigeons. (After Lyons and Thomas, 1968.)

dertaken to clarify the determinants of spatial perception, reveal its changeability or stability, and give suggestions about its ontogenetic development.

The problem of the inverted image.   At the close of the nineteenth century, George Stratton introduced a new technique for the study of spatial orientation. He constructed a system of lenses that inverted and reversed the incoming light rays to the retina. In other words, the image of the distal stimulus was rotated 180° from its normal position. The impetus for such an experiment came from the realization that the lens of the eye normally performs such a transformation. Part A of Figure 5.6 shows a normal proximal stimulus on the retina of the eye. The image is, of course, upside down relative to the object that produced it. Part B shows the condition produced by Stratton; the distal stimulus is inverted before reaching the lens. The result is a reinversion of the image on the retina. The spatial orientation of the image on the retina is now the same as the distal stimulus.

The immediate result of Stratton's lenses was that he perceived an upside-down world (Stratton, 1896, 1897). All subsequent research has demonstrated the same effect: inverting the image before it reaches the eye produces an inversion of the visual scene. The sky is seen as down and the ground as up. The controversy among subsequent investigators of inverted images centers on the results of continued viewing of the world through prisms.

Stratton wore his inverting lenses for eight days and achieved extensive improvement in overcoming the kinds of behavioral difficulties he had at first encountered. In addition, he reported that at times the world *looked* "normal," "right side up," or "upright." However, such instances of upright vision were infrequent, and when Stratton removed the lenses, he did not see things reinverted, as he would have if his perception had been totally adapted to the lenses. Later work, such as that of Ewert (1930), Snyder and Pronko (1952), and

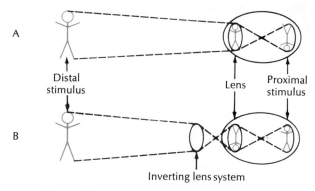

A

Distal
stimulus

Lens

Proximal
stimulus

B

Inverting lens system

Figure 5.6
A, spatial relationships of distal and proximal stimuli in normal vision. B, inversion caused by convex lens.

Kohler (1964), also reported that subjects wearing such goggles were eventually able to function quite normally. Snyder himself wore the inverting system
for over a month and adapted to the degree that he could perform complex
motor activities, such as riding a bicycle. Ivo Kohler (1964), who has conducted
numerous studies with prisms at Innsbruck in Austria, reports that a student
was even able to ski with minimum difficulty while wearing inverting goggles
for an extended period of time. As for perceptual reorientation, Kohler reported that it was considerable, whereas Snyder, having worn the apparatus
for thirty days, was unable to indicate clearly whether the world looked inverted or not. He had become so used to the inverting lenses that everything
appeared normal until he was asked to pay careful attention to whether things
looked upright. Then he noticed that, compared to his memories from before
the experiment, the world was oriented differently.

Several theories have been developed to account for these observations.
Stratton himself advanced a sensory disharmony theory to explain both why the
world sometimes looked upright and why that experience was infrequent even
after eight days of wearing the lenses. Upright vision, he said, consists of complete agreement between directions indicated by all sensory modalities (tactile-
kinesthetic and auditory as well as visual). Inverting lenses disrupt the intersensory harmony that has been achieved over a lifetime. A time-consuming
process of forming new associations between stimuli from the different modalities is required to establish a new harmony.

Walls (1951) doubted that any real perceptual reinversion took place, and
suggested that Stratton's feelings of harmony were due to his own peculiar
eidetic imagery (photographic memory) enabling him to build up a coherent
image of his inverted environment. Walls argued that the normally inverted
image on the retina is required for normal spatial orientation. In other words,
the visual pathway happens to be organized to accommodate an inverted
image. Walls drew support for his explanation from some observations with
lower animals. In a now classic experiment, Sperry (1943) removed the eyes
of mature frogs and replaced them in an inverted position. Once the nerve

endings had regenerated, the animals were tested on several visual orientation problems. Thus when a frog attempted to catch a fly located up and to the left, he moved down and to the right. L. S. Stone (1960) was able to invert the eyes of frogs in the embryonic stage. His results were similar to those of Sperry: after hatching, the young animals responded to visual targets by moving in directions opposite to the correct ones.

Rock (1966), however, suggests that experiments based on observations with animals are not necessarily relevant to the visual processes of humans. As one ascends the phylogenetic scale, less and less behavior is innate or instinctual; therefore, it is reasonable to assume that man does not necessarily display the same innate behavioral patterns as other animals. Rock argues that one cannot speak of up or down in the physical sense. Rather, these attributes describe positions in the phenomenal space of an observer; they are definable only in terms of the individual's egocentric orientation. The definitions, says Rock, of phenomenal up and down depend on the memory traces of everyday experience that are associated with egocentric orientations of the body. Hence, adaptation to a reinversion of the visual scene would be very difficult, since one could never override the effects of the sum total of all previous experience in phenomenal space.

The final theory to be mentioned, developed by Harris (1965), is based on a mechanism similar to the findings by Gibson discussed in Chapter 1, wherein the visual system can override tactile-kinesthetic information. In Gibson's case, a straight line that was optically curved also felt curved. Harris quotes Stratton's own reports to the effect that when parts of his body were seen overhead, they were eventually felt overhead. If legs and body were felt to be overhead, then the pull of gravity must also have been felt as coming from that direction. This would make that direction seem to be gravitationally downwards and so the inverted visual scene would appear properly oriented. Such a localization of legs and body would also make Stratton experience his head as inverted, and as a matter of fact, Stratton did report (1896) that sometimes it seemed "as if head and shoulders were inverted and I were viewing objects from that position, as boys sometimes do from between their legs" (p. 616).

Adaptation to prismatic distortions.[1]   As we have seen, the anecdotal and informal nature of early experiments makes it difficult to determine whether visual perception returns to normal after prolonged viewing through inverting prisms. For this reason, recent work has employed quantitative measurements of behavioral and perceptual responses. Moreover, most recent research has been conducted with prisms that produce a lesser degree of distortion than 180° inversion. These two developments in technique are not unrelated. As Rock (1966) has pointed out, perceptual adaptation to an inversion of the visual field must be all or nothing: either the field returns to the normal posi-

---

[1] Brief surveys of the extensive literature on this topic are given by Epstein (1967) and Rock (1968). An excellent detailed analysis is found in Rock (1966).

tion (undergoes a 180° rotation) or it remains inverted. It is more convenient to use lesser distortions, for which gradually increasing adaptation may be measured. In addition, adaptation to less severe distortions occurs in a matter of minutes, instead of the days or weeks required with inversion.

Wedge prisms that produce a lateral distortion are frequently used. These displace the visual field to the left or to the right. For example, a vertical line located straight in front of the observer would be perceived located 10° to the left when viewed through base-right 10° wedge prisms. Any reduction in the apparent displacement of the visual field, or in the error in pointing at visual targets, would constitute an adaptation to the prisms. Another type of prism, the Dove prism, rotates the visual scene so that true vertical and horizontal lines appear slanted.

The usual technique employed in current work follows the general procedure used by Held and Hein (1958). After first putting on the prisms, an observer is asked to carry out a spatial task or perform certain perceptual judgments; his performance is then compared with the performance on the same task or judgments after the prisms have been worn for a certain period. The amount of improvement or change is assumed to indicate the level of adaptation to the prisms. Unfortunately, this method sometimes invites confusion between perceptual adaptation and the subject's awareness of the manner in which prisms are distorting the visual experience. Hence, the observer may force himself to respond in a manner incommensurate with the visual experience he is undergoing. Because of this difficulty, the degree of adaptation is often measured without the distorting device. If adaptation has occurred, it should persist for some period after the removal of the distorting mechanism, producing an aftereffect. For example, if the subject has been seeing the world tilted to the right and has adapted to the tilt, then on removing the prisms everything should look tilted to the left. If he has been seeing things displaced to the right and has adapted his reaching, then with prisms removed he should reach to the left of his goal. As illustrated in Figure 5.7, to prevent the subject from simply correcting his reach he is usually kept from seeing his aftereffect error by having to reach under a cover that blocks his view of his hand and arm.

Two aspects of adaptation can be considered. First, what procedures are necessary to produce or to maximize adaptation? And second, what is the nature of the adaptation? What basic kind of perceptual and behavioral modification occurs? These two aspects have usually been studied separately in recent experiments.

Procedures for adaptation.   Among the wide variety of optical distortions exhibiting at least some degree of adaptation are tilt, lateral displacement, magnification, curvature, stretching in one dimension, shifting of half of the visual field, left-right reversal, and increase or reduction of apparent distance (see Rock, 1966). The general picture that has emerged matches our model of the active nature of perception in that movement by the subject and visual information about the movement are often required in order to produce good adaptation. In one clear-cut case, Held and Hein (1958) allowed one group of subjects to look through displacing prisms at their own arms moving from side

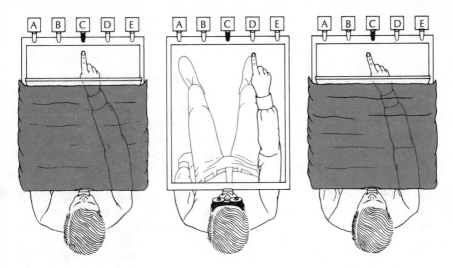

Figure 5.7
Apparatus for testing displaced vision. In control run, *left*, subject points at lettered rods without being able to see his hand. *Center,* while wearing prism goggles that displace his vision about four inches to one side, subject is asked to point repeatedly at center target with one hand. He usually misses at first due to the goggles. Finally, with goggles off, *right*, he is asked to point at various targets. Subject's head is kept steady by biting device. (After Rock and Harris, 1967. Copyright 1959 by Scientific American, Inc. All rights reserved.)

to side. A second group of subjects remained passive while their arms were moved by the experimenter. A third group simply looked at their motionless arms. When subjects removed the prisms and marked the apparent locations of visual targets, an aftereffect was demonstrated only for the first group of subjects, who had moved their own arms.

The aftereffect produced by actively moving one arm typically does not even extend to the other arm (Harris, 1963; Hamilton, 1964). However, when allowed to move their heads or whole bodies, subjects exhibit a more general adaptation which can be shown to affect pointing with either hand (Hamilton, 1964). Certain other procedures also produce aftereffects on the motionless arm (H. B. Cohen, 1966; M. M. Cohen, 1967), but such influence is always less than on the arm that was active. Held (1965) reports additional cases where adaptation is observed only following periods of active movement. He concluded that only "reafferent" information (visual stimulation resulting from *self-produced* movements) can change hand-eye coordination. Reafferent information was also considered essential for normal development of perception and coordination, based on experiments with kittens by Held and Hein (Held, 1965).

Later experiments have shown that active movement is not always necessary for adaptation. Several experiments have demonstrated appreciable adaptation with passive movement or even with no movement at all (e.g., Foley and Maynes, 1969; Mack, 1967; Rock, 1966). Usually the amount of adaptation is greater with active movement than with passive, but sometimes the two are equivalent, as in Mack's finding (1967) of 3.6° of aftereffect for active exposure to 40° tilt and 3.7° for passive (with 1.1° for stationary sitting and viewing a corridor).

In assessing the role of movement, it should be kept in mind that there are two clearly distinguishable effects of transformations of the visual field (Mikaelian and Held, 1964; Day and Singer, 1967). First, there can be an adaptation of the sensory system, as in Gibson's experiments (1933) where tilted or curved lines appeared less tilted or curved as exposure time increases, without any activity by the observer. Such effects, which are usually small and not long-lasting, will be considered in the discussion of figural aftereffects in Chapter 6.

The second kind of effect is often much larger, lasts much longer (Hamilton and Bossom, 1964), and can occur even if the visual field contains no contours; it is only for this kind that Held claims active movement is a prerequisite. In many experiments both these factors are present, but appropriate procedures can separate them. Mikaelian and Held (1964) found that when subjects were passively wheeled up and down a hallway in a wheelchair while wearing displacing prisms there was a significant aftereffect of 1.9°. However, when the experiment was repeated in a dark room randomly covered with luminous styrofoam spheres, which offered no straight contours, there was no aftereffect following passive motion, and only a 2.1° aftereffect for active walking (compared to 6.8° for walking in the hallway). The conclusion is that one sort of aftereffect occurs only when there are straight contours visible, one occurs only when there is active movement, and the two summate when there are both contours and movements.

A similar conclusion was reached by Day and Singer (1967) on the basis of a different kind of experiment. They knew that while the second effect increases with the degree of tilt, the first is maximal for moderate tilts but very small for 45° (Gibson, 1933; Morant and Harris, 1965). Therefore in their experiment they varied both the magnitude of tilt and the kind of exposure. Subjects viewed a horizontal bar through Dove prisms. For one group the bar appeared to be slanted 20°, for a second group 45°. After three minutes of viewing, subjects removed the prisms and adjusted the bar to the apparent visual horizontal. For the 20° condition the bar was adjusted on the average of 1.57° away from the true horizontal. For the 45° condition no visual adaptation was found to occur. However, if a subject was allowed to extend his hand across the bar and look at it during the three-minute transformation period, he learned to adjust the bar to compensate for the visual transformation. When he closed his eyes, the compensation persisted. Endeavoring to adjust the bar to the apparent horizontal by touch, the subjects set the bar to 6.86° after 20° distortion and to 8.23° after 45° distortion. Visual adaptation did not occur with the 45° distortion, but that condition evoked a behavioral compensation greater than for the 20° distortion.

Although the role of motion in adaptation is complex, there is no doubt that some sort of information about the optical transformation is essential for adaptation to occur. Among various possible sources of information are changes in the visual field (e.g., tilting), errors in reaching for a target, discrepancy between visual and kinesthetic localization of the hand, or abnormal

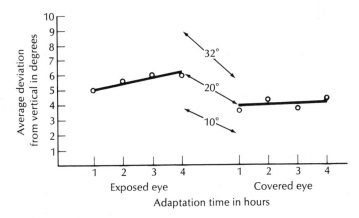

Figure 5.8
Amounts of adaptation as a function of exposure time for the exposed and covered eye. (After Ebenholtz, 1966.)

flowing of the retinal image when the subject walks. Several experiments have demonstrated that, as might be expected, the availability to the subject of greater amounts of information tends to increase the extent of adaptation. Welch and Rhoades (1969) found that there was much more adaptation when subjects had a target and could see their errors than when there was no target. Efstathiou (1969) found that increasing the amount of information by increasing the strength of the prisms led to a greater magnitude of adaptation, both in amount and in percentage of the total displacement (except for the largest displacement).

The longer the period of time the information is available, the greater the adaptation (Hamilton, 1964; Mikaelian and Held, 1964; Efstathiou, 1969). In one experiment Ebenholtz (1966) required subjects to wear prisms over one eye which tilted the visual field either 10°, 20°, or 32°. The other eye was covered. Periodically, over a total adaptation time of four hours, the amount of perceptual adaptation was measured by requiring the observer to adjust a luminescent rod to the apparent vertical. Ebenholtz's data are reported in Figure 5.8. The left part of the figure shows the amount of adaptation as indicated by the displacement of the rod after removal of the prisms. On the right are measurements taken for the unstimulated eye. Ebenholtz found that adaptation was very rapid during the first hour. The degree of adaptation reached was a function of the strength of the distorting prisms. For the subjects looking through a 10° prism, adaptation was essentially complete after one hour. The effects for the unstimulated eye are interesting in that the adaptation level did not seem to change after the first hour.

The nature of adaptation.   As with inverting lenses, one may ask if adaptation to other transformations is only an improvement in behavior, or if there are changes in visual or kinesthetic perception as well. According to Harris (1963, 1965) and Hamilton (1964), optical transformations affect the position sense of the subject's arm, due to the dominance of vision over the other senses

Table 5.1

Mean difference in inches between measurements taken before and after prismatic adaptation (Harris, 1963. Copyright 1963 by American Association for the Advancement of Science.)

Target	Adapted hand	Unadapted hand
Visual	+2.3	+0.4
Auditory	+2.0	−0.2
Straight ahead	+2.2	+0.2

that was mentioned in Chapter 1. As a consequence of seeing the arm prismatically shifted to the right, the subject's position sense also becomes shifted. The arm feels proprioceptively as though it is to the right, relative to its actual position. Therefore, although the prismatic transformation is visual, adaptation to it is nonvisual and can be measured with nonvisual tests. For example, Harris (1963) had subjects adapt by pointing at a visual target while wearing laterally displacing prisms. Subsequently they showed equal aftereffects when pointing at visual targets, auditory targets, and a kinesthetic target (pointing straight ahead with eyes closed). As Table 5.1 indicates, they showed little or no aftereffect for any of these targets when pointing with the other hand (which had not been viewed through prisms). The implication of a change in the felt position of the hand was directly confirmed by Welch and Rhoades (1969). They had subjects adapt their right arms to an 11° rightward displacement, close their eyes, and point with their left index fingers at their right index fingers. There was a large rightward error, indicating that they felt their adapted right hands were 2 cm or more to the right of their actual physical locations.

Similar changes in position sense have been found for other transformations (Rock and Harris, 1967). As mentioned, Day and Singer (1967) found that after subjects viewed their hands through prisms that tilted the visual image 20° or 45°, they would tilt a bar several degrees in the opposite direction when adjusting it to the kinesthetic horizontal. Even with a mirror-image reversal of the entire visual field, subjects' kinesthetic perceptions can be modified to such an extent that when blindfolded, they may write letters backwards but feel that they are normal (Rock and Harris, 1967).

Other experiments go beyond changes in position sense of the arm—for example, those experiments in which the aftereffects were not confined to the adapted arm but appeared in the other arm as well. Hay and Pick (1966a) found that with very prolonged exposure the initial rapid proprioceptive adaptation of the arm was replaced by a more general visual adaptation that could be measured only with visual targets. However, Hay and Pick pointed out that this visual adaptation could be attributed to changed sensing of the position of the eyes, as had been proposed by Helmholtz (1866), Hamilton (1964), and Harris (1965). Direct measurements of eye position after wearing prisms have shown that when adapted subjects attempt to position their eyes straight ahead, they are actually turned several degrees to the side (Craske, 1967;

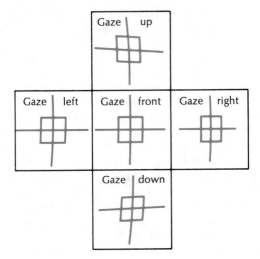

Figure 5.9
Gaze-contingent distortions produced by base-
right wedge prism spectacles with a power of
20 diopters. (After Hay and Pick, 1966.)

McLaughlin and Webster, 1967). Therefore, if a target is in the median plane,
the subject will see it as displaced to that side.

Modifications in the sensing of the positions and movements of the eyes
have been proposed as an explanation of adaptation to other conditions such
as optical curvature, magnification, depth, tilt, shape distortion, differential displacements of the two eyes, and differential displacements in the same eye produced by split-field prisms (Harris, 1965; Hay and Pick, 1966b; Ebenholtz,
1970). Of special interest here is adaptation to split-field prisms.

Kohler (1964) reported that distortions of the visual image brought about
by wedge prisms are *gaze contingent*—dependent on where the viewer is
looking. He produced photographs (1962) showing the effect of different lines
of regard when one looks through the prism. A simpler diagram of the effect
has been provided by Hay and Pick (1966b) and is reproduced in Figure 5.9. As
the figure indicates, looking up produces one distortion and looking down
another. Looking to the left produces an apparent increase in the size of the
target and looking to the right produces a decrease. The remarkable finding
is that the aftereffect of adaptation to this condition depends on the direction of view. If one views the test stimulus from below, the stimulus looks
distorted in one direction; viewing it from above produces a distortion in the
opposite direction.

Pick, Hay, and Martin (1969) carried these observations further and required groups of subjects to wear split-field prisms in which either the upper
or the lower half of the spectacles contained clear glass while the other half
contained a wedge prism producing an 11° optical displacement. Subjects
wore the spectacles for fourteen days; during the last seven days they were
given a series of tests designed to measure the adaptation level obtained for

each direction of gaze. The tests consisted of naming the lateral position of a sound presented behind a screen; aligning two lights, one above eye level and the other below; aligning the lateral position of a light to an invisible sound; pointing to the source of a sound; pointing to a number; and, finally, pointing to a light. Pointing was done in a way that prevented the observers from seeing their hands, and all tests were conducted while they looked either above or below the split level of the prisms they were wearing.

Gaze-contingent adaptation did occur, in that aftereffects were greater when the subjects viewed the test stimuli in the direction previously occupied by the prism. The two exceptions were the nonvisual point-to-sound test, where no aftereffect would be expected, and the light-to-light test, where equal adaptation should have been measured, since one light was above the horizontal midline and one was below. A further observation by Pick, Hay, and Martin (1969) clarifies the nature of the gaze-contingent shift. They took photographs of eye movements as subjects scanned up a vertical line after adapting to the split prisms, and noted that the eyes showed a lateral shift during the course of the vertical movement. They concluded: "Thus even the so-called visual change found by the present authors in a series of experiments is quite probably due to a change in position registration" (p. 131).

Beyond this, there is considerable disagreement about whether adaptation can modify visual perception per se, apart from the sensing of eye position and movement. Rock (1966), for example, argues that, given adequate visual information about the spatial properties of objects seen through distorting prisms, the subject's visual perception will actually correct for the distortion. Taylor (1962) and Festinger, Ono, Burnham, and Bamber (1967) propose that subjects first adjust their behavior to the distorted world and then, when a sufficient number of behavioral responses have been relearned, visual perception necessarily returns to normal.

In conclusion, it is clear that subjects can adjust behaviorally to a wide variety of optical distortions, and that active movement and visual feedback generally facilitate this process. In many cases the adaptation consists of modifications of position sense of the arm or eye. Whether there is in addition some visual modification has not yet been established conclusively. This is a point of some importance, since adaptation experiments are often treated as evidence about how visual perception develops in the infant—as showing, for example, that motor activity is crucial for perceptual development. In any case, the findings to date are consistent with a model of perception emphasizing the interaction of an active perceiver with the environment. If the information from the environment is distorted in some manner, the observer is able to counteract the distortion either by perceptual modification of the input or by adapting his behavior to the new situation.

The Perception of Depth

It is difficult to discuss the perception of space in terms of horizontal and vertical dimensions without reference to the third dimension of depth. A visual stimulus occupies a position in perceptual space that is defined relative to a

Figure 5.10
Apparent depth produced by squares of unequal size.

distance axis as well as to the vertical and horizontal axes. In the following discussion we will consider depth judgments made with a single eye (monocular relationships) and with both eyes (binocular relationships). Finally, we will consider the empirical evidence concerning relationships between the two, and some theoretical concepts about depth perception.

Monocular cues of depth.   That depth perception still occurs with only one eye can easily be demonstrated by viewing a scene with both eyes and then one. A definite change in the three-dimensional appearance of the scene occurs; however, one is still able to make fairly accurate depth judgments with one eye, under a variety of conditions. A number of students of perception have developed rather long lists of *depth cues* available to the perceiving organism. The lists range from about four to twelve cues in various discussions of the subject. In this section we will consider ten such cues.

Size.   The first monocular depth cue proves to be one of the most controversial. Gogel (1964), reviewing the problem of size, suggests that to accept a cue of *relative size* as an indication of depth is to assume that two objects are really the same physical size. In Figure 5.10 the two squares are physically different in size. However, they produce an apparent depth effect in which the smaller square seems to be more distant than the larger. The amount of difference in depth can be defined in terms of the visual angle subtended by the two objects at the retina: the greater the difference in visual angle, the greater the difference in distance. It is obvious that these relationships hold only when the observer assumes the targets to be of equal size.

One classic experiment involving relative size was conducted by Ittelson (1951). Subjects viewed three playing cards at a distance of 7.5 feet and were asked to estimate the distance of each. One target was a normal playing card; the second was a card twice the normal size; and the third was half the normal size. All other cues of distance were held to a minimum in the experiment. The mean distance judgment of 7.46 feet for the normal playing card was very accurate. The double-sized card was judged to be at 4.61 feet, while the half-sized card was estimated to be at 14.99 feet. Although the actual distance of

Table 5.2

Distance judgments of circles and rectangles under two conditions of suggested size
(Hastorf, 1950)

Target	Suggested size	Mean distance in feet	Standard deviation
Rectangle	Calling card (small)	5.0	1.1
Rectangle	Envelope (large)	6.5	1.6
Circle	Ping-Pong ball (small)	4.6	0.8
Circle	Billiard ball (large)	6.0	1.9

all cards was the same, differences in size led to perceptions of different distances. The relative sizes of objects, then, provide a cue of depth.

Hastorf (1950) approached the problem from a slightly different direction. Subjects viewed simple circles or rectangles of a given size. Hastorf varied the subjects' assumptions about the size of the targets by referring to them as a Ping-Pong ball or a billiard ball, and as a calling card or an envelope. Table 5.2 shows the average distance judgments for the four targets.

Ittelson, in the study previously mentioned (1951), also required subjects to judge the distances of unknown objects. Specifically, large and small irregular shapes and large and small diamonds were presented at an actual distance of 9 feet and distance estimates obtained. The small irregular shape was judged to be at a mean distance of 10.72 feet, and the large irregular shape to be at 5.83 feet. The large diamond was estimated to be 4.59 feet away, while the small diamond was seen at 7.93 feet. Again, relative size provided cues for a perception of depth difference.

Considering the results of both Hastorf (1950) and Ittelson (1951), one would conclude that size can provide two cues of depth under conditions of monocular viewing. First, depth can be judged on the basis of *relative size*. Objects subtending smaller visual angles are perceived to be farther away than similar objects subtending larger angles. This assumption is supported by a study of Hochberg and McAlister (1955) in which subjects viewed cards containing two figures. Card 1 contained a large and a small circle, card 2 displayed a large and a small square, card 3 a large circle and a small square, and card 4 a large square and a small circle. The observers estimated the smaller of the similar figures (cards 1 and 2) to be more distant than the larger figures. Dissimilar figures (cards 3 and 4) did not produce differences in depth judgments.

The second monocular depth cue may be called *familiar size*. If a familiar object is presented, the size of which is known to the observer, it will be perceived at a distance relative to the known size. Epstein and Baratz (1964) displayed pairs of photographs of a dime, a quarter, or a half-dollar. The photographs were prepared in different sizes so that the retinal sizes of the coins could be held constant or varied. Since the sizes of the objects were familiar,

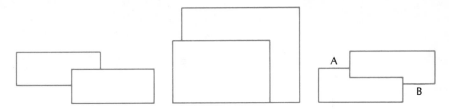

Figure 5.11
Left and center, patterns demonstrating the interposition cue of depth. *Right,* figure rendered ambiguous due to interposition. (After Ratoosh, 1949.)

it was expected that the observers would assume the dime to be the smallest and the half-dollar the largest. When retinal size was held constant, subjects perceived the depth of the objects in accordance with familiar size. That is to say, the known or familiar size determined the apparent distance.

A rather imposing number of experiments have attempted to assess the influence of familiar size as a cue of monocular depth perception. The number of experiments supporting the cue are offset by an equal number that fail to justify the subdivision of size into relative and familiar cues. The most fre-quently mentioned experiment opposing the familiar size concept was per-formed by Hochberg and Hochberg (1952). They displayed a panel containing a drawing of a man and a second panel containing a drawing of a boy of the same size. Paired judgments failed to elicit an assumption that the boy, due to familiar size, was closer than the man. More recently, Ono (1969) repeated the experiment of Hochberg and Hochberg. In one condition subjects were shown the test figures prior to presentation and asked to describe the pictures of man and boy with pairs of adjectives (e.g., mature or immature, old or young, etc.). This requirement was thought to ensure that the drawings would clearly con-note man as distinguished from boy, and vice versa. A second group received no such treatment, but was simply shown the two figures and asked to indi-cate which was the more distant. Ono found that the group that had experienced prior emphasis concerning the man-boy attributes of the test objects tended to judge the boy as closer. The second group, treated in a manner similar to that of Hochberg and Hochberg, did not tend to see the boy as closer. One concludes that familiar size does contribute to depth perception, provided the observer is well aware of the characteristics of the objects judged. Ono also presented photographs of a golf ball and a baseball which subtended the same visual angle. The results were similar to those of Hastorf's experiment (1950), in that the golf ball was seen as closer. In conclusion, the evidence seems to support a consideration of two size cues of monocular depth percep-tion: relative size and familiar size.

Interposition. As can be seen in Figure 5.11, if one object partially covers a second object, the blocked object is perceived to be behind and beyond the blocking object. Also in Figure 5.11 is an illusion prepared by Ratoosh (1949) in which the interposition cue of depth provides conflicting

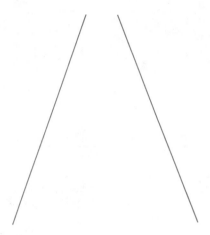

Figure 5.12
Linear perspective produced by two converging lines.

cues when the figure is viewed from point A or point B. Ittelson (1952) reports a design by Ames in which two playing cards are shown at different distances. The king is shown at 5 feet while the queen is presented at 10 feet. The cards are mounted so that the king partially obscures a corner of the queen. Observers correctly judge the king to be nearer, due to interposition. Next the scene is viewed again with the positions of the cards reversed; the queen should appear to be closer. However, the experimenter has cut out one corner of the queen (the corner formerly covered by the king) and perfectly aligned the gap with the distant king. The resulting perception is that of an off-sized (small) king mounted in front of the queen.

Linear perspective.   This cue of depth depends on the fact that as distance increases, parallel objects appear to converge. The cue is noticed when one looks down a straight road; more simply, it can be demonstrated by two converging lines, as shown in Figure 5.12. Linear perspective as a cue of depth is a product of man's modification of his environment. Parallel lines occur very

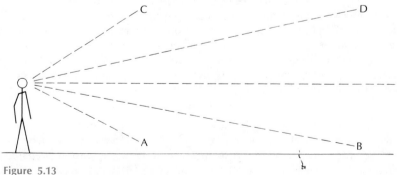

Figure 5.13
Angles of regard as cues of depth.

seldom in nature but are rather common in man-made constructions. In fact, architects occasionally use the cue of linear perspective to enhance the apparent distance of an object. A driveway can be constructed so that it actually gets narrower as it approaches a building, thereby giving it an appearance of greater length.

Angle of regard. Usually linear perspective, relative size, and familiar size combine to create a fourth cue known as the angle of regard. Objects located closer to the observer are viewed at a sharper downward angle than more distant objects, and objects located at the greatest distance require the least downward viewing angle. This holds for objects located below the midline of the visual field. For objects such as airplanes, located above the midline of the visual field, the angle of regard increases as the object nears. These relationships are depicted in Figure 5.13. Of the two targets A and B located below the midline of the visual field, A is viewed with the sharpest downward angle of regard; of the targets above the midline, C and D, the latter is seen with the sharpest angle of regard.

The Dutch artist M. C. Escher has created some fascinating drawings using the monocular depth cues of size, linear perspective, and angle of regard. One of these—a design for a perpetual motion waterfall—is shown in Figure 5.14.

Contrast, clarity, and brightness. Indications of depth and distance are also obtained by the clarity and brightness of objects. Nearer objects appear to be sharper and more distinct, while more distant objects are duller. Such contrast relationships diminish as distance increases. This kind of cue is helpful when one is viewing a wide expanse from a high vantage point.

Light and shade. The shadow cast by an object usually gives information about its distance relative to other objects. Also, due to the constant source of sunlight coming from above, contours can be perceived on the basis of light and shadow. During the flights of various spacecraft around the moon, observers on earth experienced difficulty judging whether the televised moon landscapes consisted of craters or mountains. This difficulty is demonstrated in Figure 5.15. If the photograph is viewed upright, the terrain appears to be composed of craters. Inverting the picture gives the objects the appearance of mounds. Whether one sees craters or mounds depends on the observer's judgment of the position of the sun. Usually one assumes the sunlight to be coming from above.

Texture gradient. The texture of a detailed surface becomes finer as distance increases. Hence, if one were looking at the side of the brick building shown in Figure 5.16, the increase in number of bricks per unit area from bottom to top would provide a cue of distance. This cue of depth works best if the textured surface is regular—composed of elements of uniform size. That the regularity of surface elements enhances the use of texture gradient for judgments of distance has been demonstrated by Gibson (1950). He required subjects to judge the apparent distances of textured surfaces that were regu-

Figure 5.14
M. C. Escher's perpetual motion waterfall. (Reproduced by permission
of the Escher Foundation, The Hague.)

lar or irregular. The results showed a greater degree of accuracy for the regular
surfaces.

Filled and empty space. Any object seen with intervening objects seems
more distant than when seen with only open space between it and the observer. For example, a mountain seen across a desert seems closer than a
similar mountain surrounded by forests and hills. Luria, Kinney, and Weissman
(1967) asked observers to judge the relative distance between a standard
target and a test target located at various points between 4 and 15 feet from the
subject. Both targets were 4-inch squares. On half the trials a rod was placed
between the subject and the standard target. The apparent distance of the
standard was found to increase with the rod in place. The perception of depth
changed as a result of filling the space between the observer and the target.

Motion parallax. The conditions of movement perception will be treated
thoroughly in Chapter 7, but it is appropriate to mention here the cue of mo-

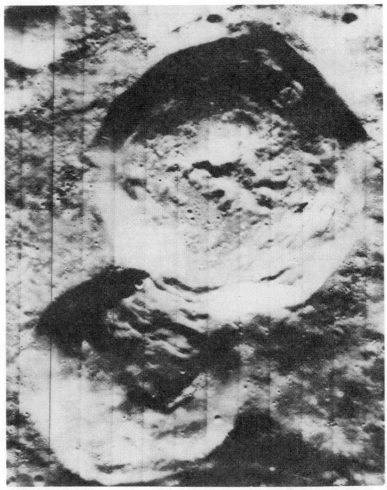

Figure 5.15
Light and shadow as cues of depth. The photograph of the lunar landscape
taken by Orbiter III seems to show two craters. Turn the picture upside down,
however, and the same surface appears to be composed of two mounds. (Photograph by NASA.)

nocular depth perception arising from movements of the observer relative to
objects in the environment. As Figure 5.17 illustrates, the images of objects
moving with the same velocity but at different distances from the observer
will traverse different distances over the retina. The farther the object from the
observer, the smaller will be the distance it appears to travel. If the observer
is in motion the perception of distal objects also varies as a function of distance.
Consider the experience of traveling at high speeds in an automobile. Objects
located immediately beside the road (e.g., telephone poles) pass rapidly from
the field of view when the observer turns his head to look out the side window.

Figure 5.16
Texture gradient as a cue of depth. *Top,* number of bricks per unit area on the side of a building. *Bottom,* relative size of rocks on rough ground.

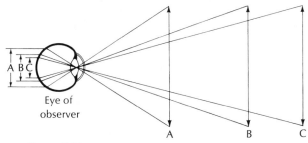

Figure 5.17
Motion parallax as experienced by a stationary observer.

Other objects located at greater distances, such as trees or shrubs in a meadow, pass from the field of view more slowly. Finally, objects at great distances, such as mountains, the sun, or the moon, actually appear to be moving in the same direction as the observer and do not pass from view over extended periods of time. Since movements by the observer can serve to improve depth judgments, researchers have been very careful to prohibit head movement during tests that seek to study other cues of monocular depth judgment. Redding, Mefferd, and Wieland (1967) have attempted to assess the amount of information gained through head and body movements in depth perception. They found that head sway or movement alone did not seem to matter, while performance improved markedly if subjects were allowed to sway from the waist.

Binocular cues of depth.   When one looks at two-dimensional objects, such as photographs or paintings, monocular cues of depth provide the sole information about apparent depth. In normal perception, however, one utilizes both eyes, whereupon several other cues of depth perception are added to the existing monocular relationships. We will first consider the binocular cues of depth and then discuss some of the research concerning the utilization of the two eyes in other perceptual processes (stereoscopic phenomena).

In addition to the rather imposing number of available depth cues in monocular vision, one would expect that some contribution to spatial perception would result from the fact that most higher organisms have two eyes. Johannes Müller (1826) considered the relationships between two eyes and distal objects and came to the conclusion that each eye receives a slightly different view of the distal stimulus. Actually, this was known and considered by Euclid in the third century B.C. Müller reasoned that one sees a single fused image due to the presence of *corresponding points* on each retina which respond to the same portion of the distal stimulus. Figure 5.18 presents the basis of Müller's concept. The eyes register a single image only if the corresponding retinal points are stimulated by the same part of the distal stimulus. When corresponding points are not stimulated, a double image results. Helmholtz (1866) worked out the general form of the law of corresponding points and advanced the theory of the *horopter*—an imaginary surface connecting all physi-

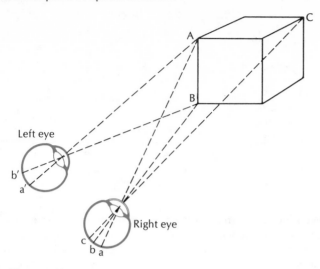

Figure 5.18
Corresponding retinal points.

cal points that for a given fixation point stimulate corresponding points on the two retinas.[2]

That the disparate image recorded by each eye could contribute to the perception of depth was discovered by Wheatstone (1828, 1852). Both Wheatstone and Brewster (1847) designed optical devices capable of presenting as a fused image two drawings or pictures taken from different perspectives. The result is a single picture with striking depth cues. Their device, known as the *stereoscope*, became a popular source of entertainment during the late nineteenth and early twentieth centuries. Today's modern version of the stereoscope, the *Viewmaster*, works on the same principle. Two photographs of the same scene are prepared from slightly different viewpoints. The separate pictures are then mounted on opposite sides of the Viewmaster reel. The apparatus presents a separate picture to each eye, focused in a way that produces a fused image of both pictures.

It has been clearly demonstrated that the image seen by each eye differs, due to the displacement of the two eyes; and that the presentation of separate two-dimensional photographs of the same scene taken from different perspectives produces a perception of depth. Of greater difficulty is, first, assessing the attributes or necessary relationships between the separate images required to produce the perception of depth, and second, evaluating the importance of binocular disparity in normal spatial vision.

Obviously the degree of disparity between the images presented to the two eyes will vary directly as a function of the distance of the viewed object. The greatest disparity will result if the object is very close. In fact, if the object

---

[2] For a discussion of the concept of the horopter the reader should consult Graham (1965a), pp. 522–24.

Figure 5.19
Random dot patterns with displaced central areas. (After Julesz, 1964. Copyright 1964 by the American Association for the Advancement of Science.)

is too close, one experiences double vision, due to the inability of the eyes to obtain two views of the stimulus on corresponding points. As distance increases the amount of disparity is reduced, with a threshold located somewhere beyond 800 to 1,900 feet (Forgus, 1966).

Julesz (1964) undertook the study of binocular disparity in a way that would isolate it from any other possible cues of depth. Using a computer he generated patterns of dots similar to those shown in Figure 5.19. When each pattern is viewed monocularly, one has no perception of depth. Both patterns are the same except for a center block of dots that is shifted several units to the left in the pattern on the right. When these two patterns are presented separately to each eye, the observer reports stereopsis (depth perception). The center portion that is shifted to the side stands out against the background of dots created by the outlying random patterns. Stereopsis occurs in this experiment when dots presented to one eye are shifted laterally in a pattern presented to the other. A number of other conditions have been identified that produce stereopsis (Kaufman, 1964, 1965).

The random dot patterns of Julesz demonstrate that contour is not a prerequisite for stereopsis. Julesz (1964) and Kaufman and Pitblado (1965) came to the conclusion that stereopsis is a product of special instances of *relative brightness disparity*. In the latter study it was found that entirely different groups of letters presented to each eye produced stereopsis, provided the relative brightness differences between disparate elements and their backgrounds were the same.

In summary, stereopsis occurs with dissimilar patterns, in the absence of contours, and even in the absence of familiar monocular depth cues, as long as the two patterns can be matched on the basis of adjacent points of similar brightness. Stereopsis can be produced by the lateral displacement of contours (Ogle, 1962), by the displacement of matrix elements (Julesz, 1964), by varying the brightness of disparate portions of the patterns (Kaufman and Pitblado,

1965), and by simply leaving out certain elements of the patterns (Lawson and Gulick, 1967).[3]

In traditional stereograms (e.g., the Viewmaster) the alignment of displaced edges produces the depth effect. In normal visual experience one must conclude that the disparate images seen by each eye provide a basis for depth perception. The experiments discussed above provide information concerning the manner in which the disparate images are matched by the brain to produce a fused image. Their results imply that relative brightness is the cue utilized to provide effective matches.

Despite the importance of disparity as the basis of stereopsis, depth can be perceived in the absence of disparity. The classic demonstration of this possibility is known as the *Panum phenomenon*. On a homogeneous background, Panum (1858) presented a vertical line to one eye and two vertical lines to the other. He found that if one of the double vertical lines is fused with the single line in binocular presentation, the subject perceives the unmatched line to be farther away than the fused line. This depth effect was found to occur only when the distance between the double lines was very small (approximately 6' of arc). The interpretation of the Panum phenomenon emphasizes that the fixation of one point in space causes other points to image at noncorresponding retinal points. Provided the disparity is not too great (Panum's limiting case), the fixated and nonfixated points will be seen at different distances. The magnitude of the spatial differences will then depend on the amount of disparity. Kaufman (1965) has shown that the fused line can be considered a reference system, with the degree of disparity dictating the localization of the line in space. The reference system can be based on edges, contours, correlated points, or brightness differences. A sensation of depth will be produced as long as some mechanism exists through which the correlations of the two separate stimuli to each eye can be obtained.

A final point worth mentioning concerning the maintenance of stereopsis comes from the report by Julesz (1968). Subjects looked at one line with the right eye and another line with the left eye. The two lines were seen as a single fused line when they were registered within 6' of arc. If the distance between the lines was any greater, two separate lines were perceived. Julesz found that once fusion occurred the amount of area separating the two lines could be increased markedly without a loss of fusion. In fact, distances of over 2° (120' of arc) could be reached before fusion was lost. Reducing the distance between the lines after a loss of fusion did not produce a single image until Panum's limits were reached again. This means that the concept of corresponding points must be considered flexible. If a fused image is obtained, then sizeable deviations from the disparate limits can occur without a loss of the single image.

If the degree of disparity indicates the spatial position of a stimulus when separate images are provided for each eye, then two other nonvisual mechanisms may also aid in depth perception. As the eyes are brought to rest on a distal object they move toward or away from each other. As Figure 5.20

---

[3] Some excellent demonstrations of stereopsis can be found in the paper by Julesz (1968).

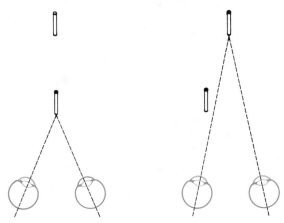

Figure 5.20
Convergence movement of the eyes in depth perception.

shows, to look at a close object requires that the eyes turn toward each other, whereas to fixate on more distant objects the eyes must move apart. This requirement is known as *convergence*. Theoretically, the position of the eyes required for fixation could provide a cue of depth, since to look across different distances should require different degrees of convergence. While most studies of depth perception are careful to control for convergence as a source of information on depth, the results of numerous studies indicate that this potential cue really provides no information. By the same token, the process of focusing the image on the retina through a flattening or bulging of the lens as a function of the distance of the distal stimulus might serve as a cue of depth. This change in lens shape is referred to as *accommodation*. Due to the finite distance of turn allowed the eyes in convergence, the cue could only be effective for distances under 80 feet. Similarly, for accommodation, the shape of the lens remains unchanged beyond a distance of 20 feet.

In normal visual experience, judgments of spatial depth are based on nonvisual cues (convergence and accommodation), on binocular disparity, and on a host of monocular cues that derive from the relationships among distal stimuli (e.g., relative size, interposition, etc.). Künnapas (1968) reported an experiment that attempted to assess the contributions to depth perception of both monocular and binocular depth cues. In five successive experiments subjects made depth judgments about circular targets located at distances ranging from 0.25 to 3.95 meters. For each experiment, Künnapas found that accuracy was a function of the available cues. The more cues the subjects could draw upon, the better were their judgments. Table 5.3 provides a summary of the experiments. Künnapas found depth judgments to be close to perfect under the full cue condition F. In contrast, under condition R1, which required distance to be estimated by means of accommodation alone, all distances were judged to be the same. Accommodation, then, did not appear to provide any information for depth perception. Condition R4, which included

Table 5.3

Available depth cues for judgments of distance
(Künnapas, 1968)

Experiment	Condition	Regard	Available cues
1	R1	Monocular	Accommodation
2	R2	Monocular	Accommodation, relative size
3	R3	Binocular	Accommodation, convergence, and binocular disparity
4	R4	Binocular	Accommodation, relative size, convergence, and binocular disparity
5	F	Binocular	All depth cues

only one monocular cue, provided accurate estimates rivaling those of the full cue condition. Actually, accuracy was rather high for conditions R2 and R3 for short distances, but performance deteriorated as the physical distance increased. Thus for short distances the monocular cues provided little information for accurate depth assessment. This is not surprising, since the other cues are particularly potent at short distances. However, at great distances (beyond 1,000 feet) one must rely more and more on the monocular cues. Depth judgments over great distances are possible but they are not particularly accurate.

Perceptual Constancies

In Chapter 3 a major concept, perceptual constancy, was introduced in the discussion dealing with *shape constancy*—the fact that known objects are recognized as the same objects despite great variations in their appearance. Some aspect of the stimulus must be remaining constant, or else we would not recognize a particular stimulus as unchanged. Consider a book lying on a table. As one moves about the room with the book clearly in view, the shape of the book in the form of the outline presented to the retina of the eye changes as a function of the angle from which the book is seen. Yet we see the book remaining essentially unchanged. The *perceived shape* of the book is *constant*. The advantages of such a mechanism for perception are obvious. If objects were seen only in terms of the shape defined by a specific retinal projection, recognition of familiar objects would be almost impossible. The same situation holds when the book is viewed from different distances. The size of the retinal projection of the book varies as a function of distance. Nevertheless, we see the book as something that maintains a constant size. This tendency is known as size constancy.

Shape constancy.   Epstein and Park (1963) defined shape constancy as the "relative constancy of the perceived shape of an object despite variations in its orientation" (p. 265). The early work of Thouless (1931) on shape constancy uncovered the interesting relationship between perceived shape and perceived slant. Consider a circular disc mounted so that a tilt can be introduced along the horizontal axis. If an observer views the tilted disc and reports the stimulus to be a true circle, one would conclude that the observer displays a tendency toward shape constancy. Further inquiry concerning the subject's perception reveals that the object is perceived as a *tilted* disc. The shape is seen as invariant or constant while the change introduced into the appearance of the disc provides a cue of the degree of tilt for the object.

Under normal viewing conditions, therefore, one would expect a known object, such as a circle, to be perceived as constant; any change would be the result of some degree of tilt given the circle. A formula with which to measure this tendency of shapes to remain invariant was introduced by Brunswik (1940). Usually called the *Brunswik ratio,* it is comprised of the following elements:

$$\text{Brunswik Ratio (BR)} = \frac{(P - R)}{(C - R)}$$

The value P represents the judged or perceived shape of the object as indicated by the observer. R equals the shape of the retinal image projected by the shape and C refers to the true invariant shape of the test object. If the judged shape is invariant, then the value of P should approximate C. The retinal shape is a constant and is subtracted from each of these values in order to avoid negative numbers. Dividing C into P should produce a value close to 1. Brunswik ratios of 1 indicate perfect shape constancy. On the other hand, if the perceived shape is seen undergoing a change, then P − R will become increasingly smaller as a function of the degree of perceived variance. Hence, if shape constancy fails, the value of the Brunswik ratio will become increasingly smaller (toward 0) as the difference between true shape and perceived shape increases.

In some of the early studies of shape constancy, Thouless (1931) found that the typical observer reported a judged shape somewhere in between the true shape and the tilted shape. In other words, the reported shape is a compromise. The deviations from shape constancy increase as the conditions of judgment are impoverished, yet even under normal viewing conditions with familiar figures, observers seldom display complete shape constancy.

Current interest in the problems of shape constancy seems to center on the instructions given to the observer. Epstein, Bontrager, and Park (1962) obtained shape judgments for simple geometric figures under three kinds of instructions. One group of subjects was asked to judge the shapes on the basis of their objective or known shape; a second group was asked to judge the shapes based on the shapes of the objects projected to the retina; and a third group was asked to judge the apparent or phenomenal shapes of the test figures. The mean Brunswik ratio for the objective condition was 0.58; for the retinal instructions, 0.21; and for the phenomenal instructions, 0.30. Objective instructions, then, produce the closest approximations of shape constancy. However, the value of 0.58 is far below the 1 value of true shape constancy.

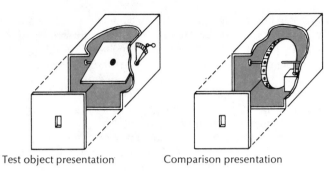

Test object presentation   Comparison presentation

Figure 5.21
Diagram of two devices for testing shape constancy. (After Meneghini and Leibowitz, 1967.)

It seems that observers are able to derive information from the same stimulus concerning the true shape of the object as well as the degree of variation introduced to the object.

Lichte and Borresen (1967) repeated the previous study with unfamiliar nonsense figures as test objects. Again, three kinds of instructions were used, and the following Brunswik ratios obtained: objective instructions, 0.93; retinal instructions, 0.45; and phenomenal instructions, 0.62. For the nonsense figures, objective instructions produced Brunswik ratios close to shape constancy and retinal instructions produced Brunswik ratios greatly influenced by the tendency toward shape constancy. The Brunswik ratios obtained with phenomenal instructions fall between those obtained with the other two varieties of instructions. This median would seem to represent a compromise between shape constancy and retinal shape. Landauer (1969) has questioned the assumption that apparent or phenomenal instructions can produce perceptions different from those obtained with objective or retinal instructions. He found that some subjects tend to respond in terms of retinal shape, and others in terms of objective shape under phenomenal instructions. The resulting average would naturally fall between the means found for retinal and objective instructions.

A tendency toward shape constancy would certainly simplify the explanation of orientation in a complex environment. One could hypothesize that the experiencing organism *learns* that objects do not change their shapes when viewed from various angles and distances. Such an expectation led Meneghini and Leibowitz (1967) to predict that the degree of shape constancy would increase as a function of age. Using the apparatus depicted in Figure 5.21, they presented a circle with one of four different degrees of tilt. Observers ranging in age from 4 to 21 years selected a matching circle that could vary in degree of circularity from a true circle to an elongated ellipse. Altogether a number of conditions were employed; Figure 5.22 gives the degree of shape constancy as a function of age for two of the degrees of tilt of the test figure. The results showed the opposite of the kind of relationship one might expect, for the degree of shape constancy was found to decrease with age. Several explanations can be offered. First, it is possible that shape constancy relations are

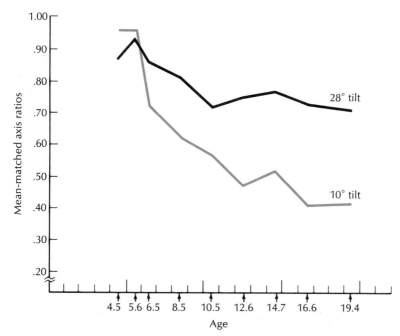

Figure 5.22
Shape constancy for two angles of tilt of a circle as a function of age. (After Meneghini and Leibowitz, 1967.)

learned at a very early age and become decreasingly important as the individual becomes older. Second, it is possible that shape constancy is not the result of experience at all; rather it may represent an innate capacity of human beings. While support for either of these possibilities is difficult to muster, Bower (1966) has shown that infants as young as two months display shape constancy. Finally, the results of the experiment by Meneghini and Leibowitz may stem from a different interpretation of the task by the subjects in each age group. Adult subjects would tend to develop their own hypotheses concerning the nature of the task and these would quite likely differ from the task as understood by four-year-old children.

Whether or not shape constancy is a product of experience remains debatable. Clearly, however, observers do tend to perceive constancy about shapes, while at the same time they are able to utilize information conveyed by the same shapes to make judgments about true shape and degree of distortion.

The perception of slant.   Beck and Gibson (1955) noted that information about the shape and the slant or tilt of an object must be obtained from a single source. The projection of the stimulus on the retina will vary in a characteristic manner when the same stimulus is viewed from different points or when the stimulus itself is placed in different positions. Realizing that any given retinal projection therefore must be the result of a distinct relationship be-

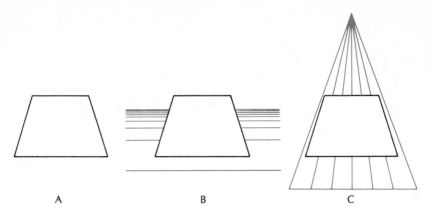

Figure 5.23
Relationship of shape to slant. A, ambiguous shape lacking information concerning slant. B, shape influenced by texture gradient. C, shape influenced by linear perspective.

tween shape and slant, Beck and Gibson proposed the *shape-slant invariance hypothesis*. While they did not introduce the concept, they helped to develop it by suggesting that impressions of shape and slant are coupled in such a manner that one cannot perceive a shape without considering its slant, and that slant determines the perceived shape. For example, in Figure 5.23 part A can be interpreted as a trapezoid or as a tilted rectangle. In part B, a background for the same figure provides information so that the perceived shape can be identified by reference to the apparent slant. In one study Gibson and Beck presented rectangular forms unaccompanied by information on slant and found that the reported perceptions on shape were variable. That is, without information on slant, the observers were unable to determine shape. By introducing a background texture indicative of a specific slant, shape constancy was evoked.

Kaiser (1967) tested the shape-slant invariance hypothesis by requiring observers to indicate the apparent shape and slant of trapezoids. He found that reports of changes in perceived shape were accompanied by corresponding reports of changes in slant. The errors made by subjects in matching shape and slant were the same for both perceptual measures. In other words, if the subject misjudged the slant of a test figure, he would usually make a corresponding misjudgment of the shape of the figure.

The accuracy with which judgments of slant can be made depends on many factors other than the perceived shape of a target. Generally speaking, performance increases in proportion to the number of depth cues, both binocular and monocular, available to the observer. Flock (1964, 1965) has argued that the texture of the background and the cue provided by motion parallax allow the most accurate judgments of slant, whereas Freeman (1965, 1966) has argued in favor of depth cues, such as linear perspective. Part C of Figure 5.23, which shows the test shape on a background defined by linear perspective, can be compared with the perceived shape of the figure in part B, in which the background is provided by texture gradients. Recent work by Willey and

Table 5.4

Judgments of size under apparent and retinal instructions as a function of physical distance
(Leibowitz and Harvey, 1967)

	Distance in feet				
	340	*680*	*1,020*	*1,360*	*1,680*
Apparent	0.39	0.36	0.30	0.27	0.22
Retinal	0.19	0.20	0.19	0.18	0.15

Gyr (1969) has indicated that neither of these explanations adequately assesses the cues of slant perception. Rather, as is the case with most perceptual problems, a complex interaction between a large number of variables provides the context within which a perception is generated.

Size constancy.   Kilpatrick and Ittelson (1953) observed that the perceived size of an object depends on its perceived distance. As in the case of shape/slant invariance, increases in perceived size are coupled with decreases in distance. They described this relationship in terms of a *size-distance invariance hypothesis*. However, the empirical observations concerning size constancy fail to confirm in full the expectations of this explanatory hypothesis. Leibowitz and Harvey (1967) asked subjects to judge the heights of human targets located at distances of 340, 680, 1,020, 1,360 and 1,680 feet. They provided three sets of instructions emphasizing the objective, retinal, and apparent sizes of the various targets. Under the objective size condition the Brunswik ratios for all five distances approached 1 and indicated a close adherence to size constancy. Table 5.4 shows the Brunswik ratios obtained under apparent and retinal instructions. Observers were able to derive information on both size and distance from the stimulus array. The apparent judgments were closer to the retinal size judgments, but this may represent an artifact in the method of calculation.

In an earlier study involving the judgment of the sizes of circles, Holway and Boring (1941) described the tendency toward size constancy as a function of the number of available distance cues. Almost perfect in a cue-rich situation, size constancy tended to decrease as the available cues were reduced. More recently, Schiffman (1967) has provided experimental evidence supporting the high degree of size constancy under conditions rich in visual depth cues. He found that in the absence of depth cues, off-sized objects were perceived at distances corresponding to the subject's memory of the correct sizes of the objects.

Auditory Space Perception

Auditory stimuli as well as visual stimuli are perceived to be localized in space. The sound is not heard within the ear, but is phenomenally positioned at the

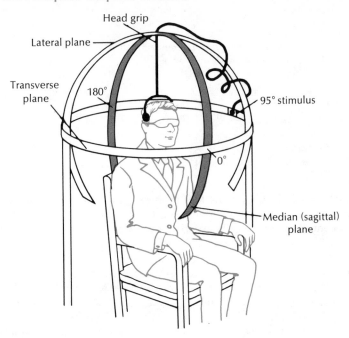

Figure 5.24
Typical sound cage for the study of auditory localization.

source of the sound. In this section we will be concerned with the auditory mechanism's ability to locate sounds in the external environment.

Sound localization. Most individuals have had the opportunity to observe a cat responding to a sound. As the sound first stimulates the ear the animal lifts its head and attempts to aim its head toward the sound. This aiming is accomplished by turning the pinna of the ear toward the sound, followed by an appropriate movement of the entire head. The animal is obviously extracting information about the sound through specific body movements. In humans the basic response is similar, although a turning of the ear does not precede the head movement toward the sound source.

Early work on the ability of observers to locate the source of a sound utilized a device similar to the apparatus depicted in Figure 5.24. The blindfolded subject could be presented with a tone, click, or noise from any direction. The usual task of the observer was to point toward or otherwise indicate the direction of the sound.

Rosenzweig (1961) reports the observations of the eighteenth-century Italian physicist Giovanni Venturi concerning the capabilities of observers to localize sounds. Venturi stationed a blindfolded subject in the middle of an open field and circled him at a distance of 150 feet. Periodically he rang a bell, and the observer attempted to indicate the position of the sound. The basic observation was that the subject could locate sounds coming from the right

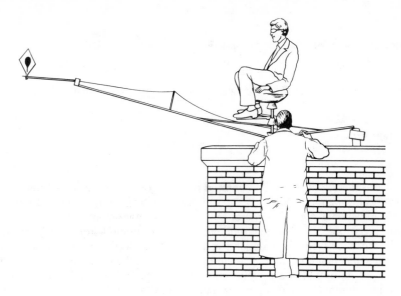

Figure 5.25
Apparatus for the study of sound localization in a free environment. (After
Stevens and Newman, 1936.)

and left but frequently made errors distinguishing between front and back.
These errors could be avoided if the sound was sustained (e.g., a note played
on a flute) and the subject allowed to turn his head during the presentation.
Similar observations were made by Pierce (1901), who also found that noises
were easier to locate than tones. After reviewing all the early literature, Newman (1948) concluded that sound localization with regard to right and left was
close to perfect, but front and back or up and down localizations proved
difficult.

Stevens and Newman (1936) studied sound localization in an open-air
situation by requiring observers to judge the direction of a sound located 12
feet from the observer. Their experimental apparatus is depicted in Figure
5.25. The sound source located on the end of the boom could be moved
360° around the observer. The experiment studied localization abilities for
tones, hisses, and clicks. Localization was also studied as a function of tone
frequency and the physical position of the sound source. Among the different
kinds of sounds, Stevens and Newman discovered fewer errors for the hiss and
click than for the tone. As far as tone frequency was concerned, they found
errors for tones between frequencies of 2,000 and 5,000 Hz to be much greater
than errors for tones with frequencies below 1,000 Hz or above 7,000 Hz.
Front-back reversals were frequently observed in this study, but subjects were
able to determine when the sound came from the median plane with greater
accuracy than when it came from the transverse. Table 5.5 gives the average
error in degrees for sounds as a function of the degrees away from the median
plane. Front-back reversals were not counted as errors in these results.

Table 5.5

Sound localization as a function of the sound position
(Stevens and Newman, 1936)

	Position in degrees from median plane						
	0°	15°	30°	45°	60°	75°	90°
Average error in degrees	4.6°	13.0°	15.6°	16.3°	16.2°	15.6°	16.0°

Considerable interest has centered on the problem of front-back reversals in sound localization. Burger (1958) attempted to analyze the contributions of head movements and the pinna of the ear to this phenomenon. For one group of subjects tones of different frequencies were presented from the front and to the right, or from the back and to the right, while the head was kept immobile with a head restraint. A second group judged the position of the sounds with head immobile and a white noise masking sound to the left ear, which forced judgments to be made monaurally. A third group listened without head restraint but with earphones over the ears in order to reduce any localization influence by the pinna. For the final control group, the head was free and neither earphones nor a white noise mask was used. Table 5.6 gives the results for several representative frequencies. The table values indicate the percentage of correct localizations for each frequency range. The control condition (4) yielded results compatible with the earlier observations of Stevens and Newman: errors are greatest in the midrange of frequencies. Performance was reduced to almost chance (50 percent) in the monaural and immobile head condition (2). Simply restraining the head or reducing the effect of the pinna of the ear resulted in accuracy less than that of the control condition. However, performance was better than chance under both of these conditions.

The role of head movement has been studied by Wallach (1940), who found a reduction in errors of localization between front and back if observers were allowed to move their heads. More recently, Pollack and Rose (1967) have studied extensively the importance of head movement in localization. They found that for sounds of brief duration performance was actually poorer when the head was allowed to move. A superiority of head movement was observed only when the sound was of sufficient duration to allow the subject to listen from several head positions. This result is not surprising, as one would expect the head movement to provide information about the sound only if the sound continues throughout the period of the movement.

In summary, sound localization is impaired by a reduction in free head movements, by monaural listening, and by disuse of the pinna. Furthermore, sound localization depends on the duration, position, and frequency of the sound.

Cues of sound localization.   There are two major sources of information for sound localization. First, when a sound source is located to the left of the

Table 5.6

Correct sound localization under four conditions of head restraint and masking
(Burger, 1958)

		Sound frequency in Hz				
		300–600	800–1,600	1,200–2,400	3,200–6,400	6,400–12,800
1	Head restraint	77%	69%	62%	80%	82%
2	Head restraint with left ear masked	58%	50%	42%	62%	71%
3	Head free with earphone	67%	65%	65%	56%	68%
4	Head free	85%	72%	82%	88%	100%

observer, the sound will be louder for the left ear than for the right. Furthermore, a *sound shadow* set up by the head will cause an additional reduction in sound intensity reaching the more distant ear. Second, due to the relatively slow speed of sound, a noticeable difference in the times sounds arrive at each ear provides information on the origin of a sound in space.

Binaural intensity differences. A sound in the sagittal plane (directly in front or directly behind the observer) will reach both ears without any difference in the intensity of its sound. As the source is displaced to the left or right of the sagittal plane, the distance to one ear increases as does the size of the sound shadow created by the head. The more the sound is displaced from the sagittal plane, the greater will be the intensity difference between the two ears. Firestone (1930) and Sivian and White (1933) carefully measured the amount of intensity reduction as a function of the angle of the sound source from the sagittal plane and the frequency of the sound. Figure 5.26 shows the results of the Sivian and White experiment for pure tones with frequencies of 300, 1,100, and 10,000 Hz. Obviously the amount of intensity difference is negligible for frequencies below 500 Hz. Using a somewhat different technique, Firestone (1930) located the lower level of frequency capable of producing a noticeable intensity difference at 2,000 Hz. He found that for a pure 4,200-Hz tone displaced 60° from the sagittal plane, an intensity difference of about 15 decibels occurred.

Stewart and Hovda (1913) provided some early data concerning the utility of an intensity difference in sound localization. They positioned tuning forks at the ends of two tubes attached to the subject's ears. The position of one fork was held constant while the distance from the end of the tube of the second fork could be varied. Increasing the distance of the variable fork produced an intensity difference for the two ears. In general, the data of Stewart and Hovda conformed to the expectations provided by the data of Sivian and White. As the intensity of the sound reaching one ear increases, the subject

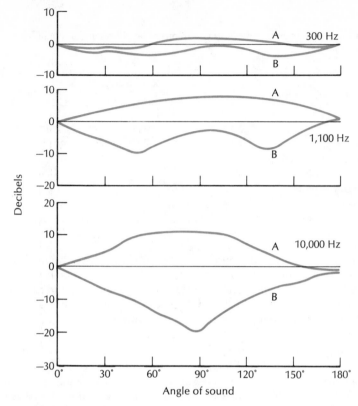

Figure 5.26
Binaural intensity differences as a function of angle of sound source and frequency of sound source. A, left ear. B, right ear. (After Sivian and White, 1933.)

reports the apparent location of the sound displaced toward the ear receiving the more intense sound. Stewart's and Hovda's results did not follow the predicted curves of Sivian and White exactly, due to variations in technique and sound-production quality.

Intensity differences, then, can provide cues of sound location at frequencies between 500 to 2,000 Hz. For complex sounds an elimination of the higher frequency elements by the sound shadow could also serve as an indicator of sound position. Stevens and Davis (1947) have provided some data supporting this expectation.

Binaural time differences. By the same reasoning that has been applied to the differences in sound intensity, one would expect a difference in the time of arrival of a sound to each ear. Woodworth and Schlosberg (1954) have computed the difference in time of arrival as a function of the angle of the sound in relation to the sagittal plane. Taking into account the speed of

Table 5.7

Differences in time of arrival (in msec) at the two ears as a function of the angle of the sound (Woodworth and Schlosberg, 1954. Copyright: 1938, 1954 by Holt, Rinehart and Winston, Inc.; 1966 by G. W. Herron and by S., W., and V. Woodworth. Reproduced by permission.)

	Angle						
	1°	10°	30°	45°	60°	75°	90°
Maximum difference	.009	.089	.266	.400	.533	.666	.799
Minimum difference	.009	.088	.260	.379	.486	.578	.653

sound (344 meters per second), they conclude that each centimeter of distance difference between the two ears will produce a time difference of 0.029 msec. Table 5.7 provides the time differences for a number of sound directions.

Again, such physical relationships can be tested by empirical observation. Wallach, Newman, and Rosenzweig (1949) presented separate clicks of equal intensity to each ear. They varied the temporal relationships between the clicks and required observers to point to the apparent source of each sound. The apparent position of the sound conformed rather well with the predicted position based on the difference in time of arrival at the two ears. However, it was also found that the frequency of the sound played an important part in localization. Subjects were able to localize pure tones accurately only when they were below 1,500 Hz.

If we return to the experiment of Stevens and Newman (1936), a rather obvious theory of sound localization emerges. They had observed that localization was accurate for tones below 2,000 and above 7,000 Hz, and that localization in between these levels was somewhat impaired. To explain these observations they advanced the *duplex theory of sound localization,* which holds that sounds are positioned in space on the basis of intensity differences for high frequency sounds and time differences for low frequency sounds. The transitional frequencies between 2,000 and 5,000 Hz yield less accurate judgments because neither mechanism is working well. More recent replications of the earlier work, such as those of Mills (1958, 1960), have provided support for the duplex theory.

It should also be remembered that in normal perception other monaural cues enter into accurate localization. Knowledge of the potential source of a sound (e.g., airplane noises from above or squeaking shoes from below) certainly aid in the correct positioning of a sound. As we shall see at the end of the chapter, visual cues also influence sound localization.

Distance judgments of sounds.   The major cue for a judgment of the distance of a sound appears to be intensity. Thus Warren, Sersen, and Pores (1958) were able to produce variations in the apparent distance of a sound by varying only the amplitude of the sound source. More recently, Cochran, Throop, and Simpson (1968) obtained distance judgments for words spoken in an open field.

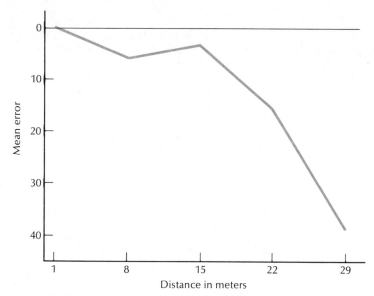

Figure 5.27
Errors in distance judgments of a sound as a function of physical distance of the sound. (After Cochran, Throop, and Simpson, 1968.)

Subjects judged the distance of a sound source located 1, 8, 15, 22, or 29 meters from the subject in relation to a standard placed at 15 meters. As Figure 5.27 indicates, very accurate judgments could be made up to 15 meters. Thereafter the error scores increased markedly.

Coleman (1963) has analyzed the available data concerning distance perception and sounds. While he concludes that the reduction in intensity over distance provides the major source of information, several other cues, both monaural and binaural, appear to contribute. Changes in the frequency spectrum of complex sounds provide cues of distance. For example, the complex noise pattern generated by a modern jet plane is reduced to a monotone at great distances. Also, the lack of overtones and harmonic relations in tones traversing large distances probably provides a cue of depth. Ingard (1953) demonstrated that higher frequencies are more subject than low frequencies to attenuation over great distances. Again, knowledge of the characteristics of a specific sound and visual information about possible distance ranges all influence the localization of a sound along the depth continuum.

Inversion of Auditory Space

In 1928 P. T. Young reported his observations concerning a device called the *pseudophone*. It consisted of a funneled tube running from the left ear over the head to a point in front of the right ear and a similar tube running from the right ear over the head to the left ear. Wearing this device produced a 180° inversion of auditory space; sounds emanating from the left were heard on the right and vice versa. Young (1928) and later Willey, Inglis, and Pearce (1937) provided data concerning the process of adaptation to the transformed auditory world created by the pseudophone.

Day and Singer (1967) have argued that the spatial adaptation process in hearing parallels the adaptation process in vision. With 180° inversions of the field, marked behavioral adaptation occurs, but the observer remains aware of the field transformation. Several experiments have dealt with the adaptation of an observer to a sound displaced to one side of the median plane (Flugle, 1921; Taylor, 1962). Taylor observed a spatial aftereffect: after adaptation to a displaced sound, subjects reported sound sources shifted in the opposite direction. In the median plane experiments in which hearing was transformed less than 180° (Freedman and Zacks, 1964), subjects rapidly learned to compensate for the distortion of the direction of sound stimuli.

Interaction of Visual and Auditory Space Relations

In normal perceptual processing the sensory information registered by visual and auditory channels is usually in accord. We see a barking dog and localize the source of the sound at the position of the visual image. In fact, due to the ambiguity of sounds lying along the median plane, the localization of a sound depends to a great extent on the accompanying visual experience. Hence, at a drive-in movie, one is strongly aware that the sound source and the visual image do not coincide. After some time, however, the discrepancy is no longer noticed, and one adapts to the displaced sound. If the expected adaptation does not occur, placing the speaker in the median plane behind the viewers quickly causes the sound to appear properly localized on the screen.

Unfortunately, few experiments have sought to trace the adaptation process for displaced sights and sounds. Harris (1963) demonstrated that the behavioral compensation learned under a visual transformation also affects pointing at sounds. However, he noted that this is not due to any change in auditory perception, but rather to a change in felt position of the adapting hand. Verbal judgments of the sound's location remained unchanged (Harris, 1965). The reverse situation, in which adaptation or compensation to displaced sounds influences visual localization, has been demonstrated by Craske (1966), who also attributed the change to the position sense of the arm. One would expect less influence in the latter case, since most observers rely primarily on visual information for exact localization of sounds.

That sounds can influence perceived verticality has been demonstrated by Chandler (1961). He required subjects to adjust a luminescent rod to the apparent vertical during monaural and binaural stimulation. Subjects tended to perceive the vertical displaced away from the side receiving monaural stimulation and away from the source of the most intense of two binaural stimuli. As the intensity of the tone increased, the magnitude of the deviation from vertical showed a proportional increase.

An experiment by Pentti (1955) demonstrated the influence of vision on auditory localization. Observers were seated within a rotating cylinder of vertical black and white stripes. A brief period of such visual stimulation produces the *nystagmic illusion*: the subject perceives himself to be turning in a direction opposite that of the rotating stripes, while the stripes appear to remain immobile. Sound localization under these conditions displayed a displacement equivalent to the strength of the nystagmic illusion.

CHAPTER 6

Perception in Context

Size, shape, pattern, and numerous other aspects of perceptual stimuli are defined as much by the surrounding context of the particular stimulus as by the attributes of the stimulus itself. While a thirty-five-story building in downtown Manhattan is not particularly large, the same structure located in Portland, Oregon would be perceived as immense. Size is a relative attribute that depends on the context in which the judged stimulus appears. In the present chapter we will discuss the influence of the surrounding area on the percep-

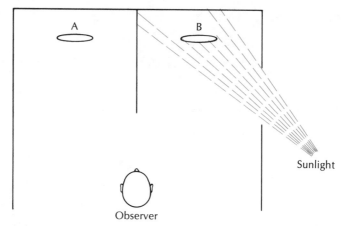

Figure 6.1
Diagram of an apparatus for testing brightness constancy. (After Katz, 1911.)

tion of a stimulus (context) as well as the influence of preceding stimuli on subsequent stimulation (anchor effects and aftereffects).

We have considered the problems of size and shape constancy in the previous chapter. Obviously these topics could have been reserved for the present discussion, as they clearly relate to the influence of context on perception. The perception of brightness, however, has not been considered, and will serve to represent constancy and contextual effects. Geometrical illusions such as the Müller-Lyer in Figure 1.1 and illusions occurring in nature will also be covered. A further topic for a discussion of context is the influence of one figure on the perception of a second figure following in time. Finally, the concept of adaptation level, or the continuing change in response patterning of the observer to groups of successive stimuli, will provide the concluding section.

The Perception of Brightness

The apparent brightness of an object can remain the same despite changes in overall illumination and therefore in amount of light reflected by the stimulus. Analogous to size constancy, such a condition is referred to as brightness constancy. Conditions also exist in which the brightness of a stimulus, although physically unchanging, appears to vary as a function of surrounding conditions. Such conditions are examples of brightness contrast. A final situation has been described in which the apparent brightness of a stimulus increases as a result of the intermittent presentation of the stimulus. This condition is called brightness enhancement.

Brightness constancy.   Assume a situation in which an observer is presented with a sheet of black paper and a sheet of white paper. Obviously the subject

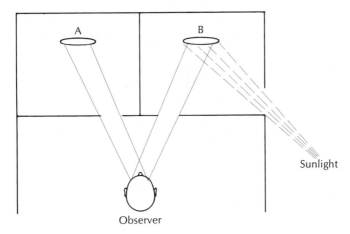

Sunlight

Observer

Figure 6.2
Diagram of an apparatus in which testing for brightness constancy
fails. (After Katz, 1911.)

will report the perception of a marked brightness difference between the two
stimuli. Physical measurements show that the white paper reflects fifty times
more light than the black paper. If we now leave the illumination of the white
paper unchanged and increase the illumination of the black paper fifty times,
the amount of light reflected by the two stimuli will be the same. Yet the perception of the two stimuli remains invariant. The white paper still appears
white and the dark paper still appears black. This is an illustration of *brightness
constancy*.

The classic experiment in brightness constancy was reported by Katz
(1911). The design of the study is diagramed in Figure 6.1. Target A consisted
of a paper disc initially half white and half black, constructed so that the proportion of white to black could be varied. When the disc was spun a uniform
gray surface appeared. Target B was constructed in the same manner but was
illuminated by direct sunlight from an adjacent window, while target A was in
the shadow of the dividing partition. The task of Katz's observers was to adjust
the gray of the right disc to match the gray on the left. Katz found that the subjects were able to do this, despite the difference in illumination provided by
the sunlight. The proportion of white to black in the subjects' matches closely
resembled the actual proportions on the test disc. The experiment demonstrates the tendency of observers to maintain brightness constancy.

Katz's procedure can be modified by placing a screen with two holes in it
between the two target stimuli and the observer, as shown in Figure 6.2. Now
the observer is able to see only the two targets. In this situation the observer is
strongly influenced by the different levels of illumination, and constancy breaks
down.

A number of psychologists have attempted to explain brightness constancy
and the loss of constancy under the reduction screen experiment. Feldman
and Weld (1935), in an extension of the line of thinking initiated by Katz, point
out that the reduction screen does more than alter perceived brightness. Under

reduced conditions the observer is unable to make any judgments about the characteristics of the discs. He sees only two spots of differing brightness. In the absence of the reduction screen, however, the objects can be judged in relation to the background, and the brightness of each disc is perceived as an attribute or part of the disc. When the reduction screen intervenes, the brightnesses do not appear to be related to specific objects; they are independent of the targets' surfaces. It was Helmholtz (1866) who pointed to the role of inferences in brightness judgments. In the situation without the reduction screen, the observer *knows* that the stimuli are composed of the same elements and must thus appear the same. Such an inference cannot be made about the spots of brightness in the reduction screen condition.

Wallach (1948) describes an experiment by A. Gelb which demonstrates the importance of relational judgment in brightness perception. A piece of black paper is suspended in the open door of a room and illuminated by a strong projection lamp. The beam of the lamp proceeds into an adjacent room so that only the suspended black paper is illuminated. Under these conditions, the black paper appears almost white. However, if a piece of white paper is held beside the black paper, the two objects are restored to their original brightnesses. The white looks white and the black appears black. In the first condition the observer is presented with no information on which to base a perception of brightness. In the second, the two objects can be judged in relation to one another. Wallach (1948) mentions a convincing extension of the Gelb experiment in which the intensity of the light beam is systematically reduced. When the black paper is presented alone, the perceived brightness seems to change from white to black as the intensity is lowered. With both the white and black papers in view, changes in intensity evoke no modification in the perceived brightnesses of the stimuli.

Various studies of this sort led Wallach to conclude that brightness is determined by the ratio of the brightness of the test surface to the entire surround. This can be simply demonstrated by holding a rolled piece of dark paper (the cardboard center of a roll of toilet paper is ideal for the demonstration) in your left hand and placing it on the open palm of your right hand. With both eyes open place the roll or tube against the left eye. Your hand should still be pressed against the other end of the roll. Inside the roll you should now see a dark area surrounded by a lighter ring. If you compare the brightness of this ring with the view of your hand afforded by the right eye, the ring certainly appears brighter. Yet in fact it is physically darker, since less light is present to be reflected inside the tube. The apparent brightness depends on the ratio of the dark center portion of the hand to the lighter ring. The view from the right eye in normal illumination provides a hand-to-surround ratio of much less contrast, hence the hand appears less bright.

Wallach (1948) described a number of experiments designed to demonstrate that brightness perception is the result of a comparison of the relative brightnesses of test figure and surround. His basic design, shown in Figure 6.3, uses four projectors in pairs. One projector illuminates a disc while the paired projector illuminates a surrounding ring. A second pair of projectors are similarly situated. When the brightness of the first projector is adjusted so that the

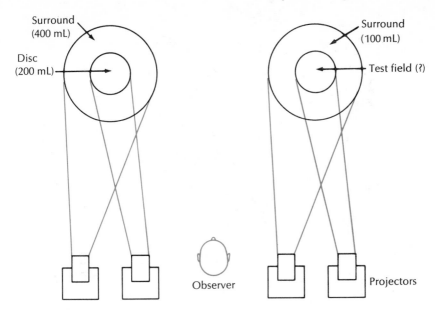

Figure 6.3
Brightness measurements as a function of the brightnesses of the surround and the test field. (After Wallach, 1948.)

disc has a luminance of 200 mL and the second projector so that the ring has a luminance of 400 mL, one perceives a light gray ring surrounding a darker gray disc. Next, the luminance of the second ring is set to 100 mL and the observer is required to adjust the brightness of the second disc to match the brightness of the first. Physical equality would exist if the observer adjusted the disc to a luminance of 200 mL. The result, as predicted by the ratio explanation, is an adjustment to 50 mL. The ratio of ring to disc in the first pair is 2 to 1 and this ratio must be maintained in order to produce an equal brightness match.

If the perception of object brightness occurs on the basis of the ratios found by Wallach, then the perceived brightnesses of a multitude of objects should be predictable from the brightnesses of the immediate surround. Hurvich and Jameson (1966) projected slides of gray squares on surfaces of varying reflectance and varied the overall illumination of the array. Observers were requested to adjust a comparison stimulus whose brightness could be varied over the entire range of brightnesses to match various portions of the complex slides. They obtained, then, brightness judgments for several portions of the complex field in which the reflectance of the test objects differed for a number of different levels of overall illumination. Their results are presented in Figure 6.4, which relates test luminances to the matching luminances of the subject. Increases in the overall illumination of each slide produced increases in the intensity of each square. However, complete constancy occurred only for area number 4, for which the matching luminance stayed the same

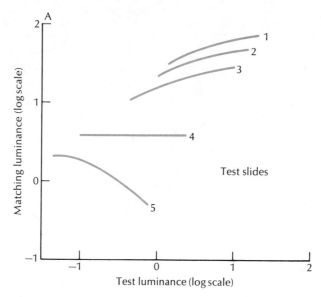

Figure 6.4
Brightness judgments for various portions of a complex visual field as a function of overall illumination. (After Hurvich and Jameson, 1966, in *The Perception of Brightness and Darkness*. Reproduced by permission of Allyn and Bacon, Inc.)

while the overall illumination increased. Areas 1, 2, and 3 required an increase in matching luminance as the overall illumination increased, whereas area 5 required a decrease. This result for area 5 means that the more the overall level of illumination increased, the darker the object appeared, even though the light from the object was more intense.

Such deviations from the expectations of the ratio concept of brightness had been noted in a study by Wallach (1948) as well as in an earlier study by Hess and Pretori (1894). The ratio concept applies only to a limited range of brightnesses. If the general level of illumination is very low, the settings of the matching stimulus will be somewhat lower than under intermediate brightnesses. Moreover, for high levels of overall illumination the matching stimulus will be adjusted brighter than the ratio would predict.

Hurvich and Jameson have isolated a number of factors that help to explain deviations from brightness constancy. In addition, Freeman (1967) has found that the range of conditions under which constancy is found to hold is limited by other factors beyond the overall illumination. It should be clear, however, that the perception of brightness does depend on some aspect of the contrast provided by the relationships of stimulus figures to one another. The more common situation, in which the brightness of an object varies as a function of its surround, provides the next topic.

Brightness contrast.   Brightness constancy appears under certain conditions in which the observer perceives certain stimuli as unchanging despite variations

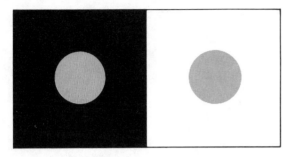

Figure 6.5
Pattern for the demonstration of brightness contrast.

in overall illumination. Under many conditions, however, constancy breaks down and perceived brightness does depend on the surrounding figures. These conditions produce *brightness contrast*. In the experiments developed by Wallach (Figure 6.3), brightness perception depends on the ratio of the surrounding luminance to the test luminance. Brightness, then, is the result of a contrast between test figure and surround. For the intermediate range of luminances, the test figure will appear darker as the luminance of the surround increases and lighter as the brightness of the surround decreases. Figure 6.5 provides an example.

Figure 6.6 contains an example of brightness perception initially developed by Musatti (1953). Although the gray areas are equal from the standpoint of luminance, the gray diagonal bars separated by white lines appear to be lighter than the gray standard on the left. In contrast, the diagonal gray lines separated by black lines appear darker than the standard. Compare these observations with those obtainable with Figure 6.5. There one finds that the gray patch appears lighter in the context of a black surrounding field, whereas in Figure 6.6 the gray bars appear darker when separated by black lines. The former is an example of a *contrast* effect, the latter of an *assimilation* effect. Contrast depends on one uniform area of the field judged in conjunction with the entire surround, and assimilation seems to depend on the proximity and subdivision of the visual field. Using a target similar to Figure 6.6, Helson and Joy (1961) found that the degree of assimilation decreased as the width of the intervening black lines increased. If the width was increased beyond a certain point, the effect reversed and contrast was observed rather than assimilation (Helson, 1964).

Beck (1966c) presented observers with 2-by-2-inch gray squares of intermediate brightness (albedo) subdivided by seven ⅛-inch lines of different reflectance values. The reflectance values of the lines were 88, 58, 49, 31, 20, 16, 10, 7, and 5 percent; the reflectance value of the gray was always 20 percent. If differences between the gray background and the lines produced contrast or assimilation, one would expect the gray to appear increasingly darker than a plain gray standard as the reflectance value of the vertical lines decreased. Conversely, one would predict an apparent lightening of the gray as the reflectance of the lines increased in value. Beck observed assimilation when the reflectance value of the vertical lines was lower than that of the background

Figure 6.6
Pattern for the demonstration of assimilation. (After Musatti, 1953.)

(analogous to the right-hand part of Figure 6.6), but contrast when the line reflectance was greater than the background reflectance.

An additional aspect of contrast is demonstrated by the bands of gray ranging from light to dark and placed side by side in Figure 6.7. The left edge of each bar usually appears to be darker than the right edge. This demonstrates a typical contrast effect: brightness on the left is influenced by the adjacent light region, and brightness on the right by the adjacent dark region. Even when the observer is aware that the gray within each of the seven bars is actually uniform, he still observes a contrast effect.

In 1935 Koffka introduced a rather fascinating design capable of demonstrating brightness constancy. Known as Koffka's gray ring, it is shown in Figure 2.18. The constancy effect can be destroyed by placing your index finger over the intersection of the two fields. The portion of the gray ring on the dark background now appears lighter than the section on the light background. Viewing the figure from a greater distance reverses the brightness effects; the

Figure 6.7
Pattern for the demonstration of simultaneous contrast.

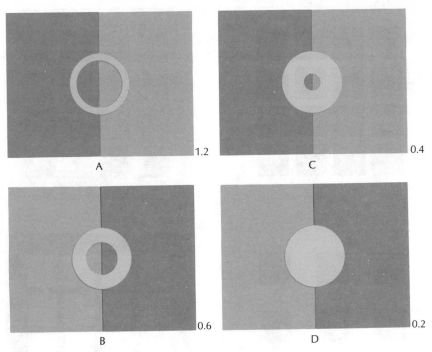

Figure 6.8
Variations on Koffka's gray ring, with mean difference ratings for twelve observers. (After Cohen, Bill, and Gilinsky, 1968.)

visual angle subtended by the gray ring becomes small enough to allow the surround to effect assimilation. After propping up the book and placing a pencil across the intersection of the light and dark surrounds, the reader should look at Figure 2.18 from varying distances, noting especially that as one moves away from the target, contrast shifts to assimilation.

Cohen, Bill, and Gilinsky (1968) reported a number of experiments that examined factors relating to contrast or constancy in the Koffka ring. In one series of experiments subjects were required to rate the difference in brightness between the two halves of the ring from 0 (minimum) to 5 (maximum). The degree of separation between the two halves was varied. For the condition in which both halves came together, subjects rated the difference with an average of 1.2. As the area of separation increased, so did the brightness ratings, with a difference average of 3.2 for the largest separation. As can be seen in Figure 6.8, increasing the width of the ring produces a reduction in contrast. To the right of each of the individual figures is the mean difference rating of the twelve observers.

Attempts to explain assimilation and contrast effects have not been entirely successful. Of the many processes contributing to these effects, an important one is that of *lateral inhibition*. Initially this mechanism was pro-

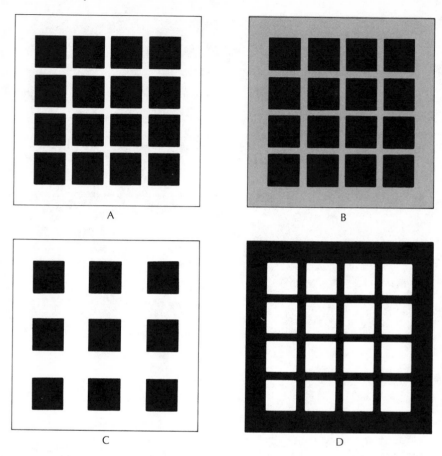

Figure 6.9
Patterns for the demonstration of induced brightness.

posed by Hering (1890), who assumed that retinal elements responding to strong stimulation would inhibit the reactions of adjacent elements. For the simple contrast situation, Hering proposed that the gray patch on a white background appeared to be darker because of the inhibitory effects of the stronger white stimulus around the gray object. Conversely, placing a gray patch on a dark background produced a lighter gray, due to the lack of inhibitory effects by the surround. Such an inhibitory mechanism has been demonstrated for the retina of the cat by Baumgartner (1961) and probably has some influence on the human visual process.

When assimilation occurs, the result is opposite the kind of effect predicted by the influence of lateral inhibition: a dark line causes the gray area to appear darker. As previously noted, however, assimilation depends on a specific degree of proximity of adjacent areas and a specific line width. If

 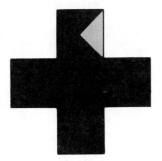

Figure 6.10

The Benary figures (1926). The gray triangle on the right should appear lighter than the gray triangle on the left.

these conditions are not met, contrast results. Figure 6.9 demonstrates what may be an underlying mechanism. If one views any intersection of white lines in part A, all other intersections appear to contain gray squares. The pattern in part B, consisting of gray rather than white lines, also produces the effect: each intersection contains an intermediate gray square. The effect can also be observed when brightness relationships are reversed: the white squares on a black background in part D produce lighter areas at each intersection except the one fixated. In part C the area between the squares is increased, and the effect cannot be observed.

Such effects induced by the grids—often called Hermann grids—are not completely understood, although the mechanism of lateral inhibition certainly plays a part. According to the theory of that mechanism, the white intersection fixated by the observer activates units sensitive to brightness and evokes an inhibitory response from surrounding units. Since the point at which two white lines cross (intersections) stimulates a greater proportion of inhibited units than the white lines outside the intersections, the input for brightness is weakened at precisely these points. During periods of involuntary eye movements over the pattern, the intersections are actively inhibited by the brightness units processing the fixated intersection.

Another factor in brightness contrast and in particular in brightness constancy was proposed by Helmholtz (1866). He suggested that the observer judges brightness by allowing for the overall illumination and thereby inferring the brightness of the target. Landauer (1964) has shown that the instructions given a subject in brightness-matching tasks (whether to attend to reflectance, luminance, or apparent brightness) dictate the brightness matches even if the physical targets remain the same. Such results certainly imply the influence of cognitive process and conscious inference in brightness perception.

A further element of brightness perception is demonstrated in Figure 6.10, introduced by Benary in 1924. The gray triangle superimposed on the cross on the right appears lighter than the triangle abutted to the cross on the left. As Coren (1969a) has demonstrated, the effect depends on the perception of the left-hand triangle as part of the ground. Contrast is enhanced by the

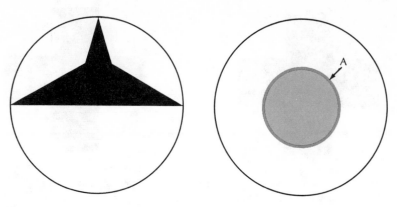

Figure 6.11
Disc pattern for the demonstration of Mach bands (1914). *Left,* stationary disc. *Right,* spinning disc.

perception of the judged area as a figure. Consider the reversible pattern shown in part A (Rubin figure) of Figure 4.28. The white appears lighter when the vase is seen than when the faces are seen; conversely, the latter appear darker when perceived as figures.

A striking illustration of contrast effects was introduced by Ernst Mach (1914) and is referred to as the demonstration of *Mach rings* or *bands.* At the left of Figure 6.11 Mach's figure is at rest. If this figure were spinning, one would expect it to show a darker center disc with a continuous increase in brightness from the outer edge of the disc (the point at which half the figure is black and half white) to the outside edge of the figure (where the ratio of black to white is about 95 percent white to 5 percent black). In fact, when it is spun at a high speed, an observer perceives the pattern shown at the right. The phenomenal ring at the intersection of the darker inner circle and the lighter outer circle of the spinning disc has no physical basis. The effect is the result of a rapid change in luminance occurring at point A in the figure; this rapid increase sets up an inhibitory effect similar to that of the edges of the gray bands in Figure 6.7. Lateral inhibition seems to account for the bands that appear in the Mach demonstration, since the greatest inhibitory effect occurs at the point where luminance increases most rapidly, and it is at this point that the Mach band appears.

Brightness enhancement.   If a light is flashed intermittently at a frequency of about 17 Hz, subjects will judge the brightness of the light to be greater than that of a steady light of similar brightness. This effect, first noted by Brücke (1864) and extensively studied by S. Howard Bartley (1961), is called *brightness enhancement.* The amount of brightness enhancement has been found to depend on specific stimulus conditions such as the initial brightnesses of the test and matching stimuli. Brightness enhancement can occur in response either to a single brief flash (Broca-Sulzer effect) or to an intermittent light situation (Brücke-Bartley effect).

Although the exact nature of brightness enhancement has not been explained, some evidence indicates that the effect is produced by an adaptation in the retina which, under conditions of steady stimulation by a light source, does not summate over the interval of intermittent stimulation. Other conditions may contribute to the phenomenon. For example, Bourassa and Bartley (1965) showed that visual acuity is impaired during periods of brightness enhancement.

The perception of brightness is a complex phenomenon, one which clearly demonstrates the need for extensive study of the influence of context on perception. The brightness of any stimulus depends on the sizes, shapes, and relationships among all other elements present in the field. This dependency is demonstrated by studies of brightness contrast and is even found in experiments involving brightness enhancement (Wasserman, 1966). While the interaction between elements of the stimulus field in brightness perception is impressive, even more striking interaction effects may be observed in the traditional geometric illusions.

Geometric Illusions

The Müller-Lyer illusion mentioned in Chapter 1 (Figure 1.1) is perhaps the best-known geometric illusion, but many others have been discovered. Titchener (1906) provided the most widely accepted definition of such an illusion: "A perception which differs in some way from the perception which the nature of the visual stimuli would lead us to expect" (page 151). This definition can be expanded to the other senses, such as the auditory, since illusions are by no means limited to the visual system. The definition also poses an implicit question: if a given set of stimuli provoke a certain perception in most cases, what is it about the stimuli that prevents us from expecting this perception in all cases? The problem hinges on the difference between physical and perceptual interpretations of the stimulus. Physically, the lines of the Müller-Lyer illusion are of equal length; perceptually, they are not. Unfortunately, the bulk of the research on illusions has centered on a search for conditions producing differences between a physical and a perceptual definition of the stimulus. To understand illusions, however, one should concentrate not on the discrepancy between the physical nature of the stimulus and the perceptual response, but rather on the mechanism by which the perceptual system processes the physical stimulus. If one considers that our senses process input solely on the basis of their capacities and capabilities, our view of the world is dependent on and a result of these capacities and capabilities. One might say that illusions are only a special case in which the inherent discrepancy between physical and perceptual worlds is noticeable.

As an example, consider the variation of the Müller-Lyer illusion shown in Figure 6.12. In the standard figures (top), the left line appears longer than the right; in the bottom part, the figures have been closed. Perhaps we take more than the lines into account in our perception of the figures and judge the size of the entire figures rather than just the length of the lines. While

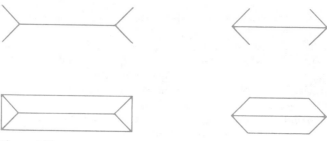

Figure 6.12
Variations on the Müller-Lyer illusion.

this interpretation of the Müller-Lyer illusion, proposed by gestalt psychology, may or may not adequately explain the illusion, it does serve to illustrate the direction of needed research with illusions.

Illusions provide insights into some of the perceptual mechanisms: we see the illusion because of the way in which the perceptual system processes the illusion. A comprehensive theory of perception must include an explanation of illusions, for they represent a fundamental aspect of the process by which the perceiving organism extracts information from the environment.

In the following sections we will consider five basic types of illusions— those of *shape, size, height, width,* and *direction*—and several theories of illusions. For now we will consider an illusion to be an instance of a contradiction between any physical attribute of a stimulus and the observed perceptual response. The ultimate goal of the discussion is to explain the manner in which the perceptual system interprets the stimulus complex. If, as our model of perception implies, the perceiving organism exists in a personal, subjective world of sensory input, then illusions are only illusions to those who choose to note a difference between perception and any other given definition of the physical attributes of the environment. The perceptual world itself constitutes the subjective reality of the observer.

Illusions of width: Several kinds of width illusions are presented in Figure 6.13: A, the Oppel illusion (Oppel, 1854–55); B, a variation of the Müller-Lyer figure; C, the Müller-Lyer and Oppel illusions combined so that the illusion fails; and D, a variation of the Müller-Lyer figure proposed by Ebbinghaus.

Dewar (1967) has conducted a comprehensive study of the underlying variables in the Müller-Lyer illusion. A total of 160 subjects adjusted the apparent length of one line of the illusion until it appeared equal to the other. Dewar varied the degree of inclination of the end angles and the length of the angle lines. Table 6.1 shows the strength of the illusion—how much longer one line had to be made before the two lines appeared to be equal—for each combination of angle and line length. As the table indicates, the illusion is influenced by both these factors. Interestingly enough, the analysis of variance showed no interaction between angle and line length, which would indicate that these two variables exert their influence on perception independently of one another.

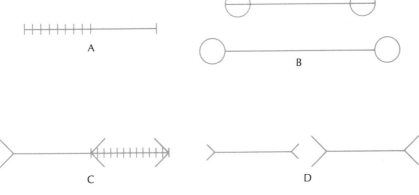

Figure 6.13
Illusions of width. *A*, Oppel. *B* and *D*, variations on the Müller-Lyer. *C*, combination of the Oppel and Müller-Lyer.

Virsu (1967) compared the magnitudes of the illusion of line length for the Oppel figure, the Müller-Lyer figure, and the variation of the Müller-Lyer figure developed by Ebbinghaus. The horizontal lines in the illusions he used were all the same length; however, in the Müller-Lyer/Ebbinghaus version the end lines were longer than in the other figures. The greatest illusion was found for the Müller-Lyer figure (3.2 cm) followed by the Müller-Lyer/Ebbinghaus (2.4 cm). The average illusion for the Oppel figure was 1.5 cm. Virsu also varied the instructions to the subjects, requiring one group to adopt a "whole-perceiving" attitude and another to adopt an "analytic" attitude. The magnitude of the illusion was reduced by the instructions to be analytic. The present author also studied the effect of instructions on perception of the Müller-Lyer figure by instructing a first group of subjects to adjust the lines until they appeared to be subjectively equal and then to readjust them so that they were objectively equal. A second group completed the same tasks but in reverse order. The magnitude of the illusion was markedly reduced under the objective instructions, but the illusion was not completely eliminated.

Table 6.1
Mean strength of the Müller-Lyer illusion
(Dewar, 1967, table 1. Reproduced by permission of author and publisher.)

| | | \multicolumn{4}{Degree of inclination of end angle} | | | |
		30°	60°	90°	120°
Length of	1 cm	6.2 mm	6.1 mm	5.0 mm	3.0 mm
angle line	2 cm	7.3 mm	6.7 mm	5.6 mm	5.9 mm
	3 cm	10.2 mm	8.4 mm	9.4 mm	5.8 mm
	4 cm	11.9 mm	8.4 mm	8.2 mm	6.9 mm

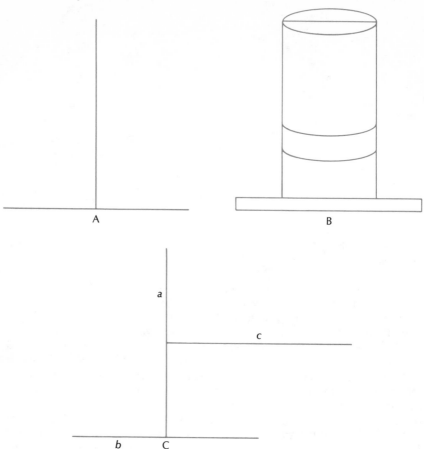

Figure 6.14
Variations on the vertical-horizontal illusion.

A rather interesting relationship between length of presentation and strength of the illusion was reported by Piaget and Vinh-Bang (1961), who worked with the Oppel illusion. They found that the strength of the illusion was greatest for a viewing duration of 200 msec, and that it decreased at longer or shorter time intervals.

Illusions of height.   Figure 6.14 presents several variations of the vertical-horizontal illusion. In each case the height of the figure is physically equal but not apparently equal to the width. Although several individuals noted in early publications that observers frequently overestimated the length of a vertical line relative to a horizontal line (Fick, 1852; Wundt, 1862), this particular variety of illusion was first studied exhaustively by Künnapas (1955a). He found that the standard illusion actually consisted of two illusions: one due to an over-estimation of the length of the vertical line relative to a horizontal line of

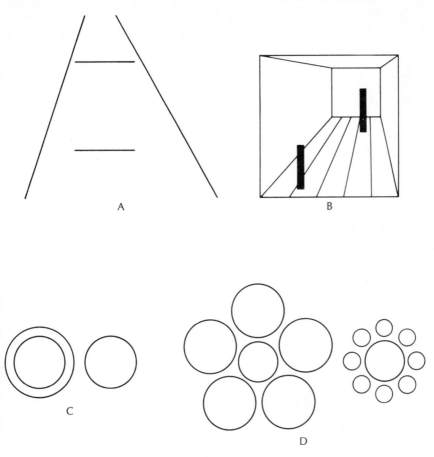

Figure 6.15
Illusions of size. A, Ponzo. B, perspective. C, Delboeuf. D, Titchener.

equal length, and the other due to an overestimation of the line dividing the base line into two halves. The latter illusion is independent of the position of the figure in space, whereas the first depends on the vertical position of the dividing line.[1] Künnapas has developed a figure—part C of Figure 6.14—that displays both illusions. Line a relative to line b provides the illusion of the over-estimated vertical line; line c relative to line b provides the illusion of the undivided line appearing much longer than the divided line.

For the illusion of the length of the vertical line, Künnapas found that if the line was moved away from the center toward either end of the horizontal line, a reduction in the illusion occurred. When the illusion is presented in the

---

[1] Many illusions are actually dual illusions, as will be seen in the following discussion. The Müller-Lyer figure is a good example in which one set of angles makes a line appear shorter and another set of reversed angles makes an identical line seem longer.

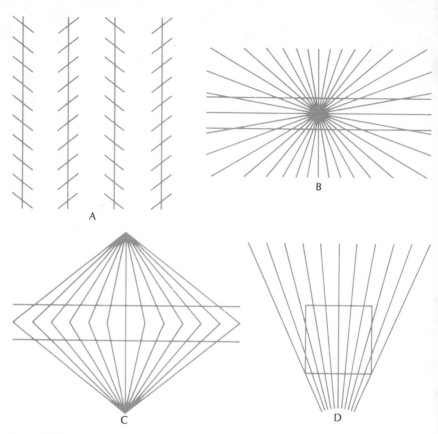

Figure 6.16
Illusions of shape. A, Zöllner. B, Hering. C, Wundt. D, Ehrenstein.

upright position both component illusions are equally active and produce the strong total effect.

Illusions of size.   A number of illusions in which the perceived and the physical sizes of objects are not the same are shown in Figure 6.15. Part A is the Ponzo illusion (1928). Part B is a variation on the Ponzo illusion frequently referred to as the perspective illusion. Part C is the Delboeuf illusion (1865). Part D is a size illusion first described by Titchener (1906).

Working with the Ponzo illusion, Sickels (1942) found an optimal slant for the two diagonal lines. Generally, the illusion increased as these lines were slanted toward the horizontal and then decreased markedly after they passed the optimal angle. The Delboeuf illusion has been extensively studied by Weintraub, Wilson, Greene, and Palmquist (1969). They required observers to indicate whether the circle within the enclosing circle was larger or smaller than a circle of equal size lacking an enclosing circle. They found a maximum illusion when the ratio of the inside circle to the surrounding circle was 2:3. They also found that the illusion could be produced by enclosing the test circle

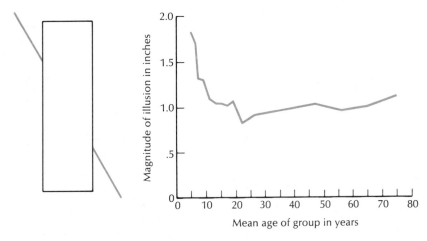

Mean age of group in years

Figure 6.17
Left, the Poggendorf illusion. Right, its magnitude as a function of age. (After Leibowitz and Gwozdecki, 1967. Reproduced by permission of the Society for Research in Child Development. Copyright 1967.)

with dots or with sections of a surrounding circle. Furthermore, varying the contrast by changing the brightnesses of the circle increased the illusion when the center circle was of lower contrast (less bright) than the enclosing circle.

Illusions of shape. Perhaps the most striking geometric illusions are found in this category. Several examples are provided in Figure 6.16. Part A is the Zöllner illusion (1860). Part B is the Hering illusion (1861). The reverse of the Hering illusion in part C is called the Wundt illusion (1896). Part D is an illusion developed by Ehrenstein (1928) which is based on a version of the Ponzo illusion.

In all the illusions the appearance of curved lines is provided by numerous diagonal lines running across parallel lines. Orbison (1939) displayed various geometric shapes on lined backgrounds and found all shapes (e.g., circle, square, triangle) subject to distortion by the diagonal lines. Wallace (1966) has studied the influence of the kinds of diagonal lines and the viewing distance of the Zöllner illusion. Generally, the more lines added to the figure, the stronger the illusion, although at increased distances (4.6 meters) an illusion of curvature was created with only a few diagonal lines.

Some general observations about geometric illusions. Perhaps the most popular kind of study with illusions relates the magnitude of illusion to age. This relationship has been explored for practically all known illusions; the results generally agree with the observations of Leibowitz and Gwozdecki (1967), who studied the Poggendorf illusion on this basis. The magnitude judgments of this illusion as a function of age are provided in Figure 6.17. The strength of the illusion decreases with age, reaching an asymptote after about the eighteenth year. However, as Rausch (1966) points out, due to the large number of

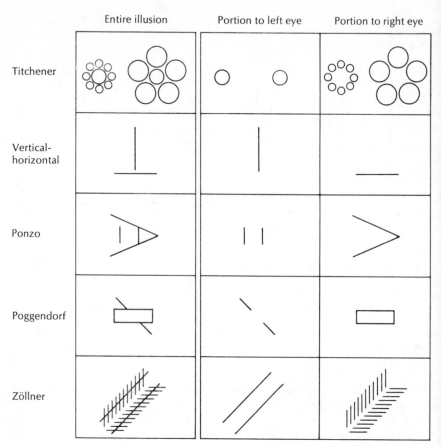

Figure 6.18
Binocular presentation of the parts of various illusions. (After Schiller and Wiener, 1962, figure 1. Reproduced by permission of authors and publisher.)

observations and the variety of conditions of observation, the results of all studies on age and illusions do not agree.

Early research also questioned the magnitude of illusory effects as a function of the frequency of presentation (Judd, 1902; Benussi, 1904). Generally, it was found that the strength of the illusion reduces with increasing frequency of presentation. Although other factors are probably influential, subjects learn that they are dealing with illusions and tend to modify their responses in accordance with the assumed strength of the particular illusion.

Theories of geometrical illusions.   Over the last several hundred years scientists and philosophers have attempted to explain the known geometrical illusions. At the outset we must realize that none of the extant theories is able to explain or incorporate all the available data. If one considers that all illusions are due to the characteristics of the perceptual process, then each theory must explain what specific aspect of the process is responsible for each illusion. However, there is no intrinsic reason for assuming that all illusions are due to the same mechanism. Robinson (1968) has pointed out that illusions can be classified generally as *distorting illusions* or *size illusions*. The former include illusions of shape (Zöllner, Hering, etc.); the latter include illusions of width (Müller-Lyer, Oppel) and of size (Ponzo). Finally, a third category is required to explain the vertical-horizontal illusion; in the opinion of the present author it represents a special case and is caused by a mechanism not operative in the other two groups of illusions.

Retinal inhibition theory.   Ganz (1964) and Robinson (1968) have argued for a mechanism of retinal inhibition to explain illusions of distortion. They suggest that in the Zöllner illusion, for example, the majority of lines running in one direction set up inhibitory processes that repulse or displace the parallel lines running against the majority. Generally, their retinal inhibition theory describes a retinal responding field, based on the pattern of the majority of lines in the field, that inhibits the perception of lines running counter to the field. Thus these lines are displaced away from the diagonal lines.

An experiment by Schiller and Wiener (1962) provides significant data concerning the retinal inhibition theory. They presented five illusions binocularly for brief durations. The element of each illusion usually perceived as distorted was presented to one eye and its distorting elements to the other eye. Figure 6.18 shows the division of the illusions in their study. Of the five illusions chosen, two are illusions of distortion (Zöllner and Poggendorf), two are illusions of size (Ponzo and Titchener), and one is representative of our third category of illusions (vertical-horizontal illusions). Schiller and Wiener concluded that most of the illusions occurred despite binocular separation. This led them to ascribe illusions to central or cognitive areas of the visual system rather than to the inhibitory processes generated in the retina. Although still present, a noticeable reduction in strength occurred in all illusions presented binocularly. The greatest reduction—perhaps to a point where one would question whether an illusion was still evoked—was for the Zöllner and Poggendorf illusions. Because many illusions transfer binocularly, retinal inhibition cannot be used to explain all illusions. However, the breakdown of the illusions of distortion under binocular presentation would lend support to the contention that these types of illusions may in fact be the result of retinal inhibition. Geometrical illusions most probably arise from a number of sources and no single theory is able to account for them all.

Perspective theory.   Thiery (1896) introduced a theory of geometric illusions based on an assumption about the way the visual system uses perspective to judge distances or depth. An excellent example is the Ponzo illusion: since its diagonal lines suggest depth, the top line seems inappropriately large for its position beyond the bottom line. Thiery's principle is demonstrated

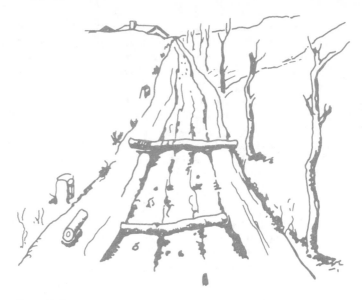

Figure 6.19
Modification of the Ponzo illusion. (After Holst, 1957.)

more clearly by a modification of the Ponzo illusion prepared by Holst (1957), shown in Figure 6.19.

The perspective theory of illusions has been developed in recent years by Tausch (1954) and Gregory (1963, 1966). In their explanation, frequently referred to as the *size constancy theory,* perceptual illusions of size depend on misjudgment of size produced by monocular cues of depth. The Holst drawing in Figure 6.19 and the perspective illusion in Figure 6.20 illustrate this principle.

Illusions frequently occur when the cues of depth are not clear enough to provide a strong perception of depth. Gregory believes that only a few of the usual depth cues are necessary to produce the inconsistency required for an illusion. While he attempts to explain all illusions in terms of depth, the explanation of the Müller-Lyer illusion provided by his theory seems rather far-fetched. According to Gregory, for a subject looking at the Müller-Lyer illusion, the outward-pointing figure is shaped like a roof seen from below; the inward-pointing figure then becomes the same view seen from above. In the view from above, the roof's apex seems closer, and hence longer than the more distant (and thus shorter) apex seen from below.

Logically, the perspective theory and size constancy theory can account for illusions such as the Ponzo illusion. The diagonal lines produce the cue of linear perspective, and therefore the top horizontal line appears more distant than the lower line. Since they are actually the same length, the apparently more distant line thus seems to be larger.

Fisher (1968) developed several versions of the Ponzo figure in which curved lines rather than angles surrounded the straight lines. The figures pro-

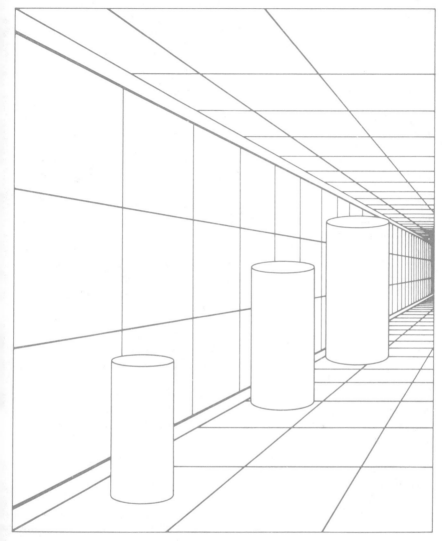

Figure 6.20
Gibson's version of the perspective illusion (1950).

vided no apparent indication of depth, yet they did produce the illusion. Fisher himself points out that the new illusion created by the curved lines may not refute the size constancy theory. Possibly the new illusion transforms the usual Ponzo illusion into an illusion involving retinal inhibition (illusion of distortion).

Sommer (1967) designed a clever examination of the perspective theory using the Zöllner illusion. He mounted the figure so that it could be tilted forward or backward from the frontoparallel plane and required subjects to adjust the figure to apparent vertical. Sommer found that the figure appeared to be vertical only when the top was tilted approximately 3° toward the subject. Displayed in this manner, the figure produces an apparent depth effect. Sommer also reported an experiment involving the Ponzo illusion. The angle of the diagonal lines was varied between 0 and 40° and judgments of the apparent length of the two horizontal lines were obtained. The size of the illusion increased directly with the angle of the diagonal lines. Sommer noted that a reduction in the illusion should have occurred for the largest angle, since the apparent depth of the figure was reduced for this condition; however, this was not the case. Such an observation could be interpreted as support for the perspective theory, since the apparent depth of the illusory figure may not have been reduced at the 40° angle. This possibility was not empirically tested by Sommer.

The results of experiments by Leibowitz and Judisch (1967) are inconsistent with expectations based on the perspective and size constancy theories of illusions. They measured the magnitude of the Ponzo illusion as a function of age and found that the two increased proportionately. This contrasts with the inverse relationship between size and shape constancy and age discussed earlier in this chapter. Therefore, it seems inappropriate to ascribe the Ponzo illusion to size constancy—a perceptual tendency which decreases with age—when the strength of the illusion increases with age.

In a related experiment, Carlson (1966) obtained measures of size constancy and the magnitude of several illusions, including the Müller-Lyer illusion. She found that subjects displaying the best degree of size constancy were no more susceptible to the illusions than those displaying poor size constancy.

Unfortunately, all of the tests of size constancy theory are necessarily indirect. If certain illusions are *caused* by the presence of depth cues, replacing one set of cues with another does not necessarily mean that the depth cues have been removed. The failure of an illusion could mean that the new cues are not sufficient as depth cues; the recurrence of the illusion under other cue conditions could be interpreted to mean that the new cues are also indicative of depth.

Confusion theory.   Many variations on the confusion theory of geometric illusions have been advanced (Woodworth, 1938). The basic assumption of each is that the observer judges more than the illusory aspects of the figure; in other words, he takes into account all the information available in the entire figure. The Müller-Lyer figure is particularly useful in demonstrating this assumption. According to the confusion theory, the subject views not only the two horizontal lines but also the entire figure and the angles that compose it. The figure with the open angles is in fact larger and is judged on that basis (see Figure 6.12). A simple experiment by Künnapas demonstrates the major tenet of the confusion theory. Subjects estimated the length of a horizontal line situated inside a square of varying area. The estimated length of the line was found to increase as a direct function of the size of the square. Hence, the more information contained in the figure (or, the larger the square), the greater the judgment of line length.

An early observation by Heymans (1896) dealt with a particular difficulty in explaining the Müller-Lyer illusion in terms of confusion theory. Heymans noticed that subjects underestimated the length of a line enclosed in angles turned inward, as compared with judgments of a line without angles on the ends. In other words, the Müller-Lyer illusion is actually a dual illusion in which a line enclosed in angles turned inward appears shorter than a line of equal length; and at the same time a line enclosed in angles turned outward appears longer than a simple line of equal length. Erlebacher and Sekuler (1969) explained this discrepancy by pointing out that the subject includes the distance between the tips of the inward-turned angles in his judgment of length. This contributes to his confused assumption that the enclosed line is shorter than the unenclosed line. Extending this argument, Erlebacher and Sekuler suggested that the length and the angle of the end lines could be varied without changing the distance between their tips: the more acute the angle, the shorter the end line. They predicted that despite such changes, the apparent length of the enclosed line would remain constant. Their test of this hypothesis showed that the magnitude of the illusion was the same for all angles under such conditions. Increasing the angles without a corresponding increase of length of angle line served to reduce the illusion.

Most critics of the confusion theory (e.g., Gregory, 1963) have expressed dissatisfaction with the theory's inability to designate exactly what it is that confuses—or gets confused—in illusions. Gibson (1966) has advocated a combination of the confusion and the perspective theory, although he has not worked out such a theory in detail. In general, he believes in the correctness of the confusion theory's emphasis on the total perceptual field. He also suggests that the confusing elements of an illusion may well be inconsistencies in depth cues provided by the gestalt of the total figure.

Optical aberration theory. Chiang (1968) has recently revived a theory of illusions originally proposed by Einthoven (1898): that aberrations of the lens of the eye render unclear the retinal image of the distal stimulus. The degree of aberration depends on the closeness of the elements of the distal stimulus. Illusions involving crossed lines may be explained by such aberrations; in particular, the Poggendorf illusion, which fails to fit squarely in our categories of size and distortion illusions, might be explained in terms of defraction and optical aberration. That is, the observer is unable to perceive the exact point at which the diagonal from the upper left (see Figure 6.17) intersects with the left vertical side of the rectangle, and hence underestimates the point of intersection that displaces the line upward. The same effect would displace the lower right diagonal downward so that the two diagonal lines do not appear to pass through the center of the rectangle. Coren (1969) has attempted to test Chiang's theory by having subjects observe the Poggendorf illusion through artificial pupils and filters designed to reduce the amount of blurring due to abberation. He found a reduction in the illusion under these conditions; however, the magnitude of the reduction was not commensurate with Chiang's predictions. He concluded that optical aberration is a contributing but not a sole factor in illusions involving the diagonal crossing of lines.

By now it should be clear that all illusions are not to be explained by a single theory. At present it appears that no such overall theory can be developed, since the illusions depend on a large number of specific attributes of the visual system. By the nature of the various illusions one should be able to deduce characteristics of the visual response mechanism utilized to process stimulus patterns. Figures composed of large numbers of fine lines—particularly diagonal lines—create illusions of distortion; such illusions probably depend on mechanisms of retinal inhibition, optical aberration, and cognitive confusion. For certain illusions of size, misinterpretations of depth are probably involved.

Theory of the vertical-horizontal illusion. In 1901 Rivers collected data on the susceptibility of observers in different cultures to optical illusions. The general conclusion derived from his experiments was that members of non-Western groups were *more* susceptible to the vertical-horizontal illusion and *less* susceptible to the Müller-Lyer illusion. In a more recent study, Segall, Campbell, and Herskovits (1966) collected data from 1,878 subjects in fifteen different cultures. Their results confirmed some of Rivers's earlier observations —that individuals in all cultures are subject to the vertical-horizontal illusion, and that the Müller-Lyer illusion is not seen readily by non-Westerners.

Künnapas (1955a) lists ten different explanations of the vertical-horizontal illusion. Koffka's (1935), one of the most popular, stresses the *anisotropic* nature of the visual world—that is, that the horizontal dimension of the visual field is much longer than the vertical dimension is high. Thus a vertical line would take up proportionately more of the visual field than would a horizontal line of equal length. The resultant overestimation of the vertical line creates the illusion. It will be recalled that Collins and Stone (1965) cited this relationship in their explanation of the golden section.

Landauer, Rhine, and Rumiz (1968) tested an alternative explanation: that eye movements are responsible for the vertical-horizontal illusion. Vertical eye movements are more restricted than horizontal movements, due on one hand to the anisotropic nature of visual space and on the other to the muscles that conduct eye movements. Thus a shorter vertical eye movement is required to cover the entire vertical field than is needed to traverse the horizontal plane. In their experiment, subjects traced the vertical and horizontal movements of a dot of light. Their estimations of the vertical movement were consistently greater than those of the horizontal.

The vertical-horizontal illusion can be explained in terms of size constancy theory. Since the size (height) of an object is a cue of depth, one could expect an overestimation of vertical elements as opposed to horizontal. The illusion may also be due in part to non-visual factors. Teldford and Tudor (1969) found that a vertical-horizontal illusion exists when the figure is pressed against the skin.

Geometric illusions have fascinated students of perception for a number of years and probably will continue to do so in the future. They will continue to provide excellent proving grounds for any theory of visual perception, because a comprehensive theory must be at home in the world of illusions as well as all other perceptual domains.

Natural Illusions

Illusions also appear in nature. In almost all areas of the world a *wrong-way hill,* a *tilted house,* or an *uphill stream* have been discovered. Each such illusion usually depends on surrounding trees and geological formations that produce an apparent downward or upward slant of the terrain opposite to its actual physical slant. A car parked on such an incline appears to be headed uphill but actually rolls forward when the brake is released.

The best known natural illusion is the *moon illusion:* the moon appears larger on the horizon than at its zenith. One popular explanation proposed that the rays of light emanating from the moon were refracted by the dense atmosphere through which the rays must pass when the moon is seen on the horizon. As Kaufman and Rock (1962) point out, however, the earth's atmosphere could serve only as a *concave* lens, producing a convergence of light rays that would decrease the moon's size.

The most acceptable explanation of the moon illusion is based on a modification of the theory proposed by the Alexandrian astronomer Ptolemy. In essence he believed the illusion depended on a judgment of the moon's size in relation to the terrain in front of it. The terrain gives an impression of great distance; this invites a judgment of larger apparent size for the moon. Such a judgment follows from the size/distance invariance hypothesis discussed in Chapter 5: if the size of the retinal image remains constant, an increase in apparent distance produces a corresponding increase in perceived size. A judgment of the size of an object depends on a knowledge of object distance, which in the case of the moon is provided by the cues of the terrain. Dees (1966) has shown that if a test object of constant retinal-image size is made to appear at various distances by manipulation of disparity and convergence cues, subjects judge the object to be increasing in size as apparent distance increases.

At its zenith the moon is judged without reference to objects of known size. Its perceived size therefore depends on the apparent distance of the sky. King and Gruber (1962) demonstrated that the perceived distance of the sky is greater at the horizon than overhead. Subjects were required to judge the size of afterimages against a blue sky. The size of the afterimage, as discussed in Chapter 2, should depend on the distance of the viewing surface. Afterimages were judged larger against the horizon than overhead, indicating that the sky appears dome-shaped, with the overhead portion closer than the straight ahead or horizon portion. The reader can test this observation by creating an afterimage of an object and viewing it against the sky straight ahead or straight up.

In their study of the moon illusion, Rock and Kaufman (1962) required subjects to look at an artificial moon placed either on the horizon or overhead. They found the estimated size of this moon increased by 1.2 to 1.6 times when it appeared on the horizon. Goldstein (1962) reports an example of the influence of terrain on viewing the moon. On a certain street in New York the moon could be seen isolated in the sky. The street sloped downward, and as the subject walked backward down the slope the moon came closer to the horizon. Size judgments indicated that the moon appeared 1.25 to 1.50 times larger when viewed against the background of trees and buildings at the lower portion of the street.

Finally, Kaufman and Rock (1962) used a series of mirrors to project the actual image of the zenith moon on the horizon. They found that the estimated size of the moon increased. When they reversed the procedure, and projected the horizon moon to zenith position, apparent moon size correspondingly decreased.

You can reduce the effectiveness of the distance cues provided by the terrain by viewing the horizon moon while bending over and looking between your legs. Upside down, the terrain is less efficient in providing distance cues. The apparent size of the moon decreases for most observers assuming this position; others simply become dizzy.

Thor and Wood (1966) cited another factor that may contribute to the moon illusion. They found that in the absence of terrain or background, subjects tended to judge overhead targets to be smaller and farther away than targets viewed straight ahead. They explained this observation with reference to the hypothetical influence of the *vestibular mechanism*. This concept, originally advanced by E. G. Boring (1946), holds that the apparent size of objects tends to be reduced under conditions of head or body tilt. Independent experiments by Wood, Zinkus, and Mountjoy (1968) and by Van Eyl (1968) have confirmed the influence of vestibular stimulation on size judgments. It is interesting to note that this relationship between vestibular stimulation and apparent size can be used to explain the earlier observations of King and Gruber concerning the size of afterimages judged straight ahead or overhead. The reduction in afterimage size is not due to the apparent domed shape of the sky, but rather to the influence of the vestibular mechanism on the processing of optic information under conditions of head tilt.

The magnitude of the vestibular effects obtained in the studies above is not great enough to account for the entire moon illusion. Therefore it appears that the illusion is a product of both factors, influence of terrain and vestibular input.

The geometric vertical-horizontal illusion has a parallel that occurs in the everyday world. Chapanis and Mankin (1967) required subjects to judge several test objects (lamp posts, parking meters, floodlight poles, etc.) by indicating their heights along a horizontal line. Although the shapes of the figures influenced the results, subjects tended to overestimate the heights of the objects tested. For example, both male and female observers overestimated the height of a four-story building by about 25 percent. Some objects evoked marked differences in judgment between male and female observers. Females overestimated a parking meter by 30 percent, males by only 11 percent. Perhaps males did better because they are more familiar with parking meters. Overestimations of vertical distance have also been observed by Kammann (1967). He obtained judgments of horizontal and vertical distances for room interiors, sloping streets, bridges and many other structures. In all cases subjects overestimated the vertical distance. Kammann also measured afterimage size in a manner similar to that of King and Gruber (1962), and noted a size decrease when the afterimage was viewed overhead.

Another interesting illusion can be termed the *tower illusion*. The height of a tower or building seems much greater when one looks from the top down than when one looks from the bottom up. Specifically, all the familiar distance cues are changed due to the new angle of regard at the top of a high observation point; this produces a disorientation in distance judgments. Such overestimation seems to lessen with increased experience in high places.

John Senders (1966) has described an interesting size illusion which he calls the *coffee cup illusion*. Place a full cup of coffee on a table so that it reflects an overhead light. Then raise the cup to your lips or move your head to the cup. The light's image in the coffee appears to *decrease* markedly in size rather than increase, as one might expect. A dull light reflected by a small mirror creates the same effect. Senders explains the illusion as the result of relative size judgments of the cup and the light. As the cup moves closer its size increases much more than the image of the light. The light now fills less of the cup and therefore appears smaller.

Goldstein (1966), who described the street in New York that afforded a particularly impressive moon illusion, has also noted an interesting illusion involving a searchlight beam. Usually such a beam is inclined at a constant angle relative to the horizon and aimed in a given direction. Nevertheless, if the beam is motionless, most observers will judge that it points directly overhead. The illusion probably depends on the lack of distance cues in the open sky and on the apparent closeness of the sky overhead. Thus the beam is located on a perceived path along the sky which passes over the observer. The illusion works only when the light is not viewed from too great a distance and when the beam is motionless.

Figural Aftereffects

The discussion of illusions described situations in which subjective perceptions of certain stimuli did not match the physical characteristics of the stimuli. In each instance the illusion is perceived immediately, when one first sees the stimulus. For this reason such illusions are frequently referred to as *simultaneous illusions*. Another sort of modification of the subjective interpretation of physical characteristics can be induced by the *temporal presentation* of sev-

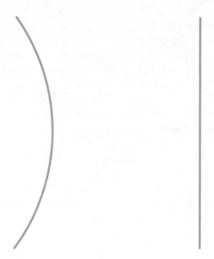

Figure 6.21
Patterns for the demonstration of Gibson's curved line effect.

eral stimuli. If prolonged viewing of a stimulus modifies perception of a second stimulus, the influence is called a *figural aftereffect*. Usually the influencing or preceding stimulus is called the inspection or *I-figure* and the following figure is called the test or *T-figure*. Figure 6.21 can be used to evoke a figural aftereffect. Look at the curved line at the left for three or four minutes while

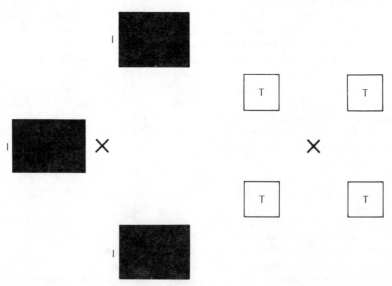

Figure 6.22
Patterns for the demonstration of figural aftereffect. (After Köhler and Wallach, 1944.)

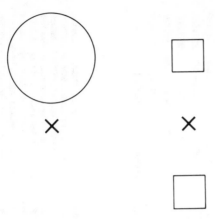

Figure 6.23
Patterns for the demonstration of figural
aftereffect. (After Köhler and Wallach,
1944.)

covering the line at the right with your hand. Move your eyes as close to the
page as possible without a loss in fused vision. After the inspection period look
at the line on the right. According to Gibson's results (1933) it should appear
slightly curved or bowed in the direction opposite that of the inspection figure.

Köhler and Wallach (1944) conducted a thorough study of figural aftereffects. Some of the figures they devised are shown in Figures 6.22 and 6.23.
With both figures you should fix your gaze on the X in the left-hand portion
of the figure. Viewing time should be held to about one minute. After this
inspection period fixate the X at the right. The aftereffect consists of a displacement of elements of the T-figure away from the portions of the visual
field stimulated by elements of the I–figure. In Figure 6.22, for example, the
two left-hand squares of the T-figure are repulsed away from the single left-
hand block of the preceding I-figure. Similarly, the right-hand squares of the
T-figure seem to move closer together as they are repulsed away from the
blocks of the I-figure.

The general conclusion of Köhler and Wallach was that lines or figural
elements tend to be displaced from the portion of the field previously stimulated. For these authors, Gibson's observation—that a straight line appears
curved to the left after prolonged inspection of a line curved strongly to the
right—represents another kind of line repulsion away from previously stimulated areas.

A new kind of figural aftereffect based on the perception of size has been
reported by Blakemore and Sutton (1969). Fix your gaze on the small horizontal
line between the two grids at the left of Figure 6.24. As in the case of the curved
line used by Gibson, a strict fixation is not required. After one minute fix
your gaze on the square located between the two grids on the right.
Rather than a displacement or repulsion of lines, such as found in the older
figural aftereffects, the Blakemore and Sutton figure produces a size aftereffect.
The upper portion of the T-figure previously stimulated by the wide lines of the

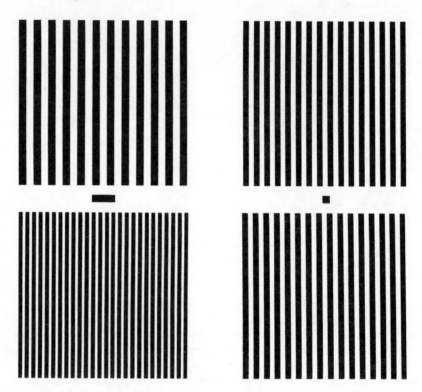

Figure 6.24
Pattern for the demonstration of size aftereffect. (After Blakemore and Sutton, 1969. Copyright 1969 by the American Association for the Advancement of Science.)

I-figure appears to have narrower lines than the lower portion previously stimulated by the narrow grid of the I-figure.

A number of variables affect the magnitude and direction of figural aftereffects. Köhler and Wallach (1944) found that if the stimulus areas of the I-figure were very close to the areas of the T-figure, displacement was slight. Moreover, if the separation between stimulated areas of the I-figure and T-figure was too great, little displacement occurred. An optimal distance, dependent on the figural elements employed, could be determined for most aftereffect demonstrations.

Sagara and Oyama (1957) summarized a number of experiments conducted by various investigators in Japan. Several studies used the Delboeuf illusion shown in part C of Figure 6.15. In the usual illusion the circle within the circle seems larger than the single circle at the right. However, when the larger surrounding circle was employed as an inspection figure and was followed in time by two circles of equal size functioning as a test figure, Sagara's and Oyama's subjects saw the encircled figure as though it were smaller than the single circle. The result is consistent with the observation of Köhler and Wallach (1944) that displacement occurs away from an area previously stimulated, but the effect is opposite that of the usual simultaneous illusion. The critical factor was found to be the time interval between the I- and T-figures.

Ikeda and Obonai (1953) varied the interval between I and T from 0 to 600 msec, as shown in Figure 6.25. The magnitude and direction of each interval's aftereffect are given in millimeters on the vertical axes; the sizes of the I-circles tested for each interval are indicated in millimeters on the horizontal axes. The diameter of the T-circle was 30 mm, so that observations for the influence of the I-figure measured to the left of the vertical dotted line are for I-figures *smaller* than the T-figure; and measurements to the right of the dotted line are for I-figures *larger* than the T-figure. For a zero delay (simultaneous illusion), subjects perceived the enclosed circle to be larger than the unenclosed comparison circle. Ikeda and Obonai found that the magnitude of the effect depended on the proximity of the two; a reversal of the effect occurred at large size differences. As the interval between I- and T-figures lengthened, an increasing displacement or shrinkage of the enclosed circle was observed.

Pollack (1963) reported similar results following an experiment in which simultaneous viewing of combined I- and T-figures produced an attraction effect while successive presentation brought about a displacement. In his study Pollack utilized rows of light and dark blocks, which indicates that the results of Ikeda and Obonai are not necessarily limited to effects of the Delboeuf illusion. That different processes underlie these effects would seem supported by the observation of Piaget and Lambercier (1944). They reported that the magnitude of the Delboeuf illusion decreases with age while the magnitude of the aftereffect produced by successive presentations of the elements of the Delboeuf illusion (Usnadze effect) increases with age. If the relationship between age and aftereffect strength differs for the two effects, one can conclude that they are indeed two distinct effects.

Hammer (1949) measured the strength of the aftereffect as a function of the duration of I-figure viewing. Displacement magnitude increased with inspection times ranging between 0 and 50 seconds, but showed little increase beyond 50 seconds. Hammer also found that the aftereffect decays rapidly after the presentation of the test figure. After the immediate maximum effects, magnitude decreased rapidly up to 90 seconds. Ikeda and Obonai (1953) found a measurable aftereffect with inspection periods as short as 1 second. Evidently an aftereffect develops almost immediately, as demonstrated by Köhler and Wallach (1944), who displayed an I-figure for 250 msec followed by 1,750 msec of darkness. When the cycle was repeated a number of times a measurable aftereffect was obtained. Both these results indicate that the effect builds rapidly and can be maintained for rather long periods.

In the typical observation of figural aftereffects, subjects are required to maintain a strict fixation point during presentation of the I-figure. An exception seems to be the curved-line effect described by Gibson (1933) and the size aftereffect demonstrated by Figure 6.25 in which fixation points are not required. Gibson (1937) has also reported an effect produced by looking at a tilted line with a strict fixation point followed by a vertical line. The latter appears slightly tilted in a direction opposite that of the previously presented tilted line. Such observations indicate that there are several kinds of aftereffects, just as there are various kinds of illusions. Evidently some aftereffects

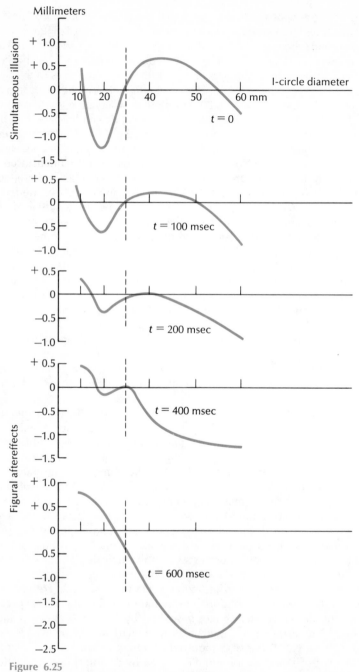

Figure 6.25

Influence of delay interval on the magnitude and direction of after-effects with the Delboeuf illusion. (After Ikeda and Obonai, 1955, as reported by Sagara and Oyama, 1957.)

Figure 6.26
Patterns for the demonstration of spiral aftereffects. (After Holland, 1965.)

depend on the stimulation of specific retinal areas while others are not local-ized. Morant and Harris (1965) have found two aftereffects of a tilted line, one localized and one nonlocalized. In addition Held (1962) has described several figural aftereffects that do not require stationary images.[2]

Spiral aftereffect.   Adams (1834) described a specific kind of aftereffect created by the prolonged viewing of moving objects. He stared at a waterfall for sev-eral minutes and noted, upon looking at the bank, an impression of movement in the opposite direction. Subsequently the effect has been called the *waterfall illusion*. Perhaps the earliest report of a motion aftereffect was recorded by Purkinje (1825), who is better known for his formulation of the chromatic sensitivity shift in dark adaptation (Purkinje effect). After viewing a military parade of horses for a period of one hour, Purkinje noticed an aftereffect while looking at the stationary horses. The aftereffect's motion was against the pre-vious line of march.

Later work on motion aftereffects has involved the use of spirals such as those in Figure 6.26, a technique first introduced by Plateau (1849). The spiral

---

[2] For a more detailed discussion of aftereffects the reader should consult the short book by Holland (1965).

is spun clockwise or counterclockwise for several minutes, then stopped. Subjects report an aftereffect in which the apparent motion of the stationary target is opposite the previous direction of the spiral.

Since the discovery of the spiral aftereffect, a number of important variables contributing to its magnitude have been identified. The effect depends, for example, on the size of the stimulus (Wohlgemuth, 1911; Freud, 1964) and the speed of rotation (McKenzie and Hartman, 1961). More important to the general discussion of aftereffects is the observation by Wohlgemuth (1911) that the maintenance of a strict fixation point during stimulation enhances the aftereffect. Holland (1957) randomly varied the position of the fixation point and compared the magnitude of the aftereffect to a condition involving a stationary fixation point. He found that the changing fixation point produced no aftereffect at all. It appears, then, that spiral as well as most figural aftereffects depend on fixation points.

An important argument concerning the nature of figural and spiral aftereffects has centered on the question of binocular transfer. It will be recalled that early work with afterimages failed to demonstrate transfer when the inducing stimulus was presented to one eye and the test stimulus to the other. Yet both figural and spiral aftereffects transfer to the unstimulated eye. In attempting to account for this, many investigators have failed to note Wohlgemuth's early observation that a binocular transfer does not necessarily imply a central location for the process. He points out that the processes set up by the inducing stimulus continue even after the previously stimulated eye is closed, and that the aftereffect could easily interact with information being relayed to the brain by the contralateral eye. Holland's observation (1965)—that the effect is markedly reduced when the test stimulus is presented to the unstimulated eye—would support this interpretation. Finally, Walls (1953) made the important discovery that binocular transfer occurs only when the inducing and test stimuli are presented to portions of the retina that transmit their information to the same cortical hemisphere.

Figure 6.27, a diagram of the experimental relationships explored by Walls (1953), shows the visual pathways leading from each retina through the optic chiasma and on to the left and right hemispheres. As indicated in the table to the left of the diagram, binocular transfer of the figural aftereffect only occurs when the inspection stimulus and test stimulus are presented to portions of each retina that report input to the same hemisphere. In other words, binocular transfer requires that the process instigated in the ipsilateral eye report to the same side of the brain as the process set up by the test stimulus in the contralateral eye.

In a study of spiral aftereffect duration, Masland (1969) asked subjects to fixate the center of a rotating spiral for 15 minutes. After delay periods ranging from 30 seconds to 24 hours the same spiral, now motionless, was presented as a test figure. When presented to the same portion of the retina previously stimulated by the moving target, the motionless spiral produced a motion aftereffect. Exposure to other portions of the retina elicited no aftereffect. Both results confirm Walls's earlier observations.

Masland (1969) also employed a technique originally proposed by Taylor (1963) in order to assess the magnitude of the aftereffect. After looking at a

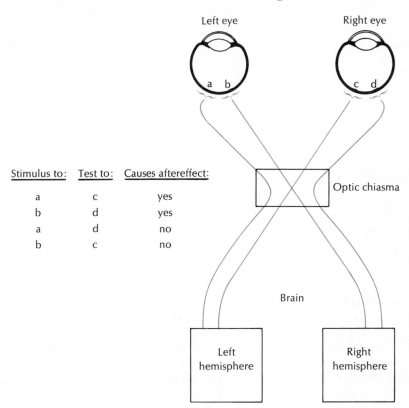

Stimulus to:	Test to:	Causes aftereffect:
a	c	yes
b	d	yes
a	d	no
b	c	no

Figure 6.27
Binocular transfer of figural aftereffects. (After Walls, 1953.)

rotating spiral, subjects were shown a motionless test spiral and asked to report their impressions. If a subject perceived rotary movement in a direction opposite to that of the original rotation, he was asked to adjust the speed of the spiral to compensate for this apparent motion. In other words, the observer set the stationary spiral in motion at a speed equivalent but opposite to the aftereffect motion, thereby eliminating the latter. The original figure, a 3.5-turn spiral similar to part B of Figure 6.26, was spun at 80 revolutions per minute. Table 6.2 shows the speed of the aftereffect computed from the compensatory speeds employed by the observers to counteract the motion aftereffect during the test period. Note that even after a period of 24 hours a marked aftereffect was found.

In his monograph on motion aftereffects Wohlgemuth noted that the magnitude of the aftereffect was greater and longer for a contracting than for an expanding spiral stimulus. Subsequent explanations of such differences by various experimenters have not been successful. Costello (1966) tested the assumption that it is easier to maintain strict fixation when the spiral's perceived motion is contracting than when it is expanding. Scott, Lavender, McWhirt, and Powell (1966) measured eye movements during stimulation but failed to find

Table 6.2

Speed of spiral aftereffect
(Masland, 1969. Copyright 1969 by the American Association for the
Advancement of Science.)

	Test figure delay				
	30 *seconds*	*7.5* *minutes*	*15* *minutes*	*60* *minutes*	*24* *hours*
Speed of aftereffect in revolutions per minute	1.8	1.6	1.4	1.3	1.1

a difference for the expanding or contracting spiral. They noted, however, that the difference between the expanding and contracting aftereffects decreased as subjects gained experience with the effects. Perhaps this decrease is the result of greater familiarity with expanding motion such as that produced when one is riding in an automobile.

Theories of aftereffects.   Köhler and Wallach (1944) and Köhler and Fishback (1950) have advanced a controversial theory of figural aftereffects based on the notion of *satiation,* which was discussed in Chapter 4. They propose that the inducing or I-figure stimulates part of the brain (or eye) until that part becomes satiated and resists further response. When the stimulus T-figure is presented, they suggest that current flows through the neuronal tissue in directions away from the area of greatest resistance, causing displacement of the T-figure.

The Köhler and Wallach theory has several shortcomings, some of which will be discussed in conjunction with other theories of figural aftereffects. One study by Pressey and Kelm (1966) dealt with the influence of sleep deprivation on the magnitude of figural aftereffects. Their stimuli consisted of modified parts of the Delboeuf illusion presented in sequence: a square surrounded by a circle to be compared to a square of equal size. Due to the increased satiation caused by sleep deprivation, the theory would predict smaller aftereffects due to a lack of sleep, and this was the result obtained. At the same time, observations by Sagara and Oyama (1957)—that attraction rather than repulsion is frequently reported for certain kinds of aftereffects—detract from the Köhler and Wallach theory.

Deutsch (1964) has attempted to relate all figural aftereffects to *lateral inhibition,* the mechanism assumed to underlie simultaneous and successive contrast. The mechanism presumably lowers or inhibits the responsiveness of receptor units close to stimulated centers. Applied to figural aftereffects, this notion explains how the I-figure inhibits areas adjacent to the stimulating area. When the T-figure appears, low response in areas surrounding the position of the previous I-figure displaces the T-figure. For spiral aftereffects, the notion suggests an inhibition of motion detectors; in the absence of physical motion, the opposite directional receptors respond. The concept can also account for the need for a fixation point to evoke most aftereffects: for there to be inhibition, there first have to be receptors under continuous stimulation. Fixation ensures that the same units will be stimulated for prolonged periods. Perhaps those aftereffects that can be evoked without a fixation point involve receptors that do not require stimulation of a specific receptive field. For example, the size aftereffect of Blakemore and Sutton involves prolonged stimulation by lines of a specific size.

Hartline (1969) recently reported studies with lower animals indicating that lateral inhibition is greatest in cells near but not adjacent to the stimulated cell. This result helps to explain the so-called distance paradox in figural aftereffects—the fact that the greatest aftereffect is obtained when the T-figure is not immediately adjacent to the area previously occupied by the I-figure.

The most recent theory of figural aftereffects has been developed by Leo Ganz (1966a, b). Whereas Deutsch seeks a relationship between contrast and aftereffects, Ganz draws a parallel between aftereffects and geometric illusions. He points out a basic similarity between the repulsion of T-figures in aftereffects and the repulsion of contours in certain kinds of perceptual illusions. As examples, he cites the Poggendorf, Hering, and Ponzo illusions. For such simultaneous illusions displacement occurs in the presence of the entire figure; for aftereffects, a time interval separates the figure's elements. In the latter condition, Ganz assumes that the I-figure forms an afterimage on the retina. This afterimage interacts with elements of the T-figure. Displacement, Ganz believes, is probably based on mutual or lateral inhibition, as proposed by Deutsch.

Ganz (1966b) marshals several kinds of evidence in support of his theory. For example, stimulus intensity exerts the same influence on aftereffects and simultaneous illusions. An earlier study by Köhler and Wallach (1944) used the Ponzo illusion either in its usual form or divided into I- and T-figures. They found the illusory effects were the same under simultaneous and successive presentation. Dreistadt (1968) used the Wundt and Hering illusions as test figures preceded by lines curved either in the same or opposite direction of the apparent curvature of the parallel lines of the illusions. He reasoned that prolonged viewing of curved-line pairs—the I-figure of part A in Figure 6.28—should reduce the apparent curvature of the lines in the Wundt illusion. Similarly, the I-figure of part B should reduce the apparent curvature of the parallel lines in the Hering illusion. If the simultaneous illusions and figural aftereffects of both figures are caused by the same mechanism, Dreistadt's technique should negate the effects of the illusion: the lines in the test figures should not appear curved. This was the result of the experiment.

Some authors (e.g., Pollack, 1967; Immergluck, 1966) have interpreted Ganz's theory to apply to all figural aftereffects and all simultaneous illusions, although serious objections can be raised to this application. The results of experiments using the Delboeuf illusion, for example, show an attraction effect during the simultaneous presentation and a contour repulsion when the illusion is divided into I- and T-figures. Spitz (1968) has also described several similar experiments in which illusions produce attraction and successive part presentations produce displacement. Pollack (1964) found a reversal of the usual illusory effect when the Müller-Lyer illusion was presented as a figural

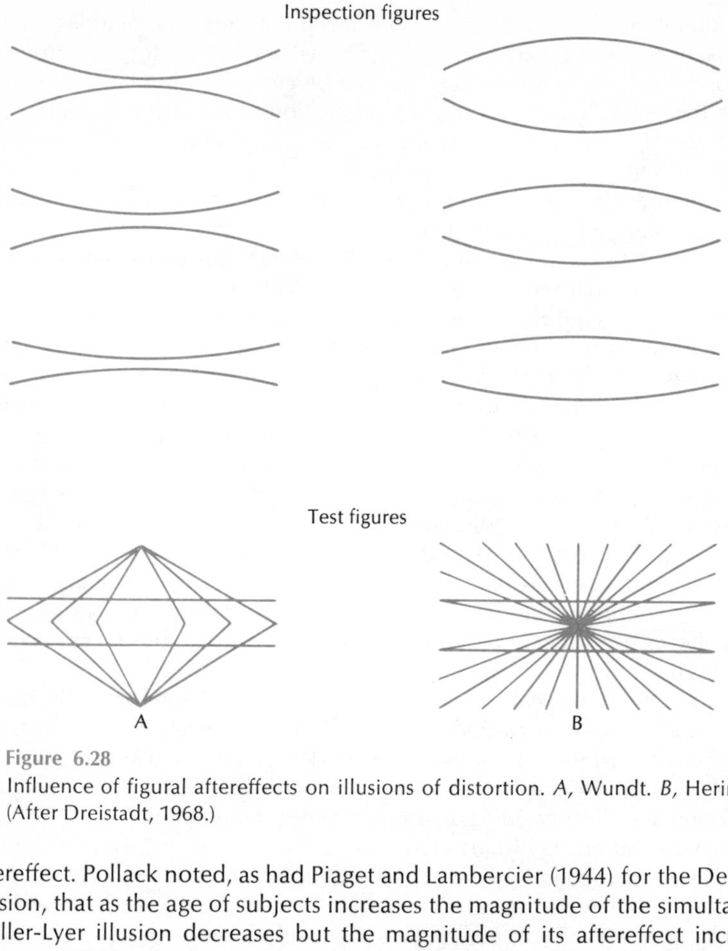

Inspection figures

Test figures

A   B

Figure 6.28
Influence of figural aftereffects on illusions of distortion. A, Wundt. B, Hering.
(After Dreistadt, 1968.)

aftereffect. Pollack noted, as had Piaget and Lambercier (1944) for the Delboeuf illusion, that as the age of subjects increases the magnitude of the simultaneous Müller-Lyer illusion decreases but the magnitude of its aftereffect increases. Wagner (1968) points out another interesting effect of the Müller-Lyer illusion that can be used to criticize Ganz's theory. If the open-angle part of the illusion is compared to a straight line of equal length without end lines, an illusion still results. This contradicts the retinal inhibition theory (Deutsch, 1964) which predicts that the single line should appear longer, since no inhibitory influences are working on it. The line with end angles, however, should be subject to inhibitory effects.

Finally, Immergluck (1966) notes that observers who saw strong figural aftereffects were not necessarily those most susceptible to the Zöllner illusion. His data are presented in Table 6.3.

Although the evidence amassed against Ganz's theory seems impressive, one must remember that Ganz did not propose to explain the relationships between all optical illusions and all figural aftereffects. In fact, Ganz introduced his theory (1966a) with the observation that "in many common geometrical illusions, such as the Poggendorf, Hering, and Ponzo illusions, con-

Table 6.3

Susceptibility to the Zöllner illusion
(Immergluck, 1966)

	Illusion	No illusion
Aftereffects	21	11
No aftereffects	7	17

tours appear to mutually repel one another when they are suitably close in the visual field" (p. 151). Since no theory has successfully accounted for all illusions, and since illusions probably depend on a number of different perceptual mechanisms, it is not surprising that Ganz's theory fails to hold for all illusions. Of the two categories of illusions proposed by Robinson (1968), Ganz's theory seems better suited to explain distortion illusions (e.g., Hering, Wundt, etc.) than illusions of size (e.g., Ponzo, Müller-Lyer, Delboeuf, etc.). Although no final conclusion can be drawn, mutual inhibition seems to be a common underlying factor in both distortion illusions and the figural aftereffects. In experiments with the latter, the suggestion that an afterimage crosses the temporal gap between the I-figure and the T-figure is the most plausible.

Any comprehensive theory of vision and perception must be able to take into account the various effects discussed in the present chapter. Work with figural aftereffects provides information similar to that derived from studies of contrast and simultaneous illusions. Such data aid in explaining the various functions of the visual system. These in turn contribute to a better understanding of the system's underlying capabilities and capacities.

Adaptation Level Theory

As indicated by the discussion of topics in this chapter, perception does not depend solely on the physical characteristics of the stimuli that give rise to a percept. An observer viewing an illusion is obviously responding to more than the isolated elements of the stimulus often used as dependent variables in experiments (e.g., length of line, circle size, line distortion, etc.). Some illusory effects can be explained in terms of the physiological mechanisms that produce particular responses. The findings concerning figural aftereffects are a case in point. A general characteristic of the perceptual process may be the ability to incorporate all aspects of any situation into its response. This characteristic of perception has been explored over a number of years by Harry Helson and co-workers. Out of their extensive research has developed an *adaptation level theory* capable of explaining and predicting behavior in an amazing number of situations (Helson, 1964a, b).

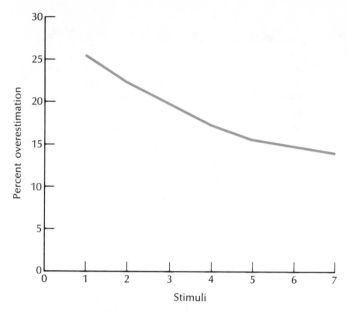

Figure 6.29
Influence of background stimuli on judgments of the size of focal stimuli. (After Helson and Bevan, 1964.)

The major tenet of Helson's adaptation level theory is that "an individual's attitudes, values, ways of structuring his experiences, judgments of physical, aesthetic and symbolic objects, intellectual and emotional behavior, learning, and interpersonal relations all represent modes of adaptation to environmental and organismic forces" (1964a, p. 37). All components of behavior are subject to a level of adaptation determined by all previous responses and by levels of adaptation currently maintained by all sensory systems. Usually the kinds of adaptation levels at work are indicated by the way the observer responds to environmental stimuli.

Helson has attempted to quantify the levels of adaptation for specific stimuli by using the concept of the *weighted mean*. The level of adaptation AL depends on the weighted mean of all *focal stimuli* X^h, the stimuli presently in the focus of attention; on the *background stimuli* Y^i, the context within which the focal stimuli are observed; and on the *residual stimuli* R^j, or the sum total of past experience, physiological state, constitutional factors, and personality variables. Thus the formula $AL = X^h Y^i R^j$.

An example of the influence of adaptation level on behavior should clarify the concept. Helson and Bevan (1964) studied the effect of variations in background stimuli on the perception of a focal stimulus. They presented a series of cards containing identical black areas in their centers. The first card was 1.5 by 2 inches, and each successive card increased in width by 1.5 inches and in height by 2 inches. Observers were asked to judge the size of each black area. The results are presented in Figure 6.29. Although the physical di-

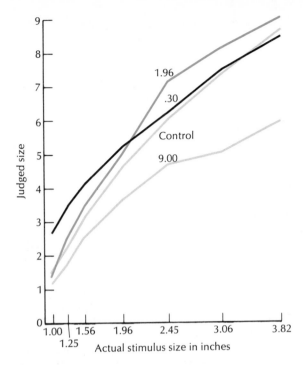

Figure 6.30
Influence of anchor stimuli on judgments of size. (After
Steger and Helson in Helson, 1964b.)

mensions of the focal stimulus remained unchanged, the observers incorporated the background size in their judgments. Furthermore, the influence of
each successive judgment produced a change in adaptation level and a correspondingly larger misjudgment of the size of the focal stimulus.

A study by Steger and Helson that was reported by Helson (1964b) demonstrates the influence of successive changes in focal stimuli and the influence
of residual stimuli. Subjects in four groups were asked to judge the size of
a series of black squares ranging from 1 to 3.82 inches. Prior to each judgment,
members of one group saw an *anchor* stimulus—a square of 1.96 inches
chosen from the geometric center of the series of squares. Two other groups
viewed anchor stimuli much smaller (0.30 inch) or much larger (9 inches)
than any square in the series. Finally, a control group made its judgments
in the absence of any anchoring stimulus. The experimental results are presented in Figure 6.30. They clearly show the influence of the anchors on
judgments of size. Preceding the estimations with a large stimulus caused
the general size of the following squares to appear smaller; in contrast, the
small anchor caused an increase in judged size. The anchor, then, established
an adaptation level for size judgment that influenced subsequent judgments
of focal stimuli. The residual effect of experience with anchors was demonstrated in a follow-up study conducted with the same subjects one week later.

Observers were asked to pick the smallest, middle-sized, and largest square used in the earlier experiment from a range of squares varying in size from 0.10 to 14.56 inches. The group exposed to the large anchor during the first study selected three squares significantly smaller than the three selected by the group exposed to small anchors. The two other groups (control and geometric mean anchor) selected three sizes falling between the extreme judgments of the anchor groups. Thus the level of adaptation produced in the earlier study displayed a residual effect on the perception of the stimuli after one week.

In Chapter 2 a discussion of Helson's work on perceived color referred to the concept of adaptation level in perception of hue. It will be recalled that the prediction of perceived color depended on a background gray that, under chromatic illumination, was actually perceived as achromatic. The hue and saturation perceived depended on the brightness of the background and on the preceding adaptation level for a given color. Hence, subjects viewing neutral gray test figures after five minutes of adaptation to red light perceived the color of the squares differently than other observers subjected to a different adapting color.

Unquestionably adaptation level theory has been used most often to predict the influence of anchor stimuli on perceptual judgments. Some of this work will be reviewed in Chapter 8. A further example from audition should demonstrate that the adaptation level concept is useful in explaining both auditory and visual phenomena. Morrison and Nazzaro (1966) investigated adaptation level theory's definition of the weighted mean as the point in a series of stimuli evoking a neutral response. From a control group they obtained judgments of pitch for tones of 600, 700, 800, 900, and 1,000 Hz. A second group judged the same tones but listened to a 1,300-Hz anchor tone after each of the five tones. As predicted by adaptation level theory, the magnitude judgments were shifted away from the anchor. That is, for the group receiving the anchor, judged pitch was generally lower than the control.

If we consider the topics discussed in this chapter in light of our active perceiver model of perception, it is clear that the process of extracting information from the environment is subject to several limitations imposed by the sensory mechanisms. The geometric and natural illusions, for example, illustrate the observer's inability to disassociate some attribute of the environment from its context. In another example, the perception of brightness depends on all other brightness relationships in the environment as well as on preceding changes in brightness levels. That the perceiver has a continuing dynamic interaction with the environment is most strongly indicated by the work of the adaptation level theorists. In their view, the perception of the moment is analyzed in terms of all the organism's preceding and concurrent sensory processes, memory variables, and physiological attributes. Despite the obvious importance of the total perceptual context, researchers frequently attempt to isolate and analyze a particular sensory stimulus without adequate control of its contextual variables.

CHAPTER 7
The Perception of Motion, Causality, and Time

Until now we have tended to regard perception as an experience based on static phenomena, and we have concentrated on the perception of single or multiple objects that are for the most part immobile. However, the perceptual environment is seldom stationary, and the constant changes introduced by the movements of objects, the observer's movements, the interaction and influence of one object on another, and the passage of time all contribute to the dynamic process of perception.

259

The Perception of Movement

Most organisms display extreme sensitivity to movement, and man is not an exception. In fact, the introduction of movement in a complex perceptual field usually influences the process of selection by which certain potential stimuli become effective stimuli. In the present section we will discuss the objective conditions of movement and attempt to analyze the mechanism by which such movement is perceived. In the sections that follow we will also consider several conditions of apparent movement and examine their relationship to the mechanism of movement perception.

There are two basic conditions for movement perception: the displacement of an object in the environment, and the motion of the observer himself. In the second instance the observer perceives his own locomotion as well as the displacement of specific objects in his environment. We will consider both of these conditions in detail.

Early attempts to analyze movement perception specified various proximal stimulations of the retina capable of producing a perception of movement. Table 7.1 lists such retinal conditions and the type of movement perception accompanying each. The various conditions emphasize the difficulty facing the theorist or would-be classifier: the same patterns of retinal stimulation produce markedly different perceptions, and in many cases the same perceptions are caused by different patterns. Despite such difficulty, Table 7.1 constitutes at least an attempt to differentiate conditions of motion on the basis of the patterns of retinal stimulation.

One's first guess might be that motion perception is due to the displacement of an image across the retina. The *retinal image displacement theory*[1] holds that as the image of the distal stimulus moves across the retina, new receptors are stimulated in a pattern of successive change. This consistent pattern of stimulation is interpreted by the perceiving organism as external object movement.

Several problems with the retinal image displacement theory are immediately obvious. First, how does the organism obtain the proper perception when several conditions are capable of producing the same pattern of retinal stimulation? Second, why does the world seem not to move when the eyes, and therefore the retinal images, are in motion? With regard to the latter it will be recalled from the discussion in Chapter 3 that the eye is constantly in motion. How, then, can the observer perceive motion when the eye's movement—a prerequisite for figure perception—is always creating new patterns of retinal stimulation? To accommodate these phenomena, the retinal image displacement theory also suggests the presence of an analytic mechanism of

[1] It is very difficult to identify the original proponent of the retinal image displacement theory. The phrase was suggested by Gibson (1968) in the context of opposition to his own theory of the ambient array. Probably Helmholtz (1866) was influential in the development of the concept, although its application reached a high point with the gestalt psychologists and in particular with Wertheimer (1912).

Table 7.1

Retinal conditions during movement

Condition	Retinal condition	Perception
Sweeping eye movements	Constant change in pattern of retinal receptors stimulated	No motion
Stationary eye, single objects in motion	Successive retinal receptors stimulated by object	Object motion
Stationary eye, entire field in motion	Constant change in pattern of retinal receptors stimulated	Observer motion
Observer fixates moving object	Constant change in pattern of retinal receptors stimulated except for fixated object	Object motion
Observer fixates object and turns head	Constant change in pattern of retinal receptors stimulated except for fixated object	Head movement
Observer in motion with fixation point maintained on single object	Constant change in pattern of retinal receptors stimulated except for fixated object	Observer motion
Observer in motion without fixation point	Constant change in pattern of retinal receptors stimulated	Observer motion

the brain that cancels out the effects of eye movements. Helmholtz (1896) called one element of this mechanism the "effort of the will" in moving the eyes; awareness of this effort enables the observer to distinguish between similar conditions of proximal stimulation. More recently Rock (1966) has referred to *central intention*. For example, the pattern of stimulation created when an observer turns his eyes would be accompanied by the knowledge that he had actually caused his own eyes to turn. This motion could then be "subtracted" from the retinal image motion that would otherwise signal movement in the environment.

Some well-known data would seem to support retinal displacement as the critical factor in movement perception. If an observer closes one eye and moves the ball of the other eye with his fingertip, the environment appears to move. Research with the waterfall motion aftereffect demonstrates that only movement across the retina creates an effect; fixating a moving object is ineffective (Anstis and Gregory, 1965). One might conclude, therefore, that all motion perception is the result of retinal displacement.

A major criticism of the retinal image displacement hypothesis can be derived from the model of perception discussed throughout the present text. In almost all perceptual processes described thus far the observer is actively involved in extracting information from the environment. The retinal displacement concept requires only a passive observer, one who deduces motion on the basis of the play of images across the retina and his knowledge of his own actions.

That the retina is involved in motion perception cannot be denied, since the retina is the initial source of visual information. However, Gibson (1966) has pointed out that it is not the image of the external object that is displaced across the retina. Rather, it is the active retina in constant motion that is displaced across the image. In an enlightening paper Gibson (1968) reconsidered the theoretical analysis of motion perception and argued that its source is not displacement of the retinal image but actual displacement of the external object.

Gibson's theory of the ambient array.   Gibson believes that the perception of movement is the result of changes in the ambient array of light reflected by objects in the external environment. Changes can occur in that environment to create five types of motion. Specifically, these include changes of:

1.   An object in the environment;
2.   The observer;
3.   Objects while the observer moves;
4.   The observer's head; and
5.   The observer's bodily extremities in the field of view.

As illustrated by the data in Table 7.1, these conditions produce retinal image displacement that can frequently describe more than one kind of actual movement. Yet, on the basis of information contained in the ambient light array coming from the environment, the visual system differentiates easily between each of these conditions. This approach—the ambient array theory of motion perception—explains perception in terms of movement in the environment rather than by an analysis of retinal stimulation.

   Movement of an external object.   Several characteristic changes or transformations occur as an object moves. Against its stable environment the object reflects varying patterns of light; portions of the background are successively covered and uncovered. In other words, as an object moves toward the observer an increasing *occlusion* develops on all sides; an object moving away from the observer produces an increasing *disocclusion*. From these relationships and from the rate by which they change the direction and speed of motion can be deduced. If a moving object is seen from different viewpoints, very specific changes are noticeable in its appearance. These changes may be termed transformations in the ambient array. In addition to the occlusion effects, transformations provide changing perspectives, textures, and brightness relationships.

   Movement of the observer.   When the observer himself is in motion the entire array is transformed. This transformation can be experienced even when the observer is stationary. For example, sitting in a train or car and observing the movement of a neighboring train or truck which covers the entire field of view can produce a compelling subjective impression of movement.

Table 7.2

Perception experience and transformations in the ambient light array
(Gibson, 1968)

Occlusion and disocclusion of environment by an object	Object motion
Transformation of the total ambient array	Observer movement
Eye sweeps over entire array without ambient transformations	Eye movement
Occlusion and disocclusion at the borders of the visual field	Head or body turning

Other sources of information, such as changes in vestibular and kinesthetic systems, usually help the observer to interpret correctly (or incorrectly) the changes in the total array that indicate subject motion.

Movement of objects while the observer moves.   This case combines the kinds of ambient light changes described in the two previous conditions. The movement of the observer is perceived by means of a transformation of the entire array, and the movement of objects is indicated by the occlusion and disocclusion of portions of the environment.

Movement of the observer's head.   To turn the head produces a different kind of transformation. As the head is turned from left to right, occlusion occurs on the left edge of the visual field and disocclusion on the right edge. Objects in the direction of turn are uncovered or come into view, while those away from the direction of turn are successively covered.

Movement of the observer's bodily extremities in the field of view.   The perceived motion of arms and legs, as Gibson points out, falls somewhere between the subjective motion of observer displacement and the movement of external objects. In addition to the fact that the object is clearly connected to the observer and also subject to kinesthetic feedback, movement is defined by occlusion and disocclusion, as with any external object placed in motion in the field of view. Gibson's theory of movement is summarized in Table 7.2, which compares the transformations occurring in the visual field to the resulting perceptions. Each specific kind of transformation produces a single perceptual experience.

Absolute movement perception.   Gibson does not discuss one other condition of movement—that of a target without contours (e.g., a small dot of light) moving across a homogeneous background. The situation is similar to the demonstration of autokinetic movement, except that the target light actually moves. Kinchla and Allan (1969) have called the perception of movement under such conditions *absolute movement perception,* as opposed to movement perception in a textured environment, or *relative movement perception*. The perception of movement cannot arise from transformations in the ambient array provided by the target because the target has no contours. Nor can one speak of occlusion and disocclusion effects in the strictest sense, because the background contains no texture.

Kinchla and Allan propose that the perception of movement occurs when the observer is able to compare the memory trace of the object in one position in visual space to a new position in the field. If the observer perceives a difference between the position of the stimulus at one time and at another time a short while later, then he is able to build a percept of motion. Movement is inferred from the cue provided by a perceived change in the position of the target within the visual field. Under these conditions, slight, discrete movements are frequently undetected, while larger or more rapid movements are noticeable.

Absolute movement perception could be considered the result of a special case of occlusion and disocclusion. Rather than covering and uncovering a portion of the background, the observer now finds the target occluding a specific portion of the visual field previously unoccupied by the target. By comparing the new position with his memory of the target's previous position, the observer infers movement.

In both absolute and relative movement perception the observer utilizes cues extracted from the environment (e.g., occlusion and disocclusion, object transformation, change in spatial position) to develop his perception of occurrences in the external world. The experience of movement is developed from the perceptual process and is based on an interpretation of input by the perceiving organism.

Movement thresholds.   Not enough research has been devoted to accurate measurements of the thresholds for the perception of movement. The reported data are based, for the most part, on thresholds established via the older techniques of psychophysics: the method of limits and the method of intervals. The classic data were obtained by Aubert (1886), who estimated the lowest velocity of a moving target at which subjects were just able to perceive movement (movement threshold). In one condition he presented a pattern of motionless lines and superimposed this background with a second pattern of fine lines. When the second pattern was set in motion, Aubert observed the velocity (amounts of displacement in minutes of arc as a function of time in seconds) necessary for movement to be detected. That is, by varying the amount of displacement, Aubert measured the threshold for movement perception. With a velocity of 1' to 2' of arc per second, the observers reported movement of the lines. In another condition, the same pattern of fine lines was set in motion without a background pattern. In this case a velocity of 10' to 20' of arc per second was required before the observers could detect movement.

Leibowitz (1955a) followed up Aubert's observation of the marked influence of background lines in the detection of movement. In one study the movement threshold for fine lines with and without background lines was obtained under several conditions of stimulus duration. The presence of background lines resulted in a lower threshold for movement only with longer stimulus durations. When the moving lines were presented for only 250 msec, the threshold was independent of any influence of background pattern.

If one attempts to perceive the movement of the minute hand on a clock, it is easier to perceive the movement in the context of one of the clock's numbers. Perhaps such slow movement is not actually perceived during long exposures, but only inferred, on the basis of a noticeable change in the relationship between the moving stimulus and the contoured background.

Leibowitz (1955b) also studied the influence of luminance on movement perception. When the luminance of the display was increased, movement could be detected at lower velocities. That is, increases in the luminance of the display could be accompanied by corresponding reductions in velocity without a loss in movement perception. Brown (1955) noted that this observation was analogous to the *Roscoe-Bunson law* which relates the threshold of visual acuity to the products of luminance and duration. If one increases the luminance of a target, a corresponding decrease in duration will not result in a loss of acuity. As the Roscoe-Bunson law had been shown to hold only for a limited range of durations—below certain critical luminance values acuity cannot be maintained by corresponding increases in duration—Brown sought to establish the limits of movement perception when luminance and duration were varied. He found the expected result: the lowest velocity capable of being reported (movement threshold) could be held constant by decreasing luminance and increasing duration. The proportional relationship held for durations up to 750 msec.

Very few researchers have sought to measure the upper limits of acuity for targets moving at high speeds. An exception is Ludvigh (1948), who reported zero levels of acuity for targets moving at angular speeds of 200° per second.

J. F. Brown (1931a, b) reported several extensive experiments involving the relationship between movement perception and the physical velocity of a moving target. Brown used a string of small black squares, any one of which could be set in motion. His results for the lowest velocity detectable were comparable to the values obtained earlier by Aubert: angular velocities of approximately 2′ of arc per second were required for movement to be perceived. After introducing successive changes in the velocity of the moving squares, Brown listed eight variations in the reported perceptions. The subjective experience and the average velocity for each perception are provided in Table 7.3.

Clearly much of the work on movement thresholds is subject to the same criticisms advanced in conjunction with the discussion of the classic studies of absolute threshold. Very few studies have applied signal detection methods to the study of movement detection. One experiment by Shaffer and Wallach (1966) measured the threshold for movement with the method of constant stimuli—a method considered acceptable by signal detection theorists (see Chapter 1). The movement thresholds were compared for two conditions of motion perception. In one condition an object in the visual field was set in motion while the rest of the field remained immobile; in the other condition

Table 7.3

Movement perception as a function of velocity
(Brown, 1931*b*)

Perception	Target velocity
1. No movement	Below 2' of arc per second
2. Square seen moving in some parts of field	2' to 6' of arc per second
3. Square seen moving in all parts of field	Below 1° per second
4. Gradually increasing velocity from slow to fast	1° to 4° per second
5. Apparent backward motion of square	3° to 9° per second
6. Two squares perceived in motion	3° to 19° per second
7. Light gray line with some darker sections	12° to 20° per second
8. Smooth gray line filling center of target area	18° to 32° per second

the visual field was set in motion and the object remained immobile. While the phenomenal experience of movement induced by the two conditions was the same, the thresholds for the detection of movement differed. With a speed of movement of 164' of arc per second, a displacement of the object of only 1.8' was necessary for the movement to be detected. However, when the field was moved and the object remained stable, a displacement of 4.8' was required for movement to be perceived.

This study is of particular importance for the discussion of the theoretical explanation of movement perception. As far as the pattern of retinal stimulation is concerned, it makes no difference whether the object is set in motion and the field left immobile or the field is in motion and the object stable. Nevertheless, Shaffer and Wallach found differences in the movement thresholds for the two conditions. For the ambient array theory proposed by Gibson, which seeks to isolate the clues of motion perception in transformations of the visual array rather than in patterns of retinal stimulation, there are differences between the two conditions. In the condition in which the object moves, the dominant cues are occlusion and disocclusion of the background by the object. The condition in which the field moves supplies the additional cues of occlusion and disocclusion at the borders of the visual field. These latter cues usually signal observer movement when accompanied by appropriate vestibular and kinesthetic cues and are seldom interpreted as an indication of the entire field's movement. Therefore they are probably involved in the maintenance of threshold differences in the two conditions.

In an earlier study, J. F. Brown (1928) analyzed the subjective estimates of the physical velocity of targets moving at velocities well above threshold. The basic design required the observer to match the velocity of a variable target to the physical speed of a standard target. In one study subjects viewed standard objects that were twice the size of the comparison targets. Furthermore, the viewing field in which the standards were presented was twice the size of the field of the comparison targets. In order to obtain a satisfactory match, the

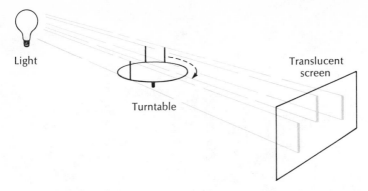

Figure 7.1
Diagram of an apparatus for the demonstration of the kinetic depth effect.
(After Metzger, 1934.)

observers adjusted the velocity of the variable target to about half the velocity of the standard; phenomenal speed depended on the relative size of the targets and on the background. Presenting different sized objects as the test object and standard object, but holding field size constant, generally brought about an overestimation of the speed of smaller targets. Judgments of speed of movement, then, depend on the frame of reference against which speed is to be judged. In a manner similar to judgments of size or brightness, observers are only able to judge motion accurately relative to the objects of the environment. Obviously if the observer is unaware of the true size of the target (as in a totally dark environment) he cannot judge velocity correctly.

Kinetic depth effect.   Metzger (1934) designed an experiment in which vertical rods were mounted on a turntable located between a light source and a translucent screen. A diagram of the basic design is shown in Figure 7.1. The subjects observed the movements of the shadows of the rods on the screen. At rest, the distal stimuli (shadows on the screen) were clearly two-dimensional and were described as such by all observers prior to the movement of the turntable. When movement was introduced, however, most subjects reported that the rods were moving in three dimensions.

Wallach and O'Connell (1953) proposed the phrase *kinetic depth effect* to describe the transformations of two-dimensional stimuli into three-dimensional stimuli when motion is introduced. In their initial experiments wire forms such as those represented in Figure 7.2 were projected as shadows on a viewing screen. Again the forms were seen as two-dimensional until they began to move.

One study by Wallach and O'Connell (1953) presented the shadows cast by a rotating figure of three rods connected at their ends and diverging at angles of 110°. The two-dimensional projections on the screen were perceived in three dimensions only if the observers could see the ends of the rods. The authors concluded that the kinetic depth effect occurs only if there are changes in both the apparent length and the direction of the shadows. Changes in direc-

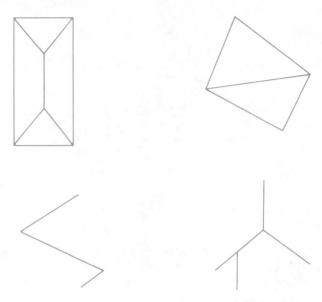

Figure 7.2
Wire figures for the demonstration of kinetic depth effects.
(After Wallach and O'Connell, 1953.)

tion alone were not sufficient to produce a depth effect. Several other studies
used Metzger's original design (Figure 7.1) to obtain descriptions of three-dimensional motion. White and Mueser (1960) found the three-dimensional effect
noticeable with as few as two moving rods. The frequency of depth-effect
reports increased with the number of elements shown in motion. Using only
two rods—the two-dimensional projections of which displayed only changes
in length but not direction—still produced depth perception. The result is
similar to that of the study by Wallach and O'Connell. Ross (1967) found that
the perceived movement or the pathway of the three-dimensional movement became more and more stable as the number of rods in the shadow
display increased. Interestingly, the stable perceptions were not necessarily
more accurate descriptions of the actual movements of the rods producing
the shadows.

In his analysis of the kinetic depth effect, Braunstein (1962) sought to explain the phenomena by identifying the retinal cues for depth found in the ambient arrays produced by objects in motion. Considering Gibson's more recent
theory of motion perception (discussed at the beginning of this chapter), one
might attempt to analyze the perception of motion as a function of the stimulus attributes of the ambient array. If we attempt to apply this theory, then
movement perception depends on a transformation of objects in the visual
field. By transforming two-dimensional arrays one would expect motion perception. Furthermore, the direction of motion would be indicated by the nature of the changes in the ambient array; such changes were discussed earlier

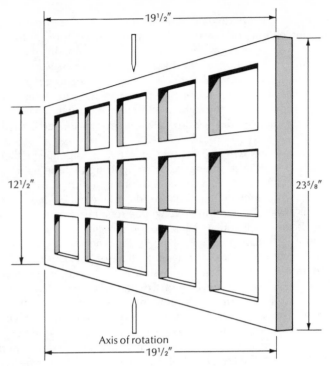

Figure 7.3
One side of the Ames trapezoidal window shown perpendicular (frontoparallel) to the line of sight. (After Ames, 1951.)

in the paragraph on movement of external objects. As the size of the shadow increases, so does the occlusion of the surrounding field. According to the theory of the ambient array, the observer is left with the conclusion that the object must be moving toward him. The kinetic depth effect is an example of the manner in which the visual system interprets the changes or transformations in the ambient light array. Such specific transformations give rise to a perception of motion in three dimensions.

Perception of rotary movement.   Figure 7.3 is a drawing of the *trapezoidal window* developed by Ames (1951). It appears to be a normal rectangular window, but is in fact trapezoidal in shape. To enhance the illusion, shadows are painted on both its sides so that when the window is viewed head on (frontoparallel plane) it appears to be a normal window seen from an angle.

When the window is rotated slowly (5–20 rpm) about the vertical axis it produces an illusion: rather than simply rotating, it appears to stop and reverse its direction once every 180°. Thus the figure creates an illusion of oscillation or reversal.

Ames believed his window demonstrated the influence of mental assumptions about perception. To the observer, his apparatus appears to be a rectangular window. However, as the window is set in motion, the perception of rotation—the true motion of the figure—is inconsistent with the assumption that the figure is a normal window. When a normal rectangular figure rotates, one edge approaches while the other recedes; alternately each edge appears longer and shorter throughout the complete rotation. However, the long edge of the trapezoidal window always appears longer than the short edge.

For Ames, the observer is presented with two possibilities. Either he can perceive the true motion of the figure by recognizing that the figure is in fact not a normal window; or he can see an illusion of motion consistent with the assumption that he is viewing a normal window. Since one edge of the trapezoidal figure is always longer, this edge will be seen nearest the observer. Thus the long edge seems to pendulate back and forth (oscillate).

The figure is designed so convincingly to appear as a normal window that most observers respond with a perception of oscillation. The window seems to rotate through 180° and then stop and reverse direction. Measurements of the illusion are given in terms of the frequency of illusory or apparent reversals (reversal rate) or in terms of oscillation frequency.

In several demonstrations Ittelson (1952) produced illusory reversal with the Ames window despite the presence in the field of a number of other objects that provided true cues of directional rotation. In one experiment a cube suspended from the long edge of the trapezoidal figure appeared to become dislodged from the window and rotate around the short edge, even though the short edge was in fact closer to the observer. The observation was interpreted to mean that the mental assumption about the window was stronger than the cues provided by the cube about the true direction of the figure's movement.

Several experiments lend support to Ames's suggestion that the illusion is based on mental assumptions about perception. Both McGree (1963) and Cappone (1966) demonstrated an influence of verbal suggestion on the perception of motion. Reinforcing the observer's assumption concerning the rectangularity of the window increased the magnitude of the illusion. Haber (1965) was also able to show that the magnitude of the illusion—frequency of illusory reversal—decreased when subjects were provided with information about the true nature of the figure. One group of Haber's subjects viewed the trapezoidal window for seven trials of three minutes each; 88 percent of their responses indicated the perception of oscillation. The frequency of apparent reversal diminished to 61 percent by trial 5. Before trial 6, subjects were shown the figure and allowed to study it. Reports of oscillatory motion decreased to 28 percent on trials 6 and 7. Another group, receiving no information during the seven trials, maintained a reversal rate of 85 percent. A final group of subjects was shown the trapezoidal window prior to the experiment. This group averaged a reversal rate of 40 percent during the seven trials. These results support Ames's contention that a misperception of the true motion of the figure depends on the subject's assumptions about the nature of the perceptual stimulus.

One interesting test of the Ames theory was provided by Burnham and Ono (1969). Subjects viewing a rotating trapezoidal window were told that it was rotating but not that it was in fact a trapezoid. They were simply asked to report the window's apparent movement. For the subjects in one group a string was attached to the upper-right-hand corner of the window (see Figure 7.3). The string was connected to a stylus held by the subject seated several yards away from the window. The subject's task was to move the stylus in accordance with the movement of the window while holding the string taut at all times. That is, the subject was to attempt to duplicate the rotary motion of the window with the stylus. When the window appeared to change direction (oscillate), the subject would expect, on the basis of visual cues, to move the stylus in one direction; but in fact he would have to move it in the opposite direction in order to follow the true direction of motion.

Subjects in a second group observed the procedure and attempted to trace the movement with a stylus that was not connected to the trapezoid. Burnham and Ono report that most subjects holding the stylus attached to the window experienced great difficulty with the task during early trials, but learned it well on subsequent trials. In fact, several subjects actually pulled over the apparatus while attempting to hold the string taut during the period of illusory motion. The experimental results showed that those subjects holding the attached stylus reported oscillatory movement of the window during only 50 percent of the trials, while the subjects with the stylus unattached reported oscillatory movement during 72 percent of the trials. But as viewing continued, the attached-stylus group increased to 72 percent while the reports of the second group of observers stayed at the same level. This seemingly strange result is explained to some degree by the results of a related test. A group of subjects viewed the window to which no indicators of true motion were attached. The subjects were informed, however, of the actual motion and told to concentrate on one of the window's edges during viewing. Initially these subjects reported oscillatory motion on 68 percent of the trials. During the second and third viewing periods the number of oscillations dropped to 30 and 28 percent, respectively. During a fourth period an increase to 50 percent occurred.

Burnham and Ono suggest that such results may be explained in terms of selective focusing. When the observers were told to concentrate on some element of the figure, the true direction of motion could be ascertained. In the previous experiment those subjects holding the attached stylus were forced to attend to the portion of the figure to which the string was attached during early trials. After some practice, however, the rotary motion of the stylus could be carried out independently of the perceived movement of the window. Such results generally complement the explanation of Ames, although some subsequent research, which will be discussed below, indicates that the illusion may depend on factors other than the assumptions of the observer.

Zenhausern (1968) attempted to produce an illusion of rotation by actually oscillating a trapezoidal window which kept its short edge always closest to the observer. The percentage of illusory reversals for three observation sessions as a function of the distance of the window are indicated in Table 7.4. Note that the frequency of the illusion Zenhausern evoked increases as a function of

Table 7.4

Percentage of apparent rotations of an oscillating trapezoidal window
(Zenhausern, 1968)

Session	Distance in feet			
	6	10	14	16
1	14	31	46	49
3	25	44	58	60
5	27	42	53	53

distance up to 10 feet. At distances greater than 12 feet, no significant increase in the frequency of the illusion was reported.

A number of experiments have demonstrated that the trapezoidal apparatus need not appear like a window. Zegers (1965) did not find a difference in the number of reversals reported for trapezoids designed to look like windows and for a plain trapezoid. Freeman and Pasnak (1968) conducted a number of studies in which trapezoidal shapes of varying size were observed from various distances. They concluded that the apparent reversals were affected by the visual angle subtended by the trapezoid and by the amount of linear perspective provided by the sloping horizontal lines of the figure from the large edge to the short edge.

Several other investigators have found that apparent reversals in rotating figures are not confined to trapezoidal shapes. Day and Power (1963) and Mulholland (1956), among others, found an apparent oscillation of circular, elliptical, and irregular shapes. Mulholland (1956) and Pastore (1952) also reported apparent reversals of rotary motion with rectangular shapes, provided that the shapes subtended small visual angles (below 10°). In a study by Cahill (1969), a comparison of the frequency of reversals showed a superiority for a trapezoidal shape over a rectangle, although reversals also occurred under some conditions for the rectangular shapes. Cahill incorporated a distance-of-viewing variable in the study so that the figures subtended angles greater than 10° at the shorter viewing distances.

Ames's explanation of the apparent oscillatory motion of rotating trapezoids seems to encounter difficulty when it is applied to the apparent reversal of non-trapezoidal forms. A misjudgment in the assumed shape of the figure would not seem applicable to rectangles and circular shapes, and a realistic trapezoidal window should reverse more often than a featureless trapezoid. Several other theories that attempt to extend the Ames explanation to the non-trapezoidal forms will be discussed after we have first considered some findings concerning the cues available to the observer during the judgment of rotary motion.

Power (1967) attempted to analyze the important cues of directional motion. He assumed that when a rectangular shape rotates around a vertical axis, two possible cues of motion are available to the observer. With reference to the patterns in Figure 7.4, cue 1 may be explained as follows: as the

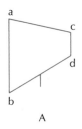 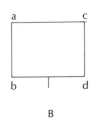 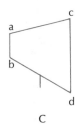

Figure 7.4
Cues of rotary motion.

square turns from view A to B to C, the vertical edges (a-b and c-d) of the square extend and contract. Cue 2 is observed in this fashion: as the square turns from view A to B to C, the horizontal lines (a-c and b-d) converge on one side and diverge on the other side.

In his experiment, Power (1967) sought to compare these cues systematically by designing shapes that eliminated either or both cues. By comparing the perceptions of such figures he could ascertain the relevant importance of each cue in the detection of true motion. The shapes he used are shown in Figure 7.5. According to Power, shape number 1 would exhibit both cues of motion, while shape number 2 would contain only the second cue provided by the changes in the horizontal lines. Shape 3, on the other hand, would exhibit only the extension and contraction of the vertical lines (cue 1), while shape 4 would provide neither cue. Finally, oscillatory movement or apparent reversals should occur with the greatest frequency for shape 4 and the least frequency for shape 1. Depending on the relative importance of the two cues of motion described above, shapes 2 and 3 should fall between.

Power's subjects viewed each figure rotating 20 times at a speed of 4.75 rpm. Table 7.5 gives the mean number of apparent reversals for each shape. As expected, the lowest number of illusory reversals occurred for the full square. However, shapes 3 and 4 exhibited an equal number of reversals. Shape 3, it will be recalled, provides only cue 1 (extension and contraction of the vertical edges). The number of reversals for shape 2 was greater than for shape 1 but far less than for shapes 3 and 4. From these results, Power concluded that the important cue for actual direction of motion is the change in the horizontal lines—the perspective cue mentioned earlier. One can also conclude that the

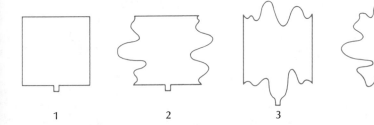

Figure 7.5
Shapes used to eliminate cues of rotary motion. (After Power, 1967.)

Table 7.5

Reversals reported for the shapes in Figure 7.5
(Power, 1967)

Shape	1	2	3	4
Mean reversals	4.7	8.1	19	18

illusion of oscillation is a result of a lack of this cue, but not that the illusion is caused by the changes in the vertical edges. Both shapes 3 and 4 exhibit equally frequent reversals, but only one shape exhibits the vertical edge cue.

The present author sought to test Power's conclusions with a modified experimental design. It was assumed that the irregular sides utilized by Power to eliminate the vertical and horizontal cues of motion (shapes 2 and 3 respectively) might not be sufficient, since the observer would be able to infer the length of the vertical line in shape 2 on the basis of the positions of the ends of the two horizontal lines. By the same reasoning, the observer could infer the positions of the horizontal lines, despite the irregular horizontal edges of shape 3, by the relative heights of the vertical lines. For the modified experiment, seven targets were made of fine wire and portions of them painted with luminescent paint; their outlines are shown in Figure 7.6. Each figure was viewed in total darkness so that the observer was able to see only the painted luminescent lines. Object 1, consisting of two parallel horizontal lines, would provide cue 1 as defined by Power (1967). Object 2 (two vertical lines) would provide a test of the effectiveness of cue 2. So that the subject could not infer the changes in the horizontal lines from the position of the ends of the vertical lines, object 3 (a single vertical line) was included. Object 4 (a single horizontal line) would produce cue 2 unconfounded by inferred changes in the vertical edges. Object 5 was a full square. Finally, two objects based on the Ames trapezoidal figure were included. Object 6 contained two diagonal lines (perspective cue) while object 7 consisted of two vertical lines of unequal length (size cue). Following a procedure similar to Power's, subjects viewed each figure for 20 rotations at a speed of 4.5 rpm. Each time the figure seemed to change rotational direction the subject was instructed to press a response key. The results of the experiment are to be found in Table 7.6. Each value represents the mean number of reversals recorded for 28 observers.

A statistical analysis of the data showed no significant differences among objects 1 (two horizontal lines), 2 (two vertical lines), and 5 (full square). Thus, in the modified study, reducing Power's cues 1 and 2 by removing the vertical or horizontal edges did not produce an increase in the frequency of apparent reversals. However, the number of apparent reversals was significantly greater for both objects 3 (single vertical line) and 4 (single horizontal line). From these results we can conclude that the perception of true directional movement is obtained from information extracted by the interplay of vertical and horizontal elements of the square. A single vertical or horizontal line transposed in space seems to provide only ambiguous information about directional motion.

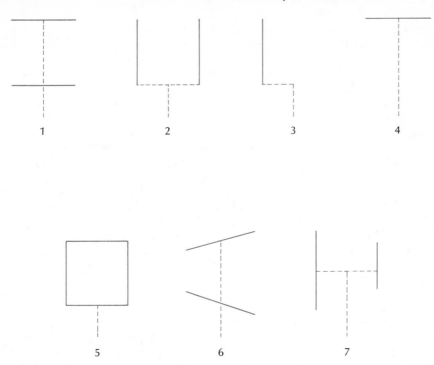

Figure 7.6
Luminescent wire figures for the study of cues of rotary motion. The solid-line portions of each figure were painted with luminescent paint and the dotted-line portions were painted flat black. (Murch, 1970.)

Finally, it is interesting to note that the greatest number of apparent reversals was observed for object 6, which displayed two converging horizontal lines. The number of illusory reversals was significantly greater for this object than for all other targets. Such a result lends support to Power's suggestion that changes in the horizontal lines constitute an important cue. This was also indicated in the Ames demonstrations. These observations also fit the model of motion perception, discussed earlier in the chapter, in which motion is deduced from transformations in the ambient array provided by the moving object. By means of these systematic changes the object can be seen as a complete figure displaying the characteristic transformations of a rotating

Table 7.6

Reversals reported for the objects in Figure 7.6
(Murch, 1970)

Object	1	2	3	4	5	6	7
Mean reversals	8.93	11.32	17.21	15.04	6.61	21.82	17.18

square. These observations would also hold for movement perception in the kinetic depth effect experiments. Object motion causing transformation of two-dimensional arrays produces a three-dimensional perception of the figure. Here the nature of the transformation determines the perception of the direction of movement.

The transformations of objects 6 and 7 do not conform to the usual transformations of a true square. By means of projective geometry one should be able to predict the successive transformations of the lines and angles of the square in a figure for which information on line length (size and perspective) is available. If the observer is unable to observe these characteristic transformations due to the absence of angle and line transpositions (objects 3 and 4), no clear perception of directional motion can result.

If in fact transformations of an object in three-dimensional space provide the cues of rotary motion, one would predict that a figure such as part A of Figure 7.7 should be perceived reversing with a frequency no greater than that of a full square (part B), since the information provided by transformations in the ambient array is the same for both figures. The author performed such an experiment as a follow-up to the study with luminescent figures. Under the same conditions of observation as that study, the mean number of reversals reported by 28 subjects for the figure in part A was 9.54, and for part B, 8.18 reversals. The difference was found to be solely due to chance.

From these studies it can be concluded that the perception of true rotary motion is a result of successive transformations in the ambient array of the rotating object. As the degree of clarity of transformation is reduced (e.g., the figure subtends a smaller visual angle) the observer experiences increasing difficulty in correctly noting the transformations. Furthermore, if the figure is designed so that it provides incorrect cues of transformation (e.g., objects 6 and 7 of Figure 7.6 or the Ames trapezoidal window), errors of judgment commensurate with the perceived transformations result. In the trapezoidal window an oscillatory movement is commensurate with the transformations of the figure projected to the observer.

During the discussion of theories of apparent reversals, the position taken by Ames (1951) has been mentioned several times. After the discovery that apparent reversals were not confined to trapezoids, Pastore (1952) proposed an alternate theory designed to explain apparent motion both in trapezoidal shapes and in other figures. Like others, he also used the notion of a misjudgment in perception as the basic factor. However, for Pastore the error was not in the shape assumed by the subject but in a discrepancy of true and apparent slant.

A similar argument has been advanced by Graham (1963). His theory emphasized, as Pastore's had earlier, that subjects' erroneous depth judgments produce oscillatory perceptions of the rotating figures. Graham believes that the motion parallax cue of depth is misleading in the illusion, due to the different angular velocities produced by the elements of the rotating figures.

Other authors agree with Graham that the apparent rotation results from conflicting depth cues, but they fail to agree about exactly what cues are

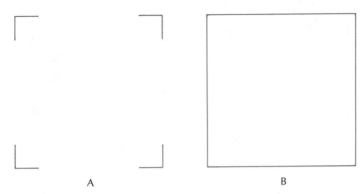

Figure 7.7
Two squares that provide equal information concerning direction of rotation. (Murch, 1970.)

in conflict. For example, Cross and Cross (1969) made a good empirical case for the contributions of interposition and shadow during the misperception of rotation with the Ames figure. They pointed out that the shadows on the window bars of the Ames window provide a false interposition cue. In a rotating figure the shadows usually would be seen during only one phase of the rotation. Also, the shadows are painted gray and retain constant brightness values throughout the rotation; for a normally rotating figure, this would not be the case. Using square and circular objects, Cross and Cross obtained judgments of directional movements for five classes of figures:

1. Objects without conflicting depth cues.
2. Objects with shadow-interposition cues.
3. Objects with linear perspective cues.
4. Objects with mutually compatible shadow-interposition and perspective cues.
5. Objects with incompatible shadow-interposition and linear perspective cues.

Figure 7.8 shows the objects Cross and Cross employed and the total number of apparent reversals for all subjects out of 1,000 observations reported. For both rectangular and circular figures the perspective cue is strongly influential in the production of the illusion (objects 3 and 4). The shadow-interposition cue increases the number of reversals (object 2) yet is also capable of reducing them, as in the example of the square in conflict with perspective (object 5). While these results do allow a prediction of reversals based on characteristics of the stimulus elements, they fail to explain the reversals for the simple rectangle, for which 14.7 percent of the trials evoked reports of oscillatory movement.

Day and Power (1965) have also advanced a theory of rotary motion which places emphasis on changes in retinal projections of the stimulus figure. In es-

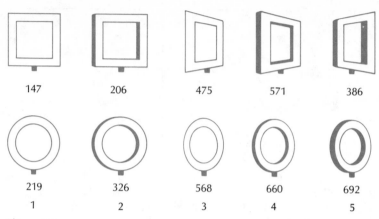

Figure 7.8
Stimulus objects and frequencies of reversals out of 1,000 observations reported. (After Cross and Cross, 1969.)

sence they assume that the changes in retinal projections are the same for an object rotating either clockwise or counterclockwise, and that the eye is therefore presented with no valid information on directional motion. They further assume that the observer, due to the ambiguity of these cues, makes a random decision about the direction of motion. Judgments in either direction are assumed to be equally probable. They conclude that subjects will be able to see either a rotation or an oscillation, since either motion can with equal probability be perceived on the basis of the available cues displayed by the object. The frequency of apparent reversals represents a random process: on some trials subjects simply develop a percept of movement in the wrong direction on the basis of the ambiguous information. With regard to this theory of Day and Power it is important to note that the equality of cues provided by counterclockwise and clockwise motion is based on an analysis of the points of the rotating figure in transformation on the retina. As Hershberger (1967) has observed, these points are in fact equivocal only if the retinal points are sufficiently close (e.g., if the figure is small or is viewed from a considerable distance).

Cook, Mefferd, and Wieland (1967) took strong exception to Day's and Power's argument that the apparent reversals occur on a random basis due to the indeterminate cues of motion. Using a number of different figures these authors demonstrated that the frequency of reversals was not random. Rather, apparent reversal occurred in a very systematic pattern. In a second study they attempted to ascertain at what point in the rotation the apparent reversals occurred. They were found to occur only when there was a difference in distance among parts of the figure—that is, when one edge was nearer the subject than the other edges.

If we evaluate the empirical observations on apparent reversals in light of the ambient array theory of motion presented in the first part of this chapter, several possibilities seem open. The apparent oscillation of the original figure by Ames would certainly appear to be based in part on the conflict of depth

Figure 7.9
Diagram of an electric neon sign utilizing apparent motion as an attention-getting device.

cues. Conflict arises not only because of the failure of the short edge to occlude an equal amount of the background during rotation, but also because of the conflicting cues of light and shadow provided by the simulated sections of the window. In the case of small non-trapezoidal figures, reversal rates are lower but occur regularly. Because the information provided during the transformations of these figures is insufficient for an accurate assessment of depth, subjects are required to make an assumption about the meaning of the cues perceived. Once the assumption is made it is not surprising, as Cook, Mefferd, and Wieland report, that the rotation or oscillation persists, since the observer has assigned a meaning to the indeterminate cues and continues to use this meaning in his perception.

In summary, the apparent oscillation of the Ames window depends on conflicting cues of depth that occur during its transformation. Reversals of other figures occur when their transformations fail to provide clear indices of the distance between the observer and the elements of the figure. Once the available information has been translated into a perception, subjects tend to persist in interpreting the available information in the same manner. The transformations of the ambient array fail to provide clear indicators of the direction of change. Finally, it seems unnecessary to explain any of this process by referring to the interplay of elements across retinal fields.

Apparent Movement

A number of conditions have been established under which an illusion of movement can be produced. Due to the extreme sensitivity to motion of most observers, such techniques are frequently applied in advertising as attention-getting devices. A typical example is shown in Figure 7.9. The arrows in the sign are illuminated in succession with slight delays between the flashing of each arrow. The perception is one of fluid movement: the arrow seems to start at the top of the sign and move rapidly downward. Certain illuminated theater marquees provide excellent examples of apparent movement. When a shadow appears to move rapidly around the marquee's band of lights, the effect is produced by successively turning off each lamp for a brief interval. The on-and-off sequence of each lamp creates the illusion of a moving shadow.

Perhaps the most striking examples of apparent movement are provided by television and motion pictures. The latter consist essentially of a series of still photographs each differing minutely in the position of its elements. Projected in rapid succession, they give an impression of natural movement.

Although several scientists dealt with the problem of apparent movement during the late nineteenth century, it was Max Wertheimer's classic presentation in 1912 that awakened interest in the topic. Prompted by his early research, psychologists have extensively investigated four basic types of apparent movement—beta, gamma, delta, and alpha—known collectively as *phi phenomena*.

Beta movement.   Wertheimer (1912) concentrated primarily on the type of apparent movement referred to as *beta* movement. When two spatially separated stationary targets are presented in succession, if the delay interval and the distance between the targets stand in the proper proportion, observers report a single target moving from the position of target 1 to that of target 2. The alternate flashing red lights at a railroad crossing or the yellow warning lights on construction projects frequently produce such beta movement. Rather than perceiving two lights flashing off and on, one sees a single light moving back and forth in a lateral direction.

The occurrence of beta movement depends, then, on an optimal interval between the sequential presentations of the targets and an optimal distance between the targets. The factor of target illumination also influences the perception of this type of apparent movement. Korte (1915) studied the interrelationships between these aspects of the experimental situation and derived several basic principles which have come to be known as *Korte's laws*. They represent an attempt to define the relationships between temporal interval, spatial distance, and target illumination which will produce optimal beta movement. According to Korte, a movement perception reported under a given set of these variables can be maintained even when the value of one variable changes, so long as a proper compensatory change is introduced in one of the two remaining variables. The following statements paraphrase Korte's observations:

1.   With temporal interval constant, optimal beta movement can be maintained with *increases* in spatial distance and proportionate *increases* in luminance.
2.   With spatial distance constant, optimal beta movement can be maintained with *increases* in luminance and proportionate *decreases* in temporal interval.
3.   With luminance constant, optimal beta movement can be maintained with *increases* in temporal interval and proportionate *increases* in spatial distance.

For any given parameters of movement, conditions can be specified within which apparent movement occurs. Increasing or decreasing the values of any of the parameters without a corresponding change in one of the other variables breaks down the apparent beta movement.

Gamma movement.   Gamma movement is a change in the apparent depth or apparent size of a stimulus produced by increasing and decreasing the illumination level of the stimulus. As the illumination of a target increases it seems to move closer or to get bigger; when the illumination decreases, subjects report the contraction or increased distance of the target. For the early gestalt psychologists gamma movement exhibited the same relationships as those that occur under conditions of figure-ground discrimination. As illumination increases, the target becomes the dominant figure and is seen in front of the ground. The observer could interpret this forward movement of the target as a change in size or in depth. Gamma movement is not confined to single targets in a field of varying illumination. A contraction effect also occurs with variations in the illumination of the entire visual field.

Delta movement.   If the stimulus conditions for beta and gamma movement are combined, a third form of apparent motion is produced in which the observer reports a lateral movement of the target from position 1 to position 2 as well as a movement in the third dimension. If target 1 is sufficiently more intense than target 2, the apparent motion is a lateral displacement to one side and back away from target 1.

Alpha movement.   A special case of apparent movement was introduced by Benussi (1912), who alternately presented the two portions of the Müller-Lyer illusion. After several alternations of the portion of the figure with closed end angles followed in time by the portion with open end angles, an apparent expansion and contraction of the horizontal lines occurred. Subjects also perceived beta movement—at slow rates of alternation the end-angle lines seemed to flip back and forth with the successive presentation of each portion of the figure. However, as the rate of alternation increased a pivotal movement occurred, and the lines appeared to rotate around the point of contact with the horizontal line, producing both a lateral movement and a movement in depth.

Sayons and Prysiazniuk (1963) produced alpha movement with the *frame illusion.* A horizontal line (1 by 30 cm) was presented as target 1 followed in time by a surrounding frame of variable size (length varied from 30 to 230 cm and width was constant at 30 cm). The observed movement of contraction and expansion of the horizontal line was spontaneously reported by 98 percent of the observers. In a similar study by Sayons (1964) subjects frequently reported a change in the apparent depth of the horizontal line rather than a shortening or lengthening of the line. When instructed to focus their attention on the horizontal line, they reported an apparent movement of the line, which came toward them and then moved away. Requiring the subjects to focus on the frame produced an apparent change in the depth of the frame, while the horizontal line appeared to maintain a constant distance.

Factors similar to those discussed by Ames in his study of the rotating trapezoidal window are probably involved in the phenomena of apparent movement of lines. Subjects tend to assume that a line is of a constant length and that the illusion is a result of a depth change in which the line moves closer and then farther away. In the alpha movement produced with the Müller-Lyer components, high speeds of alternation produce the pivoting effect of the end lines. Again, in order for the subject's perception to fit his previous experience, an assumption of a rotary movement in depth is required to account for such rapid changes in the position of the line. At slow speeds a two-dimensional, back-and-forth motion appears natural, but at high speeds such a motion would defy a subject's previous experience with moving objects.

Generally, it seems that the perception of apparent movement depends on the similarity between cues produced by the apparent movement stimuli and previously experienced cues of actual motion. This point will be considered further in the discussion of theoretical explanations of apparent movement.

Complex stimulus patterns.   Several experimenters have employed complex patterns of lights in order to evoke apparent movement. Ball and Wilsoncroft (1966) reported an interesting type of apparent movement involving the pattern shown in Figure 7.10. The four lights forming the diamond at the right were turned on simultaneously, followed in time by the single light at the left. The diamond appeared to move forward and to the left and backward to the right, and subjects reported perceiving four lights rather than five. Ball and Wilsoncroft noted that this effect resembled the perception of the gestalt factors of closure and good form (discussed in Chapter 4).

Situational and observer variables in apparent movement.   The role of observer expectancy in the perception of apparent movement has been explored by Jones and Bruner (1954). In a series of demonstrations they tested observer response to the apparent motion of numerous meaningful and meaningless objects. They found, for example, that subjects could see the apparent motion of a line drawing of a man easier than the apparent movement of a nonsense figure. In another study they evoked apparent movement of a meaningful target (an automobile) by displacing successive pictures of the target relative to the background. The perception of the car's fluid motion depended on the total number of discrete pictures and the slight displacement of each. However, they still reported apparent movement of the car even when the center picture in the sequence was deleted. The smooth movement of a meaningless target in the same context (an ellipse) was disrupted when the center picture was deleted. These results seem to support the assumption that the perception of apparent movement depends on the relationship between the cues provided by the targets and the observer's prior experience with objects in actual motion. Thus it is easier to see a car moving across a background than an ellipse.

Recently Raskin (1969) demonstrated that previous experience with forms in apparent movement can influence the subsequent perception of alternately presented forms. He asked his subjects to consider the sequential presentation of two spatially displaced arrows. After one week they returned and were shown the same arrows in a situation in which apparent movement is usually not reported by observers unfamiliar with such experiments. Nevertheless, the subjects continued to see apparent movement. Their prior experience with the forms allowed them to interpret the stimuli in this way, even though subjects lacking prior experience did not see apparent movement.

Figure 7.10
Light pattern for testing movement
perception with complex stimuli. (After
Ball and Wilsoncroft, 1966.)

A number of studies have related apparent movement to age. Gantenbein
(1952) found that young children were able to perceive apparent movement
with less difficulty than adults. Children of five years, for example, were able
to see apparent movement much more readily than older children or adults.
Again this observation probably reflects the role of prior experience in the
perception of apparent movement. Adults have more experience with the
kinds of stimuli usually giving rise to a perception of motion. They approach
the stimuli for apparent movement more analytically and as a result are less
susceptive to apparent movement. Children, however, are more able to accept a perceptual occurrence at face value.

Phenomenal versus physical change.   Early work on apparent motion emphasized the pattern of retinal interactions produced by the stimuli inducing
apparent movement. Basic to these studies was the assumption that the perception of actual movement is the result of a displacement of the proximal stimulus (image) across adjacent portions of the retina (retinal fields). While a number of experimenters have attempted to isolate conditions leading to optimal
apparent movement perception, almost all assume that stimulation of disparate
retinal fields is required. They have been more concerned with the manner
in which information from these fields is processed than with determining if
apparent movement actually depends on the successive stimulation of different
portions of the retina. But if apparent movement is interpreted in terms of
Gibson's theory of the ambient array, such an assumption may not even be
pertinent.

Rock and Ebenholtz (1962) have described several experiments in which
apparent beta movement was produced with a single target which appeared
to move from side to side (phenomenal displacement) rather than with two
separate targets flashing alternately (physical displacement). They also produced apparent movement in a condition involving target stimuli that were
always presented to the same portion of the retina. The device Rock and Ebenholtz used for the first part of their study is diagramed in Figure 7.11. The
subject was required to look through the left opening in screen A with one
eye and then move his head and look through the right opening with the same

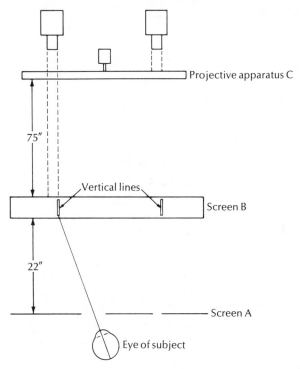

Figure 7.11
Diagram of an apparatus for the phenomenal displacement
of a light target presented to the same portion of the retina.
(After Rock and Ebenholtz, 1962.)

eye. A separate target, consisting of an illuminated vertical line on a dark
background, could be seen through each opening. The vertical lines on screen
B were flashed alternately and the observer instructed to coordinate the movement of one eye between the two openings in the screen until the illuminated lines could be seen alternately. In this way each flash of a vertical line
would stimulate the same portion of the retina. Of ten observers, six reported
seeing a single vertical line in apparent motion, while four reported two separate lines flashing on and off. However, these same four also failed to report
apparent movement when screen A was removed and the vertical lines were
alternately flashed. When apparent movement is induced by two separate
flashing targets, subjects frequently fixate the two targets alternately rather than
maintain a single fixation point somewhere between them. In such a case
separate retinal points are not stimulated, but phenomenal movement is still
reported. Rock and Ebenholtz conclude that apparent movement occurs even
though the same portion of the retina is stimulated by the successive targets.

In a second study Rock and Ebenholtz (1962) devised a situation in which
the target did in fact stimulate different portions of the retina but did not change
its objective position. The result was that it failed to move phenomenally.

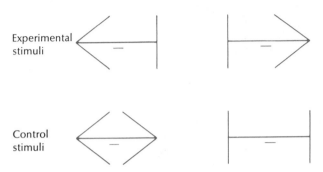

Figure 7.12
Patterns for the demonstration of phenomenal displacement without physical displacement. (After Brosgole, 1966, figure 1. Reproduced by permission of author and publisher.)

Brosgole (1966) also studied phenomenal and retinal displacement with the experimental and control stimuli shown in Figure 7.12. Since the short horizontal line is located in the same physical position below each of the four figures, if the two targets are presented alternately an apparent movement of the short horizontal line should be reported—if in fact phenomenal rather than retinal displacement is necessary to produce apparent movement. However, due to the influence of the Müller-Lyer elements, the short line appears displaced toward the end angles, and Brosgole's observers reported the line's apparent movement. Again, this movement occurs despite stimulation of the same portion of the retina. Unfortunately Brosgole failed to include a third condition in which the short line in each figure would be displaced toward the center. Under such a condition physical displacement would occur without phenomenal displacement, since the Müller-Lyer elements would compensate for the displacement. In an unpublished experiment the present author attempted to test this third condition and found that most subjects failed to report apparent movement of the short line.

In conclusion, available experimental results indicate that stimulation of successive retinal fields is not a prerequisite for apparent movement. In fact, under some conditions movement is not reported even when such disparate fields are stimulated. The important parameter seems to be the phenomenal displacement of objects relative to each other or relative to the context of background stimuli.

The importance of the phenomenal displacement of the target against the background context can be demonstrated simply by alternately viewing your upright thumb at arm's length with one eye and then the other: the thumb appears to move. Under more precise conditions observers report the same effect for a thin white rod placed several inches from a textured background. Looking alternately with each eye at a luminescent rod in an otherwise totally darkened environment fails to produce apparent motion.

Real and apparent movement. An obvious experiment would compare the perception of two targets under conditions of beta movement with a single target actually in motion. Such a study has been performed by a number of investigators (e.g., Desilva, 1929; Kennedy, 1936; and Gibson, 1954). The basic result is the inability of the observer to distinguish the real movement from the apparent movement. However, Kolers (1963, 1964) has argued that at least four distinctions must be made between conditions of real and apparent movement:

1.   Apparent movement occurs only at certain rates of stimulus presentation (approximately 15° to 25° per second), while real movement is perceived over a much wider range (1° to 125° per second).
2.   The image of the object moves across the retina during real movement and not during apparent movement. During apparent movement only two points are stimulated on the retina.
3.   Real movement produces a blur at high speeds which does not occur with apparent movement.
4.   Real movement appears to be faster than apparent movement. Thus to produce an apparent equivalence of two targets in beta movement and a single target in real movement, the real object must move more slowly than the alternation rate of the beta movement.

Kolers also reports a number of studies that help to identify the different perceptual processes that occur during real and apparent movement. In one study subjects watched a lighted vertical line move back and forth across a darkened surface. A small target light was illuminated at random in the center of this path, and the observers were asked to report its occurrence. When the target light and the moving line were in close proximity, the probability was low that the subject would report the presence of the target light, since it was masked by the moving line. In a similar test, the line was replaced by two alternately flashing lines located at either end of the surface. When the target light was flashed in the interval between them—i.e., when the line in apparent movement seemed to be passing through the center of the field—there was no reduction in the probability of identifying the light.

Under both conditions subjects reported the movement of a single line across the darkened surface. Under the first, the line was actually in motion, whereas under the second the line was only in apparent motion. Subjectively the movement observed was the same for both conditions, yet the identification of the target light was impaired only by the line in actual motion. Since the discrimination of the target light depended on the stimulus condition of real or apparent motion, it would seem difficult to ascribe both types of movement perception to a single mechanism of stimulation of disparate retinal fields.

Therefore, rather than search for a retinal mechanism for movement perception, it would seem more plausible to follow the lead of Gibson's theory of the ambient array, and to look for similarities in real and apparent movement created by the transformations of the visual array. To concentrate, in other words, on what the two types of stimulus conditions have in common rather than on what common retinal mechanism might underlie them both.

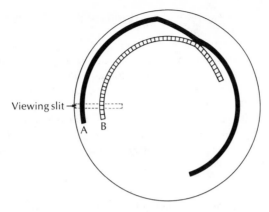

Figure 7.13
An example of the stimulus material used to study
the perception of phenomenal causality. (After
Michotte, 1963.)

Stimulus elements are displaced in space in both real and apparent movement. Lights occupying one position seem to change to a new position as a
function of time. Both real and apparent movement produce occlusion and
disocclusion of the background. There are meaningful differences between the
two, particularly in the speed of displacement, since the occlusion and disocclusion of the background are continuous in real movement and discontinuous in apparent movement. Nevertheless, the transformations of the ambient
array are very similar in both instances. Therefore if real motion perception
is the result of continued experience with objects in transformation in the
external environment, then the conditions of apparent movement would be
those producing highly similar transformations. So similar, in fact, that the observer often cannot discriminate between the two.

In conclusion, the perception of motion—real or apparent—seems to be
the result of experience with transformations of the ambient array of light
reflected from objects in the external environment to the active, moving eye
of the perceiver. Any argument holding that changes in retinal fields produce
real or apparent motion seems untenable on grounds of experimental observation.

Phenomenal Causality

A rather fascinating aspect of the perception of movement was explored in
a number of experiments by the late Belgian psychologist Albert Michotte
(1958, 1963). His experimental design, shown in Figure 7.13, essentially invited the subject to follow small colored rectangles moving horizontally across
an opening in a large screen. The rectangles could move laterally or be halted
at any point and their extent of movement, speed, and direction could be
varied by the experimenter. As Figure 7.13 shows, the rectangles were portions

of bands painted on the surface of a revolving disc seen through a 0.5-by-15-cm opening in the screen.

Consider the effect produced by the disc shown in Figure 7.13. The positions of the two figures remain the same until line A (phenomenally, rectangle A) moves toward line B. At the point of contact, rectangle A stops moving and rectangle B starts to move away from A. The usual perception is one of a *throwing effect:* the observer notes that A bumps or pushes B away. The important point in such a demonstration is that the observer perceives a causal relationship between the movement of rectangle A and the movement of rectangle B. According to Michotte, the nature of this causal relationship depends on seven variables:

1. The initial separation of objects A and B.
2. The time at which they begin to move.
3. Their speed of movement.
4. The time interval between the moment of contact of object A and initiation of movement in object B.
5. The nature of contact between the objects.
6. The direction of movement of the objects after contact.
7. The distance traversed by the objects.

Table 7.7 provides descriptions of the movement relationships between two rectangles and the kinds of phenomenal perceptions reported by observers of the movement.

The relationships between the two targets depend on the seven variables listed by Michotte. In each of the five instances cited in Table 7.7, however, the observer perceives a *causal* relationship between the movement patterns of the two targets: one target's motion is a direct result of the motion of the other. Michotte described the typical kinds of causal perceptions as the *throwing effect* (A moves to push B away), the *transporting effect* (A moves to stationary B and then both move off together) and the *tunnel phenomenon* (A is displaced to the right toward a stationary B but briefly disappears due to a break in the continuous line producing target A).

Under these experimental conditions, Michotte noted several important aspects of the way in which perception is affected by the causal patterns reported by the observers. Subjects perceived the targets to be interacting with one another and frequently described these relations in very human terms— as, for example, "A has moved over to B and shoved him away."

The assignment of human characteristics to moving objects was even more pronounced in a series of experiments conducted by Heider and Simmel (1944) in the United States. They showed a film in which several objects—such as triangles of various sizes—moved about and made contact with one another. After seeing a large triangle move over and displace a smaller triangle, subjects typically described the action as "a big fellow going over and picking on a little chap." Such perceived relationships in the movement of targets employed by Michotte and Heider and Simmel—the motion of neutral objects is interpreted in terms of human or animal interaction—have important sociopsychological implications.

Table 7.7
Some examples of the perception of causality
(Michotte, 1963)

Objective movements of targets A and B	Subjective impressions of movements of A and B
1. A displaced to B, B displaced away from A	"A bumps, pushes, or throws B"
2. A and B displaced simultaneously to the right	"A follows or pursues B" "B pulls A"
3. A displaced to right, B displaced to right after slight delay	"A repels B"
4. A displaced to right to immobile B and then back to starting position	"A bumped off or thrown off by B"
5. A rapidly displaced to B and dissolved at B	"A welds together with B or is destroyed at B"

Although all seven of Michotte's variables contribute to the perception of causality, particular importance must be assigned to the temporal relationships between moving objects. Gruber, Fink, and Damm (1957) attempted to assess a threshold for causality by requiring subjects to describe the collapse of a model bridge after the removal of a key support. Whether they assumed this removal caused the bridge to fall depended on the delay between support removal and bridge collapse. Houssiadas (1964) compared the causal relationships reported by two groups of observers, one with low-I.Q. scores and the other with high-I.Q. scores. Generally, the descriptions were quite similar. The results also showed the high-I.Q. observers to be subject to expectation effects. That is, if the experimenter stated beforehand that a certain situation would not produce causal perceptions, the subjects tended to report a lack of causality in the ensuing array.

Michotte (1963) believed that awareness of phenomenal causality does not develop as a function of experience. The experiment by Gruber, Fink, and Damm (1957) already mentioned showed changes in the threshold for causality as a function of practice. Gemelli and Capellini (1958) required observers to adopt an *analytic attitude* toward the stimulus array and reported a reduction in the number of reports of causal responses. Lastly, Houssiadas (1964) found that he could reduce the number of causal responses by evoking an inappropriate set concerning the stimulus material viewed by his subjects.

Causality is a very complicated topic even when considered independently of the perceptual process. Michotte and others have assumed that a perception of causal relations influenced the subjective reports of their observers. One may question whether or not Michotte succeeded in demonstrating the perception of causality. However, the import of this research in the present context is that observers seem to rely on their past experience with live objects in the construction of a percept for complex movement patterns. That subjects frequently describe the perceptions of movement in the Michotte design in terms of living objects indicates the utilization of past experience as a reference system for the analysis of the present perception.

Space and Time

As noted in previous sections, the passage of time obviously influences the perception of movement. That time also contributes to the perception of spatial distance has been studied extensively by Cohen (1964). In his basic experimental design the observer is presented with three flashing lights spaced well apart in a horizontal row. The observer controls the temporal interval between the flashing of each light, but the experimenter is able to position the middle light anywhere between the two outside lights. As the experimenter varies the position of the center light, the observer is asked to modify the temporal interval between flashes correspondingly to accommodate the change in distance. That is, the observer must select temporal intervals in proportion to the distance between the three lights. Generally, Cohen found that subjects tend to allot a shorter interval to the longer of the two distances. This effect, in which time and space are perceptually related, is called the *kappa effect*. Using a spatially separated pair of lights, Price-Williams (1954) studied the estimated temporal interval between flashes based on the physical distance separating the lights. His results shown in Figure 7.14 indicate that observers tend to underestimate the interval with decreases in distance.

A number of studies have attempted to relate the influence of time to perceived extent. Originally, Helson and King (1931) noted that the observer's judgment of the apparent distance between two points on the human skin was influenced by the temporal interval between successive stimulations. If point A on the forearm was stimulated, followed after a given interval by point B, subjects would judge the stimulation of a third equidistant point C to be farther away if the interval between B and C was longer than between A and B. This effect was deemed the *tau effect*. Using an apparatus with three flashing lights, Bill and Teft (1969) studied the effects of variations in the temporal interval separating the two visual targets on the apparent distances between the targets. The experimenter would set the distance between the left target and the center target and flash them at intervals of 4 seconds. The observer was required to adjust the right target to the subjectively correct distance at different temporal intervals. The time between these two targets could vary from 1 to 7 seconds. Naturally, on half the trials, the right and center light were fixed and the left light variable. Bill's and Teft's results, shown in Figure 7.15, indicate that when the interval between variable and center targets was less than between fixed and center targets, subjects moved the variable target farther away from the center target. In other words, with a larger temporal interval, the distance between targets was estimated to be greater. The opposite response occurred when the interval between the fixed and center targets was greater than the temporal separation of variable and center targets.

The perception of space is influenced by time (tau effect) and the perception of time is influenced by space (kappa effect). Cohen (1964) applied

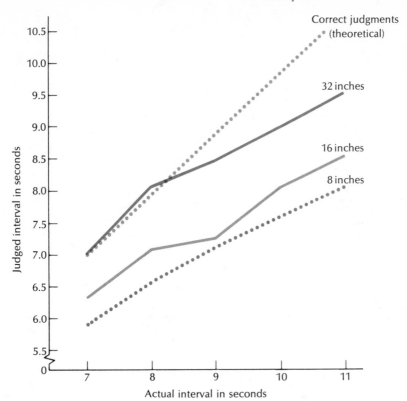

Figure 7.14
Judgment of time intervals as a function of the physical distance between visual targets. (After Price-Williams, 1954.)

these observations to a more real-life situation. He arranged to transport a blindfolded subject in an automobile for a set period under various conditions of distance covered and speed of travel. He found that a subject's estimates of elapsed time increased subjectively in proportion to changes in speed of travel, distance traveled, or both.

Cohen (1964) has also noted an auditory kappa effect. Two tones of equal duration but of different pitch are presented sequentially. The listener is asked to indicate which tone displays the greatest subjective duration. Usually the higher-pitched tone is reported to be shorter in duration than the tone of lower pitch. In a manner analogous to the three lights Cohen used to produce the visual kappa effect, three tones of different pitch levels produce a kappa effect in which the temporal separation between the tones appears to lessen as the differences in pitch are diminished.

The Perception of Time

Most of us experience occasional surprise at the amount of time that elapses during an interesting activity. Subjectively, the time often seems to fly by.

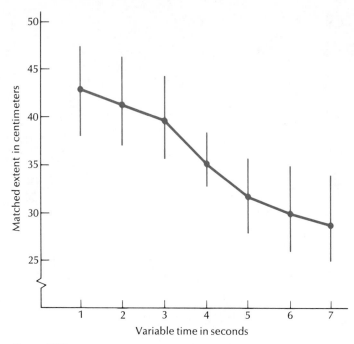

Figure 7.15
Influence of variation in temporal interval on perceived extent. Vertical bars represent standard deviations for each time interval. (After Bill and Teft, 1969.)

Experimenters have long been interested in such impressions and have extensively studied the influence of external events, motivation, physical state, and other factors on the subjective estimation of time. To determine how accurately an observer can judge the passage of a certain interval, the typical experiment uses one or more of three methods of time perception (Underwood, 1966):

1. Verbal estimation: experimenter presents a standard time interval and the observer attempts to estimate the interval in seconds, minutes, or even hours.
2. Production: experimenter requires the observer to produce a time interval of a given length (e.g., one second).
3. Reproduction: experimenter presents a standard time interval and the observer attempts to reproduce the same interval.

Unfortunately, each of these methods does not produce the same results. Clausen (1950) obtained time judgments with the methods of verbal estimation, production, and reproduction. Using verbal estimation, subjects tended to overestimate the intervals employed (5, 10, or 15 seconds). The method of production showed much variation for different individuals. The most ac-

Table 7.8

Ratio of subjective time judgments to experimental (clock) time
(Hornstein and Rotter, 1969)

Interval	Method of estimation		
	Estimation	*Production*	*Reproduction*
2	1.18	0.78	0.78
5	1.13	0.93	0.88
8	1.10	0.96	0.95
11	1.13	0.98	0.96
14	1.07	0.98	0.96
17	1.06	0.98	0.96
20	1.07	0.99	0.96
23	1.03	0.97	0.95
26	1.05	0.99	0.93
29	1.03	0.99	0.98

curate estimates could be obtained with the method of reproduction. Carlson and Feinberg (1968a) also conducted a study in which the same group of subjects assessed given intervals (1 to 10 seconds) under each of the three methods. In contrast to Clausen's work, they found a great deal of consistency among the three.

In another study, Carlson and Feinberg (1968b) compared the time judgments for one group of subjects using the methods of production and reproduction with the judgments of a second group using the methods of estimation and reproduction. The first group's estimates under reproduction varied in the same way as their estimates under production. The second group's reproduction judgments also varied in a manner similar to their verbal estimates. In other words, how subjects judged time with the method of reproduction depended on the kind of method employed during alternate trials. The reason for this result is unclear, but it does indicate that comparisons across groups of subjects will be influenced by the context of the judgments. Since such variation was not observed when the same subjects were required to make judgments under each method, one is forced to conclude that the influence of different variables on time judgments must be tested with the responses of the same subjects rather than with comparisons of groups of subjects.

Hornstein and Rotter (1969) also compared the methods of verbal estimation, reproduction, and production in a study that required the same subjects to make time estimates ranging from 2 to 29 seconds under all conditions. Their data in Table 7.8 presents the ratio of subjective time to real time as a function of the size of the estimated interval. In this experiment subjects tended to overestimate all intervals with the method of verbal estimation and to underestimate all intervals with the other two methods; the degrees of over- and underestimation were greatest for the shortest intervals.

Table 7.9

Accuracy of time judgments as a function of method of judgment and sex
(Hornstein and Rotter, 1969)

	Estimation	Reproduction	Production
Male	0.974	0.920	1.033
Female	1.191	0.947	0.881

Hornstein and Rotter (1969) also compared the performances of male and female subjects. Table 7.9 gives the mean ratios of subjective time and real time for each method employed by each sex. According to Hornstein and Rotter, then, female subjects seem to make their best time judgments with the method of reproduction; males do equally well with either verbal estimation or production.

In view of the differences in time judgments that have been obtained using these three methods, it is obvious that considerable disagreement exists concerning the influence of various judgmental factors. But with due caution some selected observations can be considered. Wallace and Rabin (1960) conducted a search of the experimental literature and analyzed time perception as a function of method. Taking the differences in method into account, they conclude that subjects tend to overestimate very brief periods of time (seconds or fractions of seconds) and to underestimate longer periods of time. Cohen (1964) places the transitional point from over- to underestimation between 0.6 and 0.8 second. Again, it must be emphasized that many experiments fail to support these observations.

The speed of subjective time has been related to the temperature of the body by Francois (1927). Subjects were required to maintain a key-tapping rate of three taps per second. As the body temperature was experimentally increased the tapping rate increased. A similar result was obtained by Hoagland (1933) but not by Bell and Provins (1963). Since other experimenters have shown that body temperature changes throughout the day, Pfaff (1968) obtained time judgments using the methods of production and estimation during different times of the day. In this way he could observe subjective time as a function of body temperature. The major advantage of this technique lies in the utilization of normal temperature changes rather than the experimentally induced changes of the earlier studies. The results of his experiment are shown in Figure 7.16. As the graph indicates, time judgments with the method of production decrease (time goes faster) as body temperature increases, while intervals judged with the method of estimation increase as temperature increases. These results corroborate earlier findings concerning the relationships between body temperature and subjective time.

Does time seem to pass more quickly during an active period? DeWolfe and Duncan (1959) required observers to judge a 26-second interval with the reproduction method. Two basic conditions of active or passive behavior were observed. In the passive condition subjects sat back in their chairs and did nothing; in the active condition they worked on anagrams. The active and pas-

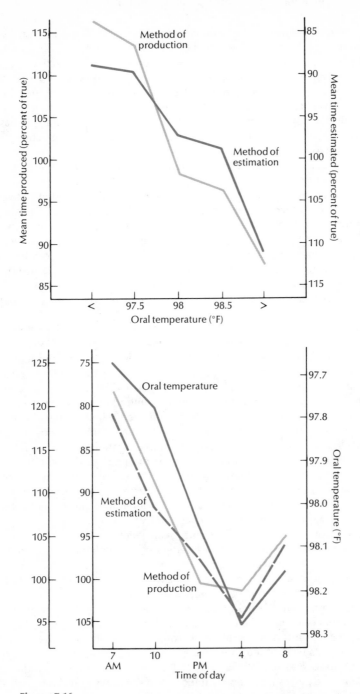

Figure 7.16
Variations in temporal intervals judged by the methods of production
and estimation. *Left,* as a function of body temperature. *Right,* as a
function of time of day. (After Pfaff, 1968.)

sive conditions occurred either during the presentation of the interval by the experimenter or during the reproduction of the interval by the observer. This procedure produced four conditions of observation: active-active, passive-passive, active-passive, and passive-active. The results showed the greatest effect for the passive-active condition. The passive period was judged longer when the observers were active while making reproduction estimates. Conversely, the shortest estimates of elapsed time occurred in the active-passive condition. There was no difference in judgments for the active-active versus the passive-passive condition.

At first glance the latter result might seem surprising, since activity is traditionally presumed to shorten subjective time. However, one would expect the subjective duration of an active period judged during active reproduction to produce the same degree of over- or underestimation as a passive period judged by passive reproduction. The influence of activity can only be assessed by comparing passively judged active periods with actively judged passive periods. Although the reported DeWolfe and Duncan tests corroborated the influence of activity, less convincing results have been reported by other experimenters. In their review of this topic, Wallace and Rabin (1960) conclude that the general effects of activity versus inactivity are still open to question.

A number of studies have shown relationships between the intensity of a tone and variations in estimates of tonal duration. Needham (1935) reported that the lengths of louder tones tend to be overestimated and the lengths of weaker tones underestimated. Some results contradict this finding, but most studies show experienced duration to be a positively increasing function of intensity. Zelkind and Ulehla (1968) used the method of verbal estimation and a comparison method in which subjects indicated whether the test interval was longer or shorter than the comparison interval. Both methods produced the expected relationship between experienced duration and signal intensity.

An obvious factor to examine in studies of apparent duration is motivation. William James (1890) hypothesized that the speed of time would be directly related to the motivational state of the perceiver; however, he supplied no experimental evidence in support of this contention. Subsequently several studies have appeared in which motivational variables have been related to time perception. In one study Filer and Meals (1949) gave separate groups of subjects the tasks of writing alternate letters of the alphabet or of copying a long list of words. Subjects of one experimental group were told that their task would require about 10 minutes, after which they would be free to leave the class. A second experimental group was informed that successful completion of the task would be rewarded with candy. A third control group was told that after completing the task they would return to their regular classwork. The tasks were interrupted for all three groups after 4 minutes and 37 seconds, and the subjects were asked to estimate the elapsed time. When both experimental groups overestimated the interval, Filer and Meals interpreted this to indicate that time passes more slowly under the motivation to reach a goal. Their observation is certainly consistent with the everyday experience of the slow passage of time in apprehension of a pleasant future event.

Several other studies have attempted to relate time perception to monotony. Burton (1943) failed to discover a change in time perception during a monotonous task. Meade (1959) allowed two groups of subjects to practice a stylus maze under different motivational instructions. One group was led to expect several hours of work on a boring, tedious task and was told that performance would not influence the amount of time to be spent on the task. A second group was given the same basic instructions but told that a good performance would foreshorten the time spent on the tedious task. After six minutes both groups were stopped and asked to judge the elapsed time. For the motivated subjects estimated duration was found to be inversely related to the rate of progress with the task (as influenced by contrived scores presented by the experimenter) and the expectations about successful completion of the task.

Falk and Bindra (1954) evoked a stress situation and found that it produced an overestimation of elapsed time. Subjects receiving electrical shocks on some time judgment trials overestimated the length of the elapsed time. Such an overestimation of elapsed time might be expected when an unpleasant stimulus is anticipated at the end of the interval. Perhaps the general overestimation of time under conditions of both positive and negative motivation is a product of a general heightening of the observer's arousal level, rather than a change in the subjective flow of time.

In their studies of time perception the adaptation level theorists have also related estimated duration to the presence of anchor stimuli. In one early study Postman and Miller (1945) preceded a brief duration (0.25 to 1 second) with an anchor duration well under the interval to be estimated. Subjects tended to judge the test interval longer in the presence of the anchor duration. Behar and Bevan (1961) interposed a 9-second anchor after every third judgment of durations ranging from 1 to 5 seconds. The long anchor stimulus caused the test intervals to be judged significantly shorter.

Some rather interesting work has attempted to compare perceived duration in the visual and auditory senses. Goldstone, Boardman, and Lhamon (1959) asked subjects to indicate whether a sound or a light displayed a duration greater or lesser than one second and found that the visual second was consistently estimated to be longer than the auditory second. Anchor lights and tones influenced both types of estimates, but the visual stimuli registered greater response to such anchor effects. These authors—as well as Behar and Bevan—also showed the intermodal effects of anchor stimuli on time judgments. That is, generally speaking, a long tone would cause the duration of a light to be underestimated and a short tone caused an overestimation of the light duration. Conversely, long light anchors reduced and short light anchors increased the estimated length of test tones.

To conclude this discussion, there have been several developmental studies of time perception as a function of chronological age. Using the methods of estimation, production, and reproduction, Gilliland and Humphreys (1943) obtained time estimates ranging from 9 to 180 seconds for fifth-grade children and for college students. As one might expect, the magnitude of errors was much greater for the children, but they still were able to produce general estimates of the intervals and, like the students, showed a tendency to improve in accuracy as the length of the intervals was increased. Of the three methods of estimation, reproduction of the interval proved more accurate than verbal estimation or production for both groups. A more extensive report of time perception in the developing organism has been presented by Smythe and Goldstone (1957). Their subjects, ranging from ages 6 to 14, used the estimation method to indicate whether a test tone was longer or shorter than one second. The youngest group of 6-year-olds displayed practically no concept of time in terms of minutes and seconds and as a result were unable to produce judgments about the length of a second. Performances by the 7-year-old group were basically similar but significantly more accurate; these subjects almost always overestimated the time interval, although not to the degree displayed by the 6-year-old children. In all, increases in accuracy were found to be discontinuous with increasing age. That is, a marked improvement occurred between ages 7 and 8, after which ability remains fairly stable up to age 11. At age 12 another rapid improvement was found, and by age 14 a fairly consistent concept of a one-second duration was evident.

In conclusion, although the perception of time has received much experimental attention, there is little concrete evidence for a comprehensive explanation of the manner in which individuals experience the passage of time. We are aware that events are separated by temporal units, but the size of these units depends markedly on a broad number of internal and external stimuli. Before psychologists will be able to make definitive statements about time perception a number of methodological problems will have to be solved. Perhaps the use of physical measurements of time is inappropriate, since they only reflect the degree of interaction between the objective units of measurement and the subjective time experienced by an individual. Future research might well concentrate on temporal events in which the amount of subjective time passing would be compared to other events, rather than to a measure of elapsed clock time.

CHAPTER 8
Some Complex Perceptual Problems

The title of the final chapter in this book should forewarn the reader of the difficult traveling to be encountered with the topics to come. The discussion will center on certain complex processes of perception, many of which have been mentioned in passing during the preceding chapters. The warning stems from a reservation that should be respected even when one is reviewing studies of seemingly simple perceptual phenomena: that the present state of available knowledge leaves many unanswered questions. The current topics, then, are almost entirely lacking in complete, concrete answers. With this admonition in mind, we will discuss the following aspects of perception in the ensuing pages: perceptual set, attention, subliminal perception, and sensory deprivation. The chapter will end with a final consideration of the perceptual model developed throughout the book.

Perceptual Set

In a number of perceptual experiments described in the preceding pages the context of a stimulus array influenced the observer's perception or at least his interpretation of the stimulus. Furthermore, numerous tests were reported in which some preceding or ongoing stimulus influenced the perception of a new and novel stimulus introduced in the field. In each case one can generalize to the statement that the test perception was affected by the *previous experience* gained by the preceding or ongoing events. The word "experience" is used here in its broadest sense, encompassing all kinds of events ranging from the inspection figure in a test of figural aftereffects to the specific instructions emphasizing retinal, apparent, or phenomenal aspects of the test stimulus in judgments of size and shape constancy. In fact, the doctrine of the role of experience in perception usually leads to the assumption that all perceptual tendencies are the result of the sum total of all previous perceptual experience as well as a product of current ongoing events. The model of perception discussed in Chapter 3 and diagrammed in Figure 3.1 emphasized the influences of short- and long-term storage and the various control processes on the perceptual response. The current discussion will consider the influences of long-term storage and of the control processes on response output. Note that we are able to provide only examples of the influences of these complicated aspects of perception. Perhaps, by isolating some specific experience and considering its influence on concurrent perceptual processing, we will at least be able to show that any perception is the result of innumerable previous experiences.

Set produced by specific experience.   One would expect that, given a potential stimulus with which the observer has had no previous experience, his perception of that stimulus would depend on his experience with similar objects. When the new automobile models appear each fall we are usually able to judge the manufacturer of a particular new model on first view. Because of our previous experience with earlier models we note similarities between the new and the old. If these similarities are great enough, we can perceive the make of the new car. In other words, we respond to attributes of the new stimulus on the basis of our stored information about such attributes.

The term *set* is usually taken to mean a predisposition to perceive or respond to a given stimulus due to preceding perceptual events. The latter may be specific, such as a certain visual or auditory stimulus; or they may be nonspecific, such as the result of the general experiences derived from life in a certain culture. As an example of the second instance, an Eskimo's perception of snow is different from that of a typical inhabitant of the United States be-

Figure 8.1
Ambiguous rat/man drawing. (After Bugelski and Alampay, 1961.)

cause the Eskimo language contains numerous terms for different kinds of snow, while English contains only one general term. An example of a set derived from a specific experience is a game in which the subject is asked to repeat the word "joke" as rapidly as possible six times. The experimenter then immediately asks the subject to name the white of an egg. Most subjects quickly respond with the word "yolk," attempting carefully to pronounce the word correctly. Naturally, the white of an egg is not the yolk, which is yellow; the white of an egg is simply the white, or albumen. The rapid repetition of "joke," then, establishes two sets. First, "yoke" comes to mind quickly due to the *clang association* (a response based on rhyme similarity) with "joke." Second, the subject expects to be caught in a pronunciation error and therefore fails to anticipate an error in response.

A number of studies have sought to determine if ambiguous visual or auditory stimuli can be organized by means of specific perceptual experiences. Bugelski and Alampay (1961) gave two groups of observers the ambiguous line drawing shown in Figure 8.1, which can be seen as a rat or as a bald, bespectacled man. One group of subjects saw one to four "human" pictures prior to the presentation, and the other group saw from one to four "animal" pictures before judging. Table 8.1 gives the percentage of man or rat responses for both groups as a function of the number of set-inducing pictures. A control group, which saw no set-inducing figures, reported the man 81 percent of the time.

The data in Table 8.1 clearly indicate the influence of preceding perceptual experience. The same ambiguous figure tends to be seen quite differently, depending on the establishment of a set to see "humans" or "animals." The frequency or number of set-inducing stimuli appears to be unimportant in the

Table 8.1

Responses to ambiguous rat/man drawing
(Bugelski and Alampay, 1961)

	Set-inducing stimuli							
	Animal pictures				Human pictures			
	1	2	3	4	1	2	3	4
Percent rat	74	82	91	100	27	25	27	20
Percent man	26	18	9	0	73	75	73	80

case of the human pictures. For the animal pictures, however, the frequency with which the rat was reported increased as a function of the number of pictures. The lack of a frequency effect for the human pictures may be the result of a predisposition to see a man rather than a rat, as demonstrated by the control group's responses.

One of the classic studies of set was reported by Bruner and Minturn (1955). One group of subjects was shown the four letters of the alphabet L, M, Y, and A, while another group saw the numbers 16, 17, 10, and 12. A control series of letters and numbers mixed together was seen by a final group. The test stimulus consisted of the letter B with a slight separation between the straight and curved portions of the letter: B . Of the subjects shown the numbers prior to the test stimulus, 83 percent reported the test figure to be the number 13. Of those shown the letters first, 71 percent reported the letter B. The subjects who saw the letters and numbers mixed together identified the test stimulus as either the letter B or the number 13 with equal frequency. Thus the essentially ambiguous test stimulus, which could be perceived as either a letter or a number, was perceived in a manner commensurate with the set produced by the preceding string of letters or numbers.

Rather than study the effects of particular stimuli presented in immediate conjunction with test figures, some experimenters have concentrated their attention on certain long-range experiences of typical observers. Toch and Schulte (1961) based one such study on a tendency known as *binocular rivalry*. When a different picture is presented simultaneously to each eye, observers sometimes report one or the other of the two, sometimes a combination (or fusion) of the two. Levelt (1968) has pointed out that binocular rivalry usually occurs when the two pictures are so different they cannot be combined meaningfully without an information loss from one or the other. Toch and Schulte reasoned that if distinctly different pictures were used and rivalry evoked, the picture favored might depend on the observer's past experiences. Accordingly, they selected one group of observers who had undergone extensive training in police work and a second group just beginning such training. All were shown a pair of drawings in a stereoscope; as in the example, Figure 8.2, each drawing featured a violent and a nonviolent scene. Out of 18 pairs of drawings, subjects with police training saw an average of 9.37 of the violent scenes; sub-

Figure 8.2
Stereogram presenting violent scene to left eye and nonviolent scene to
right eye. (After Toch and Schulte, 1961.)

jects just beginning training saw only 4.69. A third group of college students
reported an average of 4.03 violent scenes. Note that both students and beginning trainees tended to perceive predominantly nonviolent scenes. The police-
trained subjects, however, perceived more of the violent scenes. Toch and
Schulte concluded that the training provided a set for the perception of violence not present in the trainees or the college students.

Relevant to the study of perceptual set are the experiments initially introduced by Stroop (1935) in which subjects were presented with the names of
colors (e.g., red, blue, yellow, green, etc.) printed in various colors. For example, a subject might be given the visual stimulus word *blue* printed in yellow
ink. Generally, Stroop found subjects required much more time to name the
color word if it was inconsistent with the actual color of the word. Reversing
this procedure and requiring subjects to name the color rather than the word
also produced slower reaction times when the two did not match. Gholson and
Hohle (1968) compared reaction times to the words *red, green, yellow,* and
blue printed in conflicting colors to the times for nonsense words printed in
the same colors. The nonsense words were the color words transposed (e.g.,
blue = lebu). Subjects asked to name the color words averaged a tenth
of a second longer than when they were asked the colors of the nonsense
words.

Some studies have presented stimulus materials inconsistent with existing sets. Bruner and Postman (1949) prepared a number of playing cards in
which the suits were reversed in hue—clubs and spades were red and diamonds and hearts were black. Using a modified method of limits they presented each card three times at durations ranging from 10 to 1,000 msec and
asked the subjects to identify the denominations and suits of the cards. Figure
8.3 gives the cumulative percentage of correct recognitions for both normal
and reversed playing cards at each intensity level. The inconsistency between
suit color and name clearly produced a higher threshold for the correct naming of card attributes. The authors interpret these results to indicate that the
set established by the frequent experience with playing cards worked against
correct recognition of the altered cards. Note that at very short exposures no
color was probably seen, and subjects guessed. At long exposures, subjects
apparently did equally well with both kinds of cards.

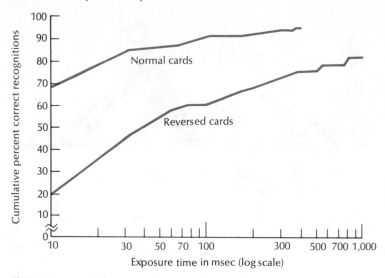

Figure 8.3
Cumulative percentage of correctly recognized normal and reversed playing cards as a function of exposure time. (After Bruner and Postman, 1949.)

A rather fascinating question about the nature of perceptual set was advanced by Robert Leeper (1935). Five groups of subjects were presented with
the ambiguous drawing shown in Figure 8.4, which can be seen either as an
old woman (or mother-in-law) or as a young woman (or wife). A first group
served as a control and was shown only this ambiguous drawing. On the average, 65 percent of these subjects spontaneously described the picture as that
of a young woman; the rest saw an old woman. A second group was given a
verbal description of the figure emphasizing the old woman alone and a third
group received a verbal description of the young woman. Prior to viewing the
test figure, groups 4 and 5 were shown part A of Figure 8.5, an unambigu-

Figure 8.4
Ambiguous wife/mother-in-law drawing.
(After Leeper, 1935.)

A   B

Figure 8.5
Unambiguous set-producing stimuli presented prior to Figure 8.4. A, unambiguous old woman. B, unambiguous young woman. (After Leeper, 1935.)

ous version of the test stimulus showing only the old woman, and part B, an unambiguous version showing only the young woman. The percentage of "young" versus "old" descriptions obtained for the subjects of each group are shown in Table 8.2.

The results indicate that verbal descriptions failed to influence the perception of the test figure, while the unambiguous visual figures produced diametrically opposed perceptions of the test figure. Leeper concluded that the mechanism of set in this instance is perceptual in nature and cannot be influenced by verbal stimulation. However, the present author has been unable to replicate this clear-cut finding. Data from classes studying the psychology of perception have been collected over a period of several years using the conditions described for groups 1, 4, and 5. These data indicate a definite tendency on the part of several hundred students to see the young woman despite preceding stimulation by the unambiguous drawing of the old woman. Furthermore, the control group (N = 237) averaged 94 percent in favor of the young woman. Perhaps the fact that the figure has become so well known influenced

Table 8.2

Subjects describing Figure 8.4 as young or old
(Leeper, 1935)

		Percent reporting young figure	Percent reporting old figure
Group 1	(Control)	65	35
Group 2	(Verbal old)	67	33
Group 3	(Verbal young)	63	37
Group 4	(Visual old)	6	94
Group 5	(Visual young)	100	0

Figure 8.6
Street's ocean-liner drawing used by
Steinfeld (1967).

the latter results. In passing, an interesting study by Koch (1968) should be mentioned. The test stimulus of Figure 8.4 was shown to patients in a home for the aged. Koch hypothesized that older persons would possess a set for elderly people and would therefore see the old woman in the picture more than the young woman, but the results did not confirm this hypothesis. Most of the older subjects tended to see the young woman, as did a control group of college-age subjects.

Steinfeld (1967) employed one of a series of drawings initially introduced by Street (1931). The picture shows an ocean liner approaching the observer with waves breaking in front of the bow (see Figure 8.6). Subjects in a first group listened to a story about the sinking of an ocean-going liner, were shown the picture, and were asked to describe it. Before seeing the picture a second group heard a story about a scrubwoman who lost her purse in a large building. Finally, a control group saw the picture without hearing any preceding story. Steinfeld measured the amount of time observers required to perceive the test stimulus as a ship. Table 8.3 gives the results for the three groups.

The subjects who listened to the ship story perceived and organized the figure as a ship much more quickly than subjects in the other two groups. Interestingly enough, group B subjects (scrubwoman story) tended to require more time to organize the figure than the control subjects. As Steinfeld points out, one might speak of a negative set in which the subjects were directed away from the possible organization of the figure as a ship.

In Steinfeld's experiment auditory input provided a set for the perception of a visual stimulus. Contradicting this result is Leeper's (1935) failure to demonstrate the influence of a verbal set on a visual stimulus. Perhaps the reason for this discrepancy is that subjects tend to perceive the Leeper figure spontaneously as an old or young woman and must overcome this spontaneous organization in order to be influenced by the set. In Steinfeld's study the picture need not be reorganized but simply organized into the meaningful ship. A possible study of this distinction might attempt to establish a set by verbal in-

Table 8.3

Recognition times for Street's ocean-liner drawing in Figure 8.6
(Steinfeld, 1967)

Set	Mean time	Standard deviation
Group A (Story about ocean liner)	4.5 seconds	3.15
Group B (Story about scrubwoman)	38.1 seconds	39.69
Group C (No story)	24.1 seconds	30.48

struction using the rat/man drawing of Bugelski and Alampay (1961). This figure can be organized in two ways, neither of which is dominant over the other. The interested student might test this by establishing a man or rat set in a group of subjects and then asking them to describe Figure 8.1.

The mechanism of set.   The set to respond to a particular stimulus in a certain manner influences the perception of the test stimulus. That set is the reason for the modified perception of the test stimulus involves the assumption of an intervening variable. That is, we observe the effect of experience A on test stimulus B, and then consider the nature of the effect to be due to a set. Assuming that such a mechanism exists and operationally demonstrating it in various experiments still tells us nothing about the mechanism itself. A classic study by Karl Duncker (1935) illustrates the problem.

Duncker prepared two stimuli from the same dark green paper: a donkey and a leaf. Each was presented alternately against a dark background and illuminated with a red light; the latter was adjusted with the green target to obtain a perfect neutral gray. After looking at the targets the subject was given a color mixer and asked to match the gray of each target by using proportions of red and green on the color mixer. Duncker found most subjects used more green to match the leaf than to match the donkey.

Interpreted in terms of set, the results indicate that subjects tend to see normally green objects as green even though they are really colorless. But did the set cause Duncker's subject to see the target as slightly green because of his previous experience with green leaves or did he adjust the color mixer to include more green because of his memory that leaves are green? In other words, does set directly affect the process of perception or is the response merely a result of memory? In Duncker's study one cannot tell whether the leaf looked greener or if the subject used more green in matching because he knew it should be green.

To reduce this possible influence of memory, Harper (1953) mounted traditionally red targets (heart, apple, and lobster) and traditionally neutral objects (oval, triangle, and the letter Y) on the front of a color mixer containing red and yellow. When the proportions of red and yellow on the mixer were equal, the color produced matched the red of the six test targets. The task of the observers was to adjust the proportion of red and yellow until the red target disappeared by becoming the same as the background provided by the color mixer. Harper found subjects tended to include more red in matches of the traditionally red objects. His results can be interpreted to mean that set modifies perception. That is, subjects required to match the targets presented in front of the color mixer used more red to match traditionally red objects than the neutral objects; and this is taken to indicate that they actually saw the targets as redder.

The present author and James Bashford replicated Harper's experiment. The study was highly similar except that after the observer had matched the color of a target (either a traditionally red or a neutral target), the target was replaced with another test target and the observer asked to readjust the color mixer if he felt that the previous match no longer held for the new target. In those cases in which the first match was to a neutral target and the replacement target was a traditionally red target, subjects tended to readjust the color mixer to include more red. The effect was small but consistent.

One popular experimental design for the study of set was originally introduced by Külpe (1904). Observers were shown groups of letters that varied in color, identity, location, and number. Prior to the presentation of each card subjects were asked to attend to one of these four attributes. Külpe found that subjects tended to be better at reporting the aspect to which attention had been directed and were often unable to report other aspects. He suggested that the clarity of the emphasized element was improved perceptually due to the set to attend to that attribute. Wilcocks (1925) introduced a control for a memory effect, since the result of Külpe's experiment might have been due to the order in which subjects chose to report the elements. In other words, once a particular aspect had been selected, subjects might have tended to report this element first and to forget some other aspects before having the opportunity to report them. To avoid this, Wilcocks dictated the order in which the elements of the stimuli were to be reported. He found that the accuracy of report diminished the later the element was reported. However, he also found a facilitating effect for the instructions to attend to a particular attribute, above and beyond the influence of order of report.

Using a modified version of the Külpe design, Chapman (1932) instructed subjects to attend to some aspect of the stimulus cards, but he was able to compare conditions in which the important attribute was indicated *before* or *after* presentation of the test card. He found accuracy of report to be greater when the instructions were provided prior to presentation of the test card, and interpreted this result to favor the perceptual hypothesis. Since the subject knew what to look for, he was better able to focus on and to perceive the important aspect of the test card. Similar effects for auditory elements have been reported by Swets and Sewall (1963). Lawrence and Coles (1954) carried the experiment one step further and displayed pictures of single familiar objects as test stimuli. Prior to or immediately following the test stimulus, the names of four alternatives for the stimulus were given; a control group received no verbal labels. Both the before and after groups gave reports superior to those of the control group. A memory aspect must be involved since one could hardly explain the superiority of the after group on the basis of perceptual enhancement.

As Haber (1966) has pointed out, the earlier results of Chapman (1932) can be explained on the basis of memory alone, if the results of Lawrence and Coles (1954) are taken into account. When the alternative is provided prior to the test stimulus, the observer is given an earlier opportunity to memorize the relevant information. The *before* condition gives him a chance to do this when the stimulus appears, instead of having to rely on a fading memory of it in the *after* condition. Nevertheless, the *after* condition allows a better utilization of memory than if no information at all were provided about the alternatives. Along the same lines, Long, Henneman, and Garvey (1960), Long, Reid, and Henneman (1960), and Reid, Henneman, and Long (1960) have reported a series of experiments in which the clarity of single letters or words was reduced through visual or auditory distortion. Alternatives from which the test words or letters were taken were provided before or after the presentation of the critical stimulus. When the number of alternatives decreased, accuracy increased, no matter whether the alternatives were made known before or after the test stimulus. The experimenters mentioned conclude that reducing the number of alternatives facilitates memory by reducing the number of elements to be held in storage. In the experiment by Steinfeld, for example, the story of the sinking of an ocean liner reduces the number of possibilities to be considered in the organization of the figure.

Memory effects are clearly involved in set. In support of this contention, Ornstein and Winnick (1968) gathered data concerning recognition thresholds for a series of words. To establish set, they presented ten words as alternatives. They next obtained the visual-recognition thresholds for these words, for a series of homonyms (words pronounced similarly but physically different in appearance, e.g., sole and soul), and for a series of unrelated words. They found that the preparatory set facilitated recognition of both the original set words and the homonyms, and that the set established by the preceding words carried over to words of similar sound even though presentation was entirely visual. Numerous other studies (e.g., Talland, 1959) involving auditory presentation of the set-inducing stimuli and visual testing of the influence of these stimuli have indicated the influence of set on such memory tasks.

At this point it appears obvious that neither an explanation based solely on memory nor one based solely on perception will be able to handle the diverse observations available concerning set. A compromise has been offered by Steinfeld (1967): that set be considered a product of a perceptual *and* a memory mechanism. One could say, then, that set enhances the clarity of the incoming percept and aids the observer's memory in developing that percept.

Another possibility has been advanced by Harris and Haber (1963; see also Haber 1964a, 1964b, and 1966). Their basic experiment used pairs of briefly flashed stimulus cards, each displaying geometrical figures that varied in number, shape, and color. Subjects were informed that special attention should be directed to one of these three aspects. On half the trials the order of report was dictated by the experimenter, on the other half it was up to the subject. With a fixed order of report most subjects reported the critical attribute more accurately than the others regardless of whether it was reported first, second, or third.

Rather than propose an effect on initial perception or on memory after the stimulus is gone, Harris and Haber (1963) concentrated on the encoding process by which the observer transforms perception of the stimulus into a verbal description for memory. For this particular task, two kinds of spontaneous encoding strategies were observed. Some subjects separated the elements of a specific card into objects on the left and right, and remembered them by saying to themselves, for example, "three blue stars, one red square." This was called the *objects strategy*. The other subjects used a *dimensions strategy*, which would interpret the previous pattern as "blue red, square star, one three." Note that with the dimensions strategy a subject could vary the order of encoding—to put first, for example, attributes that might have been emphasized by the experimenter—but that this could not be done with the objects strategy.

In a related experiment, subjects were trained to use one or the other of the two strategies. The effect of set—the emphasized attributes receiving the most accurate reports—disappeared for subjects using the objects strategy. Subjects using the dimensions strategy almost always encoded the critical attribute first, before the visual image faded, and hence displayed an improved accuracy for these aspects. From these results Harris and Haber concluded that since set is noticeable only under one encoding strategy, the effect is probably a product of that strategy rather than of enhanced perception. The experiments do not rule out the possibility of a perceptual enhancement, but it is difficult to imagine why such an effect would occur only under one kind of strategy.

Harris's and Haber's observations concerning the influence of encoding strategies do not resolve the conflict between perception and memory, as demonstrated by an experiment by Egeth and Smith (1967). They modified an older design by Lawrence and Coles (1954), mentioned earlier in this chapter, in which verbal labels for certain items were presented before and after a test picture. That study failed to find evidence of a perceptual mechanism of set, but Egeth and Smith point out that this may have been the result of reliance on verbal rather than on perceptual alternatives. Such labels would have to be translated into perceptual attributes before they could evoke a mechanism of perceptual selectivity. The use of pictures rather than verbal labels, then, would allow the observer to seek out the features of the items providing a perceptual discrimination. Egeth and Smith decided to compare the ability of subjects to isolate critical elements in pictures under several conditions. Their observers were told that the critical element was one of four items displayed before, after, or before and after the test picture. On half the trials the four alternative items were highly similar (e.g., four different kinds of shoes) and on the remaining trials highly dissimilar (e.g., radio, vacuum cleaner, sports car, man's shoe).

Egeth and Smith reasoned that if the alternative pictures were highly dissimilar, a crude memory would suffice to discriminate the critical item in the test picture, and it would make little difference whether the alternatives were provided before or after the test picture. However, if the items were highly similar, then crude memory alone would be unable to provide the information concerning the critical attribute in the after condition. In the before condition the subject could *selectively* direct his attention to the salient feature distinguishing between the similar items. Egeth and Smith (1967) predicted that

Table 8.4

Mean correct responses for critical items of a test stimulus
(Egeth and Smith, 1967)

	Condition		
	Before	*After*	*Before-after*
Similar alternatives	7.62	6.37	10
Dissimilar alternatives	13.31	14.83	14.93

"perceptual selectivity ought to result in less difference in recognition accuracy between similar and dissimilar alternatives when the sets of alternatives are presented before rather than after the test picture" (p. 544). The experimental data supported their expectation. The mean number of correct identifications for male and female subjects combined under all conditions are to be found in Table 8.4. These averages indicate less difference due to the degree of similarity under the before-after condition than under the after condition. As in the earlier studies, the comparison of before and after would be confounded by the possible effects of memory.

Although a final conclusion cannot be drawn, the results of the numerous experimental studies indicate that both memory and perceptual factors are operative in set. It seems clear that some tasks are more receptive to perceptual influence than others. In certain cases the mechanism of set may be the result of memory or of an encoding strategy; when neither of these provides discriminating information, perceptual selectivity may still occur.

Attention

From among the deluge of potential stimuli the human organism can attend only to a very few at any given moment. Limited as to the amount of information he can process, the observer is forced to perceive or to respond to less than the total array. In many ways experimental studies of attention start from the same basic premise as the studies of perceptual set. Generally, the latter are designed to isolate aspects of experience leading to a particular perceptual response. Work on attention centers on describing the manner in which the organism responds to and maintains that particular response.

As with set, attention is a term that refers to an unobservable aspect of behavior occurring between stimulus presentation and response. Egeth (1967) believes that attention is a mechanism "which enables organisms to respond selectively to important features of the environment while ignoring features which are of little or no importance" (p. 41). One of the most influential descriptions of attention was developed by Broadbent (1958). In his model he assumed that when several stimuli impinge on the senses, each evokes an initial response. Experimental observations discussed in detail in Chapter 3 indicate that the observer's capacity for processing stimuli from the environment is limited. At some point in the perceptual process, then, some of the stimuli must be selected for further processing and some disregarded. Broadbent solved this problem by assuming the existence of a *selective filter* that eliminates the irrelevant stimuli. Such a filter allows only as much information from the environment to pass on for processing as can be handled by the observer.

The technique most frequently employed in studies of attention and attention selection is *dichotic listening.* A subject listens to an auditory stimulus presented through earphones to one ear while being presented simultaneously with a second auditory stimulus to the other ear. Numerous studies have shown that if the subject is asked to attend to one of the two stimuli he is able to do so if the two messages are significantly distinguishable from one another. Usually the subject is asked to *shadow* the message to one ear; that is, he must repeat the message out loud as he hears it. Egan, Carterette, and Thwing (1954) presented different messages to each ear; each was read by a different voice and the irrelevant message was modified by a bandpass filter. Subjects experienced little difficulty in following the relevant message. Differences in intensity between the two messages were also sufficient to allow selective attention, even when the irrelevant message was actually louder than the relevant one. Explained in terms of Broadbent's model, the selective filter distinguishes the irrelevant information on the basis of differing physical characteristics, and then eliminates it.

Another classic study in dichotic listening was reported by Cherry (1953). Subjects shadowed a message presented to one ear while an irrelevant message was presented to the other ear. Throughout the experiment the nature of the irrelevant message was varied. Its first and last portions were ordinary speech, but its center portion was sometimes reversed (played backwards), spoken in another language (German), or spoken by someone of the sex opposite that of the speaker of the relevant message. After the presentation, when subjects were questioned about the speech that had been ignored, it was found that most subjects noticed the change in speakers but not the change in language or the change to reversed speech. The important point is that only a change in the physical characteristics of the irrelevant message (pitch) caused the filter to fail.

The so-called cocktail-party phenomenon would support an interpretation allowing the unattended message to have some residual effect. While engaged in a conversation at a party one is relatively unaware of the surrounding conversations. These represent irrelevant stimuli. However, if one's name is mentioned in one of these conversations, one's attention usually shifts to the new stimulus, indicating that some kind of monitoring of the other messages must have been going on. Moray (1959) has demonstrated experimentally that including the name of the observer in the context of an irrelevant message usually shifts attention to that message.

Treisman (1960) has argued that one cannot speak of a rejection of the irrelevant information, but rather of a weakening or an attenuation. The original processing of relevant and irrelevant input must be the same; however, the relevant message is processed further on the basis of some characteristic of the stimulus. In her experiment Treisman showed that if the words in the irrelevant message fit in with the meaning of the relevant message, such words were frequently reported as intrusions in the shadowed message.

In another study Treisman (1964) required subjects to shadow the message presented to one ear and to ignore the message to the other ear. Unknown to the subjects, the two messages were the same but were staggered in time; the unattended message either preceded or followed the attended one. By varying the time difference between the two, Treisman could determine the point at which subjects spontaneously remarked that they were identical. With the attended message preceding the unattended, subjects noticed they were the same when the delay interval was 4.3 seconds. When the unattended message preceded, the relationship between messages was noted with a delay of only 1.3 seconds. The time difference is not only statistically significant but also of great theoretical import, since it indicates that the incoming information—both unattended and attended—had to be stored for a brief period and then processed. That is, the unattended message still must have been in the sensory register when the same portion of the attended message entered. The realization that the messages were the same depended on content rather than physical characteristics, since observers still noted the similarity when they were read by male speakers to one ear and female speakers to the other ear.

Rather than dictate which of two separate messages requires the attention of the observer, some experimenters have presented separate auditory stimuli to each ear and observed the subject's strategy when asked to repeat or retain both items. Bryden (1962) noted that the strategies used for such tasks depended on the rate of presentation. Broadbent (1958) had found that if strings of different numbers were presented simultaneously to both ears, subjects repeated all the information to one ear and then all the information to the other ear. Bryden replicated this with fast rates, but reported that at slower presentation rates subjects repeated the information in terms of its temporal order of arrival to both ears.

Since Broadbent's filter model does not seem to account for all such observations concerning dichotic listening, several other theories have been advanced. Deutsch and Deutsch (1963) and Reynolds (1964) suggest that all stimuli are processed perceptually (i.e., enter short-term storage) but that selection occurs only as the observer responds to the stimuli. This same distinction was advanced in the discussion of set. Selective attention, then, depends on generated response rather than on a filtering of incoming stimuli. Figure 8.7 contains diagrams of both the perceptual filter and the response models of selective attention. These allow one to consider the various ways in which the two models agree with or contradict one another.

Treisman and Geffen (1967) designed an experiment that might lend support to either the perceptual filter model or the response model. Subjects shadowed a message presented to one ear while a second message was presented to the other ear, and were instructed to make a manual tapping response to critical target words that might occur in either message. The subjects responded

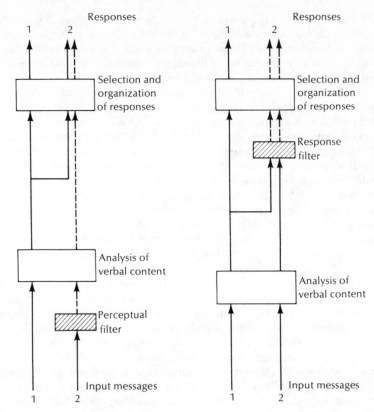

Figure 8.7
Models of selective attention. *Left,* perceptual filter model. Prior to an analysis of their verbal content, messages 1 and 2 are differentiated by means of a filter tuned to specific physical characteristics of the message. *Right,* response model. Messages are differentiated after the analysis of verbal content but before responses to them have been organized. In both models dotted lines represent unattended messages, solid lines represent attended messages. (After Treisman and Geffen, 1967. Reproduced by permission of the Experimental Psychology Society.)

to 37 percent of the critical words in the shadowed message but to only 3 percent of the critical words presented to the other ear. Treisman and Geffen concluded that such results supported the perceptual filter model. In their opinion the inability of observers to respond to critical words in the unshadowed message was due to the filtering of this message before its content was analyzed. The results fail to support the response model, according to Treisman and Geffen, because it assumes that selective attention is the result of a selection of responses. That is, the observer cannot carry out two different responses simultaneously and must therefore disregard one of the messages. However, in this study the response (tapping) was the same for either message, and the observer would not need to choose between messages in order to avoid carrying out competing responses. If, as the response model assumes, all input is initially processed, then the subject should have picked up the critical words irrespective of the ear through which the messages were entering.

Deutsch and Deutsch (1967) objected to the results of the Treisman and Geffen study, pointing out that subjects instructed to respond primarily to critical words in the shadowed message would not be highly motivated to respond to the unshadowed message. Since they already had to tap in response to certain words in the shadowed message, this could have produced different levels of motivation for monitoring the two messages. Treisman and Riley (1969) attempted to meet these objections by replicating the basic experiment and including a major modification. Each time subjects heard a critical stimulus requiring a tapping response, they were instructed to stop shadowing and to execute the required tap. Under a condition of the experiment that presented lists of digits to each ear in the same voice, subjects responded correctly to 76 percent of the critical letters in the attended message and only 33 percent in the unattended message. When the target letters were presented in a voice different from the rest of the message, responses were equally accurate for either ear.

Wilding and Underwood (1968) entered the controversy by asking about the location of the filter (Treisman = perceptual, Deutsch and Deutsch = memory) and about the characteristics of the stimulus used for filtering. Treisman's perceptual filter should eliminate irrelevant information on the basis of physical characteristics of the input; in contrast, the filter proposed by Deutsch and Deutsch should be able to discriminate inputs on the basis of their semantic features. Wilding and Underwood asked their subjects to shadow a critical message to one ear and to tap in response to critical words in a message to the unattended ear. The critical word was always "steel." The first group was instructed to listen for words with an *eel* sound, like steel, peel, heel, or feel. The second group was to listen for names of metals (e.g., steel, lead, copper, or silver). The third group was to listen simply for the word "steel." Similar instructions were developed for three other groups asked to respond to the word "gray." The average numbers of critical words detected in the unattended messages for the six groups of subjects are given in Table 8.5. The data clearly favor the notion of a perceptual filter that responds to physical characteristics of the stimulus. However, the results also show a striking difference between groups 2 and 3. While the most words were detected on the basis of sound (group 1), evidently some further processing occurs beyond the perceptual level based on an analysis of the meaning of the critical stimulus.

Despite the danger of equating the responses of human observers with those of other animals, the results of the Treisman and Geffen study bring to mind the classic experiment by Hernandez-Péon, Scherrer, and Jouvet (1956). They implanted electrodes in the auditory nerves of cats, presented auditory stimuli, and noted the responses of the auditory nerves. This technique is known as the method of evoked potentials. After a clear response pattern to a certain click had been established for an auditory nerve, the experimenters put a mouse in a jar into a cat's cage and sounded the click. On this trial no response

Table 8.5

Detection of four critical words in an unattended message as a function of instructions
(Wilding and Underwood, 1968)

Word	Group 1 (physical)	Group 2 (semantic, general)	Group 3 (semantic, specific)
"steel"	2.4	0.2	0.8
"gray"	1.2	0.2	0.8

was observed in the auditory nerve although the auditory stimulus was the same as on preceding trials. This can be interpreted as an attenuation of the auditory input by a perceptual filter. Since the auditory nerve did not respond, the nature of the filter must be perceptual rather than selective (i.e., based on responses to the visual mouse stimulus or the auditory click stimulus).

Currently two models of attention seem best equipped to deal with the existing data. Treisman (1968) has developed further the model proposed by Broadbent to include a mechanism by means of which the unattended elements of a stimulus can enter the perceptual process. This model assumes that several levels of *perceptual analyzers* deal with the sensory input, and that such analyzers respond to specific attributes of the incoming information rather than to the entire array. Analyzers for shapes, forms, and colors conduct the visual input, and analyzers of intensity, frequency, and phase transmit auditory input. Thus subjects would be very sensitive to the responses of certain analyzers carrying key stimuli even if they were utilizing another channel to process information (e.g., the cocktail-party phenomenon). The more similar the characteristics of the information entering two sensory channels, the greater the difficulty in maintaining a strict attention for one or the other of the channels.

A second model developed by Norman (1968) contains certain features of Treisman's model, but it also resembles the basic model of the perceptual process discussed in Chapter 3 of the present book. Norman's model interprets the attention mechanism in three phases. The first involves a sensory input register that records all incoming effective stimuli and evokes the first level of processing or selection. The second phase involves passing sensory input to a short-term or primary memory area, and the third involves passing input to a secondary or permanent memory area. By means of the interrelation of these phases and of a postulated retrieval system which sends out repeated queries to the two storage areas, a response and final selection of interpretation is generated. In terms of the model discussed in Chapter 3, a signal enters the sensory register and receives a first analysis, then passes to short-term storage and in some cases to long-term storage.

Norman (1968) believes that the first phase of processing in the sensory register occurs automatically and does not require a cognitive interpretation

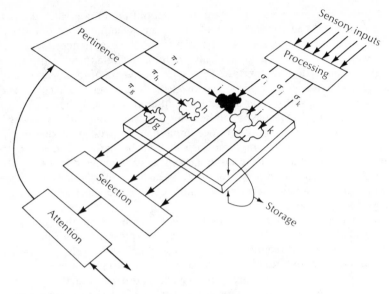

Figure 8.8
Schematic outline of the model of selective attention proposed by Norman
(1968).

of the input. Possibly, as Norman argues, the initial processing depends on the
basis of the physical characteristics of the signal: a) the signal is translated from
physical form to physiological representation in the nervous system; b) salient
features of the signal are extracted; and c) on the basis of the signal's unique
features the input is directed to the appropriate storage area in the short- or
long-term memory banks. The characteristics of short-term storage have been
discussed in detail earlier in this book. At this point it is sufficient to note that
the capacity of short-term storage is determined by the number of meaningful
elements stored at any given moment in time, and that short-term storage
processing takes longer than the initial analyzing of the sensory input by the
sensory register.

Then how does the attention mechanism respond to simultaneous sensory
stimulation of the kind encountered in dichotic listening studies? To explain
this, Norman posits an additional aspect of memory, the *pertinence value*,
which introduces a bias for one of the inputs. Figure 8.8 is a schematic outline
of Norman's model of selective attention. Effective stimuli (sensory inputs) are
processed at the level of the sensory register. Through this first stage of elimination three possible elements, σ_i, σ_j, and σ_k, pass into storage. These processed
inputs activate their representations in storage as i, j, and k. The perceiving
organism's selection of a particular input is determined by its interpretation at
this level plus the pertinence values, π_g, π_h, and π_i which are based on such factors as current attention, interest, motivation, past learning, and personality.
The input to which attention is directed, i, is the stimulus receiving the highest
pertinence value from the numerous elements processed.

Norman makes several important points about the model. First, the pertinence value and the strength of the initial sensory input need not depend directly on stimulus intensity. Thus subjects should experience no difficulty shadowing a message of lower intensity while receiving an irrelevant message of higher intensity to the other ear. The pertinence value of the lower intensity message would be greater and an analysis of the proper input could occur at the sensory register on the basis of the different physical characteristics of the two messages. Second, Norman believes that the interaction of processing and pertinence value does not produce immediate knowledge of all aspects of the stimulus. Some of the important aspects will be derived and interpreted from the memory banks of the observer only after selective attention has occurred. Third, unattended inputs are only partially interpreted. The representation of such a partially decoded stimulus may pass to short-term storage or it may be lost.

If it is true that all sensory stimuli are initially processed, then one should be able to demonstrate that the sensory register picks up more information from the environment than is actually processed and selectively attended. The classic attempt to determine the fate of unattended input was reported by Moray (1959). While shadowing a message to one ear, subjects listened to a list of thirty-five words repeated over and over to the other ear. The last word of the list occurred 30 seconds before the end of the shadowing task. When tested, subjects displayed no memory for the list of unattended words. This meant that either the concept of processing at the levels of both the sensory register and short-term storage is incorrect, or that the memory for unattended input decays after 30 seconds. In terms of the time limitations of the sensory register and the short-term storage, 30 seconds is a very long time. Norman (1969) tested both of these interpretations. Subjects shadowed English words to one ear and were tested for the memory of two-digit numbers presented to the other ear. Under several conditions of testing, the memory for the unattended items was assessed either immediately or after a 20-second delay. The results clearly indicated a memory for the unattended items tested immediately and a marked decay in memory after 20 seconds.

A rather exciting possibility for testing the assumed storage mechanism has been suggested by Inglis (1960) and experimentally tested by Inglis and Tansey (1967). They set up a dichotic listening condition that presented different digits simultaneously to each ear and required subjects to repeat as many of the digits as possible. They found that if the presentation rate was fairly rapid, subjects tended to repeat the input to each ear sequentially. That is, they repeated all of the items to one ear before starting to repeat the items to the other. This meant that the information to one ear had to be held in some kind of storage while the information to the other ear was repeated. Inglis and Tansey tested subjects at various ages, since they had noted that elderly subjects had difficulty remembering items over short periods but showed no decrement for items maintained in long-term storage. As the average age of their subjects increased they found little impairment in their ability to repeat back the digits to one ear, but a marked decrement in their ability to remember items held in storage when they were repeated back after a delay interval. Evidently the short-term storage mechanism breaks down at an earlier age than does the long-term storage mechanism. An interesting study would trace the rate of processing from the sensory register into the short-term storage as a function of age. Unfortunately, such results are not presently available.

The discussion of selective attention in this section formulated a model of perception in which many more stimuli enter the sensory system than receive the attention of the observer. As demonstrated by several different studies, much of the unattended information is actually stored for short periods of time (Norman, 1969). Perhaps some of this information is used by the observer in generating a response to an attended configuration. As Norman has argued (1968), the unattended input may not be completely encoded, and only elements or pieces of it may enter the system. When questioned about the information, the observer's responses may indicate a lack of knowledge of the characteristics of the input.

Subliminal Perception

The possibility of modifying behavior by means of sensory stimuli of which the subject is not aware has intrigued psychologists for a number of years. Attempts to demonstrate such changes in behavior date back to the nineteenth century (e.g., Suslowa, 1863; Hansen and Lehmann, 1895; and Sidis, 1898). In the early stages of such research, information pick-up was frequently judged on an all-or-nothing basis. If the subject could verbally identify the stimulus, it was defined as *supraliminal;* if he could not, it was designated *subliminal.* No possibility of partial information extraction was considered. Later experimenters realized that a subject's awareness of the characteristics of sensory input could be distinguished in terms of at least three points along an awareness continuum.

The first kind of awareness is demonstrated when a subject is asked which of two objects is located at the greater distance from his position. Under normal viewing conditions he is able to respond correctly most of the time, and the ability to make such judgments—to build a percept of depth relations—depends on a large number of cues. Although the observer uses them, he is not *aware* of this utilization. Such lack of awareness is a result of the subject's extensive prior experience with these cues. It is not that he cannot be made aware of them, but rather that he no longer needs to direct his attention to certain cues before applying them. This can be demonstrated by asking the proper questions of the subject and pointing out the specific cues. If he can be made aware of them, we have defined one kind of awareness.

A second kind of awareness is demonstrated in studies of selective attention. Questioned about the nature of unattended information, the typical subject is frequently unable to describe the stimulus accurately. But if the proper questions are posed, he can indicate portions or pieces of the information. In other words, he does maintain partially encoded sensory inputs which, under certain circumstances, may reappear in his responses. But simply asking "What did you see or hear?" seldom elicits reference to these elements.

The third point along the continuum is that of unawareness of the stimulus. Talking about this area of true subliminal perception is much easier than defining it, since demonstrations of the condition are plagued with methodological problems. But the distinctions separating this state from the other kinds of awareness become somewhat clearer in the light of a classic experiment with subliminal perception or subception reported by Lazarus and McCleary (1951). Subjects first viewed a random presentation of ten nonsense syllables, five accompanied by an electric shock to the observer and five without the shock. Measurements of galvanic skin response (GSR) were taken for each syllable. Eventually subjects displayed a marked reduction in skin resistance when a shock syllable was presented and no change at all when a no-shock syllable was shown. Next, subception was tested by presenting the ten syllables in random order at very low levels of intensity and duration and asking subjects to identify each syllable verbally. No additional shocks were given. It was found that at these low levels, verbal identification of the syllables was not possible; however, subjects still displayed a change in GSR for those five syllables that were originally accompanied by shocks. For Lazarus and McCleary, the results indicated that some unconscious process allowed the discrimination of the shock syllables at the level of the autonomic nervous system. In other words, although conscious, verbal awareness failed, an *unconscious*, nonverbal discrimination did come about.

Eriksen (1956) took rather strong exception to the Lazarus and McCleary interpretation of their results. He pointed out that they used two partially correlated observations of behavior to predict a third variable. On the one hand, perception of the syllables was judged by the verbal responses of the subjects; on the other, by changes in GSR. Each of these measures of perception would have an associated error rate. That is, each measure would correctly predict what was perceived part of the time. Let us assume that only chance produces the error rate for both verbalization and GSR. That is, that the two measures correctly predict whether or not the syllable was a shock syllable only 50 percent of the time. As a stimulus word is presented, then, the subject makes a verbal guess about its nature. Simultaneously the GSR makes a guess. If we consider only the 50 percent error rate on the verbalization response, then by chance alone the GSR response will produce 50 percent correct identifications. By the same token when we compare the GSR responses when the verbal guess was *wrong*, the GSR by chance will be correct 50 percent of the time. Naturally, Eriksen concluded, the number of correct guesses by the GSR will be greater than the verbal guesses, because we have eliminated chance from verbalization and allowed it to work freely for GSR.[1]

Even though Eriksen claimed to have detected an artifact in the Lazarus and McCleary procedure, numerous studies have attempted to demonstrate a subception effect under the same conditions. In fact, a rather heated argument centered on the ethical and moral aspects of subliminal techniques in adver-

---

[1] Cohen (1969) develops Eriksen's argument against the subception effect in a clear and understandable manner.

tising. The best-known example developed when a New York advertising firm claimed to have conducted several experiments in which advertising messages were flashed briefly on the screen during a movie in a public theater. In one experiment the message "Buy Popcorn" or "Buy Coca-Cola" was flashed on the screen for 3 milliseconds every 5 seconds. The firm claimed a 56-percent increase in Coca-Cola sales and an 18-percent increase in the demand for popcorn. However, attempts to gain information about the details of the experiment (Britt, 1958) were unsuccessful, and numerous studies trying to replicate the result have met with failure. Subliminal advertising does not seem to work.

In recent years a number of successful demonstrations of some kind of perception without awareness have been reported. However, an equal number of unsuccessful attempts have also been reported, many of these involving attempts to replicate the successful demonstrations. Such is the case with a rather well-known experiment originally conducted by Bach and Klein (1957) and repeated in several variations by Smith, Spence, and Klein (1959) and Spence (1961). In the basic design subjects were shown a neutral drawing of a face for several seconds and were asked to describe it. During the viewing period the word "happy" or the word "angry" was flashed across the face at a subliminal level low enough to prevent its verbal identification. The experimenters found that subjects tended to describe the neutral face in the direction of the word flashed. That is, if the word "happy" was flashed subliminally, subjects tended to describe that face as happy or gay, or in similar terms.

Unfortunately, a number of attempts to replicate the Bach and Klein experiment have been unsuccessful. Goldstein and Davis (1961) tested English-speaking subjects; Sagara, Tago, and Shibuya (1962) experimented with Japanese students; and Murch (1966) studied German-speaking students; but all failed to demonstrate a subliminal effect with the Bach and Klein design. In a related experiment involving the ten neutral face drawings shown in Figure 8.9, the present author attempted to use techniques other than verbal description for measuring the influence of subliminal words. Such description provides data that can only be related to the subliminal word on a subjective basis. That is, the experimenter has the responsibility of deciding whether the subject's description is closer to "happy" or to "angry." To test ways of avoiding this limitation, three groups of subjects were shown each of the ten faces in Figure 8.9 at random in a tachistoscope for 5 seconds per drawing. During each such interval either "happy" or "angry" was flashed ten times (every 500 msec) at a subliminal level which had been previously determined for each observer. The first group was asked to rate the faces on a scale of seven pairs of words such as happy-angry, gay-sad, lucky-unlucky, and so on. The second group was asked to describe the faces in the either/or manner of the Bach and Klein experiment, except that the words "happy" and "angry" were pronounced by the subjects rather than by the experimenter. Subjects in a third and final group were shown the two words "happy" and "angry" after viewing each face and were asked to choose between them. When the responses of all subjects were compared to the sequences of words presented subliminally, none of the three groups showed any measurable susceptibility to the subliminal words. In pass-

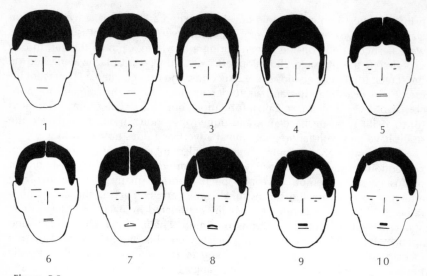

Figure 8.9
Neutral drawings used to study the influence of the subliminal presentation of the words "happy" or "angry" on descriptions of the faces. (Murch, 1968a.)

ing, most subjects considered face 10 to be angry even when the subliminal word accompanying it was "happy." They usually remarked spontaneously that the face resembled Hitler's.

Dunlap (1900) introduced another basic experimental design for the study of subliminal perception. Subjects viewed two horizontal lines and were asked which was shorter; while they were contemplating the lines, the closed and open end lines of the Müller-Lyer figure were subliminally presented in the manner shown in Figure 8.10. Dunlap reported that subjects tended to judge the line with inward angles shorter than the line with outward angles. Titchener and Pyle (1907) and Kennett (1962) successfully replicated this experiment.

A very basic difference seems to separate those experiments that can be successfully replicated and those that produce subliminal effects on some occasions and not on others. In the experiment with the neutral faces, for example, for the subliminal word to have an influence requires a cognitive processing of the input. For the experiment to succeed, in other words, the subject would have to extract the *meaning* of the subliminal word and incorporate it in the percept. Experiments by Fuhrer and Eriksen (1960), Murch (1965), Bernstein and Eriksen (1965), and McNulty, Dockrill, and Levy (1967) have all failed to demonstrate the influence of any subliminal stimulus that requires cognitive processing. (See Bevan, 1964 for a further discussion.)

In contrast, the more successfully replicated experiment with the Müller-Lyer figure does not require the subject to assimilate the meaning of the subliminal stimulus in order to perceive it. In terms of the model of selective attention discussed at the end of the previous section, it is possible that some aspects of unattended stimuli might have an influence on a perception. Norman

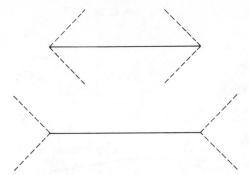

Figure 8.10
Elements of Müller-Lyer illusion used in test of subliminal perception by Dunlap (1900). Subjects compared length of solid lines while dotted portions of figures were presented subliminally.

(1968) suggested that the initial processing of sensory input prior to selective attention occurs automatically and involves only a partial encoding of the input. Perhaps under certain conditions the physical attributes of these partially encoded units could influence perception. This possibility was tested in an experiment by the present author (Murch, 1967).

While subjects viewed parts of two letters of the alphabet separated by a fixation point for 5 seconds, a pair of completed letters was repeatedly superimposed on these parts at a duration too brief to allow conscious recognition of the letters. These subliminal letters were flashed every 200 msec during the 5-second display of supraliminal letter parts. Following this presentation, subjects were shown three possible completions of the preceding parts, one of which was identical with the subliminal letter pair. Examples of the letters and parts used in this experiment are shown in Figure 8.11.

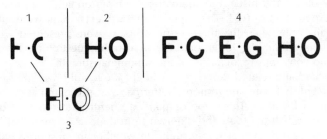

Figure 8.11
Influence of partially encoded units on perception. 1, letter parts shown supraliminally. 2, completed pair of letters shown subliminally. 3, superimposition of 2 and 1. Subjects responded by choosing one of three completed letter pairs in 4. (Murch, 1967.)

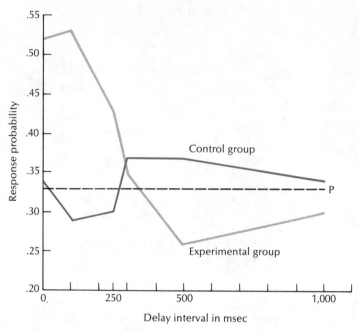

Figure 8.12
Influence of a delay between subliminal stimulation and presentation of response categories. (Murch, 1967.)

The most interesting variable of the experiment was the delay (0, 100, 250, 300, 500, or 1,000 msec) between the last subliminal projection and the presentation of the three completed letter pairs. Figure 8.12 shows the performances of the experimental group, which was flashed the subliminal stimulus letter combinations, and the control group, which was not. As the graph indicates, the experimental subjects performed well in selecting the right combination at delays of 0 and 100 msec, but thereafter their performance approached the chance expectation of 0.33. The experimental subjects, then, were influenced subliminally only when the three response pairs were presented within 100 msec of the subliminal letter pair. Upon careful questioning the subjects showed no conscious recognition of the subliminal stimuli.

A second and related experiment (Murch, 1969c) followed the same basic design except that only one response letter pair was presented after the supra- and subliminal display. This response pair was identical to the preceding subliminal pair on half the trials and different from the pair on the other half. The subject's task on each trial was to indicate whether the response pair fit the preceding supraliminal parts. Nothing was said about the subliminal letter pair. The subject responded by pushing one of two buttons located on either side of the subject's hand: a *plus* button for a fit and a *minus* button for a lack of fit. The experiment also incorporated a feedback light; subjects were told that it would come on when a correct choice was made. The purpose of the feedback was to see if subjects could learn to rely on the subliminal stimuli in making their choices.

The results of the experiment showed a significant influence for the subliminal letter pairs: when the response letter pair and subliminal letter pair were identical, subjects tended to push the plus button; when the pairs were different, they tended to push the minus button. The feedback light had no influence on their responses; that is, the frequency of correct responses tended to remain the same throughout the experiment.

If a visual stimulus can enter the sensory system without commanding the attention of the organism, such a weak stimulus might leave some trace in the sensory register. And if, before that trace decays, a second stimulus identical to the first causes a stronger sensory response and demands the observer's attention due to its high pertinence value, there might be interaction between the residual trace and the more intense stimulus.

In the present author's study (Murch, 1969c), the subject is asked to designate whether the response letter pair is a valid or an invalid extension (plus or minus response) of the previous letter parts. If the subliminal stimulus left a trace and if the subject had no other information on which to base his choice, the trace might predispose the visual system toward perceiving the response letter pair as a fit for the letter parts. The probability of responding with a plus after that letter pair had been presented subliminally would be a simple function of chance p plus the residual trace of the subliminal stimulus s:

$$r_+ = (p + s)$$

On the trials in which an alternative letter pair is presented, there should be no such predisposition. The probability of a minus response would depend on the frequency of minus responses rather than on the effects of the subliminal stimulus on the visual system. If we assume that the greatest number of plus responses will occur in conjunction with the subliminal stimuli which are identical to the response letter pairs, then as r_+ increases so does the availability of r_- as a response on those trials in which the response letter pair is not the same as the subliminal letter pair. The probability of a correct r_- response would be given by the function:

$$r_- = p_+ \frac{\Sigma(r_+/r_-)}{N r_+ r_-}$$

The probability of a minus response in conjunction with differing subliminal letter pair and response letter pair should vary as a function of the ratio of plus to minus responses prior to any given trial.

Although the data from this experiment are not sufficient for establishing the exact nature of the functions discussed, we would expect that when the subliminal letter pair and response letter pair are identical, the frequency of correct responses to subliminally presented letter pairs would remain fairly constant over trials. By the same token, we would expect the frequency of correct minus responses to increase over trials as the minus response becomes more and more available as a response possibility.

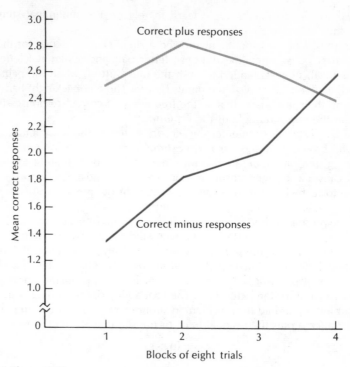

Figure 8.13
Predisposition of visual system due to residual trace of weak, unattended stimulus, as indicated by frequency of correct plus and minus responses as a function of trial blocks. (Murch, 1969*b*.)

Figure 8.13 represents the mean number of correct plus responses and correct minus responses as a function of trial blocks for the experiment under consideration. Each block represents eight trials. As the figure shows, the frequency of correct minus responses does increase over trials for the experimental group, while the frequency of correct plus responses tends to remain constant. Such results indicate that the effects of the subliminal stimulus are limited to the case in which the identical letter pair is presented subliminally and as a response letter pair. This observation fits the assumption concerning the predisposition of the visual system by the weak, unattended stimulus.

Another approach to subliminal perception comes from the work of the adaptation level theorists. Bevan and Pritchard (1963) demonstrated that weak anchor tones which could not be reported verbally served to influence the judgments of supraliminal tones. Although unable to report the anchor tones, the experimenters measured a shift in intensity judgment away from the weak anchor when tones of clearly audible intensity were rated for loudness.

That sensory input can enter the perceptual system without a cognitive analysis or response by the observer has been shown by several recent neurophysiological studies. Alberts, Wright, and Feinstein (1967) elicited responses from single nerve cells (method of evoked potentials) in the somatosensory cortex of patients undergoing stereotaxic neurosurgical therapy. The potentials were elicited by numerous physical stimuli which did not evoke a verbal response. In other words, the subjects were unaware of the stimuli. Even when a subject's attention was directed toward a particular physical stimulus, no perception was reported. However, this was true only for single stimulus presentations. When the same stimulus was repeated rapidly and frequently, a conscious perception of the input was reported.

The majority of experiments with subliminal perception indicate that meaningful material cannot be transmitted directly as unattended (subliminal) stimuli. That is, subliminal stimulation cannot modify cognition. Rather, the available data indicate that specific physical characteristics of unattended stimuli may interact—under certain conditions—with attended (supraliminal) stimuli in the development of a percept.

In formulating the model of perception discussed throughout this book, we have concluded that only a relatively small number of potential stimuli in the environment enter the sensory register. And only some of these are selected for further processing. Short-term and long-term storage and the control processes all influence such stimuli, eventually combining to produce a percept. However, this interpretation of the perceptual process must be able to account for the possible influence of environmental stimuli of which the observer is not aware. This lack of awareness may be due to extended experience on the part of the observer or due to the weak nature of the stimulus. The influence of such subliminal stimuli is limited by their physical characteristics and dependent on the close temporal proximity of the subliminal and supraliminal stimuli.

Sensory Deprivation[2]

The preceding chapter was largely concerned with the perception of specific stimulus conditions and with the selection of stimuli from the array of potential stimuli available to the perceiver. This section will consider a rather fascinating approach to perception that concentrates on the effects of a *lack* of external stimulation on the processing functions of the individual. We have previously reviewed several studies that established a kind of *perceptual deprivation* by setting up homogeneous conditions of visual or auditory stimulation. Among these were studies dealing with the Ganzfeld and with auditory white noise masks. Separate from these are the attempts to achieve *sensory deprivation*— experimental conditions which reduce as completely as possible the sensory input to the individual. The goal of such research is to study the ways in which prolonged conditions of complete darkness, total silence, lack of tactual sensations, and the absence of smell and taste affect perception.

Three basic conditions of sensory deprivation have been studied. Shurley (1960) attempted to establish complete sensory isolation by immersing nude subjects in a water tank. Each subject wore a black-out mask to which was at-

---

[2] An excellent review of the various aspects of sensory deprivation has been published by Zubek (1969).

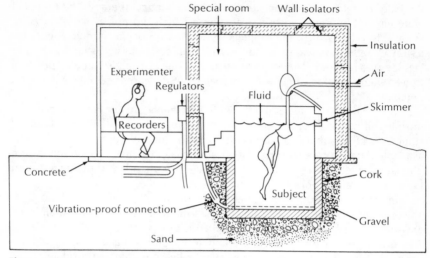

Figure 8.14
Hydrohypodynamic environment used in studies of sensory deprivation. (After Shurley, 1963. Reproduced by permission of the University of Toronto Press and of McGill University Press.)

tached a breathing tube, and the temperature of the water was a constant 98.5°. Such conditions, illustrated in Figure 8.14, brought about an almost total isolation of sensory input from the external environment. Bexton, Heron, and Scott (1954) developed a second condition, shown in Figure 8.15, in which subjects reclined on a soft bed in a sound-proofed room and wore translucent goggles that allowed low-level, diffuse light to pass to the eye but prevented the perception of distinct figures. Finally, a third condition has been created that involves monotonous stimulation rather than isolation. Wexler, Mendelson, Leiderman, and Solomon (1958) placed observers in a polio respirator on a soft mattress and encased their arms and legs in cylinders that inhibited movement and reduced tactile stimulation. Figure 8.16 shows the equipment used to achieve this type of sensory isolation.

Before we consider some of the observations gathered from experiments with these various types of isolation designs, it should be noted that many methodological problems involved in producing strict conditions of sensory isolation have not been overcome. Obviously a complete restriction of all sensory input is impossible with human subjects. If nothing else, the attempts to record the subject's observations about his perception introduce a source of stimulation. As Zuckerman (1969) points out, the subjects must be fed, toileted, and exercised during such periods of deprivation. He further warns: "The sensory deprivation experiment is a nightmare to the experimentalist who craves clean-cut, well-controlled experimental situations" (p. 47).

A first variable of interest is the extent of the period that subjects are able to endure sensory deprivation. As might be expected, the various techniques of producing isolation lead to different results. Figure 8.17 compares the lengths

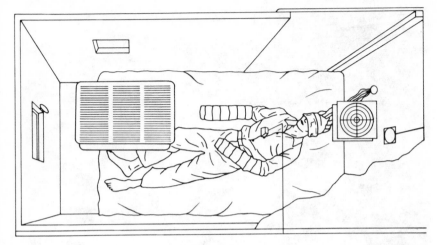

Figure 8.15
Experimental cubicle for bed confinement used in studies of sensory deprivation. (After Heron, 1961. Reproduced by permission of Harvard University Press from P. Solomon et al., *Sensory Deprivation*. Copyright 1961 by the President and Fellows of Harvard College.)

of time subjects remained in voluntary isolation as functions of the methods of deprivation. It is hardly surprising that endurance is lowest in the water-tank design, since the degree of sensory deprivation is probably greatest with this method.

Under various conditions of isolation, experiments have deprived subjects of sensory input for periods up to two weeks. Using the bed-confinement design, Zuckerman found most subjects able to endure isolation for twenty-four hours. He also noted that subjects capable of enduring three days in isolation tended to stay until the end of the experiment (up to two weeks).

Typical effects of sensory isolation on perception were demonstrated by an experiment by Zubek, Pushkar, Sansom, and Gowing (1961). Subjects attempted to remain in darkness and silence for a period of one week. Food and toilet facilities were provided, as well as a panic button if the subject wished to terminate the experiment. Before and immediately after experiencing a week of isolation, subjects were tested for the following:

1. *Visual vigilance:* subjects watched the sweep second hand of an electric clock and indicated when the movement of the hand stopped for 0.10 second.
2. *Auditory vigilance:* while watching the clock, subjects were also asked to indicate any change in the frequency of a constant tone.
3. *Depth perception:* subjects attempted binocularly to align a moveable rod with a stationary rod (Howard-Dohlman apparatus).
4. *Size constancy:* subjects adjusted the dimensions of an equilateral triangle located at 15 feet until it appeared to be the same size as a comparison triangle located at 4 feet.

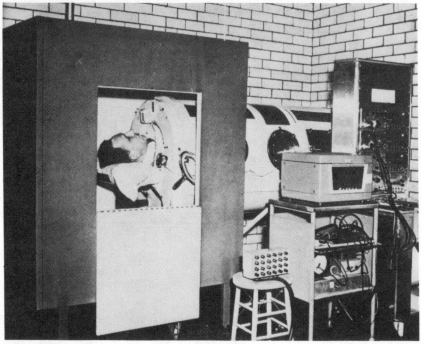

Figure 8.16
Polio tank-type respirator used in studies of sensory deprivation. (After Wexler et al., 1958. Reproduced by permission of Harvard University Press from P. Solomon et al., *Sensory Deprivation*. Copyright 1961 by the President and Fellows of Harvard College.)

5. *Reversible figures:* subjects viewed a Necker cube and indicated each time its orientation changed.
6. *Perception of colors:* subjects were shown squares of different colors and asked to describe them.

During the isolation period subjects were also required to estimate various durations of a buzzer by pressing a key to indicate their estimates of periods of 1, 3, 5, 15, 30, 60, and 120 minutes. This test was administered daily during isolation and before and after the isolation experience.

When compared to the performances of control subjects who did not experience isolation, the test results showed that isolated subjects tended to display a reduction in depth perception, a reduction in size constancy, and fewer reversals of the reversible figure; the two vigilance tasks indicated no marked differences for experimental and control subjects. Interestingly, time judgments made during isolation were highly similar for both experimental and control subjects. An exception was the 120-minute condition, which experimental subjects significantly underestimated more than the control subjects. Marnum (1968) also obtained time judgments ranging from 2 to 32 seconds from subjects isolated by a water-immersion technique. Judgments were

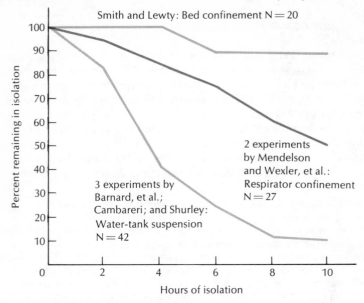

Figure 8.17
Endurance of subjects under conditions of sensory deprivation by bed
confinement, respirator confinement, and water-tank suspension. (After
Zuckerman, 1969. Reproduced by permission of Appleton-Century-
Crofts. Copyright 1969 by Meredith Corporation.)

made by the methods of production and reproduction, but no reliable differences between control and isolated subjects were found.

Of particular interest in the study by Zubek et al. (1961) is the observation
that at least eleven of the sixteen subjects reported experiencing hallucinations
during isolation. An hallucination in this context refers to an auditory or visual
perception reportedly stemming from an actual stimulus in the environment
despite the absence of a physical correlate of the stimulus. Most commonly
reported were flashes of light and ambiguous, unclear shapes. Some observers
reported more structured patterns and shapes. Finally, two observers reported
very structured animal forms. Hallucinations usually did not occur before the
third day in isolation; after that point they did not increase in frequency as the
period of isolation continued.

Reports of hallucinations and images during isolation have aroused considerable interest on the part of experimenters. After reviewing large numbers
of experiments conducted under various conditions and at various laboratories,
Zuckerman (1969) notes that only about half of the subjects in a typical experiment report some form of visual sensation. Structured hallucinations are reported by about a fifth of the observers. Generally, the results indicate that
complex hallucinations occur only after prolonged periods of isolation. Some
research also indicates that reclining subjects are more prone to hallucinations
(Morgan and Bakan, 1965). Other studies show that the occurrence and nature
of hallucinations are influenced by the instructions to the subject and by in-

trinsic or specific sets established by the experimenter prior to the isolation experience.

Zuckerman (1969) also compared the hallucinations reported during sensory deprivation experiments with those reported by psychotic patients and with drug-induced hallucinations. The differences between these groups are considerable. While psychotic hallucinations are predominantly auditory, those of sensory deprivation are primarily visual. In fact, very few sensory deprivation subjects report auditory hallucinations. Comparisons of drug-induced hallucinations with those of sensory deprivation reveal vividness and persistence in the former but ambiguity and unclear form in the latter. From his thorough study of the literature and numerous experiments, Zuckerman (1969) concludes:

> When a subject is put in an environment without patterned and changing stimulation, he may relax and fall into a state of lowered arousal and sleep, he may focus his attention on his thoughts, or he may keep scanning his interceptive and exteroceptive fields for stimuli. Either an experimental set, or his own sensitization to peripheral sensory changes, may initially lead to reports based on idioretinal phenomena, inner ear noise or illusions. Eventually the subject may become sensitized to more organized images whose site of origin lies higher in the nervous system. The discrimination between internal images and perceptions rests in the differential intensities and clarity of the phenomena, as well as in the contextual cues from the environment. Images may be intensified by a high state of arousal; or by a reduction in competing stimuli. Because the contextual cues from the environment are lacking in isolation experiments, an intense image may be localized in space in front of the subject. The subject's secondary reactions to such complex imagery will determine their persistence and whether or not he will report them in a post-isolation report (p. 125).

In the absence of external input to the sensory system, higher kinds of perceptual activity seem to continue to function. After prolonged periods of sensory deprivation or monotonous stimulation, imagery or hallucinations are probably very common (Hebb, 1968). Dreaming represents another area in which perceptual processes continue at the higher levels despite conditions of reduced external input. Due to the completely subjective nature of the hallucinatory experience and the ensuing difficulty in obtaining exact information about the nature of these experiences, little knowledge about them has been gathered. In fact, as Holt (1964) notes, the difficulties of working in this area are so pervasive that most empirically oriented researchers seem actively to avoid it. The thought-provoking observations of D. O. Hebb (1968) in Canada provide a most noted exception. On the basis of his research, Hebb believes that hallucinations and visual imagery are much more common than usually acknowledged, but because of the association with psychotic tendencies, most normal individuals are unlikely to report such experiences. Among individuals carrying out monotonous tasks, such as long-distance truck drivers, such experiences seem to be very common.

The lack of information about hallucinations in normal visual and auditory experience is hardly surprising when one considers the large gaps in knowledge about simpler processes of perception encountered throughout this presentation. The experimental observations presented herein describe many but not all of the topics of current interest to psychologists of perception. While many of the so-called facts of perception will certainly fail to stand the test of time, each new contribution aids in the understanding of techniques of study and methodology and provides insight into the most complex manner in which man interacts with his environment.

A Last Look at the Perceptual Model

Almost all of the experimental observations about perception discussed in the preceding pages isolate some specific attribute of percept development. They point out how the perceptual system deals with certain categories of physical stimuli. The information presented indicates to some degree the nature and function of the underlying physiology of vision and hearing. In fact, perception can be interpreted as the description of the relationship between some physical element of the environment and a subjective percept developed from that element. Traditionally the perceptual psychologist has attempted to collect as much data about as many diversified physical elements and subjective perceptions as possible. Over the last few hundred years much data has been collected and, gradually, meaningful relationships among independent sets of data are emerging. The explanation of the neurophysiological aspects of perception will remain the task of the psychophysiologist, while the behavioral aspects of perception will require much more cataloging by the experimental psychologists.

The observations derived from perceptual research have facilitated the identification of numerous attributes of the perceptual system. All of the observations discussed to this point in the book, for example, depend on some aspect of the perceptual system. What remains is to relate these factors to a general model within which a meaningful search can be conducted for further attributes and for the interrelationships among attributes.

With reference primarily to the model of perception presented in Chapter 3, the following sections offer some eclectic comments about the nature of perception. Each of the aspects of the model in Figure 3.1 will be discussed briefly. While the presentation is purely theoretical, it attempts to tie together the varied observations on perception presented throughout the book.

Sensory register.   Potential stimuli in the external environment which evoke a response are briefly stored in the form of sensory representations. Their nature depends in part on the characteristics of the nervous system itself and in part on the nature of the external stimulus. These stored inputs are fairly numerous and are maintained as residual traces of the external stimuli for several hundred milliseconds. Their storage and processing are also subject to the physical characteristics of other input currently held in the sensory register.

The period over which such sensory traces can be maintained by an observer seems to vary markedly from person to person. Some historical work as well as more recent studies (e.g., Haber, 1969) indicate that certain individuals are capable of maintaining a clear sensory image of the external stimulus for several seconds or even minutes after the stimulation ceases. Such persons are called *eidetikers* and the phenomenon is known as *eidetic imagery.* The frequency with which such ability is encountered in the general population is rather low. Haber (1969) screened over 500 children in pilot research in order to find 20 children capable of eidetic imagery. The frequency of eidetic imagery among adults appears to be even lower.[3]

In the normal individual, traces of the sensory experience are maintained as images in the sensory register for very brief periods. At this level it appears that the images are discriminated on the basis of physical characteristics of the sensory representations generated by the external stimulus. The sensory trace must be considered a representation, not a faithful reproduction, of the external world. The attributes of the trace are dictated by the manner in which the nervous system translates the sensation to a nervous impulse and by the nature and receptive characteristics of the sensory receptors.

Input lost at the level of the sensory register is filtered out either before the physical stimulus can evoke a representation in the register or after the item has been partially encoded. That is, the organism either does not use the stimulus at all or does not completely process it. Failure to finish processing may be due to the volume of input in the sensory register at any moment in time or to the observer's discrimination—based on the physical characteristics of the trace—that the input is unimportant or unattainable.

The filtering of input by the sensory register prevents certain stimuli from being processed. Such filtering is accomplished on the basis of the physical characteristics of the stimuli. Partially encoded items in the sensory register can undergo additional processing in short-term storage if they are selected within the time period of the residual trace of the physical stimulus; after this period, the input is lost.

Short-term storage.   From among the stimuli reaching the sensory register the organism actively selects certain items for further processing. Retrieved from long-term storage on the basis of the physical features of input held in the sensory register, these are combined with input located in short-term storage. While undergoing this interpretation, the items are also subject to the control processes, which influence the selection by assigning pertinence values to the incoming stimuli. The combination of input plus information from long-term storage produces the initial perception: the stimulus takes on meaning. To this meaning additional information from long-term storage may be added, modifying the percept.

The experience of perception centers on the activity of short-term storage. At this level a heretofore meaningless configuration of sensory data becomes recognizable as an object existing in the environment. In one's subjective awareness of the passing of time, the present is that interval involving the processing of a stimulus in short-term storage. When a stimulus leaves short-

---

[3] The eminent Russian psychologist Luria (1968) provides a fascinating description of one such individual.

term storage, it is no longer perceived to exist or to belong to the present; instead, it is relegated to the past, or to long-term storage.

Long-term storage. Input is stored in long-term storage in the form of processed percepts (coded representations) of past experiences. The strength of any of these considerably varied memories can be expressed as a pertinence value that affects the processing of new input. Some experiences will always command high pertinence values; others will not. Due to such differences, some experiences are not readily available for use in the processing of new input. Only after a search of the memory banks can certain experiences be found and applied to the processing of input. Nevertheless, the pertinence value of a particular memory does not necessarily decline or deteriorate with age. Some experiences maintain high pertinence values for very long periods, even for whole lifetimes. In particular, those memories frequently used for processing new input maintain high pertinence values.

Once a percept is filed in long-term storage, its presence there will directly influence subsequent relevant inputs. For example, after a figure has been organized in a particular manner, subsequent presentations of the figure will tend to evoke the same perceptual organization. Only with difficulty can the observer reorganize the input by calling on other representations in memory. Moreover, the organization of ambiguous material is facilitated or influenced when the observer is directed toward certain processed inputs stored in long-term storage.

Research on sensory deprivation indicates that percepts can be developed in the absence of sensory inputs. Such percepts are probably developed in short-term storage as a result of information stored in long-term storage, the control processes of the observer, and spontaneous activity in the lower visual system. Through the recombination of stored representations, the observer is able to generate new and often discomforting percepts.

Control processes. Sensory input being processed in short-term storage is influenced by pertinence values generated by the control processes. Drive level, need state, and general bodily equilibrium are typical of the factors contributing to this kind of control. For example, if an observer is hungry, fatigued, or in poor health, such bodily states will influence the processing of input. Undoubtedly much additional information is needed about the physiological nature of emotion and motivation before the influence of the control processes can be assessed. Many percepts are probably modified considerably by these subsystems. The development of hallucinations, for example, seems to depend to a great extent on activities of the control processes.

Response generator. Carrying the utilization of sensory input a step beyond actual perception, the response generator produces the observer's motor responses. Naturally, many such responses occur only after a clear percept has been developed, but some can be generated directly from input in the sensory register that has not undergone cognitive processing. Responses of this sort are probably those that have occurred frequently in the past history of the organism. Reflex actions can be prompted by certain sensory stimuli that require no past experience for processing, and thus fall into this category of unmediated response. Since the organism's ability to respond to potential stimuli is necessarily limited, part of the process of selection among percepts and inputs occurs at the level of the response generator. Input, then, can be selected at the first stage of processing (sensory filter), by short-term storage (perceptual filter), or by the response generator (response filter).

The Future of Perceptual Research

Future research in perception will require the development of exact techniques for assessing the specific influence of each aspect of the perceptual process. From future advances in the knowledge of the physiology of perception should come an understanding of the relationship between the physical world and the sensory trace within the nervous system. Frequently we are unable to ascertain whether a given percept is a product of the attributes of the input's sensory trace or a product of a particular aspect of long-term storage, short-term storage, or an active control process. Many visual illusions demonstrate current difficulties in pinpointing the exact source of a particular effect. Does the illusion arise from some attribute of the nervous system or from our interpretation of the input based on past experience? In certain cases the nature of the sensory representation has been assessed and explained in terms of the resulting percept. Phenomena satisfactorily identified in this way are simultaneous contrast effects, visual summation and masking, and the perception of brightness. Studies of the influence of specific past experiences and set have emphasized the importance of long-term storage on the building of a percept. Also, the research of the adaptation level theorists concerning anchor effects and studies by others of the motivational aspects of perception have clarified the contributions of the control processes. Finally, the traditional work of cataloging the relationships between subjective percepts and external stimuli will continue to have an important place in future interpretations of the complex process of perception.

Glossary

absolute pitch: The ability of a trained observer to name or reproduce a tone without the aid of a reference tone.

absolute threshold: The lowest value of a stimulus that can be detected on 50 percent of all presentations of that stimulus.

accommodation: A bulge or increase in thickness of the eye's lens to enable the eye to focus on near objects; or, a corresponding flattening of the lens in order to focus on distant objects.

achromatic color: A color sensation containing no dominant hue; variations from white through gray to black.

adaptation: A change in sensitivity as a result of ongoing or prolonged stimulation, e.g., dark adaptation.

additive color mixture: A mixture of colors involving the addition of component light waves.

afferent nerves: The incoming or sensory nerves.

aftereffect: The modification of the appearance of a test figure as a result of prolonged viewing of an inspection figure.

afterimage: *See* chromatic afterimage.

albedo: The proportion of incident light reflected by any given object.

allophone: A nondistinctive variant of a phoneme which fails to distinguish between letters on the basis of sound. *See* phoneme.

ambient light: Light rays reflected from objects in the environment.

ambiguous stimulus: A pattern that can be perceived in several different ways.

amplitude: The amount, size, or strength of an event.

anagram: A meaningful word formed from a set of random letters.

anchor effect: The shifting of a perception or sensation as a result of preceding sensations or perceptions.

anisotropic: Differences in the length or size of the two axes of a field.

apparent movement: The subjective impression of movement when no physical movement is occurring.

aqueous humor: The liquid filling the anterior chamber behind the cornea of the eye.

assimilation effect: A reduction in the apparent differences between two or more objects when viewed together.

attenuating sinusoids: The curve produced by a pure tone in which the amplitude (height of the swing of the curve) is reduced slightly on each successive swing.

audiokinetic effect: The apparent movement of a stationary sound source.

auditory masking: The masking or blocking out of an auditory stimulus by a second auditory stimulus.

autokinetic effect: The apparent movement of a stationary point (or points) of light seen in an otherwise darkened room or surround.

backward masking: The blocking or masking of a stimulus by the presentation of a second stimulus within a critical period *after* the initial stimulus.

bandpass filter: A device for filtering out certain frequencies or portions of the auditory spectrum.

basilar membrane: A membrane within the cochlea of the ear responsive to variations in the frequencies of a sound.

Bezold-Brücke effect: Apparent shifts in hue as a result of increases in brightness.

binaural: Relating to the two ears.

binocular: Relating to the two eyes.

binocular disparity: The difference between the proximal representations of an object on the retinas due to their separation.

binocular fusion: Combination of the input to each eye to form a single, fused image.

binocular rivalry: The failure of the input to each eye to undergo fusion; occurs when the two images are so different that a meaningful combination is not possible.

binocular transfer: The presentation of a stimulus to one eye and the measurement of the effect of the presentation of a second stimulus to the other eye.

Bloch's law: Within a critical duration, the influence on visual acuity of a reduction in the duration of a stimulus can be offset by a corresponding increase in stimulus intensity.

brightness: The amount of white or black mixed into a given hue; degree of whiteness.

brightness constancy: The tendency for the brightnesses of objects to appear the same despite changes in illumination.

brightness enhancement: The apparent increase in brightness when a previously steady light is caused to pulsate.

central intention: An action, behavior, or response carried out voluntarily.

chromatic afterimage: A color appearing after prolonged viewing of a colored area. Usually the afterimage is positive (roughly equivalent to the color studied) or negative (roughly the complement of the color studied).

chromatic color: Any color sensation displaying a dominant hue.

chromaticity space: Color-matching chart indicating the relationships among the various portions of the visual spectrum with regard to equal appearing or matching mixtures of wavelengths.

CIE (Commission International de l'Eclairage):   An international commission formed in 1931 to establish a set of primary wavelengths for use in color research.

clang associations: Word associations based on rhyme or similar sounds of words, e.g., house—mouse.

closure: The tendency to fill in the missing parts of incomplete figures and see them as complete figures.

cochlea: A series of three channels in the inner ear containing the organ of Corti.

color constancy: The tendency of hue, brightness, and saturation to remain unchanged despite variations in context and illumination.

color contrast: The apparent change in color as a result of changes in illumination or context.

complementary colors: Two hues that when mixed will produce an achromatic gray.

complex tone: A sound made up of numerous frequencies.

concave lens: A lens causing light to be bent outward or to become dispersed.

cones: Light-sensitive receptors in the eye that are sensitive to color.

contralateral eye: In studies of binocular vision, an inspection stimulus is presented to one eye and a test stimulus is presented to the other or contralateral eye. See ipsilateral eye.

contrast effect: An increase in the apparent differences between two or more objects when viewed together.

convergence: The mechanism by which the two eyes are turned inward to focus on a near object and outward to focus upon a distant object.

convex lens: A lens causing light to be bent inward or to become concentrated.

cornea: The transparent membrane covering the outer portion of the eye.

corpuscular theory of light: Newton's conception of light as a stream of particles traveling in a straight line.

corresponding points: The two portions or points of each retina stimulated by the same part of the distal stimulus.

cortical satiation: A theory that seeks to explain figural aftereffects by assuming that prolonged viewing of a figure causes an inhibition or satiation in the part of the cortex processing the figure.

critical bandwidth: A frequency range within which the separate components of a sound are summed together.

crome or croma: Units of measurement for degree of saturation of a color.

dark adaptation: A photochemical process by means of which the eye becomes more sensitive to weak light intensities.

decibel scale: A logarithmic scale of the relative loudness of a sound.

dichotic listening: An experimental technique in which the inputs to each ear differ in at least one respect.

difference threshold: The smallest change in the value of a stimulus that can be detected on 50 percent of the stimulus presentations.

diotic listening: The inputs to each ear are the same.

discrete tone: A sound containing a number of separate frequencies.

disocclusion: The uncovering of the background behind a moving object.

distal stimulus: A stimulating object or event present in the external environment.

dominant hue: The hue most prominent in a multichromatic light beam; or, the hue defining a given color sensation.

Dove prism: A prism that rotates the image with respect to the vertical without bending or changing the direction of the light.

effective stimulus: Any object or event that instigates a sensation or perception.

efference theory: A theory of perception emphasizing the motor end of responses to sensory stimuli.

efferent nerves: The outgoing or motor nerves.

egocentric vertical: Vertical defined relative to the body position.

eidetic imagery: Mental imagery with a clarity of detail similar to actual perception of the scene imagined.

electromagnetic theory: Maxwell's conception of light as an oscillating wave.

Emmert's law: The size of an afterimage is directly proportional to the distance of the area against which the afterimage is viewed.

eustachian tube: The tube connecting the middle ear with the throat; allows the maintenance of equal pressure between the middle ear and the external environment.

extraocular muscles: The muscles controlling the turning of the eyes.

field dependent: The tendency to rely on the surrounding visual field in judging the horizontal or vertical position of the body in space.

field independent: The tendency to rely on the effects of gravity in judging the horizontal or vertical position of the body in space.

figural aftereffect: Modification of a figure's shape orientation or location as a result of stimulation by a preceding figure.

figure persistence: The tendency to see a reversible figure predominantly as one of two or more possible orientations.

film color: A color independent of an object but located at a given position in space, e.g., a beam of red light.

focal stimulus: A stimulus commanding the observer's attention.

footlambert (ftL):   A measure of the intensity of a stimulus in terms of luminance.

Formant theory: A theory ascribing timbre to the relative strengthening of partial tones located in a specific portion of the musical scale.

forward masking: The blocking or masking of a test stimulus by the presentation of another stimulus within a critical period *before* the test stimulus.

Fourier analysis: A technique in physics for analyzing complex sounds and separating them into their component frequencies.

fovea: The central portion of the retina of the eye.

frequency: The number of alternations per interval of time of a sound.

frequency vibrato: Brief, rapid pulsations or variations in the frequency of a constant sound.

functional approach: The study of perception through the measurement of overt, objective responses to known effective stimuli.

fundamental tone: The lowest frequency present in a complex tone.

galvanic skin response (GSR):   A change in the electrical resistance of the skin.

Ganzfeld: A completely homogeneous field that provides the visual system with a figureless ground.

geometric illusion: An illusion observed in a line drawing.

gestalt psychology: A school of thought advocating the study of perception based on consideration of organized whole figures rather than examination of their component parts.

hallucination: A perception in the absence of physical, distal stimulation.

harmonic structure theory: A theory of harmonics emphasizing the physical characteristics of the musical instruments producing the various notes.

harmonic tone: Components of complex tones that are multiples of the fundamental tone.

Hertz (Hz):   The internationally accepted symbol of the frequency of a sound; equivalent to cycles per second (cps).

horopter: An imaginary surface connecting all physical points that for a given fixation point stimulate corresponding points on the two retinas.

Howard-Dohlman apparatus: A device for measuring accuracy of depth perception.

hue: The property of a color sensation defining the chromatic component, e.g., red, green, orange.

hue constancy: The tendency for hue to remain constant despite changes in illumination and context.

I-figure: An inspection figure used in tests of figural aftereffects.

idioretinal phenomena: Effects that are peculiar to or dependent on the characteristics of the retina.

illumination color: A color superimposed on an object but not part of the object.

illusion: A discrepancy between the physical world and the subjective impression of that world.

induced color: A color appearing on a neutral background as the result of another color surrounding the neutral background.

ineffective stimulus: A potential stimulus that is not processed as a sensation or a perception.

infrared: Light waves with lengths slightly longer (over 700 mμ) than those capable of stimulating the human eye.

inhibition: The reduction or cessation of the ability to respond in a receptor or receptive field.

interposition: The partial blocking of one object by another.

intervening variable: Some hypothesized intermediate step between the presentation of a stimulus and the generation of a response.

inverting prism: A type of lens that inverts the image presented to the eye.

ipsilateral eye: In studies of binocular vision, the eye to which both an inspection stimulus and a test stimulus are presented. See contralateral eye.

kinesthetic system: The sensory system governing the sensation of bodily movement.

kinetic depth effect: The apparent three-dimensionality of moving targets.

Land effect: Full-color projection produced by an appropriate mixture of two light sources rather than the usual three sources.

lateral inhibition: The inhibition of neighboring receptive fields after or during the stimulation of a receptor.

law of Prägnanz (law of the best figure):   An assumption in gestalt theory which holds that patterns are organized along the lines of the best possible interrelation between elements.

light adaptation: A photochemical process by means of which the eye becomes sensitive to high light intensities.

limen: See absolute threshold.

loudness: The apparent or subjective intensity of a sound.

loudness summation: If two tones of different frequencies and the same intensities are presented together, the combined tone appears louder than either of the component tones.

luminance: Light intensity adjusted in terms of the human sensitivity to various portions of the visual spectrum.

luminance masking: The blocking or masking of a visual stimulus by a flash of homogeneous light. See forward masking and backward masking.

luminosity curve: A curve relating the relative sensitivity of observers to various portions of the spectrum. It indicates how much more intense or less intense one portion of the spectrum must be in order to produce brightness levels that are apparently equal.

luminous energy: A product derived from multiplying the physical intensity of a light source by the degree of relative sensitivity for the light source obtained from the luminosity curve.

masking: Rendering a stimulus imperceptible or less perceptible by the presentation of a second stimulus.

McCollough effect: Colors seen on the white space between vertical and horizontal lines after viewing alternating chromatic patterns on vertical and horizontal lines.

mel scale: A scale relating the frequency of a tone to pitch.

memory color: The hypothetical influence of past experience with color in the perception of a color.

microgenesis of perception: The development of a percept over time.

millilambert (mL): A measure of the intensity of a stimulus in terms of luminance.

millimicron (mμ): A micron is a thousandth of a millimeter. One millimicron is one thousandth of a micron or one millionth of a millimeter. Also equivalent to one nanometer.

monaural: Relating to one ear.

monochromatic light: A light beam made up of a small portion of the spectrum, e.g., red light; also called polychromatic light.

monocular: Relating to one eye.

mono-oriented form: A figure or form usually viewed with a specific orientation, e.g., a road map.

multichromatic light: A light beam made up of a wide portion of the spectrum.

Munsell color tree: A three-dimensional model of color relations indicating the interrelationships among the dimensions of hue, saturation, and brightness.

nanometer (nm): The internationally accepted definition of wavelength; one billionth of a meter. Also equivalent to one millimicron.

natural illusion: An illusion observed in nature.

negative afterimage: An afterimage the sensation of which is roughly the complementary color of the inducing stimulus; or, an afterimage of opposite brightness to the stimulus.

negative set: A preparedness not to see or to respond to a certain kind of stimulus.

noncomplementary colors: Any combination of hues producing a new dominant hue or chromatic color.

oculomotor system: The system of motor or efferent nerves controlling eye movement.

Ohm's acoustical law: The sensation produced by a complex sound equals the sensation produced by the sum of the spectral components of the sound.

ontogenesis of perception: The development of perception as a function of the age of the observer.

opponent-processes theory: A theory of color vision based on the apparent pairing of blue-yellow and red-green hues in color sensations.

optic chiasma: The portion of the brain at which the optic tracts (nerve pathways) from each eye intersect.

organ of Corti: The portion of the inner ear containing the endings of the auditory nerve. The hair cells of the organ of Corti respond to movements of the basilar membrane; this response is transmitted to the brain as nerve impulses.

oscillation: Back and forth movement or undulation (as opposed to rotation or circular movement).

ossicles: Three bones located behind the eardrum through which sound waves are transmitted.

paracontrast: See forward masking.

parallel processing: The simultaneous processing of two or more sensory or perceptual stimuli.

pattern mask: A pattern capable of blocking or masking a stimulus. See forward masking and backward masking.

percept: The organized end product of the process of perceiving; that which is perceived.

perceptual deprivation: See sensory deprivation.

perceptual moment: The hypothesis that sensory input is processed in discrete chunks or moments rather than as a continuous flow of input.

perceptual set: See set.

periodic sound: A sound showing a repetition of wave form.

phenomenal brightness: The apparent brightness of hues; the central portion of the visual spectrum, e.g., yellow, under conditions of equal physical brightness appears to be brighter than the extremes of the spectrum, e.g., red and blue.

phenomenal causality: A perceived relationship of causality.

phenomenological approach: The study of perception on the basis of the subjective reports of the perceiver.

phi phenomena: A class of demonstrations of apparent movement.

phone: Any element of speech; a unit of sound made to produce speech.

phoneme: The smallest unit of speech capable of allowing one sound to be distinguished from another. See allophone.

photon: An element of matter making up a beam of light; a quantum of light.

photopic receptors: The color-coded cones of the eye.

pinna: The projecting portion of the external ear.

pitch: Perceived changes in sound related to the frequency of the sound. The musical scale represents changes in pitch.

plane mirror: A mirror placed in the visual plane so that it reverses the visual image.

poly-oriented form: A figure or form which can be seen and recognized in any spatial orientation, e.g., a book.

positive afterimage: An afterimage the sensation of which is roughly the same color and brightness as the inducing stimulus.

potential stimulus: Any object or event capable of instigating a sensation or perception.

primary colors: A set of three colors that when combined in proper proportions produce all visual hues. Additive color mixture utilizes red, green, and blue; subtractive color mixture utilizes red, blue, and yellow.

primitive unity: The hypothesis that the separation of figure and ground is an innate aspect of perception (Hebb, 1949).

prism: A lens capable of bending light rays.

proprioception: Individual awareness of one's own bodily movement and of the position of one's limbs.

prothetic continua: A psychophysical scale in which the just noticeable difference units vary in magnitude.

proximal stimulus: The representation of an external object or event in the sensory nervous system of the perceiver.

pseudophone: A device for reversing the input to the two ears.

psychological moment: The length of time required in order to perceive two events as separate in time; the zero time in perception. *See* perceptual moment.

pure tone: A tone containing a single frequency.

quantum theory: The theory in physics that particles are not emitted or absorbed in a continuous manner but rather in steps or packets called quanta.

radiant light: Light rays emanating from a luminous source.

rapid tremor movement: Rapid oscillation or movement of the eye not under voluntary control of the observer.

receptive field: The part of a sensory system capable of initiating a response to a stimulus.

residual trace: The continuing effect of a stimulus in the nervous system after the cessation of actual stimulation.

resolution acuity: The amount of separation between elements of a pattern required for the perception of distinct elements.

retina: The portion of the eye containing light-sensitive rods and cones.

retinal field: Portions or receptive fields within the retina.

reversible figure: A figure that can be seen in two or more distinct ways.

rods: Light-sensitive receptors in the eye most responsive to weak light.

saccadic eye movement: Rapid oscillation or movement of the eye under voluntary control of the observer.

saggital plane: An imaginary plane of orientation that divides the body longitudinally into two equal and corresponding halves.

saturation: The distinctness or clarity of the hue in a color sensation.

scotopic receptors: The rods of the eye most sensitive to low-intensity light.

selective attention: The process of actively selecting certain kinds of stimulation on which attention is focused.

sensory deprivation: Studies in which the attempt is made to reduce or eliminate all outside sensory input.

set: The preparedness to respond to a stimulus in a certain manner.

shadowing: In studies of dichotic listening, to require the listener to repeat back or "shadow" one of the messages.

shape constancy: The tendency to see objects retain their shapes or forms regardless of change in viewing angle.

size constancy: The tendency to see objects remain the same apparent size regardless of changes in viewing distance.

slow drift eye movements: Slow, involuntary, random movements of the eye while the observer attempts to hold a constant fixation point.

sone scale: A scale of the subjective loudness of tones.

sound shadow: The blocking of sounds to one ear by the head.

sound spectrum: The component frequencies and amplitudes present in a given sound.

space color: Color that fills an entire area, such as the coloration of a room illuminated with red light.

specific nerve energies: The theory that a specific receptor and neuron exist in the nervous system to correspond to each specific sensation.

spectrograph: An analysis of the energy in a spectrum; for example, the analysis of intensity differences in the frequencies of a complex tone.

spiral aftereffects: A particular kind of visual afterimage produced by viewing a rotating spiral.

stereopsis: Vision based on the difference in input to the two eyes.

stereoscope: A device for presenting disparate two-dimensional views of the same scene to each eye.

Stevens's power function: A function describing the relationship between the subjective magnitude of a stimulus and the physical intensity.

structural psychology: An early school of thought that focused on the elements of conscious experience. The major technique of study was self-observation or introspection.

subception: *See* subliminal perception.

subjective color: Color seen on a rotating black and white disc.

subjective movement: *See* apparent movement.

subjective time: The flow of time measured in subjective rather than in physical units such as minutes or seconds.

subliminal: A stimulus too weak to evoke a perceptual response.

subliminal perception: A perceptual response to a stimulus of which the observer is unaware.

subthreshold: *See* subliminal.

subtractive color mixture: The mixture of colors involving the elimination or subtraction of contributing light waves.

supraliminal: *See* effective stimulus.

surface color: A color that appears to coat or to be a property of a particular object.

tachistoscope: An apparatus used to provide brief displays of two (two-field tachistoscope) or three (three-field tachistoscope) test figures in any order or temporal sequence.

T-figure: A test figure used in studies of figural aftereffects.

timbre: The quality of a sound that allows it to be distinguished from other sound sources of the same pitch and loudness.

time-intensity reciprocity: *See* Bloch's law.

tone chroma: The distinct sound produced by the combination of overtones in a complex tone.

transformation: The change in the appearance of a target in motion.

ultraviolet: Light waves with lengths slightly shorter (under 320 mμ) than those waves capable of stimulating the human eye.

Vernier acuity: Visual acuity as assessed by the lateral displacement of a segment of a vertical line. The minimum displacement of the line that can be detected provides the measure of acuity.

vestibular mechanism: The sensory system responsible for the perception and maintenance of bodily balance.

visual acuity: The sharpness of vision.

visual angle: The angle at the eye formed by drawing to the eye two imaginary lines from the top and bottom of a distal target.

visual spectrum: The range of light waves with lengths (between approximately 320 and 700 mμ) capable of stimulating the human eye.

visual summation: The addition or integration of visual stimuli separated by very short intervals of time.

visual suppression: The masking of a visual stimulus or the elimination of vision during rapid eye movements.

vitreous humor: A liquid filling the area between the lens of the eye and the light-sensitive retina.

volume: The subjective impression that some tones appear to be larger or more "room-filling" than others.

wavelength: The length of the wave movement of photons in a light beam.

wedge prism: A lens for bending a light wave a given number of degrees.

white light: Light containing all visible wavelengths in equal intensities.

white noise: A sound source containing all frequencies of the auditory spectrum.

whiteout: The temporary loss of visual experience produced usually as a result of intense light stimulation with equal amplitude.

Young-Helmholtz theory: A theory of color vision based on the observation that three primary colors in proper combination can produce all visual hues.

References

Aaronson, D. 1968. Temporal course of perception in an immediate recall task. *J. Exp. Psychol.* 76:129–40.

Adams, R. 1834. An account of a peculiar optical phenomenon seen after having looked at a moving body. *London and Edinburgh Phil. Mag. and J. Sci.* 5:373–74.

Akita, M., and Graham, C. H. 1966. Maintaining an absolute test hue in the presence of different background colors and luminance ratios. *Vision Res.* 6:315–23.

Akita, M.; Graham, C. H.; and Hsia, Y. 1964. Maintaining an absolute hue in the presence of different background colors. *Vision Res.* 4:539–56.

Alberts, W. W.; Wright, E. W., Jr.; and Feinstein, B. 1967. Responses of human somato-sensory cortex to stimuli below threshold for conscious sensation. *Science* 158: 1597–1600.

Allport, D. A. 1968. Phenomenal simultaneity and the perceptual moment hypothesis. *Brit. J. Psychol.* 59:395–406.

Ames, A. 1951. Visual perception and the rotating trapezoidal window. *Psychol. Mono.* 65: whole no. 324.

Anstis, S. M., and Gregory, R. L. 1965. The aftereffect of seen motion: The role of retinal stimulation and eye movements. *Quart. J. Exp. Psychol.* 17:173–75.

Asch, S. E., and Witkin, H. A. 1948a. Studies in space orientation. I. Perception of the upright with displaced visual fields. *J. Exp. Psychol.* 38:325–37.

―――, and Witkin, H. A. 1948b. Studies in space orientation. II. Perception of the upright with displaced visual fields and with body tilt. *J. Exp. Psychol.* 38:455.

Attneave, F. 1954. Some informational aspects of visual perception. *Psychol. Rev.* 61:183–93. Bobbs-Merrill Reprint P-389.

―――. 1955. Symmetry, information, and memory for patterns. *Amer. J. Psychol.* 68: 209–22.

―――. 1957. Physical determinants of the judged complexity of shapes. *J. Exp. Psychol.* 53:221–27.

―――. 1959. *Applications of information theory to psychology.* New York: Holt, Rinehart and Winston.

―――, and Olson, R. K. 1967. Discriminability of stimuli varying in physical and retinal orientation. *J. Exp. Psychol.* 74:149–57.

―――, and Reid, K. W. 1968. Voluntary control of frame of reference and slope equivalence under head rotation. *J. Exp. Psychol.* 78:153–59.

Aubert, H. 1886. Die Bewegungsempfindung. *Arch. Ges. Physiol.* 39:347–70.

―――. 1887. Die Bewegungsempfindung. *Arch. Ges. Physiol.* 40:459–80.

Avant, L. L. 1965. Vision in the Ganzfeld. *Psychol. Bull.* 64:246–58.

Averbach, E., and Coriell, A. S. 1961. Short-term memory in vision. *Bell Sys. Tech. J.* 40: 309–28. Bobbs-Merrill Reprint P-607.

Ayres, J. J. 1966. Some artifactual causes of perceptual primacy. *J. Exp. Psychol.* 71:896–901.

―――, and Harcum, E. R. 1962. Directional response-bias in reproducing brief visual patterns. *Perc. Motor Skills* 14:155–65.

Bach, H., and Klein, G. S. 1957. Effect of prolonged subliminal exposure of words. *Amer. Psychol.* 12:397–98.

Bachem, A. 1950. Tone height and tone chroma as two different qualities. *Acta. Psychol.* 7:80–88.

Bagley, F. W. 1902. An investigation of Fechner's colors. *Amer. J. Psychol.* 13:488–525.

Ball, R. J., and Bartley, S. H. 1966. Changes in brightness index, saturation and hue produced by luminance—wavelength—temporal interaction. *J. Opt. Soc. Amer.* 56: 695–98.

Ball, T. S., and Wilsoncroft, W. E. 1966. Complex stimuli and apparent motion. *Psychol. Sci.* 6:187–88.

Barlow, H. B. 1956. Retinal noise and absolute threshold. *J. Opt. Soc. Amer.* 46:634–39.

Barnard, C. W.; Wolff, H. D.; and Graveline, D. E. 1962. Sensory deprivation under null gravity conditions. *Amer. J. Psychiat.* 188:921–25.

Bartholomew, W. T. 1945. *Acoustics of music.* Englewood Cliffs, N.J.: Prentice-Hall.

Bartley, S. H. 1961. A clarification of some of the procedures and concepts involved in dealing with the optic pathway. In *Neurophysiologie und Psychophysik des visuellen Systems,* ed. R. Jung and H. Kornhuber. Heidelberg: Springer.

―――. 1969. *Principles of perception.* 2nd ed. New York: Harper and Row.

Bauermeister, M. 1964. Effect of body tilt on apparent verticality, apparent body position, and their relation. *J. Exp. Psychol.* 67:142–47.

Baumgartner, G. 1961. Die Reaktionen der Neurone des zentrallen visuellen Systems der Katze im simultanen Helligkeitskontrast. In *Neurophysiologie und Psychophysik des visuellen Systems,* ed. R. Jung and H. Kornhuber. pp. 296–311. Heidelberg: Springer.

Beck, J. 1966a. Effect of orientation and of shape similarity on perceptual grouping. *Perc. Psychophysics* 1:300–302.

———. 1966b. Perceptual grouping produced by changes in orientation and shape. *Science* 154:538–40.

———. 1966c. Contrast and assimilation in lightness judgments. *Perc. Psychophysics* 1: 342–44.

———. 1967. Perceptual grouping produced by line figures. *Perc. Psychophysics* 2:491–95.

———, and Gibson, J. J. 1955. The relation of apparent shape to apparent slant in the perception of objects. *J. Exp. Psychol.* 50:125–33.

Begelman, D. A. 1968. The role of retinal orientation in the egocentric organization of a visual stimulus. *J. Gen. Psychol.* 79:283–89.

Behar, I., and Bevan, W. 1961. The perceived duration of auditory and visual intervals: Cross-modal comparison and interaction. *Amer. J. Psychol.* 74:17–26.

Békésy, G. von. 1933. Über die Hörsamkeit der Ein- und Auschwingvorgänge mit Berücksichtigung der Raumakustic. *Ann Physik.* 16:844–60.

Bell, C. R., and Provins, K. A. 1963. Relation between pyhsiological responses to environmental heat and time judgments. *J. Exp. Psychol.* 66:572–79.

Bell, R. A., and Bevan, W. 1968. Influences of anchors upon the operation of certain gestalt organizing principles. *J. Exp. Psychol.* 78:670–78.

Belsey, R. 1964. Color perception and the Land two-color projections. *J. Opt. Soc. Amer.* 54:529–31.

Benary, W. 1924. Beobachtungen zu einem Experiment über Helligkeits-kontrast. *Psychol. Forsch.* 5:131–42.

Benham, C. E. 1894. The artificial spectrum top. *Nature* 51:200.

———. 1895. The artificial spectrum top. *Nature* 52:321.

Benussi, V. 1904. Zur Psychologie der Gestalterfassens. In *Untersuchungen zur Gegenstandstheorie und Psychologie,* ed. A. Meinong. Leipzig: Barth.

———. 1912. Stroboskopische Scheinbewegungen und geometrisch-optische Gestalttäuschungen. *Arch. Ges. Psychol.* 24:31–62.

Bernadin, A., and Gruber, H. 1957. An auditory autokinetic effect. *Amer. J. Psychol.* 70: 133–34.

Bernstein, I. H., and Eriksen, C. W. 1965. Effects of subliminal prompting on paired-associate learning. *J. Exp. Res. Pers.* 1:33–38.

Bevan, W. 1964. Subliminal stimulation: A pervasive problem for psychology. *Psychol. Bull.* 61:81–89.

———., and Pritchard, J. F. 1963. Effect of subliminal tones upon the judgment of loudness. *J. Exp. Psychol.* 66:23–29.

Bexton, W. H.; Heron, W.; and Scott, T. H. 1954. Effects of decreased variation in the sensory environment. *Canad. J. Psychol.* 8:70–76.

Bill, J. C., and Teft, L. W. 1969. Space-time relations: The effects of time on perceived visual extent. *J. Exp. Psychol.* 81:196–99.

Blakemore, C., and Sutton, P. 1969. Size adaptation: A new aftereffect. *Science* 166: 245–47.

Blanton, R. L., and Odom, P. B. 1968. Some possible interference and facilitation effects of pronunciability. *J. Verb. Lern. Verb. Behav.* 7:844–46.

Bobbitt, J. M. 1942. An experimental study of the phenomenon of closure as a threshold function. *J. Exp. Psychol.* 30:273–94.

Boring, E. G. 1946. The perception of objects. *Amer. J. Physics* 14:99–107. Bobbs-Merrill Reprint P-44.

Botha, E. 1963. Past experience and figure-ground perception. *Perc. Motor Skills* 16:283–88.

Bourassa, C. M., and Bartley, S. H. 1965. Some observations on the manipulation of visual acuity by varying the rate of intermittent stimulation. *J. Psychol.* 59:319–28.

Bower, T. G. R. 1966. The visual world of infants. *Sci. Amer.* 215:80–92.

———. 1966. Slant perception and shape constancy in infants. *Science* 151:832–34.

Boynton, R. M., and Gordon, J. 1965. Bezold-Brücke hue shift measured by color-naming techniques. *J. Opt. Soc. Amer.* 55:78–86.

Braunstein, M. 1962. The perception of depth through motion. *Psychol. Bull.* 59:422–33.

Brewster, D. 1847. On the knowledge of distance given by binocular vision. *Phil. Mag.* 30:315–18.

Britt, S. H. 1958. Subliminal advertising: psychologist questions experimental design. *Adv. Agency* 51:14–16.

Broadbent, D. E. 1958. *Perception and communication.* New York: Pergamon Press.

Brooks, R. M., and Goldstein, A. G. 1963. Recognition by children of inverted photographs of faces. *Child Develop.* 34:1033–40.

Brosgole, L. 1966. Change in phenomenal location and perception of motion. *Perc. Motor Skills* 23:999–1001.

———, and Cristal, R. M. 1967. The role of phenomenal displacement on the perception of the visual upright. *Perc. Psychophysics* 2:179–88.

Brown, G. S. 1928. Perception of depth with disoriented vision. *Brit. J. Psychol.* 19:135.

Brown, J. F. 1928. Über gesehene Geschwindigkeit. *Psychol. Forsch.* 10:85–90.

———. 1931a. The visual perception of velocity. *Psychol. Forsch.* 14:199–232.

———. 1931b. The thresholds for visual velocity. *Psychol. Forsch.* 14:249–68.

Brown, J. L. 1965. Afterimages. In *Vision and visual perception,* ed. C. H. Graham, pp. 479–503. New York: Wiley and Sons.

Brown, R. H. 1955. Velocity discrimination and the intensity-time relation. *J. Opt. Soc. Amer.* 45:189–92.

Brücke, E. 1864. Über den Nutzeffekt intermittirender Netzhautreizung. *Sber. Akad. Wiss. Wien* 49:128–53.

Bruner, J. S., and Minturn, A. L. 1955. Perceptual identification and perceptual organization. *J. Gen. Psychol.* 53:21–28.

———, and Postman, L. 1949. On the perception of incongruity. *J. Pers.* 18:206–23.

———, and Potter, M. C. 1964. Interference in visual recognition. *Science* 144:424–25.

Brunswik, E. 1940. Thing constancy as measured by correlation coefficients. *Psychol. Rev.* 47:69–78.

Bryden, M. P. 1962. Order of report in dichotic listening. *Canad. J. Psychol.* 16:291–99.

———. 1966. Accuracy and order of report in tachistoscopic recognition. *Canad. J. Psychol.* 20:262–72.

Bugelski, B. R., and Alampay, D. A. 1961. The role of frequency in developing perceptual sets. *Canad. J. Psychol.* 15:205–11.

Bürck, W.; Kotowski, P.; and Lichte, H. 1935. Der Aufbau des Tonhöhenbewusstseins. *Elek. Nachrichten Tech.* 12:326–33.

Burger, J. F. 1958. Front-back discrimination of the hearing system. *Acustica* 8:301–2.

Burnham, C. A., and Ono, H. 1969. Variables altering the perception of the rotating trapezoidal illusion. *Amer. J. Psychol.* 82:86–95.

Burton, A. 1943. A further study of the relation of time estimation to monotony. *J. Appl. Psychol.* 27:350–59.

Cahill, M. C. 1969. Accuracy of position judgments of stationary targets yielded by three types of perceiver of the Ames trapezoid illusion. *Proceedings 77th Annual Convention A.P.A.*, pp. 29–30.

Cambareri, J. D. 1959. The effects of sensory isolation on suggestible and nonsuggestible psychology graduate students. *Dissert. Abstr.* 19:1813.

Campbell, I. G. 1941. Factors which work toward unity of coherence in visual design. *J. Exp. Psychol.* 28:145–62.

Cappone, M. K. 1966. The effect of verbal suggestion on the reversal rate of the Ames trapezoidal illusion. *J. Psychol.* 62:211–19.

Carlson, J. A. 1966. Effect of instructions and perspective-drawing ability on perceptual constancies and geometrical illusions. *J. Exp. Psychol.* 72:874–79.

Carlson, J. P., and Duncan, C. P. 1955. A study of autonomous change in the memory trace by the method of recognition. *Amer. J. Psychol.* 68:280–84.

Carlson, V. R., and Feinberg, I. 1968a. Individual variations in time judgment and the concept of an internal clock. *J. Exp. Psychol.* 77:631–40.

———, and Feinberg, I. 1968b. Consistency among methods of time judgment for independent groups. *Proceedings 76th Annual Convention A.P.A.*, pp. 83–84.

Cautela, J. R., and McLaughlin, D. 1960. The influence of suggestion on the audioautokinetic effect. *J. Psychol.* 60:117–22.

Chananie, J. D., and Tikofsky, R. S. 1968. Reaction time and distinctive features in speech discrimination. Report No. 49, Development of Language Functions, University of Michigan Center for Human Growth and Development. Mimeographed.

———, and Tikofsky, R. S. 1969. Choice response time and distinctive features in speech discriminations. *J. Exp. Psychol.* 81:161–63.

Chandler, K. A. 1961. The effect of monaural and binaural tones of different intensities on the visual perception of verticality. *Amer. J. Psychol.* 74:260–65.

Chapanis, A., and Mankin, D. A. 1967. The vertical-horizontal illusion in a visually rich environment. *Perc. Psychophysics* 2:249–55.

Chapman, D. W. 1932. Relative effects of determinant and indeterminant Aufgaben. *Amer. J. Psychol.* 44:163–74.

Chen, H. D., and Irwin, O. C. 1946. Infant speech: vowel and consonant types. *J. Speech Disorders* 11:27–29.

Cherry, E. C. 1953. Some experiments on the recognition of speech with one and two ears. *J. Acous. Soc. Amer.* 25:975–79.

Chiang, C. 1968. A new theory to explain geometrical illusions produced by crossing lines. *Perc. Psychophysics* 3:174–76.

Clausen, J. 1950. An evaluation of experimental methods of time judgment. *J. Exp. Psychol.* 40:756–61.

Cochran, P.; Throop, J.; and Simpson, W. E. 1968. Estimation of distance of a source of sound. *Amer. J. Psychol.* 81:198–206.

Cohen, H. B. 1966. Some critical factors in prism-adaptation. *Amer. J. Psychol.* 79:285–90.

Cohen, H. H.; Bill, J. C.; and Gilinsky, A. S. 1968. Simultaneous brightness contrast: Variations on Koffka's ring. *Proceedings 76th Annual Convention A.P.A.*, pp. 99–100.

Cohen, J. 1964. Psychological time. *Sci. Amer.* 211:116–24.

———. 1969. *Personality dynamics.* New York: Rand McNally.

———, and Gordon, D. A. 1949. The Prevost-Fechner-Benham subjective colors. *Psychol. Bull.* 46:97–135.

Cohen, L. 1959. Rate of apparent change of a Necker cube as a function of prior stimulation. *Amer. J. Psychol.* 72:327–44.

Cohen, M. M. 1967. Continuous versus terminal visual feedback in prism aftereffects. *Perc. Motor Skill* 24:1295–1302.

Cohen, W. 1957. Spatial and textural characteristics of the Ganzfeld. *Amer. J. Psychol.* 70:403–10.

———. 1958. Color perception in the chromatic Ganzfeld. *Amer. J. Psychol.* 71:390–94.

———. 1960. Form recognition, spatial orientation, perception of movement in uniform visual fields. In *Visual search techniques*, ed. Marris and Horne. Washington: National Academy of Science Publication 712.

Coleman, P. D. 1963. An analysis of cues to auditory depth perception in free space. *Psychol. Bull.* 60:302–15.

Colenbrander, M. C. 1933. Über subjektive Farbenerscheinungen. *Acta. Ophthal. Kbh.* 11:437–60.

Collins, L. A., and Stone, L. G. 1965. The golden section revisited: a perimetric explanation. *Amer. J. Psychol.* 78:503–6.

Comalli, P. E., Jr.; Werner, H.; and Wapner, S. 1957. Studies in physiognomic perception. III. Effect of directional dynamics and meaning-induced sets on autokinetic motions. *J. Psychol.* 42:289–99.

Conrad, R. 1959. Errors of immediate memory. *Brit. J. Psychol.* 50:349–59.

Cook, T. H.; Mefferd, R. B.; and Wieland, B. A. 1967. Apparent reversals of orientation (perspective reversals) in depth as determinants of apparent reversals of rotary motion. *Perc. Motor Skills* 24:691–702.

Coren, S. 1969a. Brightness contrast as a function of figure-ground relations. *J. Exp. Psychol.* 80:517–24.

———. 1969b. The influence of optical aberrations on the magnitude of the Poggendorf illusion. *Perc. Psychophysics.* 6:185–86.

Cornsweet, T. N. 1956. Determination of the stimuli for involuntary drifts and saccadic eye movements. *J. Opt. Soc. Amer.* 46:987–93.

Cornwell, H. G. 1963. Prior experience as a determinant of figure-ground orientation. *J. Exp. Psychol.* 65:156–62.

———. 1964. Effect of training on figure-ground discrimination. *J. Exp. Psychol.* 68:108–9.

Corso, J. F. 1967. *The experimental psychology of sensory behavior.* New York: Holt, Rinehart and Winston.

Costello, C. G. 1966. Direction of rotation and decay of the spiral aftereffect. *Perc. Motor Skills* 23:779–82.

Cowan, A. 1928. Test cards for determination of visual acuity. *Arch. Opthal.* 57:283–95. See also Landolt, 1889.

Craske, B. 1966. Intermodel transfer of adaptation to displacement. *Nature* (London) 210:765.

———. 1967. Adaptation to prisms: Change in internally registered eye-position. *Brit. J. Psychol.* 58:329–36.

Cross, J., and Cross, J. 1969. The misperception of rotary motion. *Perc. Psychophysics* 5:94–96.

Crovitz, H. F., and Daves, W. 1963. Tendencies to eye movement and perceptual accuracy. *J. Exp. Psychol.* 63:495–98.

Culler, E. 1926. Studies in psychometric theory. *Psychol. Mono.* 35: whole no. 163.

Davies, A. E. 1905. An analysis of elementary psychic processes. *Psychol. Rev.* 12:166–206.

Day, R. H., and Power, R. P. 1963. Frequency of apparent reversal of rotary motion in depth as a function of shape and pattern. *Aust. J. Psychol.* 15:162–74.

———, and Power, R. P. 1965. Apparent reversal (oscillation) of rotary motion in depth: An investigation and a general theory. *Psychol. Rev.* 72:117–27.

———, and Singer, G. 1967. Sensory adaptation and behavioral compensation with spatially transformed vision and hearing. *Psychol. Bull.* 67:307–22.

Dayton, G. O., Jr.; Jones, M. H.; Steele, B.; and Rose, M. 1964. Developmental studies of coordinated eye movements in the human infant. II. An electro-oculographic study of the fixation reflex in the newborn. *Arch. Ophthal.* 71:871–75.

Dearborn, G. V. N. 1899. Recognition under objective reversal. *Psychol. Rev.* 6:395–406.

Dees, J. W. 1966. Moon illusion and size-distance invariance: An explanation based upon an experimental artifact. *Perc. Motor Skills* 23:629–30.

Delboeuf, I. L. R. 1865. Seconde note sur des nouvelles illusions d'optique. *Bull. Acad. Roy. Belgique* 20.

Dember, W. N. 1960. *The psychology of perception.* New York: Holt, Rinehart and Winston.

Desilva, H. R. 1929. An analysis of the visual perception of movement. *Brit. J. Psychol.* 19:268–305.

Deutsch, J. A. 1955. A theory of shape recognition. *Brit. J. Psychol.* 46:30–37.

———. 1964. Neurophysiological contrast phenomena and figural aftereffects. *Psychol. Rev.* 71:19–26.

———, and Deutsch, D. 1963. Attention: Some theoretical considerations. *Psychol. Rev.* 70:19–26.

———, and Deutsch, D. 1967. Comments on selective attention: perception or response? *Quart. J. Exp. Psychol.* 19:362–63.

DeValois, R. L.; Abramov, I.; and Jacobs, G. H. 1966. Analysis of response patterns of LGN cells. *J. Opt. Soc. Amer.* 56:966–77.

———; Abramov, I.; and Mead, W. R. 1967. Single cell analysis of wavelength discrimination at the lateral geniculate nucleus in the macaque. *J. Neurophysiol.* 30: 415–33.

Dewar, R. E. 1967. Stimulus determinants of the magnitude of the Müller-Lyer illusion. *Perc. Motor Skills* 24:708–10.

DeWolfe, R. K. S., and Duncan, C. P. 1959. Time estimation as a function of level of behavior of successive tasks. *J. Exp. Psychol.* 58:153–58.

Dinnerstein, D. 1965. Previous and concurrent visual experience as determinants of phenomenal shape. *Amer. J. Psychol.* 78:235–42.

Dittler, R., and Eisenmeier, J. 1909. Über das erste positive Nachbild nach kurzdauer Reizung des Sehorganes mittels bewegter Lichtquelle. *Pflügers Arch. Ges. Physiol.* 126:610–47.

Djang, S. 1937. The role of past experience in the visual apprehension of masked forms. *J. Exp. Psychol.* 20:29–59.

Dorfman, D. D., and McKenna, H. 1966. Pattern preference as a function of pattern uncertainty. *Canad. J. Psychol.* 20:143–53.

Dreistadt, R. 1968. The effects of figural aftereffects on geometrical illusions. *J. Psychol.* 69:63–73.

Drösler, J. 1967. Die Kontrast-Bewertungsfunktion der visuellen Wahrnehmung von Figuren. *Bericht über den 25. Kongress der Deutschen Gesellschaft für Psychologie,* ed. F. Merz, pp. 307–11. Göttingen: Hogrefe.

Duncker, K. 1935. *Zur Psychologie des produktiven Denkens.* Berlin: Springer. On problem-solving, trans. L. S. Lees. *Psychol. Mono.* 58: whole no. 270.

Dunlap, K. 1900. Effects of imperceptible shadows upon the judgment of distance. *Psychol. Rev.* 7:435–53.

Earhard, B. 1968. Perception and retention of familiar and unfamiliar material. *J. Exp. Psychol.* 76:584–95.

Ebenholtz, S. 1966. Adaptation to a rotated visual field as a function of degree of optical tilt and exposure time. *J. Exp. Psychol.* 72:629–34.

———. 1970. On the relation between interocular transfer of adaptation and Hering's law of equal innervation. *Psychol. Rev.* 77:343–47.

Edridge-Green, F. W. 1914. The homonymous induction of colour. *J. Physiol.* (London) 48.

Efstathiou, E. 1969. Effects of exposure time and magnitude of prism transform on eye-hand coordination. *J. Exp. Psychol.* 81:235–40.

Egan, J. P.; Carterette, E. C.; and Thwing, E. J. 1954. Some factors affecting multichannel listening. *J. Acous. Soc. Amer.* 26:774–82.

Egeth, H. 1967. Selective attention. *Psychol. Bull.* 67:41–57.

———, and Smith, E. E. 1967. Perceptual selectivity in a visual recognition task. *J. Exp. Psychol.* 74:543–49.

Ehmer, R. H.; Ehmer, B. J.; Seamon, J. G.; and Cohen, H. H. 1968. Temporal relations in pure tone masking. *Proceedings 76th Annual Convention A.P.A.*, pp. 121–22.

Ehrenstein, W. 1928. Untersuchungen über Bewegungs- und Gestaltwahrnehmung 3. Mitteilung. *Arch. f. Psychol.* no. 66.

Einthoven, W. 1898. Eine einfache physiologische Erklärung für verschiedene geometrisch-optische Täuschungen. *Pflügers Arch. Ges. Physiol.* 71:1–43.

Ekman, G., and Sjoberg, L. 1965. Scaling. *Annual Rev. of Psychol.* 16:451–71.

Emmert, E. 1881. Grössenverhältnisse der Nachbilder. *Klin. Monatsbl. d. Augenheilk.* 19: 443–50.

Epstein, W. 1967. *Varieties of perceptual learning.* New York: McGraw-Hill.

———, and Baratz, S. S. 1964. Relative size in isolation as a stimulus for perceived relative distance. *J. Exp. Psychol.* 61:507–13.

———; Bontrager, H.; and Park, J. N. 1962. The induction of nonvertical slant and the perception of shape. *J. Exp. Psychol.* 63:472–79.

———, and Park, J. N. 1963. Shape constancy: Functional relationships and theoretical formulations. *Psychol. Bull.* 60:265–88.

Erickson, R. P. 1968. Stimulus coding in topographic and nontopographic afferent modalities. *Psychol. Rev.* 75:447–65.

Eriksen, C. W. 1956. Subception: Fact or artifact. *Psychol. Rev.* 63:74–80.

———. 1966. Temporal luminance summation effects in backward and forward masking. *Perc. Psychophysics* 1:87–92.

———, and Collins, J. F. 1965. Reinterpretation of one form of backward and forward masking in visual perception. *J. Exp. Psychol.* 70:343–51.

———, and Collins, J. F. 1967. Some temporal characteristics of visual pattern perception. *J. Exp. Psychol.* 74:476–84.

———, and Collins, J. F. 1968. Sensory traces versus the psychological moment in the temporal organization of form. *J. Exp. Psychol.* 77:376–82.

———, and Greenspoon, T. S. 1968. Binocular summation over time in the perception of form at brief durations. *J. Exp. Psychol.* 76:331–36.

———, and Hoffman, M. 1963. Form recognition at brief durations as a function of adapting field and interval between stimulations. *J. Exp. Psychol.* 66:485–99.

———, and Spencer, T. 1969. Rate of information processing in visual perception: Some results and methodological considerations. *J. Exp. Psychol. Mono.* 79.

———, and Steffy, R. A. 1964. Short-term memory and retroactive interference in visual perception. *J. Exp. Psychol.* 68:423–34.

Erlebacher, A., and Sekuler, R. 1969. Explanation of the Müller-Lyer illusion: Confusion theory examined. *J. Exp. Psychol.* 80:462–67.

Escher, M. C. 1967. *Graphic Works of.* Rev. ed. New York: Hawthorn.

Evans, C. R. 1967. Further studies of pattern perception and a stabilized retinal image: The use of prolonged afterimages to achieve perfect stabilization. *Brit. J. Psychol.* 58: 315–27.

Evans, R. M. 1948. *An introduction to color.* New York: Wiley.

Ewert, P. H. 1930. A study of the effect of inverted retinal stimulation upon spatially coordinated behavior. *Genet. Psychol. Monograph* 7: nos. 3–4.

Falk, J. L., and Bindra, D. 1954. Judgment of time as a function of serial position and stress. *J. Exp. Psychol.* 47:279–82.

Fantz, R. L. 1961. The origin of form perception. *Sci. Amer.* 204:66–72.

Fechner, G. T. 1838. Über eine Scheibe zur Erzeugung subjectiver Farben. *Pogg. Ann. Physik u. Chemie.* 45:227–32.

———. 1860. *Elemente der Psychophysik.* Leipzig: Breitkopf und Hartel.

Feldman, S., and Weld, H. P. 1935. Perceiving. In *Foundations of psychology,* ed. E. G. Boring, H. S. Langfeld, and H. P. Weld. New York: Wiley.

Festinger, L.; Ono, H.; Burnham, C. A.; and Bamber, D. 1967. Efference and the conscious experience of perception. *J. Exp. Psychol. Mono.* 74: whole no. 637.

Fick, A. 1852. Erörterung eines physiologisch-optischen Phänomens. *Zeit. Rat. Med.* 2: 83–94.

Fieandt, K. von. 1966. *The world of perception.* Homewood, Ill.: Dorsey Press.

Filer, R., and Meals, D. 1949. The effect of motivating conditions on the estimation of time. *J. Exp. Psychol.* 39:327–31.

Firestone, F. A. 1930. The phase difference and amplitude ratio at the ears due to a source of pure tones. *J. Acous. Soc. Amer.* 2:260–68.

Fisher, G. H. 1968. An experimental and theoretical appraisal of the inappropriate size-depth theories of illusions. *Brit. J. Psychol.* 59:373–83.

Flavell, J. A., and Dragnus, J. A. 1957. A microgenetic approach to perception and thought. *Psychol. Bull.* 54:197–217.

Fleischl, E. von. 1892. Physiologisch-optische Notizen. *Kaiserliche Akad. Wiss.* (Vienna) Bd. 86.

Fletcher, H. 1934. Loudness, pitch, timbre of musical tones and their relation to intensity, frequency and overtone structure. *J. Acous. Soc. Amer.* 6:59–69.

———. 1940. Auditory patterns. *Rev. Mod. Phys.* 12:47–65.

Flock, H. R. 1964. A possible optical basis for monocular slant perception. *Psychol. Rev.* 71:380–91.

———. 1965. Optical texture and linear perspective as stimuli for slant perception. *Psychol. Rev.* 72:505–14.

Flugle, J. C. 1921. On local fatigue in the auditory system. *Brit. J. Psychol.* 11:105–34.

Foley, J. E., and Maynes, F. J. 1969. A comparison of training methods in the production of prism adaptation. *J. Exp. Psychol.* 81:151–55.

Forgus, R. H. 1966. *Perception.* New York: McGraw-Hill.

Fraisse, P. 1966. Visual perceptive simultaneity and masking of letters successively presented. *Perc. Psychophysics* 1:285–87.

Francois, M. 1927. Contributions à l'étude du sens du temps: La température interne comme facteur de variation de l'appréciation subjective des durées. *Annee Psychol.* 28:186–204.

Freeburne, C. M., and Goldman, R. D. 1969. Left-right differences in tachistoscopic recognition as a function of order of report, expectancy, and training. *J. Exp. Psychol.* 79: 570–72.

Freedman, S. J., and Zacks, J. L. 1964. Effect of active and passive movement upon auditory function during prolonged atypical stimulation. *Perc. Motor Skills* 18:361–66.

Freeman, G. L. 1929. An experimental study of the perception of objects. *J. Exp. Psychol.* 12:241–58.

Freeman, R. B., Jr. 1965. Ecological optics and visual slant. *Psychol. Rev.* 72:501–4.

———. 1966. Function of cues in the perceptual learning of visual slant: An experimental and theoretical analysis. *Psychol. Mono: General and Applied* 80: whole no. 610.

———. 1967. Contrast interpretation of brightness constancy. *Psychol. Bull.* 67:165–87.

———, and Pasnak, R. 1968. Perspective determinants of the rotating trapezoid illusion. *J. Exp. Psychol.* 76:94–101.

Freud, S. L. 1964. Duration of spiral aftereffect as a function of retinal size, retinal place and hemiretinal transfer. *Perc. Motor Skills* 18:47–53.

Fuhrer, M. J., and Eriksen, C. W. 1960. The unconscious perception of the meaning of verbal stimuli. *J. Abnorm. Soc. Psychol.* 61:432–39.

Gantenbein, M. 1952. Recherches sur le développement des perceptions: XIV. Recherches sur le développement de la perception du movement avec l'âge. *Arch. Psychol. Genève* 33:198–294.

Ganz, L. 1964. Lateral inhibition and the location of visual contours: an analysis of visual aftereffects. *Vis. Research* 4:465–81.

———. 1966a. Is the figural aftereffect an aftereffect? *Psychol. Bull.* 66:151–65.

———. 1966b. Mechanism of figural aftereffects. *Psychol. Rev.* 73:128–50.

Garner, W. R. 1966. To perceive is to know. *Amer. Psychologist* 21:11–19.

———, and Miller, G. A. 1947. The masked threshold of pure tones as a function of duration. *J. Exp. Psychol.* 37:293–303.

Gemelli, A., and Capellini, A. 1958. The influence of subjects' attitudes in perception. *Acta. Psychol.* 14:12–23.

Gescheider, G. A. 1966. The resolving of successive clicks by the ears and skin. *J. Exp. Psychol.* 71:378–81.

Gholson, B., and Hohle, R. H. 1968. Choice reaction times to hues printed in conflicting hue names and nonsense words. *J. Exp. Psychol.* 76:413–18.

Gibson, A. R., and Harris, C. S. 1968. The McCollough effect: color adaptation of edge-detectors or negative afterimages? Paper presented to the Eastern Psychological Association, Washington, D.C.

Gibson, E. J. 1963. Perceptual learning. *Ann. Rev. Psych.* 14:29–56.

———. 1969. *Principles of perceptual learning and development.* New York: Appleton-Century-Crofts.

Gibson, J. J. 1933. Adaptation, after-effect and contrast in the perception of curved lines. *J. Exp. Psychol.* 16:1–31. Bobbs-Merrill Reprint P-128.

———. 1937. Adaptation, aftereffect and contrast in the perception of tilted lines. II. Simultaneous contrast and the areal restriction of the aftereffect. *J. Exp. Psychol.* 20: 553–69.

———. 1950. *The perception of the visual world.* Boston: Houghton Mifflin.

———. 1954. The visual perception of objective motion and subjective movement. *Psychol. Rev.* 61:304–14.

———. 1960. The concept of stimulus in psychology. *Amer. Psychologist* 15:694–703.

———. 1966. *The senses considered as perceptual systems.* Boston: Houghton Mifflin.

———. 1967. On the proper meaning of the term stimulus. *Psychol. Rev.* 74:533–34.

———. 1968. What gives rise to the perception of motion? *Psychol. Rev.* 75:335–46.

———, and Robinson, D. 1935. Orientation in visual perception: The recognition of familiar plane forms in differing orientations. *Psychol. Mono.* 46: whole no. 210.

Gilinsky, A. S. 1951. Perceived size and distance in visual space. *Psychol. Rev.* 58:460–82.

Gilliland, A. R., and Humphreys, D. W. 1943. Age, sex, method, and interval as variables in time estimation. *J. Gen. Psychol.* 53:123–30.

Gleason, H. A. 1961. *An introduction to descriptive linguistics.* New York: Holt, Rinehart and Winston.

Gogel, W. C. 1964. Size cue to visually perceived distances. *Psychol. Bull.* 62:217–35.

Goldstein, G. 1962. Moon illusion: An observation. *Science* 138:1340–41.

———. 1966. The searchlight illusion. *Amer. J. Psychol.* 79:145–47.

Goldstein, M., and Davis, D. 1961. The impact of stimuli registering outside awareness upon personal preferences. *J. Person.* 29:247–56.

Goldstone, S.; Boardman, W. K.; and Lhamon, W. T. 1959. Intersensory comparisons of temporal judgments. *J. Exp. Psychol.* 57:243–48.

Gottschaldt, K. 1926. Über den Einfluss der Erfahrung auf die Wahrenehmung von Figuren. *Psychol. Forsch.* 8:261–317.

――――. 1966. *Theorie der Wahrnehmung.* Göttingen: Psychologisches Institut.

Graham, C. H. 1963. On some aspects of real and apparent visual movement. *J. Opt. Soc. Amer.* 53:1019–25.

――――. 1965a. Color mixture and color systems. In *Vision and visual perception,* ed. C. H. Graham, pp. 370–94. New York: Wiley.

――――. 1965b. Visual space perception. In *Vision and visual perception,* ed. C. H. Graham, pp. 504–47. New York: Wiley.

――――, and Brown, J. L. 1965. Color contrast and color appearances: Brightness constancy and color constancy. In *Vision and visual perception,* ed. C. H. Graham, pp. 452–78. New York: Wiley.

Gregory, R. L. 1963. Distortion of visual space as inappropriate constancy scaling. *Nature* (London) 199:678–80.

――――. 1966. *Eye and brain.* London: Weidenfeld and Nicolson.

――――, and Warren, R. M. 1958. An auditory analogue to visual reversible figures. *Amer. J. Psychol.* 7:612–13.

Gruber, H.; Fink, C. D.; and Damm, V. 1957. Effects of experience on perception of causality. *J. Exp. Psychol.* 55:89–95.

Guirao, M., and Stevens, S. S. 1964. Measurements of auditory density. *J. Acous. Soc. Amer.* 36:1176–82.

Guttman, N., and Julesz, B. 1963. Lower limits of auditory periodicity analysis. *J. Acous. Soc. Amer.* 35:610.

Gyr, J. W.; Brown, J. S.; Willey, R.; and Zivian, A. 1966. Computer simulation and psychological theories of perception. *Psychol. Bull.* 65:174–92.

Haber, R. N. 1964a. A replication of selective attention and coding in visual perception. *J. Exp. Psychol.* 67:402–4.

――――. 1964b. The effects of coding strategy on perceptual memory. *J. Exp. Psychol.* 68: 257–62.

――――. 1965. Limited modification of the trapezoidal illusion with experience. *Amer. J. Psychol.* 78:651–55.

――――. 1966. Nature of the effect of set on perception. *Psychol. Rev.* 73:335–51. Bobbs-Merrill Reprint P-641.

――――. 1969. Eidetic images. *Sci. Amer.* 220:36–44.

――――, and Hershenson, M. 1965. Effects of repeated brief exposures on the growth of a percept. *J. Exp. Psychol.* 69:40–46.

――――, and Standing, L. G. 1968. Direct measures of short-term visual storage. *Quart. J. Exp. Psychol.* 21:43–54.

Hajos, A. 1967. Psychophysiologische Probleme bei Farbkonturen und Konturfarben. *Studia Psychol.* 10:254–66.

Hake, H. W. 1966. Form discrimination and the invariance of form. In *Pattern recognition,* ed. L. Uhr, pp. 142–73. New York: Wiley.

――――, and Rodwan, A. S. 1967. Perception and recognition. In *Experimental methods and instrumentation in psychology,* ed. J. B. Sidowski, pp. 331–81. New York: McGraw-Hill.

Hamilton, C. R. 1964. Intermanual transfer of adaptation to prisms. *Amer. J. Psychol.* 77:457–62. Bobbs-Merrill Reprint P-468.

――――, and Bossom, J. 1964. Decay of prism aftereffects. *J. Exp. Psychol.* 67:148–50.

Hammer, E. R. 1949. Temporal factors in figural aftereffects. *Amer. J. Psychol.* 62:337–54.

Handel, S., and Garner, W. R. 1966. The structure of visual pattern associates and pattern goodness. *Perc. Psychophysics* 1:33–38.

Hansen and Lehmann. 1895. Über unwillkürliches Flüstern. *Phil. Stud.* 11:471–530.

Harcum, E. R., and Friedman, S. M. 1963. Reversal reading by Israeli observers of visual patterns without intrinsic directionality. *Canad. J. Psychol.* 17:361–69.

Harper, R. S. 1953. The perceptual modification of colored figures. *Amer. J. Psychol.* 66: 86–89.

Harris, C. S. 1963. Adaptation to displaced vision: Visual, motor or proprioceptive change? *Science* 140:812–13.

———. 1965. Perceptual adaptation to inverted, reversed, and displaced vision. *Psychol. Rev.* 72:419–44. Bobbs-Merrill Reprint P-643.

———, and Gibson, A. R. 1968. Is orientation-specific color adaptation due to edge detectors, afterimages, or "dipoles"? *Science* 162:1506–7.

———, and Haber, R. N. 1963. Selective attention and coding in visual perception. *J. Exp. Psychol.* 65:328–33.

Hartline, H. K. 1969. Neural interaction in the retina and the processing of visual information. Invited address presented to the A.P.A., Washington, D.C.

Hartridge, H. 1945. The supplying of information: The special senses, bk. 4. In *Principles of human physiology,* ed. C. L. Evans. Philadelphia: Lea and Febiger.

Hastorf, A. H. 1950. The influence of suggestion on the relationship between stimulus size and perceived distance. *J. Psychol.* 29:195–217.

Hay, J. C., and Pick, H. L., Jr. 1966a. Visual and proprioceptive adaptation to optical displacement of the visual stimulus. *J. Exp. Psychol.* 71:150–58.

———, and Pick, H. L., Jr. 1966b. Gaze-contingent prism adaptation: Optical and motor factors. *J. Exp. Psychol.* 72:640–48.

Hebb, D. O. 1949. *The organization of behavior.* New York: Wiley.

———. 1968. Concerning imagery. *Psychol. Rev.* 75:466–77.

———, and Foord, E. N. 1945. Errors of visual recognition and the nature of the trace. *J. Exp. Psychol.* 35:335–48.

Heckenmuller, E. G. 1965. Stabilization of the retinal image: a review of method, effects and theory. *Psychol. Bull.* 63:157–69.

Heider, F., and Simmel, M. L. 1944. An experimental study of apparent behavior. *Amer. J. Psychol.* 57:243–49.

Held, R. 1962. Adaptation to rearrangement and visual-spatial aftereffects. *Psychol. Beitr.* 6:439–50.

———. 1965. Plasticity in sensory-motor systems. *Sci. Amer.* 213:84–94.

———, and Hein, A. 1958. Adaptation of disarranged hand-eye coordination contingent upon reafferent stimulation. *Perc. Motor Skills* 8:83–86.

Helmholtz, H. L. F. von. 1863. *Die Lehre von den Tonempfindungen als physiologische Grundlage für die Theorie der Musik.* Brunswick: Viewig.

———. 1866. *Handbuch der physiologischen Optik.* Hamburg and Leipzig: Voss.

———. 1896. *Handbuch der physiologischen Optik.* 2nd ed. Hamburg: Voss.

Helson, H. 1964a. *Adaptation level theory.* New York: Harper and Row.

———. 1964b. Current trends and issues in adaptation level theory. *Amer. Psychol.* 19: 26–38.

———, and Bevan, W. 1964. An investigation of variables in judgments of relative area. *J. Exp. Psychol.* 67:335–41.

———, and Joy, V. L. 1961. Domains of lightness, assimilation and contrast. *Psychol. Beitr.* 6:405–15.

———, and King, S. M. 1931. The Tau effect: An example of psychological relativity. *J. Exp. Psychol.* 14:202–17.

Hering, E. 1861. *Beiträge zur Physiologie.* Leipzig: Englemann.

———. 1890. Beitrag zur Lehre vom Simultankontrast. *Z. Psychol.* 1:18–28.

———. 1920. Grundzüge der Lehre vom Lichtsinne. In *Handbuch der gesamten Augenheilkunde,* ed. Graefe-Saemisch. Berlin: Springer.

Hermann, L. 1870. Eine Erscheinung simultanen Kontrasts. *Pflüger's Arch. ges. Physiol.* 3:13–15.

Hernandez-Péon, R.; Scherrer, H.; and Jouvet, M. 1956. Modification of electrical activity in cochlear nucleus during attention in unanesthetized cats. *Science* 123:331–32.

Hershberger, W. A. 1967. Comment on apparent reversal (oscillation) of rotary motion in depth. *Psychol. Rev.* 74:235–38.

Hershenson, M. 1965. Visual discrimination in the human newborn. *Disc. Abstr.* 26:1793.

———. 1967. Development of the perception of form. *Psychol. Bull.* 67:326–36.

———. 1969. Perception of letter arrays as a function of absolute retinal locus. *J. Exp. Psychol.* 80:201–2.

———; Munsinger, H.; and Kessen, W. 1965. Preference for shapes of intermediate variability in the newborn infant. *Science* 147:630–31.

Hess, C., and Pretori, H. 1894. Messende Untersuchungen über die Gesetzmässigkeit des simultanen Helligkeitskontrastes. *Graefes Arch. Ophthal.* 40:1–24.

Heymans, G. 1896. Quantitative Untersuchungen über das optische Paradoxon. *Zeit. Psychol. Physio. Sinnesorg.* 9:221–55.

Hirsh, I. J. 1959. Auditory perception of temporal order. *J. Acous. Soc. Amer.* 31:759–67.

Hoagland, H. 1933. The physiological control of judgments of duration: Evidence for a chemical clock. *J. Gen. Psychol.* 9:267–87.

Hochberg, C. B., and Hochberg, J. E. 1952. Familiar size and the perception of depth. *J. Psychol.* 34:107–14.

Hochberg, J. E., and Brooks, V. 1960. The psychophysics of form: Reversible-perspective drawings of spatial objects. *Amer. J. Psychol.* 73:337–54.

———, and Galper, R. E. 1967. Recognition of faces: I. An exploratory study. *Psychon. Sci.* 9:619–20.

———, and McAlister, E. 1955. Relative size vs. familiar size in the perception of represented depth. *Amer. J. Psychol.* 68:294–96.

———; Triebel, W.; and Seaman, G. 1951. Color adaptation under conditions of homogeneous visual stimulation (Ganzfeld). *J. Exp. Psychol.* 41:153–59.

Hocutt, M. 1967. On the alleged circularity of Skinner's concept of stimulus. *Psychol. Rev.* 74:530–32.

Höffding, H. 1891. *Outlines of psychology.* New York: Macmillan.

Holland, H. C. 1957. The Archimedes spiral. *Nature* 179:432–33.

———. 1965. *The spiral aftereffect.* London: Pergamon Press.

Holmes, D. S. 1967. Closure in a gapped circle figure. *Amer. J. Psychol.* 80:614–18.

Holst, E. von. 1957. Aktive Leistungen der menschlichen Gesichtswahrnehmung. *Stud. Generale* 10:231–43.

Holt, R. R. 1964. Imagery: The return of the ostracized. *Amer. Psychologist* 19:254–64.

Holway, A. H., and Boring, E. G. 1941. Determinants of apparent visual size with distant variant. *Amer. J. Psychol.* 54:21–37. Bobbs-Merrill Reprint P-162.

Hoppe, J. I. 1879. *Die Scheinbewegung.* Würzburg: Meiner.

Hornstein, A. D., and Rotter, G. S. 1969. Research methodology in temporal perception. *J. Exp. Psychol.* 79:561–64.

Horsten, G. P. M., and Winkelman, J. E. 1964. Electroretinographic critical fusion frequency of the retina in relation to the histological development in man and animals. *Documenta Ophthal.* 18:515–21.

Houssiadas, L. 1964. Effects of set and intellectual level on the perception of causality. *Acta. Psychol.* 22:155–61.

Howard, I. P., and Templeton, W. B. 1966. *Human spatial orientation.* New York: Wiley.

Hubel, D. H., and Wiesel, T. N. 1962. Receptive fields, binocular interaction and functional architecture in the cat's visual cortex. *J. Physiol.* 160:106–54.

————, and Weisel, T. N. 1968. Receptive fields and functional architecture of the monkey striate cortex. *J. Physiol.* 195:215–43.

Humboldt, A. von. 1850. *Kosmos* 3:73–74.

Hurvich, L. M., and Jameson, D. 1957. An opponent-process theory of color vision. *Psychol. Rev.* 64:384–404.

————, and Jameson, D. 1966. *The perception of brightness and darkness.* New York: Allyn and Bacon.

————; Jameson, D.; and Krantz, D. H. 1965. Theoretical treatments of selected visual problems. In *Handbook of Mathematical Psychology,* ed. R. D. Luce, R. R. Bush, and E. Galanter, pp. 3:99–159. New York: Wiley.

Hylan, J. P. 1903. The distribution of attention. I. *Psychol. Rev.* 10:373–403.

Ikeda, H., and Obonai, T. 1953. The quantitative analysis of figural aftereffects: I. The process of growth and decay of figural aftereffects. *Jap. J. Psychol.* 24:179–92.

Immergluck, L. 1966. Resistance to an optical illusion, figural aftereffects and field dependence. *Psychon. Sci.* 6:281–82.

Indow, T., and Stevens, S. S. 1966. Scaling of saturation and hue. *Perc. Psychophysics* 1: 253–71.

Ingard, U. 1953. A review of the influence of meterological conditions on sound propagation. *J. Acous. Soc. Amer.* 25:405–11.

Inglis, J. 1960. Dichotic stimulation and memory disorder. *Nature* 186:181–82.

————, and Tansey, C. L. 1967. Age difference and scoring differences in dichotic listening performance. *J. Psychol.* 66:325–32.

Irwin, O. C. 1947. Development of speech during infancy: Curve of phonemic frequency. *J. Exp. Psychol.* 37:187–93.

————, and Chen, H. D. 1946. Infant speech: Vowel and consonant frequency. *J. Speech Disorders* 11:123–215.

Ittelson, W. H. 1951. Size as a cue to distance: Static localization. *Amer. J. Psychol.* 64: 54–67.

————. 1952. *The Ames demonstrations in perception.* Princeton: Princeton University Press.

Jakobson, R., and Halle, M. 1956. *Fundamentals of language.* The Hague: Mouton.

James, W. 1890. *Principles of psychology.* New York: Holt.

Jones, E. E., and Bruner, J. S. 1954. Expectancy in apparent visual movement. *Brit. J. Psychol.* 45:157–65.

Jones, R. C. 1968. How images are detected. *Sci. Amer.* 219:110–17.

Judd, C. H. 1902. Practice and its effects on the perception of the Müller-Lyer illusion. *Psychol. Rev.* 9:27–39.

Judd, D. B. 1960. Appraisal of Land's work on two primary projections. *J. Opt. Soc. Amer.* 50:254–68.

Julesz, B. 1964. Binocular depth perception without familiarity cues. *Science* 145:356–62. Bobbs-Merrill Reprint P-485.

————. 1968. Experiment in perception. *Psychology Today* 2:16–23.

Juring, J. 1738. Essay on distinct and indistinct vision. In *Smith's optics.* Cambridge: University Press.

Kahneman, D. 1964. Temporal summation in an acuity task at different energy levels— a study of the determinants of summation. *Vis. Research* 4:557–66.

————. 1966. Time-intensity reciprocity under various conditions of adaptation and backward masking. *J. Exp. Psychol.* 71:543–49.

————, and Norman, J. 1964. The time-intensity relation in visual perception as a function of observer's task. *J. Exp. Psychol.* 68:215–20.

————; Norman, J.; and Kubovy, M. 1967. Critical duration for the resolution of form: Centrally or peripherally determined? *J. Exp. Psychol.* 73:323–27.

Kaiser, P. K. 1967. Perceived shape and its dependency on perceived slant. *J. Exp. Psychol.* 75:345–53.

Kammann, R. 1967. The overestimation of vertical distance and slope and its role in the moon illusion. *Perc. Psychophysics* 2:585–89.

Kaswan, J., and Young, S. 1963. Stimulus exposure time, brightness, and spatial factors as determinants of visual perception. *J. Exp. Psychol.* 65:113–23.

Katz, D. 1911. Die Erscheinungsweisen der Farben und ihre Beeinflussung durch die individuelle Erfahrung. *Zeit. Psychol. Ergeb.* 7.

———. 1935. *The world of colour.* London: Kegan Paul.

Katz, M. S. 1967. Feedback and accuracy of target positioning in a homogeneous visual field. *Amer. J. Psychol.* 80:405–10.

———; Petlay, W.; and Cirincione, P. A. 1965. Effects of stimulus and field size in the accuracy of orientation in the homogeneous environment. *Perc. Motor Skills* 20: 167–72.

Kaufman, L. 1964. On the nature of binocular disparity. *Amer. J. Psychol.* 77:393–402.

———. 1965. Some new stereoscopic phenomena and their implications for the theory of stereopsis. *Amer. J. Psychol.* 78:1–20.

———, and Pitblado, C. 1965. Further observations on the nature of effective binocular disparities. *Amer. J. Psychol.* 78:379–91.

———, and Rock, I. 1962. The moon illusion, I. *Science* 136:953–61. Bobbs-Merrill Reprint P-490.

Keele, S. W., and Chase, W. G. 1967. Short-term visual storage. *Perc. Psychophysics* 2: 383–86.

Kennedy, J. L. 1936. The nature and physiological basis of visual movement discriminations in animals. *Psychol. Rev.* 43:494–521.

Kennett, J. R. 1962. Influence of subliminal stimuli on comparative judgments of length. *Perc. Motor Skills* 14:383–89.

Kilpatrick, F. P., and Ittelson. W. H. 1953. The size-distance invariance hypothesis. *Psychol. Rev.* 60:223–31. Bobbs-Merrill Reprint P-306.

Kinchla, R. A., and Allan, L. G. 1969. A theory of visual movement perception. *Psychol. Rev.* 76:537–58.

King, W. L., and Gruber, H. E. 1962. Moon illusion and Emmert's law. *Science* 135: 1125–26. Bobbs-Merrill Reprint P-490.

———, and Wertheimer, M. 1963. Induced colors and colors produced by chromatic illumination may have similar physiological bases. *Perc. Motor Skills* 17:379–82.

Kinney, J. A. S. 1962. Factors affecting induced color. *Vis. Research* 2:503–25.

———. 1965. Effect of exposure time on induced color. *J. Opt. Soc. Amer.* 55:731–36.

———. 1967. Color induction using asynchronous flashes. *Vis. Research* 7:299–318.

Koch, R. 1968. Perception of the Boring figure by aged persons. Mimeographed. Portland, Oregon: Portland State University.

Koffka, K. 1935. *The principles of gestalt psychology.* New York: Harcourt, Brace.

Kohler, I. 1962. Experiments with goggles. *Sci. Amer.* 206:62–72.

———. 1964. The formation and transformation of the perceptual world. *Psychol. Issues* 3:1–173.

Köhler, W. 1940. *Dynamics in psychology.* New York: Liveright.

———, and Fishback, J. 1950. The destruction of the Müller-Lyer illusion in repeated trials: I. An examination of two theories. *J. Exp. Psychol.* 40:267–81.

———, and Wallach, H. 1944. Figural aftereffects. *Proc. Amer. Phil. Soc.* 88:269–357.

Kolers, P. A. 1963. Some differences between real and apparent visual movement. *Vision Research* 3:191–206.

———. 1964. The illusion of movement. *Sci. American* 211:98–106.

————; Eden, M.; and Boyer, A. 1964. Reading as a perceptual skill. *M.I.T. Res. Lab. Electr. Quart. Prog. Rep.* 74:214–17.

Korpell, H. S. 1965. On the mechanism of tonal chroma in absolute pitch. *Amer. J. Psychol.* 78:298–300.

Korte, A. 1915. Kinematoscopische Untersuchungen. *Z. Psychol.* 72:193–296.

Krauskopf, J., and Riggs, L. A. 1959. Interocular transfer in the disappearance of stabilized images. *Amer. J. Psychol.* 72:248–52.

Külpe, O. 1904. Versuche über Abstraktion. *Bericht über den Internationaler Kongress fuer experimentelle Psychologie* 56–58.

Künnapas, T. M. 1955a. An analysis of the vertical-horizontal illusion. *J. Exp. Psychol.* 49:134–40.

————. 1955b. Influence of frame size on apparent length of a line. *J. Exp. Psychol.* 50: 168–70.

————. 1960. Scales for subjective distance. *Scand. J. Psychol.* 1:187–92.

————. 1968. Distance perception as a function of available visual cues. *J. Exp. Psychol.* 77:523–29.

Land, E. H. 1959a. Color vision and the natural image. Part I. *Proc. Nat. Acad. Sci.* 45: 115–29.

————. 1959b. Color vision and the natural image. Part II. *Proc. Nat. Acad. Sci.* 45:636–44.

————. 1959c. Experiments in color vision. *Sci. Amer.* 200:84–99.

Landauer, A. A. 1964. The effect of instructions on the judgment of brightness. *Quart. J. Exp. Psychol.* 16:23–29.

————. 1969. Influence of instructions on judgments of unfamiliar shapes. *J. Exp. Psychol.* 79:129–32.

————; Rhine, C. A.; and Rumiz, L. 1968. Overestimation of vertical movement. *Psychon. Sci.* 10:59–60.

Landolt, E. 1889. Tableau d'optotypes pour la determination de l'acuité visuelle. *Soc. Francais d'Opththal.* Also see Cowan, 1928.

Lawrence, D. H., and Coles, G. R. 1954. Accuracy of recognition with alternatives before and after the stimulus. *J. Exp. Psychol.* 47:208–14.

Lawson, R. B., and Gulick, W. L. 1967. Stereopsis and anomalous contour. *Vision Research* 7:271–97.

Lazarus, R. S., and McCleary, R. A. 1951. Autonomic discriminations without awareness: A study of subception. *Psychol. Rev.* 58:113–22.

Leeper, R. 1935. A study of a neglected portion of the field of learning: The development of sensory organization. *J. Genet. Psychol.* 46:41–75.

Lehman, R. S. 1965. Eye-movement and the autokinetic illusion. *Amer. J. Psychol.* 78: 490–92.

Leibowitz, H. 1955a. Effect of reference lines on the discrimination of movement. *J. Opt. Soc. Amer.* 45:829–30.

————. 1955b. The relation between the rate of threshold perception of movement and luminance for various durations of exposure. *J. Exp. Psychol.* 42:209–14.

Leibowitz, H. W. 1965. *Visual perception.* New York: Macmillan.

————, and Gwozdecki, J. 1967. The magnitude of the Poggendorf illusion as a function of age. *Child Dev.* 38:573–80.

————, and Harvey, L. O., Jr. 1967. Size matching as a function of instructions in a naturalistic environment. *J. Exp. Psychol.* 74:378–82.

————, and Judisch, J. M. 1967. The relation between age and the magnitude of the Ponzo illusion. *Amer. J. Psychol.* 80:105–9.

————; Toffey, S. E.; and Searle, J. L. 1966. Intensity/time relationship and perceived shape. *J. Exp. Psychol.* 72:7–10.

Levelt, W. J. M. 1968. *On binocular rivalry.* The Hague: Mouton.

Lichte, W. H., and Borresen, C. R. 1967. Influence of instructions on degree of shape constancy. *J. Exp. Psychol.* 74:538–42.

Licklider, J. C. R. 1951. Basic correlates of the auditory stimulus. In *Handbook of psychology*, ed. S. S. Stevens, pp. 985–1039. New York: Wiley.

Lit, A. 1968. Visual acuity. *Ann. Rev. of Psychol.* 19:27–54.

London, I. D. 1960. A Russian report on the postoperative newly seeing. *Amer. J. Psychol.* 73:478–82.

Long, E. R.; Henneman, R. H.; and Garvey, W. D. 1960. An experimental analysis of set: The role of sense-modality. *Amer. J. Psychol.* 73:563–67.

———; Reid, L. S.; and Henneman, R. H. 1960. An experimental analysis of set: Variables influencing the identification of ambiguous stimulus-objects. *Amer. J. Psychol.* 73: 553–62.

Luckiesh, M., and Moss, F. K. 1933. A demonstrational test of vision. *Amer. J. Psychol.* 45:135–39.

Ludvigh, E. 1948. The visibility of moving objects. *Science* 108:63–64.

Luria, A. A. 1968. *The mind of a mnemonist.* New York: Basic Books.

Luria, S. M.; Kinney, J. A. S.; and Weissman, S. 1967. Distance estimates with filled and unfilled space. *Perc. Motor Skills* 24:1007–10.

Lynn, R. 1961. Reversible perspective as a function of stimulus intensity. *Amer. J. Psychol.* 74:131–33.

Lyons, J., and Thomas, D. R. 1968. Influence of postural distortion on the perception of visual vertical in pigeons. *J. Exp. Psychol.* 76:120–24.

Mach, E. 1914. *The analysis of sensations.* Chicago: Open Court.

McCollough, C. 1965. Color adaptation of edge-detectors in the human visual system. *Science* 149:1115–16.

McGree, J. M. 1963. The effect of group verbal suggestion and age on the perception of the Ames trapezoidal illusion. *J. Psychol.* 56:447–53.

McKendry, J. M.; Snyder, M. B.; and Gates, S. 1963. Factors affecting perceptual integration of illustrated material. *J. Appl. Psychol.* 47:293–99.

McKenzie, R. E., and Hartman, B. O. 1961. The effects of size, speed and inspection time on the duration of the spiral aftereffect. Mimeographed. Houston: U.S.A.F. School of Aerospace Med. Report, 62–73.

Mack, A. 1967. The role of movement in perceptual adaptation to a tilted retinal image. *Perc. Psychophysics* 2:65–68.

Mackworth, J. F. 1963. The relation between the visual image and post-perceptual immediate memory. *J. Verb. Learn. Verb. Behav.* 2:75–85.

McLaughlin, S. C., and Webster, R. G. 1967. Changes in straight-ahead eye position during adaptation to wedge prisms. *Perc. Psychophysics* 2:37–44.

MacNichol, E. F., Jr. 1964. Three-pigment color vision. *Sci. Amer.* 211:48–56.

McNulty, J. A.; Dockrill, F. J.; and Levy, B. A. 1967. The subthreshold perception of stimulus meaning. *Amer. J. Psychol.* 80:28–40.

Mann, C. W. 1950. Factors influencing the perception of the vertical. In *A symposium on psychophysiological factors in spatial orientation*, pp. 30–35. Pensacola, Fla.: Office of Naval Research.

———, and Berry, N. H. 1949. The perception of postural vertical: II. Visual factors. Joint Report No. 5. Mimeographed. Pensacola, Fla.: Tulane University and U.S.N. School of Aviation Medicine.

———, and Dauterive, J. H., Jr. 1949. The perception of postural vertical: I. The modification of non-labyrinthine cues. Joint Report No. 4. Mimeographed. Pensacola, Fla.: Tulane University and U.S.N. School of Aviation Medicine.

Marnum, K. D. 1968. Reproduction and ratio-production of brief duration under conditions of sensory isolation. *Amer. J. Psychol.* 81:21–26.

Masland, R. H. 1969. Visual motion perception: Experimental modification. *Science* 165: 819–20.

Matin, L., and MacKinnon, E. G. 1964. Autokinetic movement: Selective manipulation of directional components by image stabilization. *Science* 143:147–48.

Meade, R. D. 1959. Time estimates as affected by motivational level, goal distance, and rate of progress. *J. Exp. Psychol.* 58:275–79.

Mendelson, J.; Kubzansky, P. E.; Leiderman, P. H.; Wexler, D.; Dutoit, D.; and Solomon, P. 1960. Catechol amine excretion and behavior during sensory deprivation. *Arch. Gen. Psychiat.* 2:147–55.

Meneghini, K. A., and Leibowitz, H. W. 1967. Effect of stimulus distances and age on shape constancy. *J. Exp. Psychol.* 74:241–48.

Metzger, W. 1929. Zur Phänomenologie des homogenen Ganzfeldes. *Psychol. Forsch.* 13:6–29.

———. 1934. Beobachtungen über phänomenale Identität. *Psychol. Forsch.* 19:1–60.

———. 1937. Das Sehen von Formen und Dingen und das Problem der Seelenblindheit. In *Gegenwartsprobleme*, ed. R. Thiel. Leipzig.

———. 1953. *Gesetze des Sehens*. Frankfurt: Kramer.

———. 1966. Figural-Wahrnehmung. In *Handbuch der Psychologie,* band 1, ed. W. Metzger, pp. 693–744. Göttingen: Hogrefe.

Michotte, A. 1958. The emotions regarded as functional connections. In *The international symposium on feelings and emotions,* ed. M. L. Reymer, pp. 56–93. New York: McGraw-Hill.

———. 1963. *The perception of causality*. New York: Basic Books.

Mikaelian, H., and Held, R. 1964. Two types of adaptation to an optically-rotated visual field. *Amer. J. Psychol.* 77:257–63.

Miller, G. A. 1956. The magical number seven, plus or minus two: some limits on our capacity for processing information. *Psychol. Rev.* 63:81–97. Bobbs-Merrill Reprint P-241.

———, and Nicely, P. E. 1955. An analysis of perceptual confusion among some English consonants. *J. Acous. Soc. Amer.* 27:338–52.

Miller, J. W., and Hall, R. J. 1962. The problem of motion perception and orientation in the Ganzfeld. In *Visual problems in the armed forces,* ed. M. A. Whitcomb, pp. 14–20. Washington: National Academy of Science.

Miller, N. D. 1965. Visual recovery from brief exposures to high luminance. *J. Opt. Soc. Amer.* 55:1661–69.

———. 1966. Positive afterimage following brief high-intensity flashes. *J. Opt. Soc. Amer.* 56:802–6.

Mills, A. W. 1958. On the minimum audible angle. *J. Acous. Soc. Amer.* 30:237–46.

———. 1960. Lateralization of high-frequency tones. *J. Acous. Soc. Amer.* 32:132–34.

Mirabella, A.; Taub, H.; and Teichner, W. H. 1967. Adaptation of loudness to monaural stimulation. *J. Gen. Psychol.* 76:251–73.

Montague, W. P. 1908. Consciousness: A form of energy. In *Essays, philosophical and psychological, in honor of William James* ed. W. P. Montague. New York: Longmans, Green.

Morant, R. B., and Harris, J. R. 1965. Two different aftereffects of exposure to visual tilts. *Amer. J. Psychol.* 78:218–26.

Moray, N. 1959. Attention in dichotic listening: Affective cues and the influence of instructions. *Quart. J. Exp. Psychol.* 11:56–60.

Morgan, C. T. 1965. *Physiological Psychology*. New York: McGraw-Hill.

———, and King, R. A. 1966. *Introduction to psychology*. New York: McGraw-Hill.

Morgan, R. F., and Bakan, P. 1965. Sensory deprivation hallucinations and other sleep behavior as a function of position, method of report and anxiety. *Perc. Motor Skills* 20:19–25.

Morinaga, S. 1942. Beobachtungen über Grundlagen und Wirkungen anschaulich gleichmässiger Breiter. *Arch. Ges. Psychol.* 110:309–48.

Mörner, M. 1963. Voice register terminology and standard pitch. Royal Institute of Technology Report No. 4. Mimeographed. London: Speech Transmission Laboratory.

Morrison, L. J., and Nazzaro, J. R. 1966. Anchoring of pitch judgments. *J. Gen. Psychol.* 74:307–11.

Moustgaard, I. K. 1963. A phenomenological approach to autokinesis. *Scand. J. Psychol.* 4:17–22.

Mulholland, T. 1956. Motion perceived while viewing rotating stimulus objects. *Amer. J. Psychol.* 69:96–99.

Müller, J. 1826. *Zur vergleichenden Physiologie des Gesichtssinnes des Menschens und der Tiere.* Leipzig: Barth.

Munsell, A. H. 1941. *A color notation.* 9th ed. Baltimore: Munsell Color Co.

Münsterberg, H. 1899. The physiological basis of mental life. *Science* 9:442–47.

Murch, G. M. 1965. A simple laboratory demonstration of subception. *Brit. J. Psychol.* 56:467–70.

———. 1966. *Über subliminale Reizwirkungen bei der Wahrnehmung optischer Figurationen.* Göttingen: Psychologisches Institut.

———. 1967. Temporal gradients of responses to subliminal stimuli. *Psychol. Rec.* 17:483–91.

——— 1968a. A comparison of several methods of measuring the effects of subliminal stimuli. *Psychology* 5:20–26.

———. 1968b. McCollough afterimages and Emmert's law. *Proceedings 76th Annual Convention A.P.A.,* pp. 103–4.

———. 1969a. Size judgments of McCollough afterimages. *J. Exp. Psychol.* 81:44–48.

———. 1969b. Responses to incidental stimuli as a function of feedback contingency. *Perc. Psychophysics* 5:10–12.

———. 1969c. Growth of a percept as a function of interstimulus interval. *J. Exp. Psychol.* 82:121–28.

———. 1970. Perception of rotary movement. *J. Exp. Psychol.* 86:83–85.

———, and Hirsch, J. 1972. The McCollough effect created by complementary afterimages. *Amer. J. Psychol.,* in press.

Murdock, B. B., Jr. 1961. The retention of individual items. *J. Exp. Psychol.* 62:618–25.

———. 1968. Modality effects in short-term memory: Storage or retrieval? *J. Exp. Psychol.* 78:79–86.

Murray, D. J. 1968. Articulation and acoustic confusability in short-term memory. *J. Exp. Psychol.* 78:679–84.

Musatti, C. 1953. Luce e colore nei fenomeni del contrasto simultaneo, della constanze e dell' eguaglimento. *Arch. Ps. Neur. Psich.* 5:105–20.

Needham, J. G. 1935. The effect of the time interval upon the error at different intensity levels. *J. Exp. Psychol.* 18:530–43.

Neisser, U. 1964. Visual search. *Sci. Amer.* 210:94–102.

———. 1967. *Cognitive psychology.* New York: Appleton-Century-Crofts.

Nelson, T. M., and Vasold, T. M. 1965. Dependence of object identification upon edge and surface. *Perc. Motor Skills* 20:537–46.

Newhall, S. M.; Nickerson, D.; and Judd, D. B. 1943. Final report of the O.S.A. subcommittee on the spacing of Munsell colors. *J. Opt. Soc. Amer.* 33:385–418.

Newman, E. B. 1948. Hearing. In *Foundations of psychology,* ed. E. G. Boring, H. S. Langfeld and H. P. Weld. New York: Wiley.

Norman, D. A. 1968. Toward a theory of memory and attention. *Psychol. Rev.* 75:522–36.
————. 1969. Memory while shadowing. *Quart. J. Exp. Psychol.* 21:85–93.
O'Connell, D. C.; Weintraub, D. J.; Lathrop, R. G.; and McHale, T. J. 1967. Apparent verticality: Psychophysical error versus sensory tonic theory. *J. Exp. Psychol.* 73:347–53.
Ogle, K. N. 1962. The optical space sense. In *The eye*, ed. H. Davson, vol. 4. New York: Academic Press.
Olson, R., and Orbach, J. 1966. Reversibility of the Necker cube: VIII. Parts of the figure contributing to the perception of reversals. *Perc. Motor Skills* 22:623–29.
Ono, H. 1969. Apparent distance as a function of familiar size. *J. Exp. Psychol.* 79:109–15.
Oppel, J. J. 1854–55. Über geometrish-optische Täuschungen. *Jahresbericht physik. Verein. Frankfurt* 37–47.
Orbach, J.; Ehrlich, D.; and Heath, H. A. 1963. Reversibility of the Necker cube: I. An examination of the concept of satiation of orientation. *Per. Motor Skills* 17:439–58.
Orbison, W. D. 1939. Shape as a function of the vector field. *Amer. J. Psychol.* 52:31–45.
Ornstein, P. A., and Winnick, W. A. 1968. Influence of set in tachistoscopic threshold determination. *J. Exp. Psychol.* 77:504–6.
Ostwald, W. 1921. *Die Grundlage der messenden Farblehre.* Berlin: Grossbrother Verlag.
Oyama, T., and Hsia, Y. 1966. Compensatory hue shift in simultaneous color contrast as a function of separation between inducing and test fields. *J. Exp. Psychol.* 71:405–13.
Page, H. A.; Elfner, L. F.; and Jamison, N. 1966. Autokinetic effect as a function of inter-mittency of the light course. *Psychol. Rec.* 16:189–92.
Panum, P. L. 1858. *Physiologische Untersuchungen über das Sehen mit zwei Augen.* Kiel.
Pastore, N. 1952. Some remarks on the Ames oscillatory effect. *Psychol. Rev.* 59:319–23.
Pelton, L. H., and Solley, C. M. 1968. Acceleration of reversals of a Necker cube. *Amer. J. Psychol.* 80:585–88.
Pentti, L. 1955. Auditory localization during rotation of the visual environment. *Reports from the Psychological Institute, University of Helsinki,* no. 2.
Perkins, F. T. 1932. Symmetry in visual recall. *Amer. J. Psychol.* 44:473–90.
Pfaff, D. 1968. Effects of temperature and time of day on time judgments. *J. Exp. Psychol.* 76:419–22.
Piaget, J., and Lambercier, M. 1944. Essai sur un effect d'Einstellung survenant au cours de perceptions visuelles, successives (effect Usnadze). *Arch. Psychol.* 30:139–96.
————, and Vinh-Bang. 1961. L'evolution de l'illusion des espaces divises (Oppel-Kundt) en presentation tachistosopique. *Arch. Psychol. Genève* 38:167–200.
Pick, H. L.; Hay, J. C.; and Martin, R. 1969. Adaptation to split-field wedge prism spectacles. *J. Exp. Psychol.* 80:125–32.
Pierce, A. H. 1901. *Studies in auditory and visual space perception.* New York: Longmans, Green.
Plateau, J. 1849. Quatrieme note sur de nouvelles applications curieuses de la persistance des impressions de la retine. *Bull. Acad. Roy. Sci. Belg.* 16:254–60.
Plomp, R. 1964. The ear as a frequency analyzer. *J. Acous. Soc. Amer.* 36:1628–36.
Pollack, I. 1968. The apparent pitch of short tones. *Amer. J. Psychol.* 81:165–69.
————, and Pickett, J. M. 1964. Intelligibility of excerpts from fluent speech: Auditory versus structural content. *J. Verb. Learn. Verb. Behav.* 3:79–84.
————, and Rose, M. 1967. Effect of head movement on the localization of sounds in the equatorial plane. *Perc. Psychophysics* 2:591–96.
Pollack, R. H. 1963. Effects of temporal order of stimulus presentation on the direction of figural aftereffects. *Perc. Motor Skills* 17:875–80.
————. 1964. Simultaneous and successive presentation of elements of the Müller-Lyer figure and chronological age. *Perc. Motor Skills* 19:303–10.
————. 1967. Comment on "Is the figural aftereffect an aftereffect?" *Psychol. Bull.* 68:59–61.

Ponzo, M. 1928. Urteilstäuchungen über Mengen. *Arch. Ges. Psychol.* 65:129–62.

Posner, M. 1967. Short-term memory systems in human information processing. *Acta. Psychol.* 27:267–84.

Postman, L., and Miller, G. A. 1945. Anchoring of temporal judgments. *Amer. J. Psychol.* 58:43–53.

Poutlon, E. C.; Simmonds, D. C. V.; Warren, R. M.; and Webster, J. C. 1965. Prior context and fractional versus multiple estimates of the reflectance of grays against a fixed standard. *J. Exp. Psychol.* 69:496–502.

Power, R. P. 1967. Stimulus properties which reduce apparent reversal of rotating rectangular shapes. *J. Exp. Psychol.* 73:595–99.

Pressey, A. W., and Kelm, H. 1966. Effects of sleep deprivation on a visual figural aftereffect. *Perc. Motor Skills* 23:795–800.

Price-Williams, D. R. 1954. The kappa effect. *Nature* 173:363–65.

Pritchard, R. M. 1961. Stabilized images on the retina. *Sci. Amer.* 204:72–78.

———; Heron, W.; and Hebb, D. O. 1960. Visual perception approached by the method of stabilized images. *Canad. J. Psychol.* 14:67–77.

Purkinje, J. 1825. *Beobachtungen und Versuche zur Physiologie der Sinne II: Neue Beiträge zur Kenntnis des Sehens in subjektiver Hinsicht.* Berlin: Reimer.

Radner, M., and Gibson, J. J. 1935. Orientation in visual perception: The perception of tip-character in forms. *Psychol. Mono.* 46: whole no. 210.

Raskin, L. M. 1969. Long-term memory effects in the perception of apparent movement. *J. Exp. Psychol.* 79:97–103.

Ratoosh, P. 1949. On interposition as a cue for the perception of distance. *Proc. Nat. Acad. Sci.* 35:257–59.

Rausch, E. 1966. Probleme der Metrik (Geometrish-optische Täuschungen). In *Handbuch der Psychologie,* band 1, ed. W. Metzger, pp. 776–865. Göttingen: Hogrefe.

Redding, B. M.; Mefferd, R. B.; and Wieland, B. A. 1967. Effect of observer movement on monocular depth perception. *Perc. Motor Skills* 24:725–26.

Reese, T. S., and Stevens, S. S. 1960. Subjective intensity of coffee odor. *Amer. J. Psychol.* 73:424–28.

Reid, L. S.; Henneman, R. H.; and Long, E. R. 1960. An experimental analysis of set: The effect of categorical restriction. *Amer. J. Psychol.* 73:568–72.

Rethlingshafer, D., and Sherrer, T. I. 1961. Supplementary report: Effect of practice on an illusion. *J. Exp. Psychol.* 62:95–96.

Révész, G. 1946. *Einführung in die Musikpsychologie.* Bern: Francke.

Reynolds, D. 1964. Effects of double stimulation: Temporary inhibition of response. *Psychol. Bull.* 62:333–47.

Riggs, L. A. 1965. Visual acuity. In *Vision and visual perception,* ed. C. H. Graham. New York: Wiley.

———; Armington, J. C.; and Ratliff, F. 1954. Motions of the retinal image during fixation. *J. Opt. Soc. Amer.* 44:315–21.

———, and Ratliff, F. 1951. Visual acuity and the normal tremor of the eyes. *Science* 114:17–18.

———; Ratliff, F.; Cornsweet, J. C.; and Cornsweet, T. N. 1953. The disappearance of steadily fixated visual test objects. *J. Opt. Soc. Amer.* 43:495–501. Bobbs-Merrill Reprint P-684.

Rivers, W. H. R. 1901. Introduction and Vision. In *Reports of the Cambridge anthropological expedition to the Torres Straits,* ed. A. C. Haddon, vol. 2. Cambridge: Cambridge University Press.

Robinson, J. O. 1968. Retinal inhibition in visual distortion. *Brit. J. Psychol.* 58:29–36.

Rock, I. 1964. The perception of the egocentric orientation of a line. *J. Exp. Psychol.* 48:367–74.

———. 1966. *The nature of perceptual adaptation.* New York: Basic Books.

————. 1968. When the world is tilt. *Psychology Today* 2:24–31.

————, and Ebenholtz, S. 1962. Stroboscopic movement based on change of phenomenal rather than retinal location. *Amer. J. Psychol.* 75:193–207. Bobbs-Merrill Reprint P-544.

————, and Engelstein, P. 1959. A study of memory for visual form. *Amer. J. Psychol.* 72:221–29.

————, and Harris, C. S. 1967. Vision and touch. *Sci. Amer.* 216:96–104.

————, and Kaufman, L. 1962. The moon illusion, II. *Science* 136:1023–31. Bobbs-Merrill Reprint P-490.

————, and Kremen, I. 1957. A reexamination of Rubin's aftereffect. *J. Exp. Psychol.* 53:23–30.

Rood, O. N. 1860. On a new theory of light proposed by John Smith. *Amer. J. Sci. and Arts* 30:182–86.

Rosenzweig, M. R. 1961. Auditory localization. *Sci. Amer.* 205:32–42.

Ross, B. M. 1969. Sequential visual memory and the limited magic of the number seven. *J. Exp. Psychol.* 80:339–47.

Ross, P. L. 1967. Accuracy of judgments of movement in depth from two-dimensional projections. *J. Exp. Psychol.* 75:217–25.

Royce, J. R.; Stayton, W. R.; and Kinkade, R. G. 1962. Experimental reduction of autokinetic movement. *J. Exp. Psychol.* 75:221–31.

Rubin, E. 1921. *Visuelle wahrgenommene Figuren.* Copenhagen: Gyldendalska.

Rule, S. J. 1969. Equal discriminability scale of number. *J. Exp. Psychol.* 79:35–38.

Sagara, M., and Oyama, T. 1957. Experimental studies on figural aftereffects in Japan. *Psychol. Bull.* 54:327–38.

————; Tago, U.; and Shibuya, Y. 1962. The influence of subliminal stimuli upon the impressions of a line drawing of a face. *Jap. Psychol. Res.* 4:178–84.

Saldanha, E. L., and Corso, J. F. 1964. Timbre cues and the identification of musical instruments. *J. Acous. Soc. Amer.* 36:2021–26.

Sayons, K. 1964. Kinetic frame effects: II. Vista motion. *Perc. Motor Skills* 18:857–63.

————, and Prysiazniuk, A. W. 1963. Kinetic frame effects: I. Alpha motion. *Perc. Motor Skills* 16:581–84.

Scharf, B. 1962. Loudness summation and spectrum shape. *J. Acous. Soc. Amer.* 34:228–33.

Schiffman, H. R. 1966. Golden section: Preferred figural orientation. *Perc. Psychophysics* 1:193–94.

————. 1967. Size estimation of familiar objects under informative and reduced conditions of viewing. *Amer. J. Psychol.* 80:229–35.

Schiller, P., and Smith, M. 1968. Monoptic and dichoptic metacontrast. *Perc. Psychophysics* 3:237–39.

————, and Wiener, M. 1962. Binocular and stereoscopic viewing of geometric illusions. *Perc. Motor Skills* 15:739–47.

Schumacher, G. M., and Klingensmith, J. E. 1968. Refinement of the power function relationship in the loudness estimation of pure tones. *Proceedings 76th Annual Convention A.P.A.,* pp. 116–17.

Schurman, D. L.; Eriksen, C. W.; and Rohrbaugh, J. 1968. Masking phenomena and time-intensity reciprocity for form. *J. Exp. Psychol.* 78:310–17.

Scott, T. R.; Lavender, A. D.; McWhirt, R. A.; and Powell, D. A. 1966. Directional asymmetry of motion aftereffect. *J. Exp. Psychol.* 71:806–15.

Segall, M. H.; Campbell, D. T.; and Herskovits, M. J. 1966. *The influence of culture on visual perception.* Indianapolis: Bobbs-Merrill.

Sekuler, R. W., and Abrams, M. 1968. Visual sameness. A choice time analysis of pattern recognition processes. *J. Exp. Psychol.* 77:232–38.

Senders, J. 1966. The coffee cup illusion. *Amer. J. Psychol.* 79:143–45.

Shaffer, O., and Wallach, H. 1966. Extent of motion thresholds under subject-relative and object-relative conditions. *Perc. Psychophysics* 1:447–51.

Sherif, M. 1936. *The psychology of social norms.* New York: Harper.

Shiffrin, R. M., and Atkinson, R. C. 1969. Storage and retrieval processes in long-term memory. *Psychol. Rev.* 76:179–93.

Shlaer, S. 1937. The relation between visual acuity and illumination. *J. Gen. Physiol.* 21: 165–88.

Shurley, J. T. 1960. Profound experimental sensory isolation. *Amer. J. Psychiat.* 117: 539–45.

———. 1963. The hydro-hypodynamic environment. *Proceedings Third World Congress of Psychiatry* 3:232–36. Toronto: University of Toronto Press.

Sickels, W. R. 1942. Experimental evidence for the electrical character of visual fields derived from a quantitative analysis of the Ponzo illusion. *J. Exp. Psychol.* 30:84–91.

Sidis, B. 1898. *Psychology of suggestion.* New York: Appleton.

Siegal, R. J. 1965. A replication of the mel scale of pitch. *Amer. J. Psychol.* 78:615–20.

Sivian, L. J., and White, S. D. 1933. On minimum audible sound fields. *J. Acous. Soc. Amer.* 4:288–321.

Smith, F., and Carey, P. 1966. Temporal factors in visual information processing. *Canad. J. Psychol.* 20:337–42.

Smith, J. W.; Spence, D. P.; and Klein, G. S. 1959. Subliminal effects of verbal stimuli. *J. Abnorm. Soc. Psychol.* 59:167–76.

Smith, S., and Lewty, W. 1959. Perceptual isolation using a silent room. *Lancet* 2:342–45.

Smythe, E., and Goldstone, S. 1957. The time sense: A normative, genetic study of the development of time perception. *Perc. Motor Skills* 7:49–59.

Snellen, H. 1862. *Probebuchstaben zur Bestimmung der Sehschärfe.* Utrecht: Weijer.

Snyder, F. W., and Pronko, N. H. 1952. *Vision with spatial inversion.* Wichita, Kan.: University of Wichita Press.

Solomon, P.; Kubzansky, P. E.; Leiderman, P. H.; Mendelson, J.; and Wexler, D. 1961. *Sensory deprivation.* Cambridge: Harvard University Press.

Sommer, J. 1967. Die Quantifizierung der Perspekitive-Theorie der geometrisch-optischen Täuschungen. In *Bericht über den 25 Kongress der D.G.P.*, ed. F. Merz, pp. 317–23. Göttingen: Hogrefe.

Spence, D. P. 1961. An experimental test of schema interaction. *J. Abnorm. Soc. Psychol.* 62:611–15.

Spencer, T. J. 1969. Some effects of different masking stimuli on iconic storage. *J. Exp. Psychol.* 81:132–40.

Sperling, G. 1960. The information available in brief visual presentations. *Psychol. Mono.* 74: whole no. 498.

Sperry, R. W. 1943. Effect of 180 degree rotation of the retinal field on visuomotor coordination. *J. Exp. Zoo.* 92:263–79.

Spitz, H. H. 1968. Ganz's hypothesis on figural aftereffects. *Amer. J. Psychol.* 80:462–64.

Standing, L.; Haber, R. N.; Cataldo, M.; and Sales, B. D. 1969. Two types of short-term visual storage. *Perc. Psychophysics* 5:193–96.

Steffy, R. A., and Eriksen, C. W. 1965. Short-term, perceptual recognition memory for tachistoscopically presented nonsense forms. *J. Exp. Psychol.* 70:277–83.

Stein, W. 1928. Tachistoskopische Untersuchungen über das Lesen. *Archiv. Ges. Psychol.* 64:301–46.

Steinfeld, G. J. 1967. Concepts of set and availability and their relation to the reorganization of ambiguous pictorial stimuli. *Psychol. Rev.* 74:505–22.

Stevens, S. S. 1934a. The volume and intensity of tones. *Amer. J. Psychol.* 46:397–408.

———. 1934b. Tonal density. *J. Exp. Psychol.* 17:585–92.

———. 1936. A scale for the measurement of psychological magnitude: loudness. *Psychol. Rev.* 42:517–27.

————. 1955. The measurement of loudness. *J. Acous. Soc. Amer.* 27:815–29.

————. 1956a. Calculation of the loudness of complex noise. *J. Acous. Soc. Amer.* 28: 807–32.

————. 1956b. The direct estimation of sensory magnitudes—loudness. *Amer. J. Psychol.* 69:1–25.

————. 1959. Cross-modality validation of subjective scales for loudness, vibration, and electric shock. *J. Exp. Psychol.* 57:201–9.

————. 1964. Concerning the psychophysical power law. *Quart. J. Exp. Psychol.* 16: 383–85.

————; Carton, A. S.; and Shickman, G. M. 1958. A scale of apparent intensity of shock. *J. Exp. Psychol.* 56:328–34.

————, and Davis, H. 1947. *Hearing: Its psychology and physiology.* 2nd ed. New York: Wiley.

————, and Newman, E. B. 1936. The localization of actual sources of sound. *Amer. J. Psychol.* 48:297–306. Bobbs-Merrill Reprint P-335.

————; Volkmann, J.; and Newman, E. B. 1937. A scale for measurement of the psychological magnitude of pitch. *J. Acous. Soc. Amer.* 8:185–90.

Stewart, G. W., and Hovda, O. 1913. The intensity factor in binaural localization: An extension of Weber's law. *Psychol. Rev.* 25:242–51.

Stone, L. S. 1960. Polarization of the retina and development of vision. *J. Exp. Zoo.* 145: 85–93.

Stratton, G. M. 1896. Some preliminary experiments on vision without inversion of the retinal image. *Psychol. Rev.* 3:611–17.

————. 1897. Vision without the inversion of the retinal image. *Psychol. Rev.* 3:341–60.

Street, R. F. 1931. *A gestalt completion test: A study of a cross-section of intellect.* New York: Bureau of Publication, Teachers College, Columbia University.

Stroop, J. R. 1935. Studies of interference in serial verbal reactions. *J. Exp. Psychol.* 18: 643–62.

Stumpf, C. 1890. *Tonpsychologie,* vol. 2. Leipzig: Hirzel.

Suslowa, M. 1863. Veränderung der Hautgefühle unter dem Einfluss elektrischer Reizung. *Z. Rat. Med.* 18:115–60.

Swets, J. A. 1961a. Detection theory and psychophysics: A review. *Psychometrika* 26: 49–63.

————. 1961b. Is there a sensory threshold? *Science* 134:168–77. Bobbs-Merrill Reprint P-340.

————, and Sewall, S. T. 1963. Stimulus vs. response uncertainty in recognition. *J. Acous. Soc. Amer.* 33:1586–92.

————; Tanner, W. P., Jr.; and Birdsall, T. G. 1961. Decision processes in perception. *Psychol. Rev.* 68:301–40.

Swink, C. W. 1963. Informal comment on a study by King and Wertheimer. *Perc. Motor Skills* 17:718.

Talland, G. A. 1959. Intersensory perceptual set. *Brit. J. Psychol.* 50:231–34.

Tanner, W. P., Jr., and Swets, J. A. 1954. A decision-making theory of visual detection. *Psychol. Rev.* 61:401–9.

Tausch, R. 1954. Optische Täuschungen als artifizielle Effekte der Gestaltungsprozesse von Grössen- und Formenkonstanz in der natürlichen Raumwahrnehmung. *Psychol. Forsch.* 24:299–348.

Taylor, J. G. 1962. *The behavioral basis of perception.* New Haven: Yale University Press.

Taylor, M. M. 1962. The distance paradox of the figural aftereffect in auditory localization. *Canad. J. Psychol.* 16:278–82.

————. 1963. Tracking the neutralization of rotary movement. *Perc. Motor Skills* 16: 119–29.

Teldford, W. H., Jr., and Tudor, L. L. 1969. Tactual and visual illusions in the T-shaped figure. *J. Exp. Psychol.* 81:199–201.
Templin, M. C. 1952. Speech development in the young child: 3. The development of certain language skills in children. *J. Speech Hearing Disorders* 17:280–85.
Thiery, A. 1896. Über geometrisch-optische Täuschungen. *Philos. Studien* 12:67–125.
Thompson, J. H. 1966. What happens to the stimulus in backward masking? *J. Exp. Psychol.* 71:580–86.
Thor, D. H., and Wood, R. J. 1966. Visual space perception and the moon illusion. Paper presented to the A.P.A., New York.
Thouless, R. H. 1931. Phenomenal regression to the real object, part 2. *Brit. J. Psychol.* 22:1–30.
Tikofsky, R. S., and McInish. J. R. 1968. Consonant discrimination by seven year olds: A pilot study. *Psychon. Sci.* 10:61–62.
Titchener, E. B. 1906. *Experimental psychology.* New York: Macmillan.
———, and Pyle, W. H. 1907. The effect of imperceptible shadows on the judgment of distance. *Proc. Amer. Phil. Soc.* 46:94–109.
Toch, H. H., and Schulte, R. 1961. Readiness to perceive violence as a result of police training. *Brit. J. Psychol.* 52:389-93.
Treisman, A. M. 1960. Contextual cues in selective listening. *Quart. J. Exp. Psychol.* 12: 242–48.
———. 1964. Monitoring and storage of irrelevant messages in selective attention. *J. Verb. Learn. Verb. Behav.* 3:449–59.
———. 1968. Strategies and models of selective attention. Mimeographed. Oxford: Institute of Experimental Psychology, Oxford University.
———, and Geffen, G. 1967. Selective attention: Perception or response? *Quart. J. Exp. Psychol.* 19:1–18.
———, and Riley, J. G. A. 1969. Is selective attention selective perception or selective response? A further test. *J. Exp. Psychol.* 79:27–34.
Treisman, M., and Watts, R. R. 1966. Relation between signal detectability theory and the traditional procedures for measuring sensory thresholds: Estimating d' from results given by the method of constant stimuli. *Psychol. Bull.* 66:438–54.
Underwood, B. J. 1966. *Experimental psychology.* New York: Appleton-Century-Crofts.
Vanderplas, J. M., and Garvin, E. M. 1959. The association value of random shapes. *J. Exp. Psychol.* 57:147–54.
Van Eyl, F. P. 1968. Vestibular hypothesis for the moon illusion. *Proceedings 76th Annual Convention A.P.A.,* pp. 87–88.
Vernon, M. D. 1952. *A further study of visual perception.* Cambridge: University Press.
Virsu, V. 1967. Geometric illusions: I. Effect of figure type, instructions and pre- and inter-trial training on magnitude and decrement of illusion. *Scand. J. Psychol.* 8:161–71.
Vitz, P. C. 1964. Preferences for rates of information presented by sequences of tones. *J. Exp. Psychol.* 68:176–83.
Wagner, H. L. 1968. The illusions and Ganz's theory of contour displacements. *Brit. J. Psychol.* 59:361–67.
Wallace, G. K. 1966. The effect of background on the Zöllner illusion. *Acta. Psychol.* 25: 373–80.
Wallace, M., and Rabin, A. I. 1960. Temporal experience. *Psychol. Bull.* 57:213–36.
Wallach, H. 1940. The role of head movements and vestibular and visual cues in sound localization. *J. Exp. Psychol.* 27:339–68.
———. 1948. Brightness constancy and the nature of achromatic colors. *J. Exp. Psychol.* 38:310–24. Bobbs-Merrill Reprint P-359.
———; Newman, E. B.; and Rosenzweig, M. R. 1949. The precedence effect in sound localization. *Amer. J. Psychol.* 62:315–36.

————, and O'Connell, D. N. 1953. The kinetic depth effect. *J. Exp. Psychol.* 45:205–17.

————; O'Connell, D. N.; and Neisser, U. 1953. The memory effect of visual perception of three-dimensional form. *J. Exp. Psychol.* 45:360–68.

Walls, G. L. 1951. The problem of visual direction. *Amer. J. Optom.* 28:55–83.

————. 1953. Interocular transfer of afterimages. *Amer. J. Optom.* 30:57–64.

————. 1960. Land! Land! *Psychol. Bull.* 57:29–48.

Wapner, S. 1968. Age changes in perception of verticality and of the longitudinal body axis under body tilt. *J. Exp. Child Psychol.* 6:543–55.

————, and Werner, H. 1957. *Perceptual Development.* Worcester, Mass.: Clark University Press.

Warren, R. M.; Sersen, E. A.; and Pores, E. B. 1958. A basis for loudness judgments. *Amer. J. Psychol.* 71:700–709.

Wasserman, G. S. 1966. Brightness enhancement in intermittent light: Methods of measurement. *J. Exp. Psychol.* 72:300–306.

Weintraub, D. J.; O'Connell, D. C.; and McHale, T. J. 1964. Apparent verticality: Fundamental variables of sensory tonic theory reinvestigated. *J. Exp. Psychol.* 68:550–54.

————; Wilson, B. A.; Greene, R. D.; and Palmquist, M. J. 1969. Delboeuf illusion: Displacement versus diameter, arc deletions, and brightness contrast. *J. Exp. Psychol.* 80:505–11.

Weisskopf, V. F. 1968. How light interacts with matter. *Sci. Amer.* 219:60–71.

Weisstein, N. 1968. A Rashevsky-Landahl neural net: simulation of metacontrast. *Psychol. Rev.* 75:494–521.

Welch, R. B., and Rhoades, R. W. 1969. The manipulation of informational feedback and its effects upon prism adaptation. *Canad. J. Psychol.* 23:415–28.

Werner, H. 1935. Studies on contour. I. Qualitative analysis. *Amer. J. Psychol.* 47:40–64.

————, and Wapner, S. 1952. Toward a general theory of perception. *Psychol. Rev.* 59: 324–38. Bobbs-Merrill Reprint P-363.

Wertheimer, M. 1912. Experimentelle Studien über das Sehen von Bewegungen. *Z. Psychol.* 61:161–265.

————. 1923. Untersuchungen zur Lehre von der Gestalt. II. *Psychol. Forsch.* 5:301–50.

————. 1945. *Productive thinking.* New York: Harper & Row.

————. 1958. Principles of perceptual organization. In *Readings in perception,* ed. D. C. Beardslee and M. Wertheimer. Princeton, N.J.: Van Nostrand.

Wexler, D.; Mendelson, J.; Leiderman, P. H.; and Solomon, P. 1958. Sensory deprivation: A technique for studying psychiatric aspects of stress. *Arch. Neurol. Psychiat.* 79: 225–33.

Wheatstone, C. 1828. Contribution to the physiology of vision: Part 1. *Phil. Trans. Roy. Soc., London* 371–94.

————. 1852. Contributions to the physiology of vision: Part 2. *Phil. Mag.* 35:504–23.

White, B. J., and Mueser, G. E. 1960. Accuracy in reconstructing the arrangements of elements generating kinetic depth displays. *J. Exp. Psychol.* 60:1–11.

White, C. T. 1963. Temporal numerosity and the psychological unit of duration. *Psychol. Mono.* 77: whole no. 575.

Wickelgren, W. A. 1965. Acoustic similarity and intrusion errors in short-term memory. *J. Exp. Psychol.* 70:102–8.

Wilcocks, R. W. 1925. An examination of Külpe's experiments on abstraction. *Amer. J. Psychol.* 36:324–41.

Wilcox, W. W. 1932. The basis of dependence of visual acuity on illumination. *Proc. Nat. Acad. Sci.* 18:47–56.

Wilding, J. M., and Underwood, G. 1968. Selective attention: The site of the filter in the identification of language. *Psychon. Sci.* 13:305–6.

Willey, C. F.; Inglis, E.; and Pearce, C. H. 1937. Reversal of auditory localization. *J. Exp. Psychol.* 20:114–30.

Willey, R., and Gyr, J. W. 1969. Motion parallax and projective similarity as factors in slant perception. *J. Exp. Psychol.* 79:525–32.

Winnick, W. A., and Bruder, G. E. 1968. Signal detection approach to the study of retinal locus in tachistoscopic recognition. *J. Exp. Psychol.* 78:528–31.

Witkin, H. A. 1959. The perception of the upright. *Sci. Amer.* 200:50–56.

———, and Asch, S. E. 1948. Studies in space orientation. IV. Further experiments on perception of the upright with displaced visual fields. *J. Exp. Psychol.* 38:762–82.

Wohlgemuth, A. 1911. On the aftereffect of seen movement. *Brit. J. Psychol.* Monograph suppl. no. 1.

Wood, R. J.; Zinkus, P. W.; and Mountjoy, P. T. 1968. The vestibular hypothesis of the moon illusion. *Psychon. Sci.* 11:356.

Woodworth, R. S. 1938. *Experimental psychology.* New York: Holt.

———, and Schlosberg, H. 1954. *Experimental psychology.* Rev. ed. New York: Holt.

Worchel, S., and Burnham, C. A. 1967. Reduction of autokinesis with information about the registration of eye position. *Amer. J. Psychol.* 80:434–37.

Wright, H. N. 1964. Temporal summation and backward masking. *J. Acous. Soc. Amer.* 36:927–32.

Wright, W. D. 1928–29. A re-determination of the trichromatic coefficients of the spectral colours. *Trans. Opt. Soc.* (London) 30:141–64.

———. 1947. *Researches on normal and defective colour vision.* St. Louis: C. V. Mosby.

Wulf, F. 1922. Über die Veränderung von Vorstellungen (Gedächtnis und Gestalt). *Psychol. Forsch.* 1:333–73.

Wundt, W. 1862. *Beiträge zur Theorie der Sinneswahrnehmung.* Leipzig: C. F. Winter.

Wundt, W. 1896. *Grundriss der Psychologie.* Leipzig: Engelmann.

Yin, R. K. 1969. Looking at upside-down faces. *J. Exp. Psychol.* 81:141–45.

Yntema, D. B. 1964. Immediate recall of digits presented at very high speeds. Paper presented to the Psychonomic Society, Niagara Falls, Ontario.

Young, L. R. 1963. Measuring eye movements. *Amer. J. Med. Electronics* 2:300–307.

Young, P. T. 1928. Auditory localization with acoustical transposition of the ears. *J. Exp. Psychol.* 11:399–429.

Zegers, R. T. 1965. The reversal illusion of the Ames trapezoid. *Trans. N.Y. Acad. Sci.* 26:377–400.

Zelkind, I., and Ulehla, J. 1968. Estimated duration of an auditory signal as a function of its intensity. *Psychon. Sci.* 11:185–86.

Zenhausern, R. 1968. The perception of rotation with an oscillating trapezoid. *Psychon. Sci.* 13:79–80.

Zöllner, F. 1860. Über eine neue Art von Pseudoskopie und ihre Beziehungen zu den von Plateau und Oppel beschriebenen Bewegungsphänomenen. *Ann. Physik. Chem.* 186:500–520.

Zubek, J. P., ed. 1969. *Sensory deprivation: Fifteen years of research.* New York: Appleton-Century-Crofts.

———; Pushkar, D.; Sansom, W.; and Gowing, J. 1961. Perceptual changes after prolonged sensory isolation. *Canad. J. Psychol.* 15:83–100.

Zuckerman, C. B., and Rock, I. 1957. A reappraisal of the roles of past experience and innate organizing processes in visual perception. *Psychol. Bull.* 54:269–96.

Zuckerman, M. 1969. Variables affecting deprivation results and hallucinations, reported sensations and images. In *Sensory deprivation,* ed. J. P. Zubek. New York: Appleton-Century-Crofts.

Zwicker, E.; Flottorp, G.; and Stevens, S. S. 1957. Critical bandwidth in loudness summation. *J. Acous. Soc. Amer.* 29:548–57.

Index of
Personal Names

Index of
Subjects